BUILDING ANTEBELLUM
NEW ORLEANS

Lateral Exchanges: Architecture, Urban Development, and Transnational Practices

A Series Edited by Felipe Correa, Bruno Carvalho, and Alison Isenberg

ALSO IN THE SERIES

Ana María León, *Modernity for the Masses: Antonio Bonet's Dreams for Buenos Aires*

Burak Erdim, *Landed Internationals: Planning Cultures, the Academy, and the Making of the Modern Middle East*

Mary P. Ryan, *Taking the Land to Make the City: A Bicoastal History of North America*

Fabiola López-Durán, *Eugenics in the Garden: Transatlantic Architecture and the Crafting of Modernity*

Tara A. Dudley

Building Antebellum New Orleans

FREE PEOPLE OF COLOR
AND THEIR INFLUENCE

UNIVERSITY OF TEXAS PRESS   AUSTIN

This publication has been generously supported by a grant from Furthermore: a program of the J.M. Kaplan Fund.

Copyright © 2021 by the University of Texas Press
All rights reserved
Printed in the United States of America
First edition, 2021
First paperback printing, 2023

Requests for permission to reproduce material from this work should be sent to:
Permissions
University of Texas Press
P.O. Box 7819
Austin, TX 78713–7819
utpress.utexas.edu/rp-form

♾ The paper used in this book meets the minimum requirements of ANSI/NISO Z39.48–1992 (R1997) (Permanence of Paper).

LIBRARY OF CONGRESS CATALOGING-IN-PUBLICATION DATA

Names: Dudley, Tara A., author.
Title: Building antebellum New Orleans : free people of color and their influence / Tara Dudley.
Other titles: Lateral exchanges.
Description: First edition. | Austin : University of Texas Press, 2021. | Series: Lateral exchanges: architecture, urban development, and transnational practices | Includes bibliographical references and index.
Identifiers: LCCN 2020056880
ISBN 978-1-4773-2855-2 (paperback)
ISBN 978-1-4773-2303-8 (PDF)
ISBN 978-1-4773-2304-5 (ePub)
Subjects: LCSH: African American architects—Louisiana—New Orleans—History—19th century. | African American architecture—Louisiana—New Orleans—19th century. | Architecture—United States—History—19th century. | Free African Americans—Louisiana—New Orleans—History—19th century. | Free blacks—Louisiana—New Orleans—History—19th century. | Architects and builders—Louisiana—New Orleans—History—19th century.
Classification: LCC NA738.N5 D83 2021 | DDC 720.9763/3509034--dc23
LC record available at https://lccn.loc.gov/2020056880

doi:10.7560/323021

Melinda Mangham
(July 30, 1940–April 30, 2020)

CONTENTS

LIST OF TABLES ix
LIST OF FIGURES xi
INTRODUCTION 1

PART I
OWNERSHIP: POSSESSING THE BUILT ENVIRONMENT

CHAPTER 1
The *Gens de Couleur Libres'* Acquisition of Property 24

CHAPTER 2
The Ramifications of Use and Location 54

PART II
ENGAGEMENT: FORMING AND TRANSFORMING THE BUILT ENVIRONMENT

CHAPTER 3
The Architecture of the Dolliole and Soulié Families 78

CHAPTER 4
"Uncommon Industry": *Gens de Couleur Libres* Builders in Antebellum New Orleans 118

CHAPTER 5
"Raised to the Trade": Building Practices of *Gens de Couleur Libres* Builders in Antebellum New Orleans 141

CONTENTS

CHAPTER 6
The Status Quo: French, Creole, and Anglo Builders and Architects in Antebellum New Orleans   156

PART III
ENTREPRENEURSHIP: CONTROLLING THE BUILT ENVIRONMENT

CHAPTER 7
Money, Power, and Status in the Building Trades   196

CONCLUSION   213
ACKNOWLEDGMENTS   222
NOTES   226
BIBLIOGRAPHY   272
INDEX   290

TABLES

TABLE I.1. New Orleans population, 1769–1850   12

TABLE 1.1. Properties owned by Louis Dolliole, Geneviève Azémare *dit* Laronde, and their children, 1794–1868   28

TABLE 1.2. Select properties acquired by the first-generation Souliés, 1819–1845   48

TABLE 1.3. Bernard and Albin Soulié's business addresses in city of New Orleans directories   51

TABLE 1.4. Rental properties in the Soulié family ledgers, May 1843 through January 1845   52

TABLE 2.1. Business movement of the Dolliole and Soulié families from city of New Orleans directories, 1805–1850   71

TABLE 2.2. Residential movement of the Dolliole and Soulié families from city of New Orleans directories, 1805–1850   72

TABLE 3.1. Entries for building-related occupations in city of New Orleans directories, select years   80

TABLE 3.2. Creole cottages built by the Dolliole family   99

TABLE 3.3. Known Soulié built works   114

TABLE 4.1. Select built works by Dolliole and Soulié contemporaries   138

TABLE 5.1. Titles/roles of *gens de couleur libres* builders   142

TABLE 5.2. Number of adult enslaved males owned by *gens de couleur libres* builders in New Orleans   147

TABLE 5.3. Apprenticeship indentures in the building trades involving select *gens de couleur libres* builders   150

TABLES

TABLE 5.4. Occupations of male members of the Dolliole family, 1763–1994   154

TABLE 6.1. Featured public buildings in New Orleans, 1820–1850   179

TABLE 6.2. Apprenticeship indentures in the building trades involving select builders, 1809–1843   181

TABLE 6.3. Select participation in antebellum architecture competitions among New Orleans architects   185

TABLE 6.4. Select built works by white architects for nonwhite clients   186

TABLE 7.1. Property values of free people of color in New Orleans, 1850   200

TABLE 7.2. Select entries from 1852 and 1853 real estate tax registers for New Orleans   201

TABLE 7.3. Estate values of select *gens de couleur libres* builders   203

FIGURES

FIGURE I.1. Dolliole family tree   8

FIGURE I.2. Soulié family tree   9

FIGURE I.3. Lucien Soulié (1789–1862), Norbert Soulié (1793–1869), Bernard Soulié (1801–1881), and Albin Soulié (1803–1873)   10

FIGURE I.4. Eliza Courcelle Soulié (1808–1882)   11

FIGURE I.5. Plan de la Ville de la Nouvelle-Orléans avec les noms des propriétaires   14

FIGURE 1.1. Chronicle of Dolliole-owned property in the 900 block of St. Philip Street, 1794–1854   32

FIGURE 1.2. Approximate locations of Louis and Jean-Louis Dolliole properties on Bayou Road   35

FIGURE 1.3. Dolliole properties in the 1100 and 1200 blocks of St. Philip Street   36

FIGURE 1.4. Lots 30 and 31 purchased by Jean-Louis and Pierre Dolliole and Norbert Fortier in 1816   37

FIGURE 1.5. 1436 Pauger Street   38

FIGURE 1.6. Map showing location of Madeleine and Rosette Dolliole purchases on former Collège d'Orléans property (1200 block of St. Philip Street)   39

FIGURE 1.7. Plan of Soulié property at North Rampart and Barracks Streets   46

FIGURE 2.1. Location of neighborhoods (faubourgs), showing the Vieux Carré and Faubourgs Tremé, Marigny, New Marigny, and Franklin   56

FIGURE 2.2. Dolliole- and Soulié-owned properties in the Vieux Carré   57

FIGURE 2.3. Plan of "Soulié Property" bound by Love (now North Rampart), Soulié, Good Children (now St. Claude), and the Caffin property, 1868   65

FIGURES

FIGURE 2.4. Faubourg Annunciation and Faubourg Livaudais   69

FIGURE 2.5. Properties purchased by Norbert Soulié at the north corner of Bacchus (now Baronne) and Euterpe Streets   70

FIGURE 3.1. 628–632 Dumaine Street ("Madame John's Legacy")   82

FIGURE 3.2. 937–941 Bourbon Street ("Lafitte's Blacksmith Shop")   84

FIGURE 3.3. 931–933 St. Philip Street (Dolliole-Masson Cottage)   86

FIGURE 3.4. Sketch plan of 931–933 St. Philip Street   86

FIGURE 3.5. 931–933 St. Philip Street   87

FIGURE 3.6. Layout of an *habitation* on Esplanade Avenue similar to that which Louis Dolliole owned on Bayou Road   88

FIGURE 3.7. 1436 Pauger Street   89

FIGURE 3.8. Roof system of 1436 Pauger Street   90

FIGURE 3.9. Floor plan of 1436 Pauger Street   91

FIGURE 3.10. 1227 St. Philip Street   94

FIGURE 3.11. 1125 and 1127 St. Philip Street   95

FIGURE 3.12. Side gallery of (and rear addition to) 1125 St. Philip Street   95

FIGURE 3.13. 1010 Burgundy Street   97

FIGURE 3.14. 927–929 St. Philip Street   98

FIGURE 3.15. 935–937 St. Philip Street   98

FIGURE 3.16. The Orleans Theatre, 1816   102

FIGURE 3.17. Floor plan of Chabot Cottage   103

FIGURE 3.18. 509–511 Bourbon Street   105

FIGURE 3.19. 810 Dumaine Street   106

FIGURE 3.20. 814 Governor Nicholls Street   107

FIGURE 3.21. 330–332 Bourbon Street (demolished late 1960s)   108

FIGURE 3.22. 229 and 231 North Rampart Street   109

FIGURE 3.23. Elevations and floor plans of townhouses at Rampart and Conti Streets   110

FIGURE 3.24. Louisiana Sugar Refinery   111

FIGURE 3.25. 1226 Tremé Street   113

FIGURE 3.26. Extant *gens de couleur libres*–associated properties by type   115

FIGURE 3.27. Extant building types as constructed by identified *gens de couleur libres* builders in Faubourg Tremé and the Creole faubourgs   116

—

FIGURES

FIGURE 4.1. Detail of site plan of 1133–1135 Chartres Street, showing the original façade design and floor plan   120

FIGURE 4.2. Detail of Plan de 14 lots de terre situés au Faubourg Tremé showing properties owned by François Boisdoré and Jean-Louis Dolliole on Villeré Street   121

FIGURE 4.3. 1428 Bourbon Street   122

FIGURE 4.4. 1729–1731 Laharpe Street   124

FIGURE 4.5. 830–832 St. Philip Street (Dr. Daret House)   127

FIGURE 4.6. Floor plan and section for Roman Vionnet House on St. Philip Street   129

FIGURE 4.7. Plan of Sophia Philips cottage on St. Ann Street   130

FIGURE 4.8. Assembly of houses by Joseph Chateau: 422 Burgundy Street, 416–418 Burgundy Street, and 412–414 Burgundy Street   131

FIGURE 4.9. Elevation and floor plan of house on Magazine Street   132

FIGURE 4.10. 1035 North Rampart Street   134

FIGURE 4.11. 1024 Governor Nicholls Street (Helen Lepage *maisonette*)   135

FIGURE 4.12. 2340 Chartres Street   137

FIGURE 5.1. Floor plans and elevations for Marguerite Dauphine House   152

FIGURE 6.1. Cabildo, St. Louis Cathedral, Presbytère   159

FIGURE 6.2. 339–343 Royal Street (Vincent Rillieux House)   160

FIGURE 6.3. Halles des Boucheries (Meat Market)/French Market   161

FIGURE 6.4. Buildings by Jean Felix Pinson and Maurice Pizetta   162

FIGURE 6.5. St. Louis Hotel   163

FIGURE 6.6. *Exchange Place: Entrance to Hotel Royale*   163

FIGURE 6.7. St. Louis Cathedral   164

FIGURE 6.8. Collège d'Orléans   165

FIGURE 6.9. Mortuary Chapel of St. Anthony of Padua   166

FIGURE 6.10. 713–719 Royal Street (Vignié townhouses)   166

FIGURE 6.11. 711 Bourbon Street   167

FIGURE 6.12. 1009 and 1013 St. Ann Street   169

FIGURE 6.13. 1113 Chartres Street (Le Carpentier-Beauregard-Keyes House)   170

FIGURE 6.14. 535–541 Royal Street/708–710 Toulouse Street (Vincent Nolte House/"Court of Two Lions")   172

FIGURE 6.15. 403–407 Royal Street (Louisiana State Bank)   172

FIGURES

FIGURE 6.16. 818–820 St. Louis Street (Hermann-Grima House) 173

FIGURE 6.17. 423 Canal Street (U.S. Custom House) 174

FIGURE 6.18. 228, 232, 236–238 North Rampart (not extant) 175

FIGURE 6.19. Works of Dakin and Gallier 176

FIGURE 6.20. 500–546 St. Peter Street (Upper Pontalba Apartment Buildings) 177

FIGURE 6.21. 545 St. Charles Street (Municipal Hall/City Hall/Gallier Hall) 178

FIGURE 6.22. Advertisement for James Mooney, 1823 184

FIGURE 6.23. Detail of Sanborn Fire Insurance Company Map, Sheet 23, showing location of Norbert Soulié townhouses at corner of Baronne and Lafayette (formerly Hevia) Streets, 1876 187

FIGURE 6.24. Drawings of comparative townhouses in Faubourg Sainte-Marie 188

FIGURE 7.1. Average value of property declared in marriage contracts by period, gender, and race 199

FIGURE 7.2. Bayou Road properties of Joseph Dolliole and François Boisdoré 210

BUILDING ANTEBELLUM
NEW ORLEANS

INTRODUCTION

There is no State in the Union, hardly any spot of like size on the globe, where the man of color has lived so intently, made so much progress, been of such historical importance and yet about whom so comparatively little is known. His history is like the Mardi Gras of the city of New Orleans, beautiful and mysterious and wonderful, but with a serious thought underlying it all. May it be better known to the world some day.

ALICE DUNBAR NELSON, "PEOPLE OF COLOR IN LOUISIANA" (1917)

A few weeks after the New Year, on January 19, 1832, first cousins Bernard Soulié and Eliza Sylvie Courcelle entered into a marriage contract. He was thirty years of age, she twenty-two. The contract was signed at the prospective bride's residence—the house of her father, cotton broker Léon Courcelle, at the corner of Carondelet and Hevia Streets in New Orleans's Faubourg Sainte-Marie.[1] The document was witnessed by Vincent Rillieux, the consort of the couple's maternal aunt, and François Pierre Duconge, the groom's friend of fifteen years. The affianced couple was married at eight o'clock p.m. a few days later, on January 23. After the evening nuptials, Bernard Soulié began writing a journal that would span almost half a century.[2] In the preamble to his personal journal, Soulié does not begin by writing about himself or the day's events. Instead, he establishes his paternal lineage, noting the birth and death of his French father and the births of his paternal aunt and uncle: "My father, Jean Soulié was born at Roquecourbe, Department of Tarn on 15 September 1760. He died at Paris 10 December 1834. My uncle, Bernard Soulié was born in the same place on 11 April 1764. My aunt Louise was born in the same place on 11 September

1765."[3] In another introductory anecdote, Bernard Soulié notes that his mother died on May 16, 1825.[4] Unlike that given for his father, however, no information is imparted about Soulié's maternal heritage; neither his mother's name, date and place of birth, nor close relatives are disclosed. Soulié then officially begins the diary in the present, simply noting the date and time of his wedding that day and the bride's name.[5] Though Bernard Soulié emphasizes his French lineage and omits his maternal heritage from one of New Orleans's oldest families of *gens de couleur libres* (free people of color), his journal commences during the city's rise as an important metropolis and goes on to provide insight into the activities of many individuals—Black and white—in antebellum New Orleans.

Also in 1832, *homme de couleur libre* Joseph Dolliole, with his neighbor François Boisdoré, began a five-year battle with the city of New Orleans in opposition to the city's widening and extension of Esplanade Avenue through their properties on Bayou Road, a "back-of-town" thoroughfare active since precolonial times when Native Americans used it as a trade route between Lake Pontchartrain and the Mississippi River.[6] Frenchman Louis Dolliole and his mixed-race son Jean-Louis Dolliole had inhabited portions of Bayou Road since 1806 and 1807, respectively, when French Creole Claude Tremé began selling portions of his "back-of-town" plantation. Through the legal suit, Joseph Dolliole, another of Louis Dolliole's sons, refused to relinquish the property he inherited from his white father. His, and Boisdoré's, actions served to solidify the *gens de couleur libres'* claim to property rights and ownership as the city expanded outside of its colonial boundaries.

In 1832, the year of Soulié's marriage and the commencement of Dolliole's suit, Louisiana celebrated its twentieth anniversary as the eighteenth state admitted to the Union. New Orleans, with a population of approximately 46,000, was the state capital.[7] The city, long the crucible of the colony cum territory cum state's unique Creole heritage, was well on its way to becoming one of the United States' most prominent antebellum cities. The nation's rapid expansion, stimulated in part by the 1803 Louisiana Purchase, spurred the development of a strong capitalist economy.[8] With American ownership and statehood, as well as advances in steam-powered transportation, New Orleans became an important shipping center. The year 1832 saw just a few of the social and cultural changes brought about by the city's advanced status and the arrivals of Americans from the eastern seaboard and European immigrants to take advantage of all that the city had to offer. For one, the Bank of New Orleans relocated from the original French core of the city, the Vieux Carré, to Faubourg Sainte-Marie, a newer section of the city primarily inhabited by American newcomers.[9] To support this rapidly expanding area of the city, the digging of the New Orleans Navigation Canal, also called the

INTRODUCTION

New Basin Canal, connected Lake Pontchartrain to this booming commercial and residential "American" section of the city. Farther upriver, the former Livaudais plantation was laid out as another residential enclave for American businessmen and their families; the suburb was later incorporated as part of the city of Lafayette and came to be known as the Garden District.[10]

Business houses, factories, and manufacturing plants also thrived in the city that year. The Levee Steam Cotton Press, introducing the first steam-powered cotton press in the city, opened below the French Quarter just over one mile upriver from where Bernard Soulié's brother and cousin, Norbert Soulié and Edmond Rillieux, had begun construction of the Louisiana Sugar Refinery the year before.[11] The Pontchartrain Railroad was built to accommodate the new factory and to increase lake trade to the older, Creole part of the city, in direct competition with the New Basin Canal. Other infrastructure to accommodate the city's population, physical, and economic growth included the development of roads, such as the extension of Esplanade Avenue, which Joseph Dolliole and his neighbors opposed.

The Mississippi River, the city's river road, carried newly developed steam-powered ships that brought both goods and people to New Orleans. Among the goods and people that moved through New Orleans by way of water and land were bales of cotton and thousands of enslaved men, women, and children. By the 1830s, New Orleans had become the nexus for the cotton industry and domestic slave trade—inseparable components of the US economy. The only major metropolis in the US South, the city was a significant crossroads for the development and expansion of American capitalism as it intersected with international trade routes and movement of people through the Atlantic and Caribbean spheres.[12]

River and steamboat trade also brought a scourge to a city already prone to yellow fever outbreaks. In October 1832, a cholera epidemic broke out in the city after a steamboat arrived with infected passengers. Ultimately, six thousand persons, almost one-fifth of the city's population, died.[13] The less fortunate affected by the disease were accommodated in the newly completed Charity Hospital on Tulane Avenue in Faubourg Sainte-Marie. The outbreak knew no race or ethnic boundaries. Irish immigrants digging the New Basin Canal were particularly susceptible to the disease. The epidemic also claimed the life of teenager Jean Pierre Lafitte, the mulatto (and only) son of the infamous pirate Jean Lafitte.[14] No members of either the Soulié or Dolliole families died from the disease. Rather, amid the significant socioeconomic change and health crisis experienced by the city, the families celebrated life. Marie Eugenie, the last child of Jean-Louis Dolliole, was born on April 11, 1832, three weeks before the anniversary of statehood. Gustave Adolph

–

3

Soulié, the first-born son of Bernard and Eliza Soulié, was born on October 28 as cholera was beginning to grip the city.[15]

Like many families in New Orleans—Creole or American, white or Black—the Dollioles and Souliés lived during a time of great transition. The years from 1820 to 1850 saw New Orleans become an important American urban metropolis and industrialized shipping center. The Dollioles' and Souliés' activities are unique in this time and place in that both families were part of the *gens de couleur libres* community—people with a mixture of Black and European (usually French or Spanish) ancestry.[16] The *gens de couleur libres* thrived amid the economic and cultural ups and downs of the mid-antebellum period (1830s and 1840s) and were greatly involved in the expansion of New Orleans brought on by the city's growth in size and population. The need for architecture and infrastructure provided a canvas for free Black building artisans, developers, and patrons in the antebellum period. This played out visibly in New Orleans, where free people of color were a dominant ethnic and socioeconomic group. The contributions of the *gens de couleur libres* in the areas of music, literature, and cuisine are well known. Scholarship abounds with material trying to place free people of color within color lines and establish their place in the canon of American history and the history of New Orleans, expounding on issues such as racial conflict, racial passing, miscegenation, and sexual propriety and impropriety where New Orleans's free people of color are involved.[17] By its very nature, Creole architecture invites focus on form and typology. In general, New Orleans's Creole architecture is a unique style or type created from a synthesis of Western European and non-European building traditions.[18] Creole architecture was prevalent in the West Indies, the US Gulf Coast, and the Mississippi River valley from about 1732 to 1911. The most important characteristics of Creole buildings include:

- galleries or verandas;
- a broad, spreading roofline;
- gallery roofs supported by lightweight wooden colonnettes (posts);
- placement of main rooms above ground level;
- timber-frame construction infilled with bricks (briquette-entre-poteaux) or infilled with a mixture of mud and moss (bousillage);
- multiple French doors; and
- French wraparound mantels.

Interior spaces in Creole buildings consisted of a systematic core of main rooms, often with surrounding secondary spaces. Though vernacular in nature—derived from local building traditions, adhering to a specific time and place, and used by particular groups—Creole architecture had varying stages of development and nuances in form and style that were ultimately utilized by builders and professional architects, but especially by New Orleans's many *gens de couleur libres* practitioners.

NEW ORLEANS'S FREE PEOPLE OF COLOR

Free people of color were consistent and persistent in many US cities,[19] particularly antebellum New Orleans, in their acquisition, development, and management of property—a largely unexplored aspect of mainstream architectural history. Various classes of Blacks—enslaved persons, manumitted slaves, and free persons of color—contributed to the built world of Louisiana from its beginnings under the French, through its occupation by the Spanish, and beyond its annexation by the United States. Though frequently further distinguished by the proportion of African ancestry one had or by one's physical appearance (i.e., *négresse*, mulatto, quadroon, octoroon), in colonial and antebellum legal records in Louisiana, any free Black men and women could be recorded as free persons of color. In French records, they were *gens de couleur libres*; in Spanish, *personas de color libres*. Due to the significant proportion of mixed-race free people in colonial New Orleans, the term *gens de couleur libres* became increasingly associated with Afro-Creoles in the late colonial and antebellum eras.[20] In *Building Antebellum New Orleans*, the phrases *gens de couleur libres* and "free Blacks" are used as they would have been historically and refer to any nonenslaved person regardless of ethnicity. The term "Afro-Creole" denotes someone of African and European ancestry.

In its infancy, the Louisiana colony—claimed by the French in 1682 and settled in 1699 at present-day Mobile, Alabama, and Biloxi, Mississippi—was sparsely settled. The colony's "curiously blended Franco-African host culture of the city" was formed during this period in a process that the historian Arnold R. Hirsch, among others, terms "Creolization" or a process through which European forms are transformed under colonialization.[21] The first African slaves were brought to the colony in 1717. At this time, white female inhabitants were practically nonexistent, and white men established partnerships with female slaves. "Sexual relations among European settlers, African slaves, and Native Americans during the period of French rule in Louisiana (1718–1768) resulted in the creation of a third race of people neither white nor Black and neither slave nor completely free."[22] Initially, this group increased primarily through the manumission of Black and mulatto females and their offspring, who were involved in formal or informal unions with white settlers.[23]

INTRODUCTION

The nature of these interracial relationships has become mythicized in the historic record and in literature. Scholarship and fiction abound with the stories of women who were consorts of white men. Supposedly, upon embarking on an extramarital interracial relationship, a woman (or her family) might demand a residence as part of the agreement; the property would remain hers should the relationship end. In many cases, partners and children of these relationships received donations of real estate from their lover/father. These "startup" properties would then serve as the basis for greater involvement in the real estate market.[24] "Once given a house and investments," writes the journalist and women's movement supporter Mary Gehman, "these women had to be savvy in the ways of business and law in order to hold on to what they had been given, improve it, and pass it on to their children. There is also no doubt that other free women, through hard work and frugality, were able to purchase property on their own."[25] In recent scholarship, however, historians such as Emily Clark and Jennifer Spear show that neither denizens of New Orleans nor outsiders had a term for extramarital or long-term interrelationships. They also underscore that so-called *plaçage* contracts between white men and Black women or their families are not known to exist. The demographic and economic circumstances in New Orleans and its environs, as well as the kinship and business relationships, were the basis for families such as the Dollioles and Souliés.[26]

THE ORIGINS OF THE AFRO-CREOLE DOLLIOLE AND SOULIÉ FAMILIES

New Orleans's free community of color had its origins in and expanded as a result of informal relationships between white men and women of color (Black, mulatto, quadroon, and octoroon). The demographic, social, and political circumstances in the colony made these relationships—whether extramarital or long-term and equivalent to common-law marriages—possible. When the Spaniards took physical control of the Louisiana colony in 1769 by sending government officials,[27] Governor Alejandro O'Reilly ordered a census that showed that of New Orleans's 1,902 free inhabitants, 31 were free Blacks and 69 were of mixed blood.[28] Subsequent Spanish governors were sympathetic to the predominantly French settlement and did little to nothing to change or influence the culture. In a conscious attempt to maintain peace with the city's primarily French inhabitants and to encourage and retain settlement, the Spanish colonial government did not enforce laws regarding interracial relationships established in the French Code Noir (1724) and Code Noir ou Loi Municipale (1778). Some restrictive laws were enacted by Governor Esteban Rodríguez Miró (1782–1791), including the Spanish Código Negro (1789).[29] These French and Spanish laws, however, were not realistic to

INTRODUCTION

the economic and social status of New Orleans's free Black community.[30] In fact, some Spanish laws were more lenient regarding interracial relationships. This hands-off approach contributed to the natural increase of a mixed-race class. In 1788, the number of free people of color was 823 in a city of 5,319; at 15 percent of the total population, the *gens de couleur libres* composed a significant portion of the city's inhabitants.[31] The Dollioles and Souliés are among those mixed-race *gens de couleur libres* families who can trace their origins in New Orleans to the Spanish colonial period.

Brothers and natives of the province of Provence, Louis Antoine Dolliole (1742–1822) and Jean-François Dolliole (1760–1816) immigrated to New Orleans, sailing from La Seyne sur Mer on France's Mediterranean coast during the Spanish colonial period (1762–1803).[32] The brothers established long-term relationships with women of color, becoming white patriarchs of *gens de couleur libres* families (figure I.1).[33] Louis became involved with the *négresse libre* (free Black woman) Geneviève "Mamie" Azémare (*dit*, or "called," Laronde).[34] Their first son, Jean-Louis, was born in 1779. Three other children followed: Madeleine (ca. 1783), Pierre (ca. 1790), and Joseph.[35] With the *négresse libre* Catherine, Jean-François also fathered four children—Etienne Adam (1799), Louis Laurent (1806), Joseph Pantheleon (1809), and Edmond (1816). These eight mulatto offspring, Louis's three sons in particular, owned significant amounts of property in the Vieux Carré and Faubourg Tremé, often improving them with buildings that they constructed or commissioned.

These two neighborhoods were also the domains of the Soulié family (figure I.2). François Cheval, a descendant of Frenchmen from Normandy who settled in the Côte des Allemands (German Coast) area above New Orleans, arrived in New Orleans in the late eighteenth century.[36] As a partner in a tannery, he became a successful businessman. One of his natural children was Louison Cheval (1747–1839). Louison gave birth to daughters Eulalie and Henriette before embarking on a relationship with Frenchman Jean Charles Vivant.[37] Louison's daughter Eulalie Mazange (sometimes referred to as Eulalie Vivant) was the long-term consort of Jean Soulié, a native of Roquecourbe in the French province of Languedoc and a member of the New Orleans militia.[38] Eulalie and Jean's children were Lucien (1789), Marie Louise (1801), Norbert (1793), Eulalie (1798), Bernard (1801), Benedie/c (1802), Albin (1803), Marie Louise (1808), Marie Celeste (1810), and Marie Coralie (1811)[39] (figure I.3). While the Soulié sons Norbert, Albin, and Bernard were influential builders, all of the children owned and managed a significant amount of property in New Orleans. Several of Louison Cheval's and Eulalie Mazange's siblings also had long-term relationships with or married

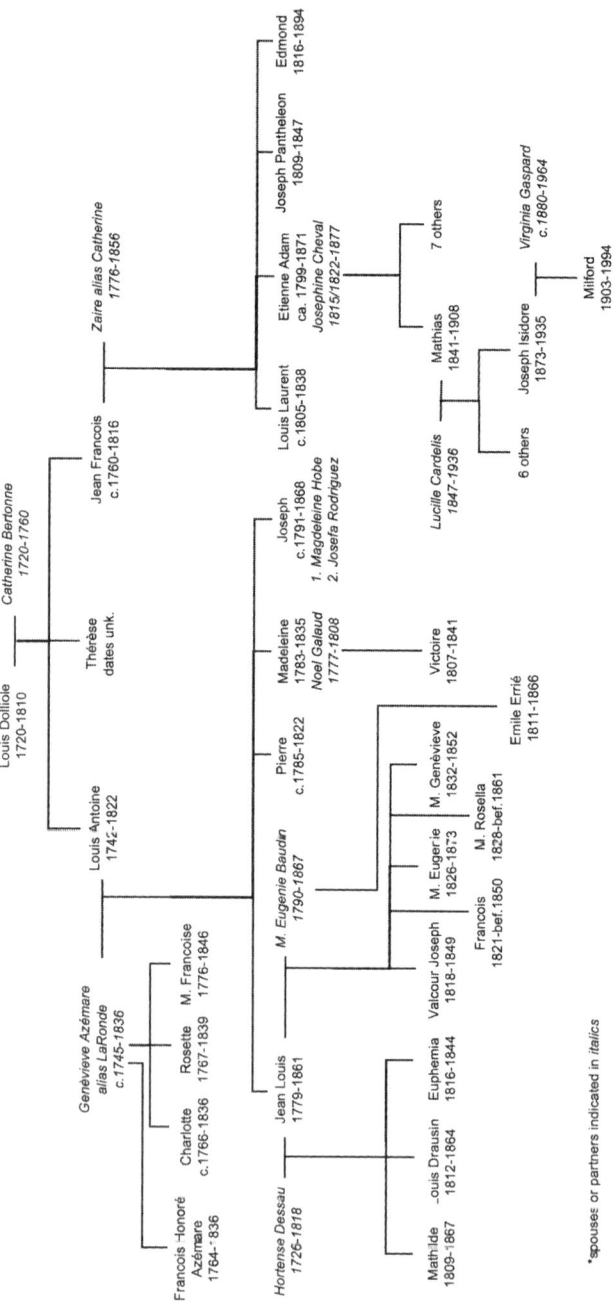

Figure I.1. Dolliole family tree.

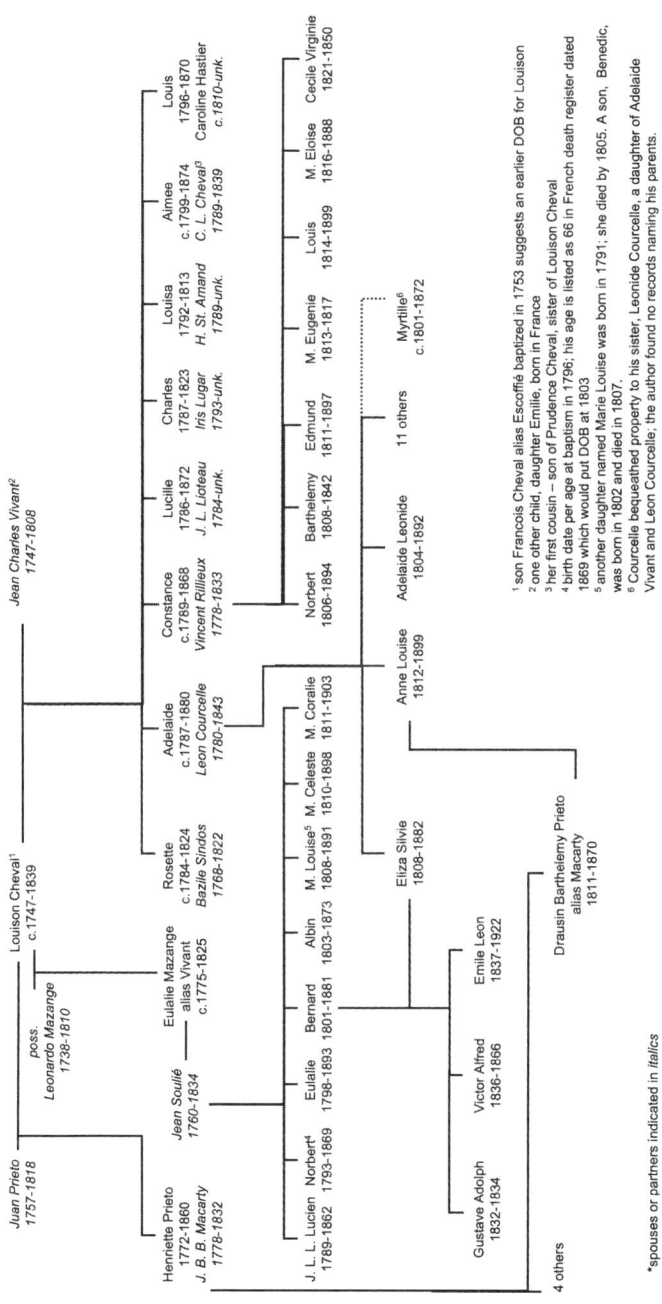

Figure I.2. Soulié family tree.

Figure I.3. Clockwise from top left: Lucien Soulié (1789–1862), Norbert Soulié (1793–1869), Bernard Soulié (1801–1881), and Albin Soulié (1803–1873). No known photographs exist of the Soulié sisters Eulalie, Louise, Celeste, and Coralie. Dates and photographers/artist unknown. Courtesy of Soulié Family, Paris, France.

INTRODUCTION

Figure I.4. Eliza Courcelle Soulié (1808–1882). Date and photographer unknown. Photograph courtesy of Soulié Family, Paris, France.

prominent New Orleanians; their offspring also influenced the built environment of the city (figure I.4). By the time the events surrounding the Haitian Revolution (1791–1804) began to affect the city, both the Dolliole and Soulié families were well established in New Orleans.

THE HAITIAN REVOLUTION AND NEW ORLEANS'S
GENS DE COULEUR LIBRES COMMUNITY

Large numbers of white and Black Saint-Dominguans fled the West Indies in the early nineteenth century, leaving Saint-Domingue due to the uprising led by Toussaint L'Ouverture or fleeing Cuba, which was hostile to Napoleon's sympathizers. At the outset of the revolution, Saint-Dominguans emigrated en masse to the Atlantic seaboard in the 1790s and to Jamaica in 1798.[40] In the late 1790s, a small number of *gens de couleur libres* arrived in New Orleans in spite of the colonial government's attempts to prohibit their immigration. Until this point, immigration of people of color had been virtually nonexistent.[41] In 1803,

INTRODUCTION

Saint-Dominguans made a mass exodus to Cuba after France failed to regain control of the colony.[42] In 1803 and 1804, the Saint-Dominguan refugees in Jamaica were expelled to New Orleans. The Jamaican refugees were joined by additional countrymen, including 3,102 free persons of color deported from Cuba in 1809.[43] The majority of Saint-Dominguan refugees to Louisiana were not white. As a result, the population of free persons of color increased from 1,500 in 1803 to 4,950 in 1810, accounting for almost one-third of the city's total population and half of the population of all free residents.[44] By 1830, that number rose to 11,562, accounting for 26 percent of the city's total population.[45] The 1840 population of free people of color was 15,000 due to natural increase and some manumission and migration.[46] The next decade saw a decline of the *gens de couleur libres* population in absolute numbers and as a percentage of the city's population; by 1850, the total was just under 10,000, less than one-tenth of New Orleans's entire population (table I.1).[47]

Though the percentage of *gens de couleur libres* in the city decreased over the course of the antebellum period due to American and European immigration and outmigration as increasingly repressive legislative measures were enacted from the 1830s through the 1850s, their sheer number allowed for their activities to inform the types of economic endeavors suitable for free people of color.[48] Their considerable presence also allowed for the persistence of Francophone culture at a time when Creoles' identity as an ethnic group came into question. Increasing cultural influences from Americans, European immigrants, and even manumitted slaves created different viewpoints as to who was considered Creole and how Afro-Creoles were indistinguishable from other Blacks. The *gens de*

TABLE I.1. NEW ORLEANS POPULATION, 1769-1850

Year	Free persons of color (% of total population)*	Whites	Enslaved	Total
1769	99 (3.2%)	1,803	1,227	3,129
1788	823 (15.5%)	2,370	2,126	5,319
1805	1,566 (19%)	3,551	3,105	8,222
1810	4,950 (28.7%)	6,331	5,961	17,242
1820	6,237 (23%)	13,584	7,355	27,176
1830	11,562 (25.1%)	20,047	14,476	46,085
1840	15,072 (18%)	50,697	18,208	83,977
1850	9,905 (8.5%)	89,452	17,011	116,368

*Includes free Afro-Creoles and other free Blacks

couleur libres were considered a part of the free Francophone population, not enslaved Afro-Creoles or Anglophone free Blacks.[49] In addition to their French speech, manners, and attitude, the "legacy of semi-legitimate sexual relationships across the color line and an ensuing degree of autonomy and control over their own financial and spatial mobility" separated the majority of New Orleans's *gens de couleur libres* from manumitted and enslaved Blacks.[50]

THE *GENS DE COULEUR LIBRES* AND NEW ORLEANS'S ANTEBELLUM ARCHITECTURE

The relationships of free persons of color with Creole and Anglo whites and the economic stability of the *gens de couleur libres* enabled them to purchase property and establish homes and businesses throughout the city, most notably in distinctly Creole enclaves—the Vieux Carré, Faubourg Marigny, and Faubourg Tremé—in the antebellum period. Despite the decline in the percentage of *gens de couleur libres* in the overall population of the city during the 1830s and 1840s, they maintained prevalent roles as property owners but a somewhat diminished role in the creation of buildings. This was partially due to the introduction of popular Anglo styles and forms of architecture that were not feasible for the majority of *gens de couleur libres* master builders to fund or for their patrons of color to finance. For younger *gens de couleur libres* practitioners, the stature of the master builder had weakened with the introduction of a different type of professionalism to the building trades. And, while speculators were still active at the end of the antebellum period, the altered human and architectural demographic distribution of the city played an increasingly limiting role in their transactions.

The work of the geographer Richard Campanella relates the demographics of antebellum New Orleans's private and public architecture and population to the contributions of the *gens de couleur libres* within the changing attitudes of the city's historic and architectural context. Even with the end of the colonial period brought about by the Louisiana Purchase in 1803 and the process of Americanization begun with the city's incorporation in 1805, New Orleans remained a predominantly Creole city. As the city had yet to formally expand outside of its colonial fortification boundary, "all of New Orleans was Creole."[51] When the last names of the property owners listed on city surveyor Joseph Pilié's 1808 plan of the city (figure I.5) are classified into Francophone versus Anglo-sounding last names, the developing pattern shows the predominance of Creole residents with a scattering of Anglo residents in the upper portion of the Vieux Carré, moving toward the developed, but still sparsely settled, Faubourg Sainte-Marie. During the territorial period (1804–1812) and the early years of statehood, an overlapping of residents, builders/architects, and

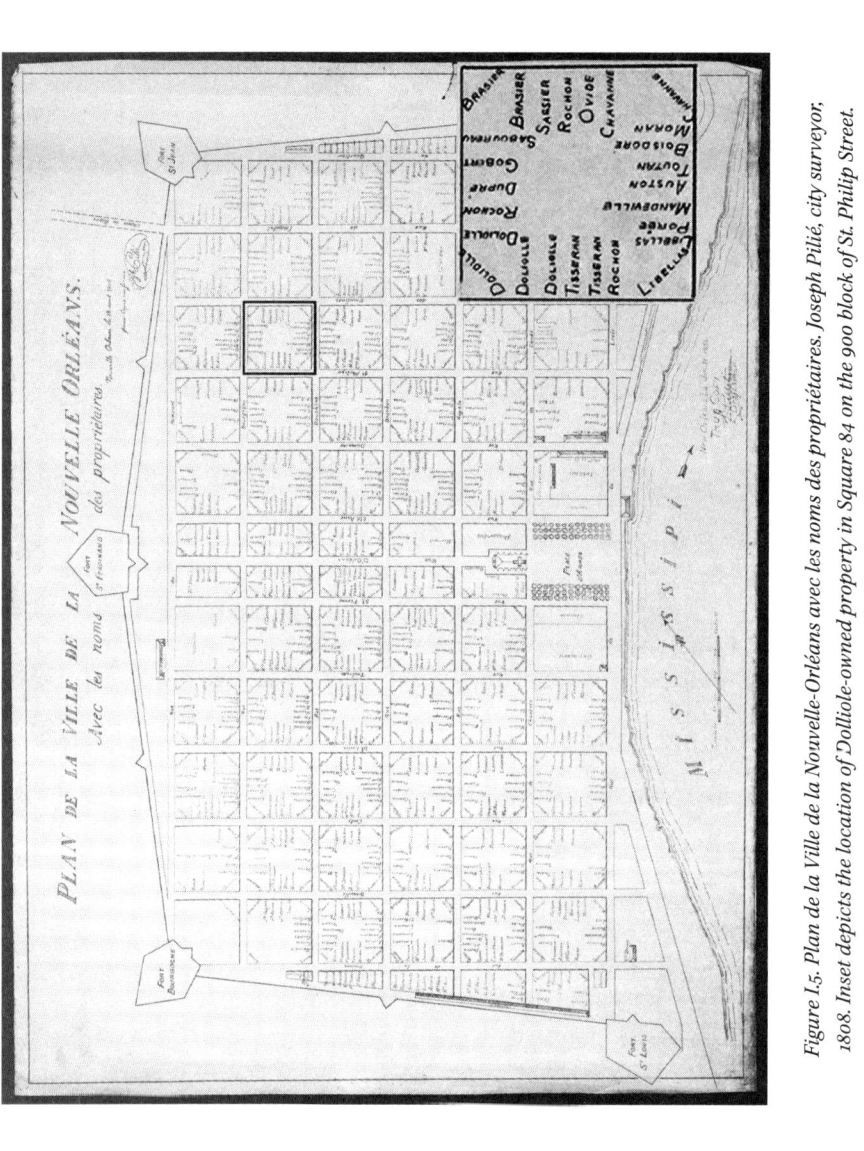

Figure I.5. *Plan de la Ville de la Nouvelle-Orléans avec les noms des propriétaires.* Joseph Pilié, city surveyor, 1808. Inset depicts the location of Dolliole-owned property in Square 84 on the 900 block of St. Philip Street. *The Collins C. Diboll Vieux Carré Digital Survey at The Historic New Orleans Collection.*

architectural forms and styles occurred. The increase in American arrivals from the East Coast after the Louisiana Purchase, as well as the immigration of the Saint-Dominguan refugees, saw a shift in New Orleans's demographics. As a result, Faubourg Sainte-Marie began to be settled, and Faubourgs Marigny and Tremé were developed in 1805 and 1810, respectively. But the city's premier cultural venues—first Orleans Theatre (Latour, 1809), St. Philip Theatre (architect unknown, 1810), second Orleans Theatre (Latrobe, 1816), and third Orleans Theatre (Brand, 1817)—were all located in the original city. In 1820, the city was primarily sited on the natural levee (high ground along the Mississippi River) and dominated by one- and two-story buildings.[52] Though they were located in the Vieux Carré, the construction of buildings in the newly popular Federal Style—Perseverance Lodge and Louisiana State Bank—signaled change. Further, the personal, anti-American prejudices of Bernard Marigny influenced his refusal to allow American developers to establish a commercial presence in his well-laid-out suburb in 1822, encouraging them to look upriver.[53] In 1823, James Caldwell's American Theatre was built and added impetus to the trend of non-Creole buildings replacing long-established forms and styles. In addition to introducing interior and gas lighting, the American Theatre illuminated the path for development outside of the Vieux Carré.

A complete turning point came about in 1836 when tensions between Creoles and Anglo-Americans resulted in the division of the city into three municipalities. The developmental ambitions (or lack thereof) of white Creoles, *gens de couleur libres*, and Anglo-Americans drove the city's demographics at that time. Campanella's work shows that by 1842, Creoles outnumbered Anglos by a 3.2 to 1 ratio below Canal Street, and that above Canal Street, Anglos outnumbered Creoles by 2.8 to 1.[54] The location and density of a larger ratio of Creoles beyond (on the side toward Lake Pontchartrain) Rampart Street in Faubourg Tremé is also apparent. The geography of Creole New Orleans, concentrated in the Vieux Carré in the early part of the antebellum period, shifted below and behind the old city by the end of the antebellum era.

TELLING THE STORY THROUGH AN EXPANDED METHODOLOGY

Focus on the first-generation members of the Dolliole and Soulié families allows for presentation of an unusually crisp picture of the *gens de couleur libres* and their circumstances relevant to the construction and appearance of antebellum New Orleans's built environment as builder-architects, owners, developers, and speculators. These two *gens de couleur libres* families in particular took advantage of opportunities in real estate. Their pursuits in all aspects of the building trades—

INTRODUCTION

as property owners, developers, and builders—are well documented and present the opportunity for both individual *and* collective examination of their influence on the architecture, which yields a historic and methodological process ignored in thematic studies.⁵⁵ *Building Antebellum New Orleans* encompasses a study of individual lives and works of the Dollioles and Souliés while addressing the group experience of the free people of color to highlight their architectural influence in the unique environment of antebellum New Orleans. Various historic documents reveal the Dollioles' and Souliés' stories. A methodology that utilizes these readily available resources as a group to specifically identify people and property further exposes the *process* by which many *gens de couleur libres* constructed individual and group identity through their ownership and development of property. In exploring the influence of the *gens de couleur libres* on New Orleans's antebellum architecture, *Building Antebellum New Orleans* focuses on three processes: ownership, engagement, and entrepreneurship.

Ownership: Possessing the Built Environment

What it meant for the *gens de couleur libres* to live and own property in New Orleans is little discussed in scholarly works.⁵⁶ *Building Antebellum New Orleans* grounds free persons of color in antebellum New Orleans, looking at acquisition and ownership as an identity-building process whereby the origins of the Dolliole and Soulié families are detected, their biographies expanded, and their lives in New Orleans established.

Real property owned by "single" Black or mixed-race mothers such as Eulalie Mazange and Geneviève Azémare or inherited from white fathers like Jean-Louis Dolliole often formed the foundation of *gens de couleur libres* families' architectural legacies. Part One of *Building Antebellum New Orleans* describes how *gens de couleur libres* acquired property, whether through inheritance or outright purchase; details how this property was used; and examines the significance of the locations where *gens de couleur libres* owned property. Though New Orleans's political geography was complicated in its changes and expansions throughout the antebellum period, the *gens de couleur libres* navigated all areas of it.⁵⁷ The act of ownership—the legal act of possession—was an important component, and often the first step, in the architecture-driven identity-building process by which many builders and developers of color established their place in antebellum New Orleans. They came into possession of property primarily via two methods—by birthright or by contract.

Privileges entitled by birth were recognized in the establishment of the first-generation Dollioles as property owners. Louis Dolliole arranged for his children to receive and purchase property that he owned during his lifetime and at his death by providing them with the necessary funds or by making them available for purchase at his death through a third party. The Dollioles circumvented legal limitations on the ability of mixed-race children to inherit property from their white fathers by purchasing property independently of one another and then combining it or dividing it among themselves. For the Souliés on the other hand, ownership came via monetary exchange as part of contractual transactions with neighbors and strangers. Though the process of acquisition emphasized gaining property for one's self through independent actions or efforts, the Souliés worked together and for one another to obtain property in such large numbers that they created their own birthright. The means of acquisition of property also appears to have been related to the use of property on some level. The Dollioles, whose status as owners emphasized birthright, used their properties for home building for themselves and others (or to fund home building). The Souliés, who acquired most of their real property through contract, primarily acquired income by using their properties for speculation and as rentals. While the Dollioles and Souliés, like their contemporaries, possessed land and buildings primarily in Faubourg Tremé, Faubourg Marigny, and other Creole-dominated neighborhoods, they expanded their property ownership across physical and racial boundaries throughout the city in a time of increasing racial and geographic separation.

Engagement: Forming and Transforming the Built Environment

Scholarship on the professions, personal habits, and socioeconomic situations of the *gens de couleur libres* and the building trades has increasingly focused on their roles as builders. Still, articles, chapters, and books on the subject are limited in their focus on this particular constituency and often present brief and repetitive biographical information.[58] The transmission of Creole forms into rural and urban environments by *gens de couleur libres* is an already acknowledged area of investigation. Studies such as those by the art historian Peter Mark and the anthropologist Jay Edwards that analyze the transmission of forms and ideas between European settlers and West African ethnic groups from the fifteenth through the eighteenth centuries are one example.[59] The study of building typology has enabled historians to trace the influence of American forms on Creole buildings and whether or not they were utilized more by Black or white builders.[60] *Building Antebellum New Orleans* investigates the larger context of *gens de couleur libres'* influence on antebellum architecture. These works do little to explore the possibilities of how and why the personal lives and motivations of their subjects intertwined with the building forms that they employed and only hint at circumstances of training and education.⁶¹ Further, these sources present neither the particulars of becoming and being a Black builder or architect nor a comprehensive narrative of the interrelationship between free builders of color and patrons, their place in the community of the *gens de couleur libres*, or their influence on the architecture of the city at large.

While the names of many *gens de couleur libres* builders and architects are known, the particulars of their education and training are not. The socioeconomic status of *gens de couleur libres* builders and architects in the nineteenth century played a role in their continuing or diminishing involvement in the building trades as well as the types of skills they gained and were able to pass on. Understanding how these male builders received their training offers additional insight into their abilities. For example, the brothers Jean-Louis and Joseph Dolliole were from a particularly prolific family.⁶² Descendants of two brothers, Frenchmen who emigrated to New Orleans in the late 1700s, the Afro-Creole Dollioles are a prime example of a family in which building skills were passed down from generation to generation. In addition to learning by doing, some *gens de couleur libres* builders received more formal training. *Building Antebellum New Orleans* compares and contrasts the circumstances and output of family- or self-taught builders like the Dollioles with *gens de couleur libres* who received formal apprenticeships in the building trades or architectural education, such as Norbert Soulié.

In terms of their built works, the principal contribution of New Orleans's *gens de couleur libres* builders in the antebellum period was their ability to refine Creole forms while expanding their knowledge and use of American types and styles in various parts of the city for clients from all walks of life—Black and white, American and Creole. Particularly in the urban context, free builders of color combined various types and forms, including newer ones from the northeast Atlantic seaboard, to serve their own and their clients' needs. Free men of color, however, were most likely to be involved with the construction of domestic forms in New Orleans. Civic and religious architecture were the domain of white builders and architects. Contemporaries such as Frenchmen J. N. B. de Pouilly and Claude Gurlie; Creoles Joachim Courcelle and Jean François Correjolles; and Americans William Brand, Benjamin Henry Latrobe, James Dakin, and James Gallier Sr. designed in European Classical Revival styles and ushered in the Federal and Greek Revival styles. The antebellum "Americanization" of forms and styles, as well as new sources of labor in the building trades in the form of American, immigrant, and emancipated builders, caused free persons of color to increasingly lose their stature socially and economically after Louisiana statehood and the Civil War. More of a total shift in architectural practice and design, this trend

—

18

was a direct contrast to the "Creolization" or mixture that occurred during the colonial era. The dividing line between vernacular and monumental forms was meaningful for the loss of the *gens de couleur libres'* influence on New Orleans's architecture from the antebellum period onward. But their ability to manipulate property as developers and speculators allowed them to retain a stronghold in specific neighborhoods where their persistence allowed for retention of a communal identity that is maintained to the present day.

Entrepreneurship: Controlling the Built Environment

Various types of architectural patronage—the acquisition of property and commissioning of structures for personal use or commercial pursuits as well as real estate speculation—persisted within the *gens de couleur libres* community. As the experiences of the Dolliole and Soulié families show, initial property ownership provided a financial base for future purchases and to support the expense of property development and speculation. Here the families' ownership of enslaved individuals also comes into question. Various scholars assert that slave ownership for the *gens de couleur libres* was complicated; on the one hand, the institution provided a means to have control over and emancipate family members, and on the other hand, it was an economic matter.[63] Whatever the case for the Dollioles and Souliés, neither family engaged in the slave trade at a level that would finance their real estate endeavors.

Over the course of the antebellum period, the first-generation Dollioles owned at least thirty-six properties in the city. The Souliés' property ownership was just as abundant; the first-generation members owned at least thirty-four diverse properties between 1819 and 1850. Many of these, and dozens of others, were utilized by the Soulié siblings as rental property. Their success as property owners and developers underscored additional business achievements and informed the manner in which they handled their business affairs.[64]

Architecture was used to reinforce the financial strength of family groups and the *gens de couleur libres* community as a whole. The Dollioles and the Souliés forged personal and business relationships related to building, development, and speculation with many other prominent *gens de couleur libres*. The Dollioles' prominence provided them with a stature in the *gens de couleur libres* community whereby Jean-Louis and Joseph Dolliole were frequently called upon to serve in a legal capacity as estate executors, appraisers of estate inventories, mortgage and money lenders, and witnesses for other *gens de couleur libres*, including other builders. While most of the first-generation Souliés were French expatriates after 1831, they, likewise, were involved in the financial well-being of the *gens de couleur*

INTRODUCTION

libres community throughout the antebellum period. They remained active not only as absentee landlords but also as money lenders and mortgage holders. Members of both families, individually and collectively, developed personal ties to Black and white Creoles by virtue of their status as builders and wealthy property owners. Jean-Louis Dolliole's oldest son married the daughter of free builder of color Laurent Ursain Guesnon. Joseph Dolliole and *homme de couleur libre* builder and landowner François Boisdoré were neighbors who demanded fair compensation from the city when their land was sought for the expansion of Esplanade Avenue. Several *hommes de couleur libres* builders, including Jean-Louis Dolliole, Joseph Dolliole, Nelson Fouché, and Henry Fletcher, were so connected in the free community of color that the philanthropist Marie Couvent selected them, among others, to oversee her estate and carry out the founding of what became known as the École des Orphelins Indigents (School for Indigent Orphans) after her death.[65] The Souliés' financial and personal records capture their involvement with many other prominent New Orleans families of color. While many of these ties were by virtue of their network of white Creole ancestors and relatives, Bernard Soulié, the only sibling to permanently remain in the city, became a staunch advocate for the rights of the *gens de couleur libres* in the years following the Civil War.

Well-to-do New Orleanians of all ethnic groups recognized the importance of creating kinship and business partnerships to further their personal interests. Particularly for the *gens de couleur libres*, however, their independent pursuits also established and emphasized their identity as a distinct class. Scholarship on the *gens de couleur libres* as a unique ethnic class is presented via a wide range of sources.[66] The manner in which the Dollioles' and Souliés' (among many others') architectural pursuits strengthened group identity in the antebellum period played out physically in space to influence contemporary experience remains evident in present-day perceptions of New Orleans's architectural, social, and economic history, and, in turn, those perceptions influence how the city's architecture and the story of the *gens de couleur libres* is told and preserved.

The architectural legacy of the *gens de couleur libres* reveals intertwined layers of cultural and social meaning relevant to a specific time and place. The cultural aspects of *gens de couleur libres'* endeavors as builders, property owners, and developers encompass their artistic and intellectual undertakings in the built environment, the development of those pursuits through education and training, and the transmission of customary practices literally built up and transmitted from one generation to another.[67] These cultural accomplishments in architecture in turn became integral to the life, welfare, and relations of the entire *gens de couleur libres* community.[68] Thematic study does not tell this whole narrative. Rather, the process by which the *gens de couleur libres* affected New Orleans architecture follows a trajectory of change directly related to the transitional nature of city, race, profession, and architectural style in antebellum New Orleans. Through the experiences of the Dollioles and Souliés, *Building Antebellum New Orleans* navigates the changing physical landscape of the city and reviews the transmission of architectural forms into the urban environment of antebellum New Orleans by the *gens de couleur libres*, examining their effect on the city's built environment within the context of antebellum architectural history. The Creole architecture of New Orleans is one of its most significant character-defining features and was greatly influenced by the *gens de couleur libres*. This work treats *gens de couleur libres'* contributions to the city's physical fabric in a new light, taking a more holistic approach than thematic studies already in place and offering viewpoints in areas as diverse, yet related, as history, economics, education, and material culture, to name a few. My goal is consideration not only of the integrity of the buildings but also of the identity and heritage of the unique group of people who built and lived in them.

The *gens de couleur libres* built, developed, and invested in property for other free people of color. But they were also hired by many white clients and did work outside of the Tremé and the Creole faubourgs. Across the board, the *gens de couleur libres'* architectural ambitions aided the persistence of Creole forms in antebellum Louisiana as well as individual economic survival and growth. Though the rural and urban conditions of many an American landscape in which they were involved would not have been the same without the influence of free people of color, the widespread influence of one ethnic group or class of people is not so pervasive elsewhere. The participation of New Orleans's *gens de couleur libres* places them in a unique position in the wider picture of American architectural, social, and cultural history, as there was little to no distinction among free Blacks (Creole or not) or between *gens de couleur libres* and their white counterparts in architectural endeavors before the Civil War. The architecture of the *gens de couleur libres* is more than a significant number of houses built by and for this ethnic class. Through further examination of specific people and places, *Building Antebellum New Orleans* reveals cultural patterns apparent in the individual and collective activities of two *gens de couleur libres* families and highlights the extent to which their participation in the building trades informed the geography of New Orleans as well as the social and economic independence, creativity, and autonomy of free people of color.

PART I

OWNERSHIP

Possessing the Built Environment

CHAPTER 1

THE *GENS DE COULEUR LIBRES'* ACQUISITION OF PROPERTY

*As a man is said to have a right to his property,
he may be equally said to have a property in his rights.*

JAMES MADISON, "PROPERTY" (1792)

While under Spanish rule from 1762 to 1800, the Louisiana colony transitioned from a struggling territory based on subsistence agriculture to a thriving plantation economy with New Orleans as its commercial, shipping, and cultural center.[1] Many free families of color trace their roots to the latter part of the Spanish period, including those stemming from relationships between Louis Dolliole and Geneviève Azémare and between Jean Soulié and Eulalie Mazange. During this formative period for the colony, members of these and other *gens de couleur libres* families acquired property in numerous instances via familial relationships and contractual arrangements with other New Orleanians—Black and white, Creole and Anglo—that allowed them a stronghold in the city that many white residents of both sexes did not possess.

Though New Orleans was not yet under the dominion of the United States when James Madison sought to explain the meaning of property as invoked by the English philosopher John Locke and others,[2] the protection of property via the government was of paramount importance in the European colony with its stratified society of free whites, *gens de couleur libres*, and enslaved persons. While much of the law dealt, obviously, with the issue of slavery, much also touched upon landownership. The French codified the Louisiana colony's tripartite racial system with the Code Noir of 1724, and the Spanish reinforced it in the late 1760s, albeit through more liberal policies.[3] Increased voluntary manumissions without government approval were recorded beginning shortly after the first Spanish governor, Alejandro O'Reilly, introduced his Ordinances and Instructions implementing Spanish law in November 1769.[4] The new government introduced the legal practice of *coartación*—petition of freedom for a price—which allowed enslaved individuals to legally sue for their freedom (even while the slave trade was reopened in 1777). Spanish land grants were made to free people of color, land was transferred to *gens de couleur libres* from white colonists for services rendered or for filial affections, and many *gens de couleur libres* purchased property outright from early colonists and their neighbors regardless of race.[5]

With the Louisiana Purchase in 1803, free people of color were not promised the rights of full citizenship.[6] In 1805, despite ambiguous wording in New Orleans's incorporation act, it became evident that the city council did not intend to enfranchise free Black people. *Gens de couleur libres* taxpayers and property owners continued to be ignored even though many free men of color provided invaluable militia service during the slave insurrection of 1811 that occurred on plantations upriver from New Orleans. Further, many provisions of the 1812 state constitution were explicitly limited to "free male white persons."[7] While the state constitution denied *gens de couleur libres* political rights, jury service, and militia service, it retained their rights to trial by jury and to testify in court, make contracts, and own property.

BIRTHRIGHT VERSUS CONTRACT

Ownership, the legal act of property possession (having land or buildings belonging to one),[8] was the first step in the architecture-driven identity-building process by which many builders and developers of color established their place in antebellum New Orleans. They primarily acquired or came into possession of property via two methods—by birthright or by contract. Birthright, "any right of privilege to which a person is entitled by birth,"[9] involved property that was passed from one family member to another. This usually occurred when a parent bequeathed land (with or without improvements) to children via a last will and testament (also known as a testamentary donation). In antebellum New Orleans, however, *inter vivos* (between living people) donations, whereby property was transferred or gifted to another party during one's lifetime, were also common. Contractual transfer of property, on the other hand, was a legal agreement between two or more parties enforceable by law. The primary difference between transfer and acquisition of property via birthright or contract was that the former was usually between family members or close acquaintances, and the latter involved monetary exchange.

The historian Shirley Thompson notes that birthright is traditionally and historically the most prominent claim to territory, endowing one with the responsibility to refine and defend that territory.[10] Establishing birthright was often difficult to do for the offspring of mixed-race relationships in antebellum New Orleans. The Code Noir of 1724 forbade miscegenation and legal marriage between Black and white persons.[11] Recognition as "natural" offspring conveyed a status of pseudo legitimacy on children of these unions. A natural child was one born of an extramarital union but acknowledged by the father. Natural children could be of white, Black, or mixed-race parentage and became legal heirs upon recognition before a notary and two witnesses.[12] Prior to changes in the Code Noir, it was not unheard of for white fathers to bequeath real and movable property to their mixed-race children. The Louisiana Civil Code of 1808, revised in 1825, however, prevented interracial couples from legitimizing their unions and favored inheritance of property to white offspring and relatives by limiting the property that white fathers could bequeath to their "natural" children.[13] With tighter restrictions by 1825, even if a man had no legitimate children and only "collateral relatives such as cousins," he could only bequeath one-third of his estate to his natural children.[14] The Dolliole and Soulié families found ways to circumvent the *gens de couleur libres'* predicament of being able to inherit and accumulate only prescribed quantities of real wealth because of restrictions placed on illegitimate interracial relationships.[15] The Dolliole matriarch and patriarch purchased property independently of one another that could then be combined or divided between their children. The Dollioles, as well as the Souliés, owned a number of properties that were transferred via *inter vivos* donations. The Soulié family, however, acquired most of their real property through contractual transaction with neighbors and strangers as opposed to transferring property among one another. While the concepts of birthright and contract coexist, especially in terms of one's birthright being potentially contracted (or recontracted) upon one's death by way of probate proceedings, contracts, according to Thompson, have the "ability to supersede past arrangements and attempt to proceed anew from a space of 'cleared ground.'"[16] Not having inherited significant amounts of property from their father or from their mother, the Soulié siblings purchased their property outright, establishing for themselves the right to own and claim property.

BIRTHRIGHT: THE DOLLIOLES

By virtue of their individual status as property owners and partners in a long-term relationship, *négresse libre* Geneviève Azémare (ca. 1745–1836) and Frenchman Louis Dolliole (1742–1822) set the stage for their children to establish a foothold as some of New Orleans's most distinguished *gens de couleur libres* property owners. Documents from Geneviève's estate file reveal that she was born about 1745.[17] She is generally referred to as a *négresse libre*, or "free negro woman," in legal documents during her lifetime; it is not known when Geneviève was manumitted, but historians have revealed that she was the daughter of Louis d'Azémare and an unidentified enslaved woman.[18] Geneviève had three daughters early in the Spanish colonial period: Charlotte (1766), Rosette (1767), and Marie Françoise (1776). Their father(s) is (are) unknown. Louis and Geneviève began a relationship and possibly were living together by 1779 as evidenced by the birth of their first son, Jean-Louis.[19] Later offspring included Madeleine (1783), Pierre (ca. 1785), and Joseph (ca. 1791). None of the births of Louis and Geneviève's four children are documented in church or civil records.[20] On August 28, 1794, Geneviève purchased a 30' × 60' piece of property fronting St. Philip Street from free woman of color Mariana St. Jean. Geneviève, Louis, and their minor offspring (Jean-Louis would have been the oldest at fifteen years old) likely lived here together after the acquisition.

The historical record has not indicated where Louis Dolliole resided from his arrival in New Orleans until the late 1780s. His real estate activities in various parts of the city shed light on his personal and the Dollioles' family life. On July 12, 1788, Louis purchased a lot at 922–924 Dauphine Street.[21] The property contained a house that had been destroyed by the Great Fire of New Orleans of March 12, 1788. It is possible that Dolliole purchased the land at a bargain and sought to profit from that disaster; however, he does not appear to have developed the lot before selling it in 1804.[22] In 1801, Louis purchased a large lot on St. Philip Street. It was adjacent to the property Geneviève had purchased in 1794.

The Dollioles' St. Philip Street, Bayou Road, and Faubourg Franklin properties were among many owned throughout the city by the family, dating from Geneviève's 1794 acquisition to Joseph's death in 1868 (table 1.1). Like many *gens de couleur libres*, the Dollioles began amassing property at a time when the growth of a free Black population was encouraged.[23] New Orleans's *gens de couleur libres* community originated in the Spanish colonial period due to a demographic, economic, political, and military environment rooted in a tolerant Caribbean community.[24] The first-generation Dollioles came of age in the Spanish regime

TABLE 1.1. PROPERTIES OWNED BY LOUIS DOLLIOLE, GENEVIÈVE AZÉMARE *DIT* LARONDE, AND THEIR CHILDREN, 1794-1868

Current street address/location	Faubourg (municipality)	Date of purchase	Date of sale	Family member(s)
927–929 St. Philip	Vieux Carré (1st)	1794/1804	1844	Geneviève Jean-Louis
931–933 St. Philip	Vieux Carré (1st)	1801/1804	1854	Louis Jean-Louis
935–937 St. Philip	Vieux Carré (1st)	1801	1843	Louis Pierre Geneviève Jean-Louis
939–941 St. Philip	Vieux Carré (1st)	1801	1843	Louis Jean-Louis
1010 Burgundy	Vieux Carré (1st)	1804	1842	Jean-Louis Madeleine Victoire
1300 block of Governor Nicholls (Bayou Road)	Tremé (1st)	1806	1841	Louis Joseph
1502 Governor Nicholls	Tremé (1st)	1807	1861*	Jean-Louis
Dauphine at Kerlerec (History at Greatmen)	Marigny (3rd)	1811	unknown	Pierre Joseph
Bagatelle	Marigny (3rd)	1814 (before)	unknown	Jean-Louis Joseph
Bayou Road	Tremé (3rd)	1814 (before)	1822	Jean-Louis Joseph
1123 St. Philip	Tremé (1st)	1816	1869*	Jean-Louis Pierre Geneviève Joseph
1125 St. Philip	Tremé (1st)	1816	unknown	Jean-Louis Pierre
1127 St. Philip	Tremé (1st)	1816	1857	Jean-Louis Pierre
1129 St. Philip	Tremé (1st)	1816	1821	Jean-Louis Pierre
1436 Pauger	Marigny (3rd)	1820	1858	Jean-Louis
909–911 Orleans	Vieux Carré (1st)	1826	1834	Jean-Louis
1200 block of St. Philip	Tremé (1st)	1826/1830	1831	Jean-Louis
1201 St. Philip	Tremé (1st)	1826	unknown	Madeleine

Address	Faubourg	Acquired	Sold	Owner
1205 St. Philip	Tremé (1st)	1826	1850	Madeleine Victoire
1223–1225 St. Philip	Tremé (1st)	1827	1869	Rosette Joseph
1227 St. Philip	Tremé (1st)	1827	1854	Rosette Joseph
1029 Bourbon	Vieux Carré (1st)	1829	1860	Joseph
1300 block of St. Philip	Tremé (1st)	1830	1831	Joseph
1523 Ursulines	Tremé (1st)	unknown	1833	Jean-Louis
1518 Governor Nicholls	Tremé (1st)	ca. 1834	ca. 1838	Jean-Louis
1522 Governor Nicholls	Tremé (1st)	ca. 1834	ca. 1838	Jean-Louis
Washington Promenade (Sq. 102)	Franklin (3rd)	1835	1835	Joseph
Faubourg Franklin (Sq. 184)	Franklin (3rd)	1835	unknown	Joseph
729 Governor Nicholls 1200–1210 Bourbon	Vieux Carré (1st)	1836	1836	Joseph
1455–57 Pauger	Marigny (3rd)	1838	1841	Jean-Louis
923–925 N. Robertson	Tremé (1st)	1838	1839	Joseph
Villeré between Bayou Road and Ursulines (Lot No. 19)	Tremé (1st)	ca. 1841	unknown	Jean-Louis
Villeré between Bayou Road and Ursulines (Lot No. 20)	Tremé (1st)	1841	1861*	Jean-Louis
822–824 Governor Nicholls	Vieux Carré (1st)	1841	1845	Jean-Louis
		1847	1857	Joseph
1200 block Governor Nicholls (Lot No. 7, Bayou Road near Tremé)	Tremé (1st)	1845	1861*	Jean-Louis
1200 block Governor Nicholls (Lot No. 8, Bayou Road near Tremé)	Tremé (1st)	1845	1861*	Jean-Louis

TABLE 1.1, CONTINUED

Current street address/location	Faubourg (municipality)	Date of purchase	Date of sale	Family member(s)
500 block Marais Street (Lot No. 2 in square bound by Marais, St. Louis, Villeré, and Toulouse)	Tremé (1st)	1848	unknown	Jean-Louis

Note: An asterisk indicates that property was listed on last owner's estate inventory. This list includes some properties owned by Geneviève's daughters Rosette and Charlotte, as they relate to properties later belonging to their half siblings. Rosette and Charlotte were older than Geneviève's children with Louis but adopted the surname Dolliole; the two women are not discussed at length in this work. Property owned independently by Louis or Geneviève is not included in table 1.1.

and were well established in the Vieux Carré and Faubourg Marigny by the territorial period and years of early statehood.[25] The properties they obtained prior to 1830 set the stage for the family's real estate endeavors; most of it was retained or obtained during and through the 1830s and 1840s. Property acquisitions—located in the Vieux Carré and Faubourgs Marigny and Tremé—in the latter part of the antebellum period served as income for the family members. The first-generation Dollioles took advantage of these peak decades in New Orleans's economic history to continue to acquire property for their residences and to generate development opportunities as the city's population and boundaries expanded.

Creating the Family Compound

The real estate acquisitions of Geneviève Azémare and Louis Dolliole laid the foundation for the establishment of a family compound that allowed the couple, their children, and even grandchildren to be stakeholders in property ownership through the middle of the next century. In 1794, Geneviève Azémare purchased property on St. Philip Street. On the surface, this transaction was completed solely by Geneviève. And it was under another alias, Laronde. Presumably, Louis and Geneviève moved there with their children, and Louis built a house on the property. It is clear that Louis and Geneviève were both living on the property in 1801 when, in transactions for the adjacent lot, ownership of the Laronde/Dolliole land was credited to Louis in January 1801 and then to Geneviève in July 1801.[26] Regardless of who was behind the purchase, the family became established on St. Philip Street, and Louis expanded their holdings at this location. On July 11, 1801, he acquired a large, 92′ × 60′ lot in Square 84 at St. Philip and

THE *GENS DE COULEUR LIBRES'* ACQUISITION OF PROPERTY

Burgundy Streets adjacent to Geneviève's property.[27] Louis Dolliole lived there, at 67 St. Philip Street, according to the 1805 New Orleans directory and census.[28] He was the only white occupant, while four *gens de couleur libres* were in residence— one female over the age of sixteen and three males under the age of sixteen. Three of the individuals would have been Geneviève, Joseph, and Pierre.[29] Daughter Madeleine, age twenty-two, was listed—under her husband, Noel Galaud—as living on the family property (at 63 St. Philip, probably Geneviève's lot).[30] Jean-Louis likely resided on adjacent property facing Burgundy Street; he purchased a 30' by 120' lot from *femme de couleur libre* Louison Desprès bordering the rear of his parents' St. Philip Street holdings on July 26, 1804.[31] Expansions to and divisions of the family land on St. Philip and Burgundy Streets were made to accommodate the Dolliole children as they grew older and established families of their own (figure 1.1).

1010 Burgundy Street

After Madeleine Dolliole's marriage at about age fifteen to *homme de couleur libre* Noel Galaud in 1798, the newlyweds resided at Geneviève's St. Philip Street property. Louis Dolliole provided the funds for Jean-Louis to purchase the 30' × 120' lot facing Burgundy Street, and adjacent to his own, from Louison Desprès in July 1804 for the use of his two eldest children, Jean-Louis and Madeleine.[32] Accordingly, Jean-Louis transferred the lakeside half of the property to Noel Galaud ("in the name and as spouse of" Madeleine Dolliole) later in the year.[33] An act of sale dated November 8, 1805, indicates that ultimately Jean-Louis transferred all interest in the Burgundy Street property to his sister for $250.00.[34] Madeleine lived at present-day 1010 Burgundy Street with her daughter (husband Noel died in July 1808)[35] until they moved to the 1100 block of St. Philip Street in the 1820s. When Madeleine died in 1835, her daughter Victoire Galaud Urquhart inherited the property. Victoire retained the property for seven years; it was sold with the extant ca. 1835 three-bay cottage and outbuildings upon her death in 1842.[36]

927–929 St. Philip Street

At an unknown date, and without benefit of a formal notarized transaction or written title, Jean-Louis sold or gave the riverside quarter of his Burgundy Street property—a 30' × 30' portion—to his mother. When added to her existing property purchased in 1794, Geneviève had a 30' × 90' lot facing St. Philip Street under her ownership (present numbers 927–929). She lived here until the 1820s. In 1838, two years after Geneviève died in 1836, an order to sell the property was made

OWNERSHIP

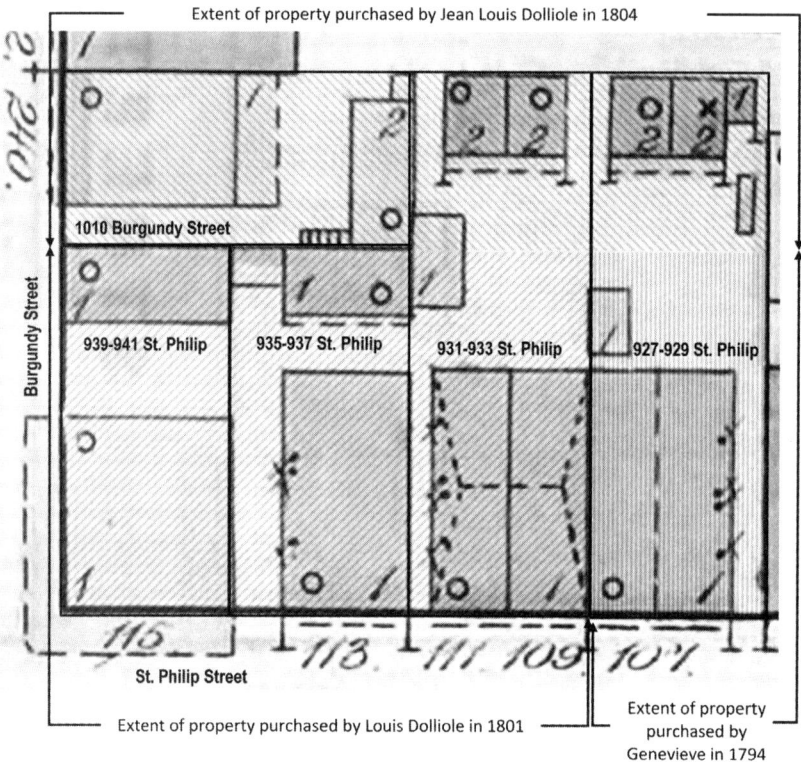

Figure 1.1. Chronicle of Dolliole-owned property in the 900 block of St. Philip Street, 1794–1854, overlaid on detail of 1876 Sanborn Fire Insurance Company map. Sanborn Fire Insurance Maps, New Orleans, Louisiana, 1876, sheet 34, Collection 125, Southeastern Architectural Archive, Tulane University Special Collections, New Orleans, Louisiana.

by the court of probates.[37] By this time, the lot contained the main dwelling, a four-bay cottage, and other outbuildings. Jean-Louis purchased the property from Geneviève's succession for $5,600.00 on May 11, 1839. He owned it for another five and a half years before selling it to Mathilde Duralde in 1844.[38]

931–933 St. Philip Street

In December 1804, Louis sold approximately one-third of his large St. Philip Street property to Jean-Louis for $250.00.[39] The rear of said property abutted another 30' × 30' portion of Jean-Louis's Burgundy Street property. Jean-Louis now owned a 30' × 90' lot facing St. Philip at present-day numbers 931–933. In 1805, he built the extant four-bay cottage.⁴⁰ In his midtwenties by this time, Jean-Louis established residence outside of his parents' home. He would have lived here with his family—consort Hortense Dusuau and their young children (born between 1809 and 1816)—until moving to a house built in Faubourg Marigny on land purchased from Hortense's mother in 1820. After this time, the St. Philip Street lot served as income property. The property at 931–933 St. Philip Street remained in the Dolliole family the longest—for fifty-three years; Jean-Louis sold it in 1854.⁴¹

935–937 St. Philip Street

In 1812, Louis Dolliole sold the central 25' × 60' portion of his large St. Philip Street lot to second son Pierre for $400.00.⁴² Pierre, a shoemaker, had already been living on the property, as he is listed in residence in the 1811 city directory. According to the act of sale, the lot contained buildings that had been built by or for Pierre with Louis's permission. Since Pierre was a shoemaker by trade, one of his older brothers probably built the house. When Pierre died in 1822, the land and buildings were bequeathed to his mother, Geneviève.⁴³ Jean-Louis then purchased the property from his mother's estate in 1839 for $3,800.00.⁴⁴ He owned this portion of the St. Philip Street land until he sold it to Marie Laure Popin in 1843.⁴⁵

939–941 St. Philip Street

Jean-Louis ultimately acquired the corner lot of the Dollioles' St. Philip Street holdings, placing the entire compound under his ownership. He purchased the 35' × 60' lot—with a tile-clad, four-room brick-between-post house; a brick kitchen with tile roof; and outhouses—from his father's estate for $4,500.00 on March 9, 1822.⁴⁶ By this time, Jean-Louis owned other property in Faubourgs Marigny and Tremé. Still, he retained possession of this corner lot until April 1843.⁴⁷

City surveyor Joseph Pilié's "Plan de la Ville de la Nouvelle-Orléans avec les noms des propriétaires" clearly labels the Dolliole family's landholdings in Square 84 of the Vieux Carré (see figure I.5). In the first two decades of the nineteenth century, the properties were subdivided among the Dolliole children as they came into adulthood. In 1804, 1822, and 1839, all of the lots facing St. Philip Street came into Jean-Louis's possession. A survey of New Orleans city directories shows that members of the Dolliole family resided in the 900 block of St. Philip Street at least until 1811 (Louis at no. 63, Pierre at no. 65, and Louis at no. 67).⁴⁸ Starting in the 1820s, the lots and buildings appear to have been rented until they were sold in the 1840s and 1850s. Though the Dollioles no longer resided on St. Philip Street and had other holdings on Bayou Road, the decades from 1810 to 1850 saw a significant amount of property come under the ownership of the Dolliole siblings (as well as their half sisters Charlotte and Rosette) through a variety of means.[49]

Dolliole Family Ownership through the 1840s

During the second half of the first decade of the nineteenth century, the Dollioles established a presence outside of the city proper. Like many other New Orleanians, white and Black, Louis Dolliole purchased property along Bayou Road. Claude Tremé sold lots that he and his wife inherited from the former Morand-Moreau plantation to many *gens de couleur libres* between 1798 and 1810, including free man of color Charles Montreuil.[50] On June 7, 1806, Louis purchased a former Tremé property—a 60' × 270' lot on Bayou Road (present-day 1300 block of Governor Nicholls)—from Charles Montreuil.[51] By this time, or soon thereafter, it appears that Louis and Geneviève had ended their relationship—they are listed separately as heads of household at different addresses in the 1810 census. Thus, with the Bayou Road purchase, Louis gained a residence elsewhere. Regardless of Louis Dolliole's motivations, his son Jean-Louis followed suit, also purchasing a lot on Bayou Road from Claude Tremé in March 1807 (figure 1.2).[52] Jean-Louis established his residence there, building a house at present-day number 1502.[53] Whether this, or the house at 931–933 St. Philip, was the primary residence for Jean-Louis, Hortense Dusuau, and their children is not known. It is listed as his primary residence in 1822 and from 1841 on. This property was sold out of the family after Jean-Louis died in 1861; it was the property that he owned individually for the longest, at fifty-four years.

Once the youngest Dolliole sons, Pierre and Joseph, came into adulthood, land bequests or monetary assistance for the purchase of property was not so immediately forthcoming from their parents as it was for their older siblings. If Louis and Geneviève had indeed ended their relationship by the 1810s, this may have been a reason. In 1811, Pierre and Joseph jointly purchased a lot at the corner of Greatmen and History Streets (present-day Dauphine and Kerlerec Streets) from Zaire (alias Françoise Grammont) in the newly developed Faubourg Marigny (1806).[54] As mentioned above, Pierre received his share of the family's St. Philip Street property in 1812. Joseph, on the other hand, had come into his own to the extent that he was able to assist family members via land transactions. In 1814, Jean-Louis sold to Joseph properties on Bayou Road and Bagatelle Street (purchased at an unknown date), two enslaved individuals, and the tools of his trade.[55] A cash down payment was exchanged between the brothers, with the balance to be applied to several of Jean-Louis's debts, including

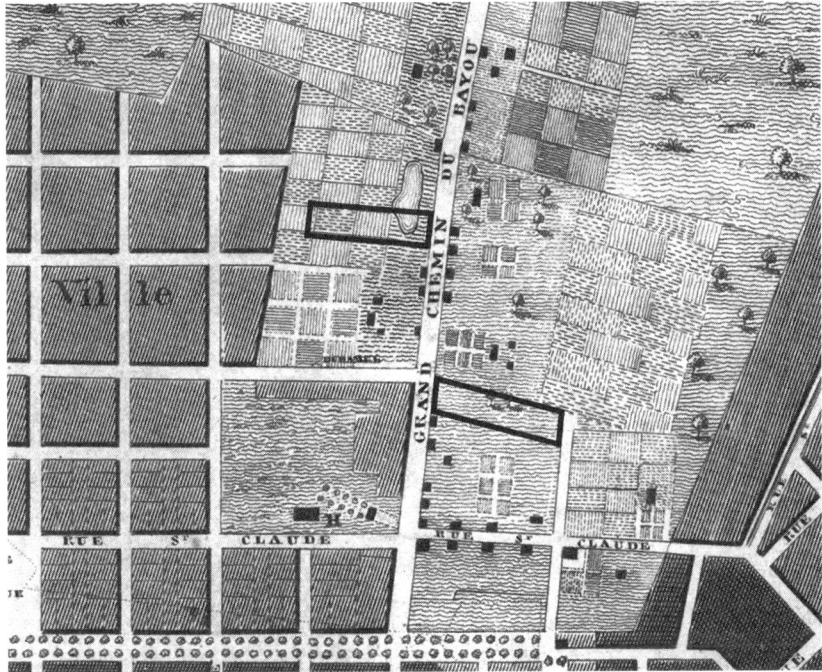

Figure 1.2. Approximate locations of Louis (right) and Jean-Louis Dolliole (left) properties on Bayou Road shown on plan of the city and suburbs of New Orleans: from an actual survey made in 1815 by J. Tanesse. Published by Charles Del Vecchio (New York) and P. Maspero (New Orleans), 1817. The Collins C. Diboll Vieux Carré Digital Survey at The Historic New Orleans Collection.

one to their mother, Geneviève, and another to their brother Pierre. Whatever financial problems Jean-Louis experienced at this time, his situation improved as he continued to acquire property and work as a carpenter and builder in the early years of Louisiana statehood. The latter part of the 1810s saw the Dolliole brothers start a second St. Philip Street family compound, on the lake side of Rampart Street in the 1100 block (figure 1.3). In 1816, Jean-Louis Dolliole, Pierre Dolliole, and Norbert Fortier purchased a 120' × 120' lot (including present-day nos. 1127–1129). The property appears as lots 30 and 31 on an 1816 survey by Jacques Tanesse (figure 1.4).

In 1819, Jean-Louis Dolliole began constructing a house on Pauger Street on property belonging to Catherine Dusuau, his deceased wife's mother (figure 1.5).[56] He purchased the majority of the lot and the house that was under construction a few months later in February 1820.[57] Jean-Louis developed and purchased this

OWNERSHIP

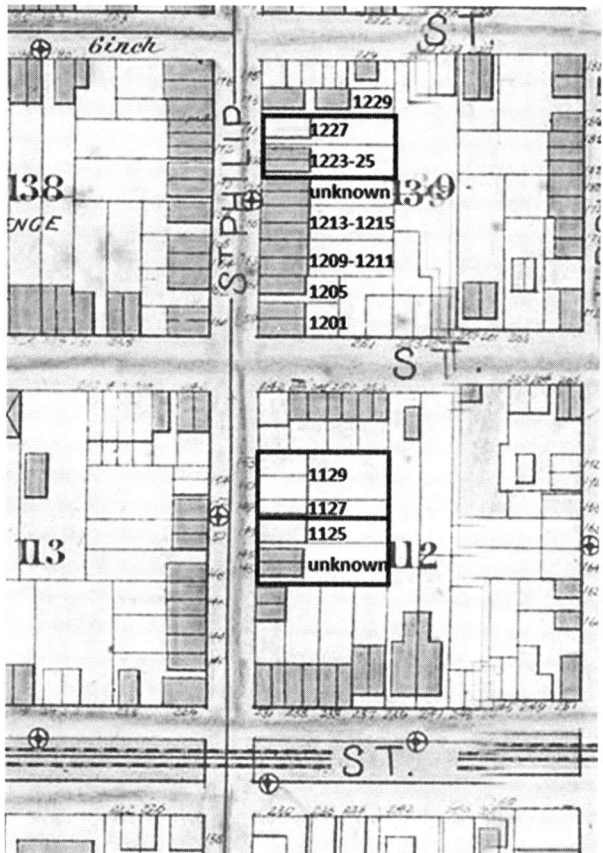

Figure 1.3. Dolliole properties in the 1100 and 1200 blocks of St. Philip Street indicated on the Robinson Atlas, plate no. 7, 1883. Courtesy of Hon. Chelsey Richard Napoleon, Clerk of Civil District Court, Parish of Orleans.

property to provide for his three minor children. A month and a half after he acquired it, Jean-Louis made an *inter vivos* donation of the property to his minor children to provide for their support but reserved the right to use it during his lifetime.[58] Ultimately, Dolliole sold the property in 1858.

The years 1821 and 1822 saw various transitions leading up to and as a result of the deaths of two family members. In June 1821, Jean-Louis and Pierre Dolliole and Norbert Fortier confirmed partition of their joint property in the 1100 block of St. Philip Street whereby each received a lot approximately 42' × 130' in size (see figure 1.4).[59] Jean-Louis built two cottages on his lot (present-day numbers 1125 and 1127);

Figure 1.4. Lots 30 and 31 purchased by Jean-Louis and Pierre Dolliole and Norbert Fortier in 1816. Note the location of the Collège d'Orléans. Plan de division d'une portion de terre situee, au N.N.O. de la Nouvelle Orleans, et appurtenant a la corporation, aux droits de Monsieur Tremé. Plan by Jacques Tanesse, 1810. Louisiana Map Collection, Louisiana Division/City Archives, New Orleans Public Library. The inset indicates the partition of the property and floor plan of the house that Joseph Dolliole constructed on lot "E" (1123 St. Philip Street) in the 1830s. Detail of plan by J. A. d'Hémécourt, 1869. Attached to Succession of Joseph Dolliole, Joseph Cuvillier notary, volume 83, act 7, December 16, 1868. Courtesy of Hon. Chelsey Richard Napoleon, Clerk of Civil District Court, Parish of Orleans.

they were occupied by Jean-Louis or his son Louis Drausin through the 1840s. On the same day that the brothers made the partition, Pierre authorized a general procuration whereby he gave Jean-Louis the authority to act on his behalf in legal matters.[60] The following month, Pierre sold his share of the Bagatelle Street property to Joseph;[61] the latter made this location his primary residence, as it is listed as his address in the 1822 city directory. The reason Pierre divested himself of these two properties is not clear in the acts of sale. However, it is noted that the partition clarified the ownership of each third by its respective owner to avoid future confusion. Perhaps he did so to prepare for and fund his trip or permanent relocation to Port-de-Paix, Saint-Domingue. In fact, he died there the next year. While his succession records cannot be found, property records note that Pierre willed his properties in the 900 and 1100 blocks of St. Philip Street to his mother,

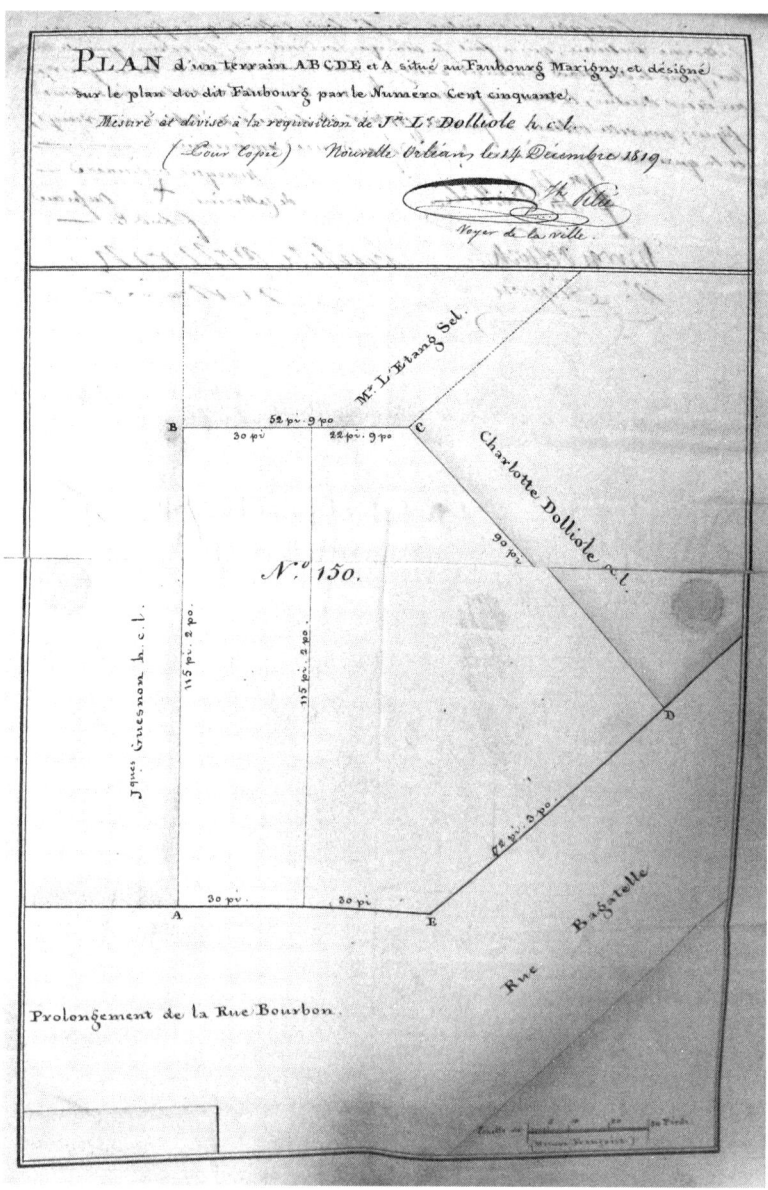

Figure 1.5. 1436 Pauger Street. Plan of a lot of land ABCDE situated in Faubourg Marigny and designated on the plan of said faubourg by the number 150. Joseph Pilié, city surveyor, December 14, 1819. Attached to sale of land from Catherine Dusuau to Jean-Louis Dolliole, Carlile Pollock notary, volume 2, açt 126, February 4, 1820. Courtesy of Hon. Chelsey Richard Napoleon, Clerk of Civil District Court, Parish of Orleans.

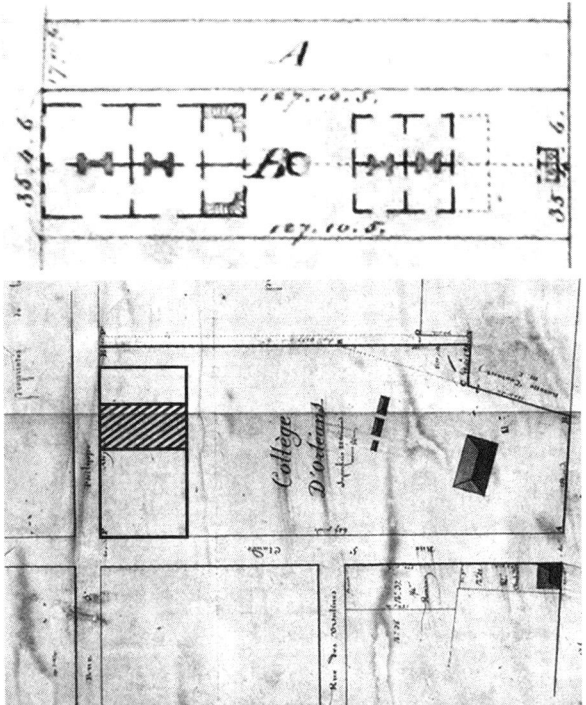

Figure 1.6. Map showing location of Madeleine and Rosette Dolliole purchases on former Collège d'Orléans property (1200 block of St. Philip Street). Plan of the Collège d'Orléans by Jacques Tanesse, 1811. Louisiana Map Collection, Louisiana Division/City Archives, New Orleans Public Library. The inset indicates the property and floor plan of the house that Joseph Dolliole constructed at 1223–1225 St. Philip Street in the 1830s. Detail of plan by J. A. d'Hémécourt, 1869. Attached to Succession of Joseph Dolliole, J. Cuvillier notary, volume 83, act 7, December 16, 1868. Courtesy of Hon. Chelsey Richard Napoleon, Clerk of Civil District Court, Parish of Orleans.

Geneviève. The transfer of ownership to his brothers and bequests to his mother made settling Pierre's estate easier.

Earlier in the year, the family had suffered another loss. Family patriarch Louis Antoine Dolliole died on February 13, 1822, at the age of eighty.[62] In his will, he noted that half of the furnishings in the house belonged to Geneviève. He bequeathed the other half of the furniture and all of the house plate, linen, and utensils to her. Inheritance laws limited Louis from leaving his landed property to either Geneviève or his four recognized children—Jean-Louis, Madeleine,

Joseph, and Pierre. Instead, he left the children monetary bequests of 300 piastres each to be remitted by his executor, Joseph Aicard, after his death.[63] Aicard was also placed in charge of seeing to the sale of the immovable property from Louis's estate. He fulfilled these duties in March 1822 when he sold, undoubtedly through a previously arranged agreement, Louis's corner lot at St. Philip and Burgundy Streets to Jean-Louis and the lot in the 1300 block of Bayou Road to Joseph.[64] Because of restrictive inheritance laws, he arranged for Geneviève to receive the maximum that she could in movable property—the household goods—and for his children to receive his immovable property through a third party. Furthermore, with these purchases, Jean-Louis and Joseph saw to their mother's financial stability; they made *inter vivos* donations of Louis's former properties to Geneviève for her use during her lifetime as signs of their love and filial gratitude.[65] Geneviève's financial needs were further solidified when she inherited Pierre's properties. Indirectly, the first-generation Dollioles received their birthright and, as a result, were able to support their mother and acknowledge her left-handed marriage to Louis Dolliole.

In the latter half of the 1820s, the Dollioles invested in property of the Collège d'Orléans (figure 1.6). The school was built on the grounds of the former Morand-Tremé plantation in 1812. The institution failed five short years later, and in the 1820s, the city corporation began auctioning off the property. The Dolliole women took advantage of this opportunity. In 1826, Madeleine Dolliole purchased two properties on St. Philip Street (present-day numbers 1201 and 1205), in the square above her brothers' lots in the 1100 block; she retained them until her death in 1835, at which time they were passed down to her only child, daughter Victoire Galaud.[66] In 1827, Dolliole half sister Rosette purchased former Collège d'Orléans property at present-day numbers 1223–1225 and 1227 St. Philip. She sold the undeveloped fifty-foot-wide lot to Joseph in 1834.[67] Joseph created two lots; on one (1227), he built a two-bay cottage that he sold in 1854, and on the other (1223–1225), he built a cottage that was sold after his death by his widow, Josefa Rodriguez, in 1869.

The notarial archives reveal an interesting partnership in which Joseph Dolliole was involved. In May 1835, he and Nelson Fouché, another *homme de couleur libre* builder, purchased several properties in Faubourg Franklin (the uptown portion of Nouvelle Marigny—an extension of Faubourg Marigny, created in 1826). After the neighborhood began to be developed in 1830, Dolliole and Fouché acquired eight lots in Square 102 on Washington Promenade (present-day St. Roch Avenue) and all of Square 148.[68] They began capitalizing on their investment in Square 102, replatting it into nine lots and then selling one of the lots on December 29, 1835, and another on February 11, 1836.[69] Though the fate of the other lots is not known, it is clear that the two builders purchased the properties to develop and sell them for their own profit as the city of New Orleans continued to grow outside of its colonial boundaries in the antebellum period.

In addition to retaining property within their immediate family, the Dollioles also often transferred property between their extended family members. This was first done between Jean-Louis Dolliole and his first wife's mother in 1821. In 1841, Jean-Louis acquired property on Governor Nicholls Street from Joseph's mother-in-law, Marguerite Jason, and her brother and sister, Gabriel and Helene.[70] Four years later, he resold the property to Helene Jason. Then, in 1847, she again sold the property, this time to Joseph Dolliole and Magdeleine Hobe (Joseph's wife and the seller's niece). The couple retained the property until 1857. Again, the Dolliole's practices of property acquisition and ownership emphasized family ties and longevity.

CONTRACT: THE SOULIÉS

The notion of property ownership through an established birthright did not play into the role of property acquisition for the first-generation Souliés, even though they were born into families who were well established in New Orleans and owned various properties by the antebellum period. Instead, they used the legalized purchase and sale of property to create their own rights and privileges. Research does not reveal when Jean Soulié (1760–1834) arrived in New Orleans or substantiate that he had any family residing in New Orleans.[71] Eulalie Mazange (1775–1825), on the other hand, descended from Black and white families who had resided in the city since the French colonial period and had ties to many other old New Orleans families. Her mother was Louison Cheval (ca. 1754–1839), the daughter of an unknown enslaved woman and François Cheval (1727–1793), a resident of the German Coast whose parents emigrated to the Louisiana colony from Grenoble, France, in 1731.[72] Louison was around sixteen years old when inventoried as part of François Liotau's estate in 1768.[73] François Cheval purchased Louison from Marie Louise Liotau in 1774 and emancipated her about three years later.[74] Louison and her mixed-race half siblings were among the *gens de couleur libres* who owned significant amounts of property in the city and other parts of the Louisiana colony.[75]

Eulalie Mazange was born enslaved around 1773. She was an infant when her mother was manumitted but remained enslaved by the Liotau family. The widow Marie Louise Liotau freed Eulalie in 1784.[76] In the 1788 city census, two female children are listed in Louison's household, suggesting that Eulalie and Henriette lived with their free mother as if they were free even though the children were still enslaved.[77] The historic record and familial relationships imply that Eulalie's father was the New Orleans notary Leonard Mazange or that she took his name since he endorsed her act of emancipation.[78] After the births of Eulalie and her half sister Henriette, Louison entered into a long-term relationship with Jean Charles Vivant, a wealthy French merchant and landowner. Notarial and other archival records, as well as secondary sources, indicate that Charles Vivant and Jean Soulié were business associates, which is likely how the latter and Eulalie Mazange became acquainted.[79]

Jean Soulié and Eulalie Mazange commenced their long-term relationship by late 1788 (their oldest son, Lucien, was born on May 27, 1789). Over the course of the next two decades, the couple had at least nine more children: Marie Louise (1791), Norbert (1793), Eulalie (1798), Bernard (1801), Benedic (1802), Albin (1803), Louise (1808), Celeste (1810), and Coralie (1811), all of whom carried the Soulié surname.[80] Although the births of most of Jean and Eulalie's children are recorded in sacramental records, archival research reveals little on the real estate activities or domicile(s) of the combined Soulié-Mazange household(s) during the last decade of the eighteenth century. Jean Soulié's first recorded property purchase was in 1794 at present-day 818–820 Royal Street. Eulalie Mazange purchased property at present-day 819 Bourbon Street in 1803. In the New Orleans directory and census of 1805, Eulalie Mazange is listed as head of household on Dumaine Street.[81] Interestingly, she and her four minor sons and minor daughter are listed as white, and they are not identified as *gens de couleur libres*.[82] No adult males are present in the household, indicating that Jean did not reside with his consort and children.[83] Although Jean Soulié is not listed in the 1805 directory, he owned several properties in the Vieux Carré between 1808 and 1827.[84] Likewise, Eulalie Mazange came into possession of numerous city lots in the first decades of the century. According to a search of the Vieux Carré Survey, she purchased present-day 819 Bourbon Street in 1803. In 1815, she inherited 129–133 Chartres Street, 130 Exchange Alley, 132–134 Exchange Alley, and 620 Iberville Street from Marie Louise Liotau, the daughter of her former enslavers.[85]

For all intents and purposes, Eulalie Mazange and Jean Soulié maintained separate residences and kept their business transactions independent as well. Their interracial relationship did not hinder Jean Soulié's ability to perform as a public servant. Soulié was a Freemason; he was a founding member of the Grand Consistory of Louisiana formed in 1811 and the lodge's second Grand Master.[86] He served in the New Orleans militia during the 1815 Battle of New Orleans like many other French Creoles and *gens de couleur libres*. Soulié served as an alderman on the city council, representing the Third District during the term of Mayor

James Mather (1807–1812).⁸⁷ Furthermore, he was elected as the city recorder in September 1815 and voted in for two additional terms in 1818 and 1820.⁸⁸

By the 1820 federal census, Jean Soulié lived on Bourbon Street with eight free persons of color. Two years later, Jean and his son Norbert represent the family in the 1822 directory at 117 Bourbon Street. The oldest son, Lucien, an accountant, is listed at the corner of Tchoupitoulas and Poydras Streets in his only appearance in a city directory. Jean and Norbert are then both listed in the 1824 directory at 241 Bourbon Street (Eulalie's property at present-day number 819).⁸⁹ Eulalie Mazange died there on May 16, 1825.⁹⁰ Jean Soulié served as *curator ad bona* (administrator of the estate property) for the minor children—Louise, Celeste, and Coralie.⁹¹ The Soulié children inherited their mother's Bourbon Street property and lived there for three years after Eulalie's death; inheritance laws permitted women to leave their natural children the full amount of any donations or bequests.⁹² They sold the house and land—including an adjacent lot purchased by Norbert in 1826—to Marc Lafitte on May 23, 1828, for $8,500.00.⁹³ The proceeds from the sale went to the account of daughter Eulalie Soulié, with the stipulation that Eulalie Mazange's heirs (her children) be permitted to live rent free in the house, only paying property taxes, for one year following the sale.⁹⁴ No other property from Eulalie Mazange's estate was willed to or purchased by her children. Unlike the Dolliole siblings, the Soulié brothers Lucien, Norbert, Bernard, and Albin—as well as their sisters Eulalie, Louise, Celeste, and Coralie—did not receive a significant amount of property owned by their parents, Jean Soulié and Eulalie Mazange, either during their parents' lifetime or after their deaths. Apparently, Jean Soulié felt that, by this time, his mixed-race children could provide for themselves. He appears to have left New Orleans for good, returning to France in 1827. Jean gave Norbert the right to act in his stead over his affairs (including real estate) and left him to act as sole guardian of the minor Soulié women.⁹⁵

"Transforming Contract into Birthright"

The Soulié patriarch placed his children and personal and financial interests in good hands. Norbert had independently started acquiring property in 1819 and in the 1820s. These transactions helped Norbert build a reputation as a reputable speculator and accumulate capital for future purchases from the profits. It was not until the 1830s, however, that Norbert and his brothers began buying property on a large scale, developing most immediately and retaining some for longer periods of time. They accomplished this in spite of increasing restrictions on free people of color, who, like themselves, traveled abroad for extended periods of time. "An Act to Prevent Free Persons of Colour from Entering into This State and for Other Purposes" specifically targeted wealthy free persons of color, like the Souliés, who traveled to France for education.[96] After the law was amended, *gens de couleur libres* still could not travel to the West Indies. Ship passenger lists show one or more Soulié family members returning to New Orleans from Europe via diverse ports from the 1820s on.[97] Contractual documents often have Léon Courcelle (before 1835) or one of the younger brothers (usually Bernard) acting as agent for other siblings who are out of the country. In 1830, native *gens de couleur libres'* entitlement to legal residence was challenged. They were prohibited from returning to Louisiana if they traveled outside of the United States. In 1831, lawful residents, property owners, or permanent residents "who exercise a useful trade, and have always conducted themselves in an orderly and respectful manner" were exempted from this law.[98] The Soulié family—with builder Norbert, merchants Bernard and Albin, and all of the siblings' prolific real estate activities—certainly fit this description.

In 1830, Norbert purchased several Vieux Carré lots (present-day street numbers shown in parentheses):

May 12	Dumaine Street, 31' × 65'-8" lot (nos. 522 and 526)
May 31	Dumaine Street, 2'-6" × 65'-8" lot (no. 522)
September 8	Bourbon Street, 40' × 50' lot (nos. 330–332)
October 19	Dumaine Street (no. 810)

All of these lots had previously been improved with buildings.[99] The next year, he acquired a 77' × 103' lot on Dauphine Street at the intersection with Bienville Street (present-day nos. 301–311).[100] In 1832, Norbert, Bernard, and Albin are listed in the city directory as residing at 19 Dumaine Street.[101] Norbert's absence in subsequent city directories lends validity to the story that he moved to France permanently after disagreements arising during the establishment of the Louisiana Sugar Refinery. In 1831, Norbert and his cousin Edmond Rillieux were contracted to build the Louisiana Sugar Refinery. After some type of conflict regarding the project and disagreements between the refinery head Edmund Forstall and the wealthy cotton factor Vincent Rillieux (Edmond's father and Norbert's white "uncle"), Edmond Rillieux disappeared from New Orleans for a year.[102] Likewise, Norbert and his oldest brother, Lucien, left New Orleans for France.[103] While Norbert retained the properties that he acquired in the early 1830s, they were rented and overseen by his brothers Bernard and Albin. These two men became the family's dominant landowners in the latter part of the decade. On October 3, 1835, Bernard and Albin purchased a lot of land bound by Bayou Road and Rampart,

Barracks, and St. Claude Streets from François Pierre Duconge.[104] It was already developed with two four-bay cottages facing Rampart Street.[105] A few weeks later, the brothers purchased two lots on Marais Street (in the present-day 100 block) from Charles Montfort.[106] The Marais properties were retained until 1848, when they were sold undeveloped to various parties.

The year 1837 provides a cross section of different types of property transactions in which the Soulié brothers were involved. In March 1837, Bernard acquired two lots of land with buildings on Tremé Street (present-day 1222–1224 and 1226 Tremé Street).[107] On May 1, 1837, Norbert purchased a Vieux Carré lot on Governor Nicholls Street.[108] Three days later, Emile Sainet sold three lots out of the former Cazelar plantation, across the river in what is now Algiers, to Bernard and Albin along with Léon Courcelle and François Pierre Duconge.

In the spring of 1838, Lucien, living abroad and represented by Bernard, purchased several properties on Ursulines Avenue—four lots from the estate of Félicité Dupin (deceased wife of Achille Barthélémy Courcelle; 1529–1533 Ursulines Avenue) and one lot from Appolinaire Perrault (1511 Ursulines Avenue). The five lots were sold together in June 1845.[109] Bernard and Albin continued to purchase property for themselves in the late 1830s. In 1838 and 1839, Bernard purchased two additional lots on North Rampart Street adjacent to the one he acquired in 1835 on behalf of both of the brothers (Albin was living in France). The extent of the property was depicted when it was sold in 1867 (figure 1.7).[110] Norbert's younger brothers continued to act as his representatives in real estate transactions. By June 1839, Norbert owned a lot at the corner of Baronne and Hevia (now Lafayette) Streets; with Albin acting in his name, he commissioned the builder Alexander Baggett to construct four townhouses on the site.[111]

The Souliés continued acquiring property in the 1840s. In September 1843, Norbert received property on North Rampart Street via a *fieri facias* ruling against Sophia Meisson Kennedy.[112] The following year, Norbert acquired property in Square 96 in the Vieux Carré (222–224 North Rampart and 1022–1024 Bienville); he retained the property for only a few months.[113] Finally, in 1845, Albin, represented by Bernard, purchased a half lot of property on Bienville Street between Villeré and Marais Streets (1500 block).[114]

The Soulié Sisters

The relationship between Jean Soulié and Eulalie Mazange resulted in the birth of four daughters. The women never married and, given their brothers' frequent travel, were likely educated abroad.[115] The income from the short-lived sale of their mother's house and property on Bourbon Street in 1828 was to go to the

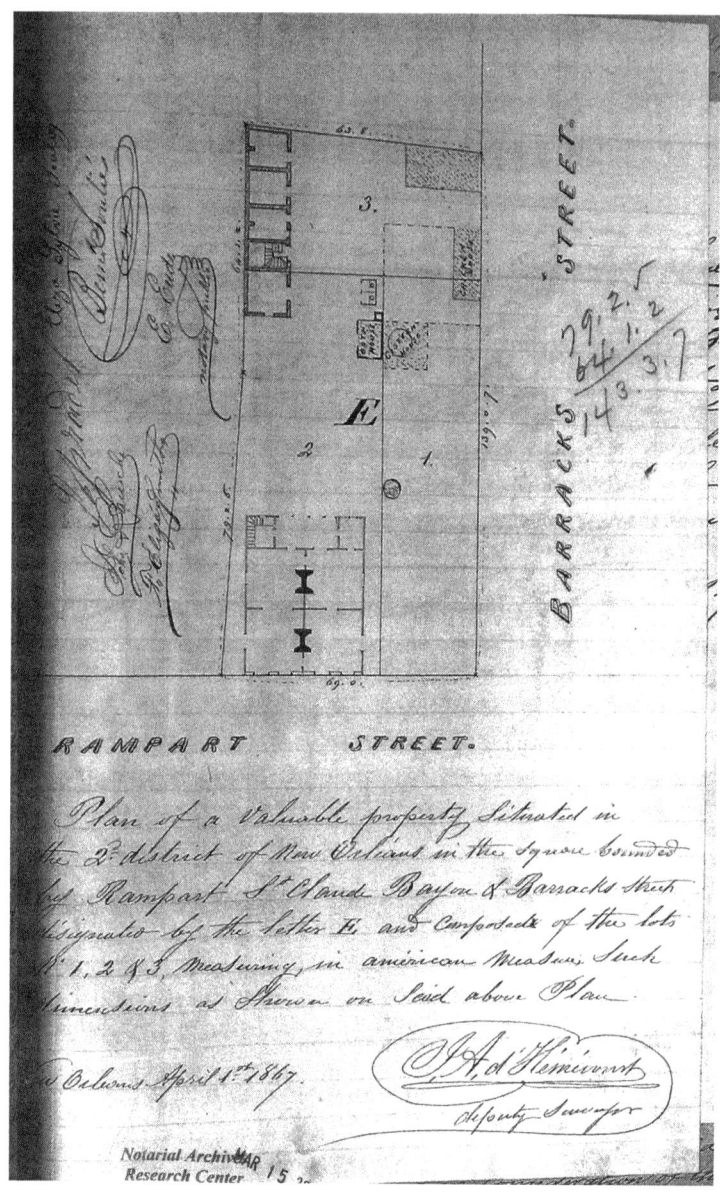

Figure 1.7. Plan of Soulié property at North Rampart and Barracks Streets. Plan by J. A. d'Hémécourt, 1867. Attached to sale of property from Bernard and Albin Soulié to Balise Pradel, Ernest Eude notary, volume 2, act 146, April 11, 1867. Courtesy of Hon. Chelsey Richard Napoleon, Clerk of Civil District Court, Parish of Orleans.

account of Eulalie, the eldest of the first-generation Soulié females, to provide for herself and her younger sisters. A survey of notarial indices in the 1830s does not reveal the sisters' involvement in any real estate activity. They were living in Paris by November 1832.[116] By the 1840s, the younger Soulié sisters—Louise, Celeste, and Marie Coralie—had come of age and begin to appear in notarized transactions.[117] The women, with Lucien, purchased a lot with buildings and dependencies on Customhouse Street (present-day 823–827 Iberville Street) on September 12, 1840. In February 1843, Eulalie, Celeste, and Marie Coralie acquired five enslaved individuals and several properties from their cousin Myrtille Courcelle for $3,258.00.[118] On September 6, 1843, the sisters acquired a lot on Dauphine Street (nos. 1131–1133) via sheriff's sale after winning a suit against *femme de couleur libre* Adelaide Ferrand.[119] They retained the property for just over a year, selling on September 24, 1844. On June 18, 1845, the sisters resold properties on St. Philip Street and Dumaine Street to Courcelle for $2,500.00, with Bernard acting as agent. Two days later, the siblings sold the Iberville Street property they owned with Lucien to François Pierre Duconge at a loss of $1,000.00.[120] Two sales so close together (both to individuals known to the family and who had entered into real estate transactions with them before) that raised rather significant income suggest that the women needed funds for some reason.

Like their mother, Eulalie Mazange, as well as Geneviève and Madeleine Dolliole, the four Soulié women were actively involved in property ownership. Unlike the passive lovers and daughters presented by the nineteenth-century British traveler Harriet Martineau and further asserted by contemporary historians, these women of color and many others played a central role in the acquisition and selling of property throughout the antebellum era.[121] Like many free women of color throughout the Atlantic world from the seventeenth through the nineteenth centuries, the Soulié and Dolliole women brought considerable wealth—via property ownership—into their families.[122] A review of archival land records and chains of title indicate that the Soulié women were more involved in real estate transactions than Madeleine Dolliole. This is probably due to the fact that, unlike Madeleine, they did not receive monetary bequests from their parents or have husbands to support them. Like their brothers, the Soulié women collectively owned land and buildings throughout the city (table 1.2). Through their brothers, who were well known as builders, merchants, and developers, they conducted real estate transactions with Black and white New Orleanians of both sexes. Through the business of buying and selling property, the first-generation Souliés established their own stakeholding in the city of New Orleans and gained a means by which to provide for themselves, establishing birthright via contractual agreements.

TABLE 1.2. SELECT PROPERTIES ACQUIRED BY THE FIRST-GENERATION SOULIÉS, 1819-1845

Current address or historic description	Faubourg (municipality)	Date of purchase	Date of sale	Family member(s)
819 Bourbon	Vieux Carré (1st)	1803/1826	1833	Eulalie Mazange, Norbert, Eulalie
227, 229, 231, 233 Rampart	Tremé (1st)	1819	1852 unknown	Norbert
1019–1025 Bienville	Vieux Carré (1st)	1820	1825	Norbert
1027–1031 Bienville	Vieux Carré (1st)	1820	1822	Norbert
1111 Bourbon	Vieux Carré (1st)	1822	1827	Norbert
1113 Bourbon	Vieux Carré (1st)	1822	1827	Norbert
814 Governor Nicholls	Vieux Carré (1st)	1829	1830	Norbert
509–511 Burgundy	Vieux Carré (1st)	1829	1831	Norbert
1017 Canal	Vieux Carré (1st)	1830	1833	Lucien
330–332 Bourbon	Vieux Carré (1st)	1830	1858	Norbert
522 Dumaine	Vieux Carré (1st)	1830	1866	Norbert
526 Dumaine	Vieux Carré (1st)	1830	1866	Norbert
810 Dumaine	Vieux Carré (1st)	1830	1858	Norbert
301–311 Dauphine	Vieux Carré (1st)	1831	1851	Norbert
1225 Rampart Street (Lot No. 1, bound by Bayou Road, Rampart, Barracks, and St. Claude)	Tremé (1st)	1835	1867	Bernard, Albin
1122 Marais	Tremé (1st)	1835	1848	Bernard, Albin

Address	Neighborhood	Acquired	Sold	Owner
1126 Marais	Tremé (1st)	ca. 1835	1848	Bernard, Albin
714 Governor Nicholls	Vieux Carré (1st)	1837	1848	Norbert
1222–1224 Tremé	Tremé (1st)	1837	unknown	Bernard
1226 Tremé	Tremé (1st)	1837	1885	Bernard
Three lots in Cazelar habitation	(5th)	1837	unknown	Bernard, Albin
1511 Ursulines	Tremé (1st)	1838	1845	Lucien
1529–1533 Ursulines	Tremé (1st)	1838	1845	Lucien
1225 Rampart Street (Lot No. 2, bound by Bayou Road, Rampart, Barracks, and St. Claude)	Tremé (1st)	1838	1867	Bernard, Albin
1114–1116 Barracks (Lot No. 3, bound by Bayou Road, Rampart, Barracks, and St. Claude)	Tremé (1st)	1839	1867	Bernard, Albin
600 block of Baronne	Ste. Marie (2nd)	by 1839	unknown	Norbert
823–827 Iberville	Vieux Carré (1st)	1840	1845	Lucien, Eulalie, Coralie, Celeste
Carondelet Street (Lot Nos. 23–25, bound by Carondelet, Hevia, St. Charles, and Poydras)	Ste. Marie (2nd)	1842	1843	Norbert, Lucien, Eulalie, Coralie, Celeste
520 N. Rampart	Vieux Carré (1st)	1843	1847	Norbert
1509–1511 Dumaine	Tremé (1st)	1843	1845	Eulalie, Celeste, Coralie
Partial lot on St. Philip Street (part of Lot No. 4, between Marais and Villeré)	Tremé (1st)	1833	1833	Bernard, Albin
Partial lot on St. Philip Street (part of Lot No. 4, between Marais and Villeré)	Tremé (1st)	1843	1845	Eulalie, Celeste, Coralie

TABLE 1.2, CONTINUED

Current address or historic description	Faubourg (municipality)	Date of purchase	Date of sale	Family member(s)
Lot on St. Philip Street (Lot No. 5, between Marais and Villeré)	Tremé (1st)	1843	1845	Eulalie, Celeste, Coralie
2339 Columbus 2300 block of Laharpe Street (lots in Faubourg Gueno)	Tremé (3rd)	1843	1849	Eulalie, Celeste, Coralie
1131–1133 Dauphine	Vieux Carré (1st)	1843	1844	Eulalie, Celeste, Coralie
1024–1026 Bienville	Vieux Carré (1st)	1844	1844	Norbert
222–224 N. Rampart	Vieux Carré (1st)	1844	1844	Norbert
1500 block of Bienville	Tremé (1st)	1845	unknown	Albin
Square bound by Carondelet, Sixth, Baronne, and Seventh Streets (Square 116)	Livaudais (Lafayette)	1847	unknown	Albin
Bacchus at Euterpe (street no. unknown)	Annunciation (2nd)	1848	1848+	Norbert
Chestnut (street no. unknown)	Livaudais (Lafayette)	1848	unknown	Norbert

Income Property

The significant number of properties owned by the Souliés, most for a short period of time, and the fact that Lucien, Norbert, Eulalie, Louise, Celeste, and Coralie lived abroad indicate that they did not reside in them. Only Bernard maintained a permanent residence in New Orleans throughout the antebellum period.[123] Albin resided with Bernard and his wife when he was not abroad (except for 1842, when he had a residence on North Rampart Street in Faubourg Marigny—formerly 50 Love Street).[124] As builders and commission merchants, Bernard and Albin utilized several addresses to conduct their business (table 1.3). By and large, the majority of the properties owned by the Souliés were utilized as rentals to generate income. The Souliés did not distinguish between race, ethnicity, or gender in their rental activities. Examination of the Soulié family's ledger books from June 1843 through January 1845 reveals no fewer than forty-three locations for which family

TABLE 1.3. BERNARD AND ALBIN SOULIÉ'S BUSINESS ADDRESSES IN CITY OF NEW ORLEANS DIRECTORIES

Address	Years of Occupancy	Business Type
19 Dumaine	1832	Builders
55 Bienville	1838–1842	Commission Merchants
48 Conti	1846	Commission Merchants
139 Royal	1850	Commission Merchants
84 Bienville	1851–1853	Commission Merchants
88 Bourbon	1854–1859	Commission Merchants
43 Bienville	1861	Commission Merchants

Note: In the 1830s, Bernard and Albin Soulié's office was located in the 300 block of Chartres Street in the pharmacy of François Pierre Duconge until the building burned in April of 1837; Bernard Soulié, "Journal of Bernard Soulié," 324; Cautionnement, Bernard and Albin Soulié and Leon Courcelle to Pierre Aime Becnel, Felix De Armas notary, vol. 52, act 199, May 22, 1837.

members collected rents (table 1.4).[125] In January 1842, the family group purchased properties on Carondelet Street from John Minturn. Each received their percentage of the rents every month.[126] For the eight-month period from May 1843 to January 1844, the account of Norbert (with Bernard and Albin) was credited $4,571.21 from rents collected. Eulalie, Celeste, and Marie Coralie earned $1,183.55 from May 1, 1843, to February 27, 1844. Lucien's account shows an income of $564.20 from rents collected between April 1844 and September 1846.[127] The monies earned from rental properties would have supplemented additional income from Bernard and Albin's business and from all of the family members' property sales, lending activities, or, for those living abroad, financial endeavors in France.

A LEGACY OF OWNERSHIP

The cases of both the Dolliole and Soulié families illustrate that *gens de couleur libres* acquired property through the same means as other free New Orleanians—through *inter vivos* donations and by engaging in property purchases and sales with friends, acquaintances, and strangers alike. Where the *gens de couleur libres* are concerned, previous scholarship has placed emphasis on the property ownership of free women of color, especially when bequeathed or gifted with property from their white fathers or "husbands." In their own right, *femmes de couleur libres* owned significant amounts of property in New Orleans. The independent property purchases of Geneviève Azémare and Eulalie Mazange provided foundations for the real estate activities of their families—a family compound that was later expanded by lover and children on the one hand (Geneviève), and the creation of

TABLE 1.4. RENTAL PROPERTIES IN THE SOULIÉ FAMILY LEDGERS, MAY 1843 THROUGH JANUARY 1845 (CURRENT STREET NUMBERS AND NAMES IN PARENTHESES)

ACCOUNT OF NORBERT WITH BERNARD AND ALBIN	
Baronne Street	21 Dumaine Street
Maison Rue Baronne (Kelly)	111 Dumaine Street
Maison Rue Baronne (Boucher)	House on Hevia Street
House on Bayou Road	House on Hevia Street (Taylor)
134 Bienville Street	House at corner of Hevia and Baronne
½ of 138 Bienville Street	79 Hospital Street
½ of 142 Bienville Street	41 Rampart Street (227 N. Rampart Street)
Kitchen of ½ of 142 Bienville Street	42 Rampart Street (222 N. Rampart Street)
88 Bourbon Street	43 Rampart Street (229 N. Rampart Street)
Shack on Carondelet Street	45 Rampart Street (231 N. Rampart Street)
Carondelet Street	47 Rampart Street (233 N. Rampart Street)
½ of store at 17 Dumaine Street	½ of house on Tremé Street (Daunoy)
Top of 17 Dumaine Street	½ of house on Tremé Street (Labatut)
19 Dumaine Street	½ of house on Tremé Street (south side)
ACCOUNT OF LUCIEN WITH BERNARD AND ALBIN	
House on St. Philip (P. E. Courcelle)	House on St. Philip at Marais (Levis)
House on St. Philip at Marais (Tintut)	House on St. Philip at Marais (Raboteau)
Lot and kitchen on Ursulines Avenue	House on Dauphine
ACCOUNT OF EULALIE, CELESTE, AND MARIE CORALIE	
Rue Philippa (various tenants) (O'Keefe Street)	House on Dumaine (Mlle. Menard)
½ of house on Dauphine (Eugene Macarty) ½ of house on Dauphine (T. Ragland)	Carondelet Street properties (various tenants)

a nest egg for the children, particularly the females, on the other (Eulalie). Neither woman's daughters engaged in any known extramarital or common-law relationships. When Madeleine Dolliole was widowed in her midtwenties, she remained single. Eulalie, Louise, Celeste, and Marie Coralie remained unmarried and were as self-sufficient as they could be in that day and age through their ownership of property. As their records of buying and selling property in New Orleans indicate, they surpassed the property ownership of their parents.

The Dollioles collectively established themselves as property owners through family-oriented acquisitions early in the nineteenth century. They capitalized on the properties that were bequeathed by or purchased from their parents to later buy and develop additional property. The family's longevity in New Orleans originated with (and has remained to the present day due to) the establishment and maintenance of birthright via property ownership in the nineteenth century. The Souliés were part of the generation that came of age early in the antebellum period and participated in the upward trend of property ownership.[128] By way of individual and joint property acquisition, they created a collective influence as property owners, thereby establishing their own financial success and birthright to the extent that their real estate activities were not hindered with most of the family members living abroad. By the 1830s and 1840s, both families owned significant amounts of property despite the increasing obstacles *gens de couleur libres* faced to obtaining equitable civil rights. The historian Shirley Thompson notes that because of challenges to free status, "to own and deal in property in New Orleans in the middle decades of the nineteenth century was risky business for anyone, and particularly for people of African descent."[129] The Dollioles and Souliés persevered. Individuals in both families managed to maintain financial security—and parity with their white peers as far as architecture was concerned—despite changing attitudes toward the status of *gens de couleur libres* and the banking crises of 1837 and 1839. In 1843 and 1844, Jean-Louis sold all but one of the family lots and homes in the 900 block of St. Philip; he and Joseph maintained their other properties. The Souliés, even as absentee landlords, maintained most of the properties they acquired by and between 1820 and 1850 until well after the Civil War. Bernard Soulié was one of five free people of color who were the largest landowners in New Orleans in 1850.

The location of the properties the Dollioles and Souliés acquired was as important, if not more important, as the manner in which they acquired it. Both families increasingly purchased both developed and undeveloped property outside of the Vieux Carré. This shift coincided with the establishment of Faubourg Tremé (1810), the sale of former Tremé/Collège d'Orléans property by the city of New Orleans (1826–1827), the coming of age of the second generation of Dollioles in the 1830s, and pervasive development of the American Sector and other suburbs upriver during the antebellum period.

CHAPTER 2

THE RAMIFICATIONS OF USE AND LOCATION

*New Orleans, beyond Royal Street toward the swamp,
retains its old character without variation.*

BENJAMIN HENRY LATROBE, *THE JOURNAL OF LATROBE* (1819)

*I returned, with great interest, to wander in the old French town....
Among the houses, one occasionally sees a relic of ancient Spanish
builders, while all the newer edifices have the characteristics of the
unartistic and dollar pursuing Yankees.*

FREDERICK LAW OLMSTED, *A JOURNEY IN THE SEABOARD SLAVE STATES;
WITH REMARKS ON THEIR ECONOMY* (1856)

The first of the city's "suburbs"—Faubourg Sainte-Marie—was planned in 1788 upriver from the Vieux Carré on the former plantation of the city's founder, Jean Baptiste Le Moyne de Bienville. Faubourg Marigny came next, developed downriver from Vieux Carré in 1806 out of the plantation of French Creole Bernard Marigny de Mandeville. Although Claude Tremé began selling portions of the plantation inherited from his wife's grandmother in the late eighteenth century, Faubourg Tremé was not officially platted until 1810. Each of these "suburbs"—or *faubourgs*—developed a distinct cultural and economic identity that hastened the division of the city of New Orleans into three municipalities with separate governing bodies in 1836. The Vieux Carré and Faubourg Tremé made up the First Municipality; Faubourg Sainte-Marie, the Second; and Faubourg Marigny and the other so-called "Creole faubourgs" adjacent downriver made up the Third Municipality (figure 2.1). The *gens de couleur libres* owned and built property in all of these neighborhoods, albeit to varying degrees. This municipal and cultural division—in a city considered distinctive due to its unique collective cultural and social mores—resulted in a dichotomy of the sense of place.[1]

The physical aspects of New Orleans, despite or due to geographic limitations, were more or less concrete even as the city expanded in area and population and larger lots continued to be subdivided. Yet the movement of people and the way they utilized property was not static. In particular, the land ownership patterns of the *gens de couleur libres* leave room for interpretation of the world in which the *gens de couleur libres* moved.[2] The Dollioles and Souliés owned and built personal and business property in the city's various suburbs as well as the Vieux Carré. Examination of the use and the locations of these lots and buildings provides a new perspective on the *gens de couleur libres*' movement in and interaction with the city of New Orleans from its origins as a European colony to its peak years as a major American metropolis.

THE VIEUX CARRÉ

With relaxed settlement policies and a laissez-faire attitude toward encouraging immigration, New Orleans's colonial population was relatively small under both French and Spanish rule. The Vieux Carré, sited on the high ground between the river and the back swamp, was planned to include sixty-six blocks bound by the Mississippi River and what would later be named Customhouse (Iberville), Rampart, and Barracks Streets. At the beginning of the Spanish period, however, development was limited to approximately thirty-four blocks within the city's walls—a less formal wooden palisade than the grand fortification often depicted on historic maps. Except for those flanking and behind the Cathedral-Basilica of St. Louis King of France (St. Louis Cathedral), the squares were divided into twelve lots, with five lots on each side of the square facing the streets parallel to the river and two slightly larger "key" lots at the center of the square with frontage on perpendicular streets.[3] Cottages and raised houses were typically set back from the street with gardens in the rear. After the 1794 fire, the Vieux Carré was defined by the Spanish colonial block with cottages and townhouses set at the front of property lines.[4] As lots became subdivided among heirs or due to development, the density of the Vieux Carré increased. The Dollioles were among *gens de couleur libres*—New Orleans natives and Saint-Dominguan refugees—who settled in the undeveloped perimeter of the Vieux Carré during the latter years of the Spanish colonial period and the region's period as a US territory. While Soulié patriarch Jean owned property throughout the Vieux Carré, his sons did not come of age until after Louisiana obtained statehood in 1812. Between that year and the division of the city into municipalities in 1836, Jean's son Norbert acquired lots in various squares of this oldest part of the city, while Jean-Louis and Joseph Dolliole spread out from the family enclave to other areas of Vieux Carré, but on a limited scale (figure 2.2).

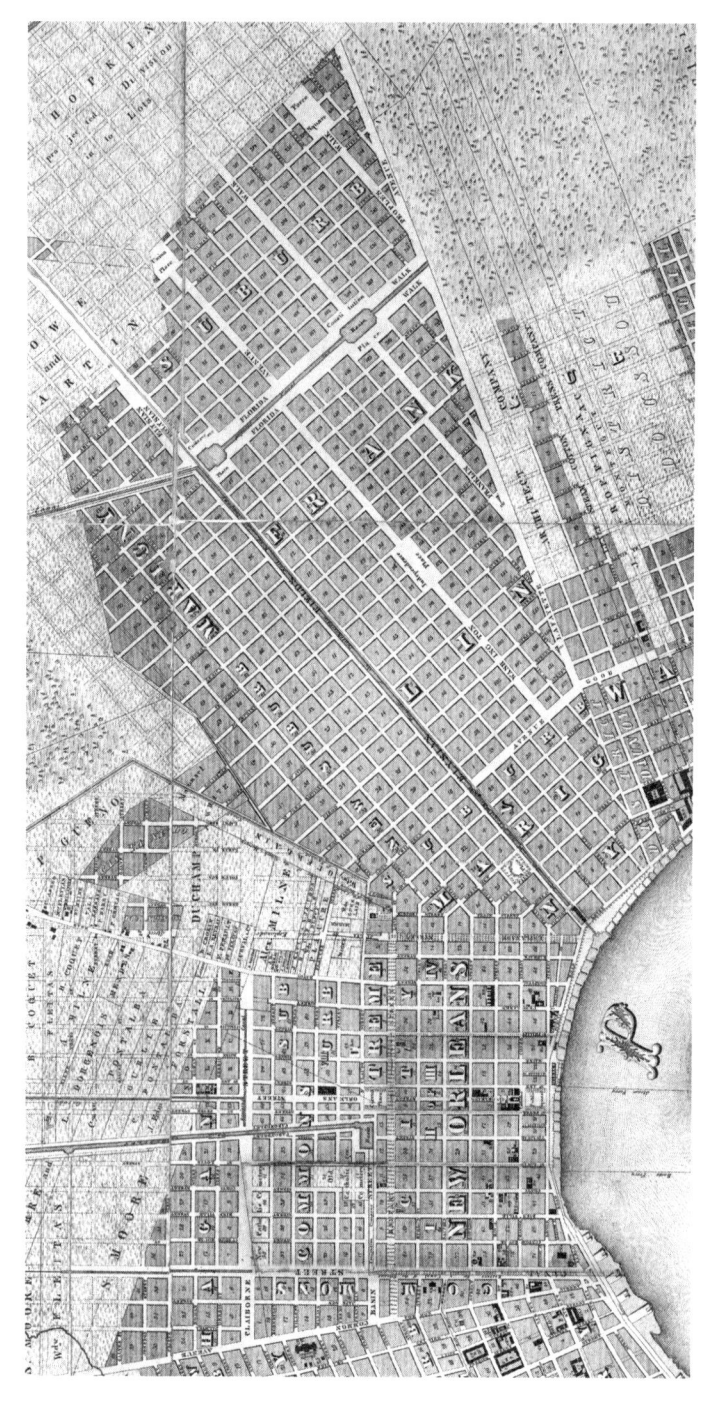

Figure 2.1. Location of neighborhoods (faubourgs), showing the Vieux Carré and Faubourgs Tremé, Marigny, New Marigny, and Franklin. Detail from Topographical Map of New Orleans and Its Vicinity. Charles F. Zimpel, surveyor, 1833. The Collins C. Diboll Vieux Carré Digital Survey at The Historic New Orleans Collection.

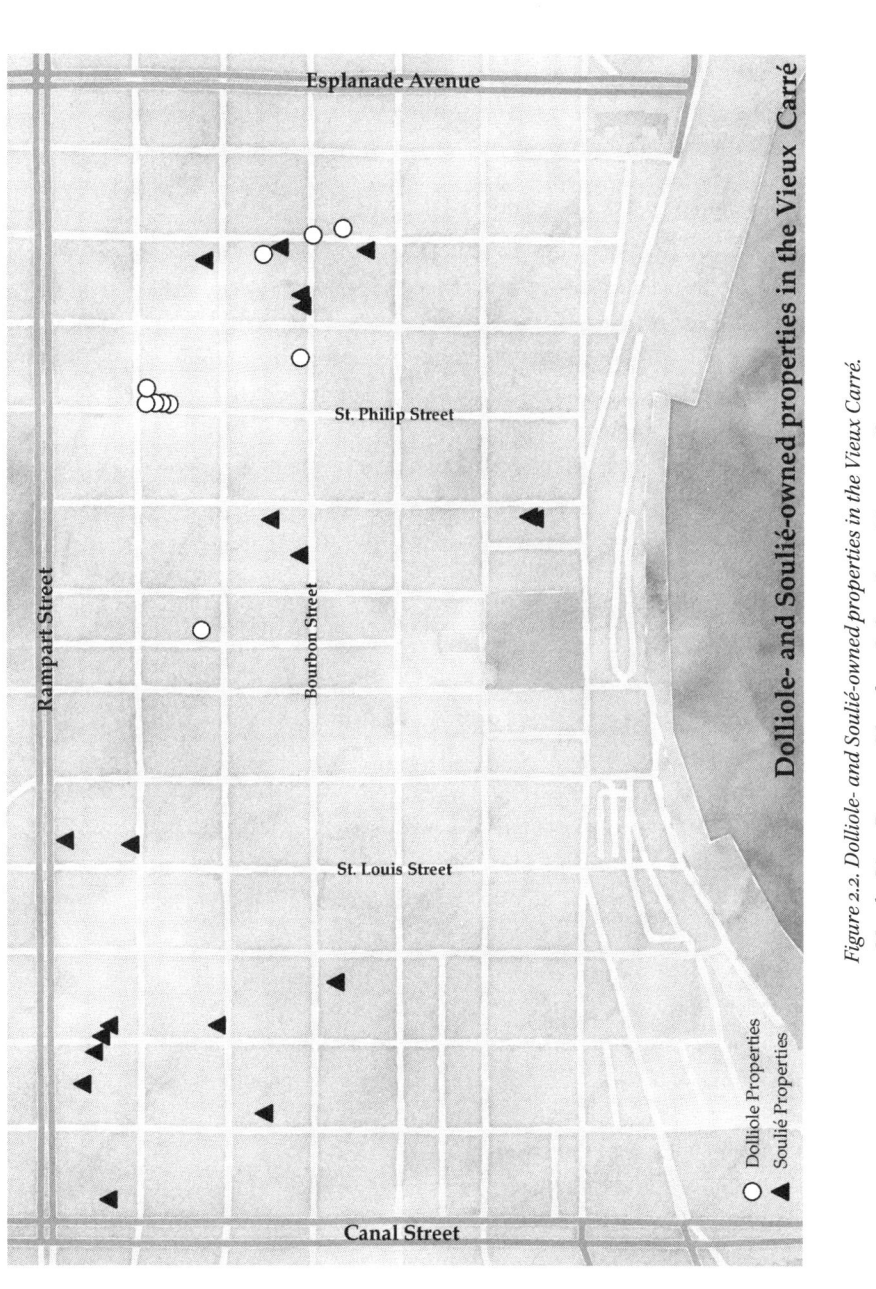

Figure 2.2. Dolliole- and Soulié-owned properties in the Vieux Carré. Map by Lissa Pearson. Map data © OpenStreetMap contributors.

The 1830s and 1840s coincided with New Orleans's division into three municipalities (1836–1852) and saw Joseph Dolliole obtain properties in kitty-corner lots, again in the Vieux Carré's periphery. The Souliés also continued to acquire property in the Vieux Carré. Most were near properties that they already owned at the edges of the Vieux Carré.

On the Margins: Bayou Road and Rampart Street

By virtue of the city's expansion into faubourgs with different layouts and street names (even where routes continued between faubourgs) immediately adjacent to the Vieux Carré, the old city became locked in. With earlier French and Spanish settlers and their descendants ensconced in the core of the Vieux Carré, secondary sites at the old city edges, near Congo Square and in Tremé and New Marigny, became the enclaves of choice for the *gens de couleur libres*.[5] While these secondary areas of development may have been considered increasingly unimportant or insignificant by white Creoles and Americans, they were important to the development of the city as a whole and to the sustainability of the *gens de couleur* community.[6]

From the earliest days of French settlement, the Chemin du Bayou Saint John, or Bayou Road, was the primary artery between the old city and Bayou St. John.[7] This in-between path served as a secondary water route to the city (the Mississippi River being the primary one).[8] Large land grants were increasingly divided into *habitations* (plantations) that stretched back from the Bayou Road. Like their white counterparts, "along Bayou Road, the old colonial thoroughfare, families of *gens de couleur* also formed economic bonds and marriage ties with one another that served to keep title and ownership status relatively consolidated."[9] The Dollioles, then, were in good company when they purchased their Bayou Road properties in 1806 and 1807.

In the 1830s and 1840s, Faubourg Tremé and farther lakeward along the Bayou Road was still a less densely settled area of the city.[10] Correspondingly, little property in this area was purchased by Dollioles or Souliés. One exception is the acquisition of property by the Soulié sisters in Faubourg Gueno in 1843. By 1815, Pierre Gueno (1759–1821), a native of Barrè, France, consolidated his properties to create the single largest *habitation* on Bayou Road at that date.[11] In 1835, ten years after Gueno's death, his property was subdivided. Soulié relative Myrtille Courcelle obtained a portion of the former Gueno plantation, selling it to his female cousins in 1843. The builder Nelson Fouché and the carpenter Bernard Couvent were among the *gens de couleur libres* who purchased some of this property.[12] The practice by free people of color of buying and selling property along the

Bayou Road, often between family members, was maintained well into the 1840s and 1850s. The Faubourg Gueno properties were among the latest purchased by members of the Soulié or Dolliole families anywhere in the city during the antebellum period. This area of the city downriver of Esplanade Avenue is now part of the Seventh Ward.

Another dividing line, North Rampart Street was initially sparsely developed but evolved into a mixed commercial and residential corridor linking the old city to the new suburb. Faubourg Tremé, initially consisting of portions of the City Commons and a portion of the Morand-Tremé plantation, was platted in 1810. Among Norbert Soulié's first purchases was his acquisition of four lots on the lake side of Rampart Street between Customhouse (Iberville) and Bienville Streets in 1819. This land was at the very edge of the former City Commons, used for public grazing and firewood gathering in the eighteenth century, and still mostly uninhabited.[13] On other end of Rampart, at the intersection with Barracks Street (formerly along the riverside boundary of the Morand-Tremé plantation), Norbert purchased several lots in 1835, 1838, and 1839 to create a 69' × 139' holding. A few years later, he acquired two properties on the river side of Rampart Street, technically in Vieux Carré; one was across the street from the lots purchased in 1819. As opposed to simply being an inferior no-man's-land sheltering those involved in controversial relationships and their offspring, the area where the old city and Tremé's subdivision merged was home to diverse families and individuals as well as commercial enterprises to serve them, and offered development opportunities. Today, Rampart Street appears as a significant dividing line, both in its graphic representation on maps and physically in person. In the antebellum period, however, it served as a much more fluid boundary between the Vieux Carré and Faubourg Tremé.

FAUBOURG TREMÉ

Once beyond the former ramparts, Faubourg Tremé became dominated by Creoles of color and was far from the "never-never land" it is often described as.[14] Today, the boundaries of Faubourg Tremé vary slightly depending on the source. Tremé is generally considered the swath of land from North Rampart Street to North Broad Street, between Canal and St. Bernard Streets. Historically, the suburb consisted of former plantations lakeside of the Vieux Carré along the Bayou Road and of the City Commons beyond the fortifications. The Commons included St. Jean's Hospital (1764–1809), the Old Burying Ground (St. Louis Cemetery No. 1, 1788), and the Carondelet Canal (Old Basin Canal, 1792).[15] In 1810, the city of New Orleans purchased the Tremé plantation and set aside the house, outbuildings, and their immediate environs for the Collège d'Orléans.[16] This institution, founded for the city's (white and male) French-speaking population, was short-lived, existing only from 1812 to 1823. Faubourg Tremé, formally laid out in 1812, featured a public square and market, now famous as Congo Square. A new Catholic cemetery (St. Louis Cemetery No. 2, 1820) and a mortuary chapel (Our Lady of Guadalupe Church, 1826) were amenities added to the new suburb.[17] As far as location, this area of back swamp behind the Vieux Carré was better than the back swamp farther upriver that was fast being settled by newly arriving Americans. At Tremé, the natural levee of the Mississippi joins the natural levee of Bayou Gentilly, resulting in the Esplanade Ridge.[18] The *gens de couleur libres* slowly pushed into Tremé's less desirable "inland margin" of the natural levee.[19] Their significant presence resulted in Faubourg Tremé being joined with the old city—both areas being dominated by black and white Creoles—as the First Municipality in 1836.

Since the Spanish colonial period, 80 percent of the lots in Faubourg Tremé have been owned by persons of color at one or more times.[20] Investigation of the properties researched and surveyed for *New Orleans Architecture*, Volume 6, *Faubourg Tremé and the Bayou Road* reveals a significant number of structures extant in 1980 that were historically associated with free persons of color in Faubourg Tremé from 1816 to 1860.[21] The involvement of *gens de couleur libres* for these properties included thirty-three original owners, six builder-owners, six builders, and six speculative developers. Among these properties are those that were owned by members of the Dolliole and Soulié families.

In Tremé, the Dollioles were principally ensconced on St. Philip Street near or on former Collège d'Orléans property (see figures 1.4 and 1.6). In essence, they created a second family enclave a few blocks toward the back of town from the family properties on St. Philip Street in the Vieux Carré. It was at their respective residences on St. Philip Street in Faubourg Tremé that Madeleine (1835), Geneviève (1838), and Joseph Dolliole (1868) died on property purchased between the dates the faubourg was platted and became part of the Third Municipality (1810–1836). During this period, Bernard and Albin Soulié acquired land nearby on Marais Street as speculative property; they later sold these lots undeveloped.

After the municipalities were recombined in 1852, the *gens de couleur libres* continued to buy and sell in Tremé. Joseph Dolliole purchased a property on North Robertson Street, and Jean-Louis bought land on Villeré and Marais Streets and on Bayou Road.[22] The Souliés also continued to be prolific in their real estate activity, acquiring property farther lakeside and uptown on Tremé (Bernard),

Dumaine (sisters), St. Philip (sisters), and Bienville (Albin) Streets and Ursulines Avenue (Lucien), in the 1830s and 1840s.

In the antebellum era, the settlement and building patterns of the *gens de couleur libres* were focused in Faubourg Tremé. It was more than undesirable land on which an in-between socioeconomic group built houses and lived. Many wealthy and influential *gens de couleur libres* not only resided in this neighborhood in their traditionally Creole houses; they also created residences and livelihoods for their Black and white neighbors and established churches, lodges, and clubs to support the *gens de couleur libres* community. While religious resources were added to the suburb when it was newly developed in 1812, both white and Black Creoles were involved with the establishment of St. Augustine Catholic Church at the corner of St. Claude and Hospital Streets in the early 1840s.[23] Economy Hall, at 1422 Ursulines Avenue in the vicinity of Soulié- and Dolliole-owned properties, was built as the meeting place of the Société d'Économie et d'Assistance Mutuelle (Economy and Mutual Aid Society, founded 1836) in 1856.[24] The benevolent society also allowed other benevolent and mutual aid groups to use the building and hosted social and fund-raising events there. First- and second-generation members of both families maintained strongholds in Faubourg Tremé in the 1850s and after the Civil War as residents and landlords. Today, Faubourg Tremé retains its historic significance as an enclave for *gens de couleur libres* and, after emancipation, other free Blacks.

FAUBOURG MARIGNY, NEW MARIGNY, AND THE CREOLE FAUBOURGS

Faubourg Marigny as "Foreign Territory"

Though the *gens de couleur libres* were a prevalent force in Faubourg Tremé, Faubourg Marigny was developed earlier in 1806, in direct response to the needs of the Creole community as refugees flooded into New Orleans fleeing the Haitian Revolution and its aftermath. Bernard Xavier Philippe de Marigny de Mandeville, owner of the plantation that became the first suburb below the city, preferred to keep the environment residential and sell property to his Creole friends and neighbors as opposed to Anglo developers.[25] Marigny was not a stranger to the *gens de couleur libres* community, as he had familial ties to it. His father, Pierre Philippe de Mandeville (Sieur de Marigny and Chevalier de St. Louis), sired a daughter—Eulalie de Mandeville—with a woman of color. Eulalie de Mandeville entered into a long-term interracial relationship with a member of a leading Creole family and became one of the wealthiest women, white or Black, in New Orleans. In Faubourg Marigny, with street names such as Rue d'Amour (Love Street) and Rue des Bons Enfants (Good Children Street), Bernard Marigny supposedly acknowledged extramarital interracial partnerships.[26] Given the relationships between white and Black Creoles, the openness of white landowners to conducting business with free persons of color, and prime real estate conditions for Black émigrés to purchase property, Faubourg Marigny possessed a large population of free Blacks. The community was located downtown of the Vieux Carré, bound by the Mississippi River and Esplanade Avenue, Good Children Street (St. Claude Avenue), and Enghuien Street (Franklin Avenue). On either side of the canal that had provided water from the Mississippi River to the Marigny plantation sawmill (then flowed onward to the back swamp and Bayou St. John) was Elysian Fields Avenue, intended by Marigny and French engineer Nicolas de Finiels to be the neighborhood's main street and a grand promenade like its namesake in Paris, the Champs-Élysées. Like New Orleans's other suburbs, Faubourg Marigny also had a designated public space—Washington Square—facing Elysian Fields. Lots in Faubourg Marigny were manipulated to allow for changes in the street angles where the new suburb met the Vieux Carré. Thus, the faubourg's namesake and planners ensured maximum residential development by those of more modest means. The allotment of ten to twelve lots per block and prices at $300 to $400 per lot would have been appealing for the small homeowner, including many *gens de couleur libres*.[27] Based on the inventory of Volume 5 of the *New Orleans Architecture* series, in 1974, thirty-five antebellum sites and buildings with known associations with the *gens de couleur libres* were extant in Faubourg Marigny.

Three-quarters of the sites in Faubourg Marigny were owned by free people of color at least one time by the Civil War.[28] Except for Eulalie Mazange's properties on Casa Calvos (Royal) and Frenchmen Streets, which were sold at her death in 1828, the Souliés do not appear to have had any stake in Faubourg Marigny.[29] The Dollioles, on the other hand, had a small presence. After starting a house on the property the year before, in 1820 Jean-Louis purchased a uniquely shaped corner lot where Bourbon Street curves and changes into Pauger Street. In 1822, Joseph, the youngest of Louis and Geneviève's sons, lived on History Street (now Kerlerec Street) below Greatmen Street. He apparently set up a household with his new wife, Magdeleine Hobe, away from the family compound on St. Philip Street in the Vieux Carré.[30]

The character of the neighborhood changed little over the antebellum years. One exception was the construction of the Pontchartrain Railroad. It was built from 1830 to 1831 over the infilled Marigny canal down the center of Elysian Fields Avenue, taking advantage of the thoroughfare being the only street in the city that extended all the way from the Mississippi to Lake Pontchartrain.[31] Otherwise, Faubourg Marigny remained a tight-knit community with property often exchanging hands among neighbors who already owned land. In 1838, Jean-Louis inherited from Joseph Prieto a lot with a cottage that he probably built (1455–1457 Pauger Street), one block from the house he already owned on Pauger Street. He did not retain this property for long, selling it in 1841 to another *homme de couleur libre*, Francisco Tio. Tio purchased another cottage on Elysian Fields at that time that was also likely the workmanship of Jean-Louis Dolliole.[32]

In the early part of the nineteenth century, Faubourg Marigny was primarily settled by white Creoles and *gens de couleur libres* émigrés expanding out of the Vieux Carré.[33] Later, German and Irish immigrants began to settle in the neighborhood from the 1820s through the 1840s.[34] Toward midcentury, unlike the Vieux Carré and Faubourg Tremé, "to the proper Creole [Faubourg Marigny] was foreign territory, too."[35] By the 1840s, the operation of Catholic churches catering to different ethnicities—Annunciation (French, 1844), Holy Trinity (German, 1847), and Saints Peter and Paul (Irish, 1849)—reflected the neighborhood's mixed Creole and immigrant population.[36]

Nouvelle Marigny

Lots in Faubourg Marigny quickly sold, prompting Bernard Marigny to extend his original subdivision into "New Marigny" in 1810.[37] Lot sales gained impetus after the Pontchartrain Railroad was completed and began operation in 1831, running along Elysian Fields Avenue.[38] Initially, New Marigny consisted primarily of the area bound by Good Children Street (North Rampart/St. Claude), Bernard Street (St. Bernard Avenue), Prosper Street (North Derbigny), and Marigny Street. The suburb also encompassed six blocks toward the back of town, three on either side of Elysian Fields, to Celestine Street (North Johnson). By 1833, the area had developed farther lakeside from Faubourg Marigny between St. Bernard and Elysian Fields Avenues. Like Rampart Street and Bayou Road, the suburb of New Marigny was another of the city's "marginal" areas, and, like its predecessor, catered to French Creoles, *gens de couleur libres*, and European immigrants. Louis Drausin Dolliole, Jean-Louis's son, had building commissions in New Marigny,[39] but in the 1830s and 1840s, the neighborhood did not house the residences of the first-generation Souliés or Dollioles. Dolliole cousins, the children and grandchildren of Louis's younger brother Jean François and his partner Catherine, lived in New

Marigny from the 1840s onward, however. Their descendants were among the *gens de couleur libres* who called what is now New Orleans's Seventh Ward home well into the twentieth century.

Faubourg Franklin

Faubourg Franklin was another Creole-dominated neighborhood. In 1826, the property owner Nicolas Destrehan subdivided his plantation located downtown from Nouvelle Marigny. Faubourg Franklin was located beyond Good Children (St. Claude Avenue) between Marigny Street and Lafayette Avenue (Franklin/Almonaster Avenues).[40] Washington Promenade (St. Roch Avenue) was originally platted as Poet Street, the neighborhood's primary thoroughfare, with a large two-block public square, Independence Place (St. Roch Playground), between Solidline (N. Roman) and Liberal (N. Johnson) Streets. Development of Faubourg Franklin began in earnest after the Pontchartrain Railroad was built one block beyond the suburb's uptown boundary in 1830.[41] Joseph Dolliole took advantage of real estate availability in this new suburb. In 1835, he and Nelson Fouché acquired two groups of properties from Nicolas Destrehan. The first was nine lots facing Washington Promenade at the corner of Girod (Villeré) Street. The second property was located near the first and consisted of an entire square bound by Music, St. John the Baptist (North Robertson), Arts, and St. Avide (South Claiborne) Streets. The family maintained a presence in Faubourg Franklin—a Pierre Dolliole (relationship undetermined) was listed as residing on Music Street well into the 1860s. Like New Marigny, this suburb extended toward the back swamp over time. Faubourg Franklin became known as Faubourg St. Roch when a shrine and a cemetery at Independence Place were dedicated to the saint in 1867.[42]

The Other "Creole Faubourgs"

New Orleans's Bywater neighborhood downriver from Faubourg Marigny was once several plantations that were subdivided into street grids and developed over time.[43] Faubourg Daunois was subdivided from the plantation of Nicolas Daunois in 1810. It was not intended to be a continuation of Faubourg Marigny and was actually separated from the earlier neighborhood by a rope walk at Franklin Avenue.[44] By 1831, the Levee Steam Cotton Press Company had acquired former Daunois plantation land to develop the world's largest cotton press.[45] Immediately downriver was Faubourg Montegut, platted in 1830 by the heirs of Joseph Montegut.[46] By 1834, the former Darby and Coustillas concessions below Faubourg Montegut consisted of Faubourg Clouet (1807); Faubourg Montreuil; the Delphine Macarty-Martin Duralde property; the L. B. Macarty plantation;

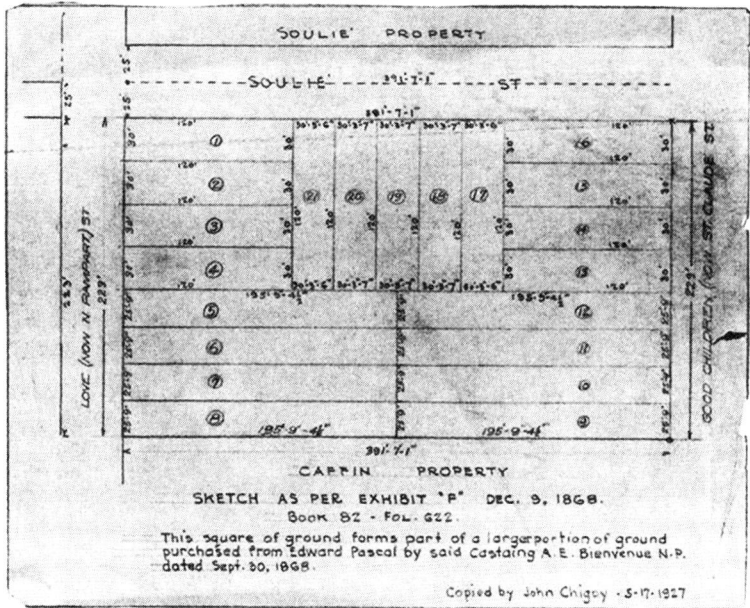

Figure 2.3. Plan of "Soulié Property" bound by Love (now North Rampart), Soulié, Good Children (now St. Claude), and the Caffin property, 1868. Louisiana Map Collection, Louisiana Division/City Archives, New Orleans Public Library.

Faubourg Carraby (1833); Faubourg Lesseps (1832); plantations owned by G. Salkeld, A. Lesseps, and Manuel Andry; and the Ursuline Convent (1823). The area from the Faubourg Daunois to the Ursuline Convent became known as Washington.[47] As in Faubourg Tremé, three-fourths of the sites in these lower suburbs were probably owned by a free person of color at one time or another before the Civil War.[48] Dollioles and Souliés do not appear in real estate transactions in these suburbs.

The Holy Cross neighborhood, once a continuation of the downriver plantations cum suburban developments, is located on the downriver side of the Inner Harbor Navigation Canal (construction on which commenced through the Ursuline Convent and Deslonde properties in 1918).[49] When depicted on Zimpel's 1834 map of the city of New Orleans, this area still consisted of large plantations stretching back from the Mississippi. One of these plantations belonged to Edmund J. Forstall, who took a portion of his land to develop the Louisiana Sugar Refinery in 1831, with buildings designed and built by Norbert Soulié and Edmond Rillieux. This association—far from their other property holdings in the city (in addition to Jean Soulié's work relationship with Pierre Misotiére)—probably familiarized the family with the area and prompted Albin Soulié to later purchase property on Flood Street on what was the Misotiére plantation (figure 2.3).[50]

THE "AMERICAN SECTOR"

Though immediately adjacent to the Vieux Carré and not extending as far as the downriver Creole suburbs, the area that developed upriver beyond the original city grid as Faubourg Sainte-Marie was considered a world apart for the city's Creoles and *gens de couleur libres*. Historic maps indicate that between 1764 and circa 1770, the Vieux Carré expanded outward, following the fortification walls, lakeside of Dauphine Street beyond Bienville and Barracks Streets. At the end of the Spanish colonial period, this area was occupied by a few landowners and government buildings. On the uptown side of the Vieux Carré, beyond the City Commons, part of the former plantation of New Orleans's founder Jean-Baptiste Le Moyne de Bienville came under the ownership of Maria Deslondes, the future wife of Beltran Gravier, in 1785.[51] The Graviers subdivided their plantation after the 1788 fire in the Vieux Carré, allowing the city to expand upriver beyond the fortifications. Per the second plan of the suburb drawn on April 24, 1788, Villa Gravier consisted of seven streets running parallel to the Mississippi River, four perpendicular streets, and one oblique street. Roughly at the center was a public square (Place Gravier, later Lafayette Square). The neighborhood was renamed Faubourg Sainte-Marie after Maria Deslondes died in 1798.[52] By the late eighteenth century, some of the public lands or commons between Faubourg Sainte-Marie and the city wall had been sold and built upon.[53]

With the transfer of the Louisiana territory to the United States in 1803, several developments took place that quickly transformed the former commons and Faubourg Sainte-Marie, a colonial suburb, into a vibrant residential and commercial district—the "American Sector." By 1805, citizens had demolished the city walls for firewood; the physical distinction between the upper suburb and the Vieux Carré was further diminished when Magazine Street (named for the Spanish colonial powder magazine that was at its head) and Levee Street were connected.[54] Magazine Street would become one of several commercial arteries in the American Sector, establishing the city's Central Business District. In 1807, a portion of the former commons was reserved for a continuation of the Carondelet Canal (which ended at the rear of the city in what would become Faubourg Tremé) to the Mississippi River. The canal extension was never developed, but the thoroughfare on either side of it is still known as Canal Street. The right-of-way reserved for the waterway became the median. The emergence of Canal Street as the city's primary business center emphasized the cultural and economic differences between the old French Creole city and the upriver area fast being settled by American newcomers and businessmen. Thus, the street became (and still is) considered an imaginary divider between the conflicting sections of the city. The canal bed became known as a dividing line, but also a place where Americans and Creoles could ostensibly meet in concord. Thus, the medians of all split thoroughfares in New Orleans are still today called the "neutral ground."

Historical research suggests that Canal Street also served as a barrier for the involvement of Creoles, including the *gens de couleur libres*, in the physical development of the American Sector. In *The American Sector* volume of the *New Orleans Architecture* series, free people of color are rarely mentioned. While this may stem from the fact that the constantly changing nature of the American Sector from residential suburb to commercial core resulted in the demolition of buildings with which they were involved, the fact remains that few free persons of color owned property in this area of the city. Popular belief had it that Julia Street was named for a *femme de couleur libre* who owned property along the banks of the New Basin Canal (built in the lakeside portion of the American Sector from 1832 to 1838 to serve the area and provide competition with Carondelet Canal).[55] As opposed to being named for Julia Mathew, the Black cook of Julien Poydras, the man himself was the inspiration for the street name. Poydras encouraged Gravier to subdivide his plantation and purchased the first lot—at the corner of Poydras Street (also named for him) and the Camino Real (Tchoupitoulas).[56] Julia Street (Julie Street—short for Julien—on early maps of the suburb) was named in his honor. While Eulalie Mazange inherited property in the area formerly between the original colonial city grid and fortifications, it was sold in 1828 after her death. Her children, on the other hand, made their own investments in the American Sector, purchasing properties close together. The first-generation Souliés were not strangers to the area. Léon Courcelle, their Aunt Adelaide's consort and Bernard's father-in-law, lived on Magazine Street in 1822 and 1824. He is listed as residing at the corner of Carondelet and Hevia (Lafayette) Streets in 1832; this was one block riverside of Norbert's properties at Baronne and Hevia Streets acquired by 1839. The Soulié ledger books reveal that Norbert collected rents for several properties on Baronne Street in the 1840s. His sisters were landladies for a rental on Philippa Street (O'Keefe Avenue). The women, and older brother Lucien, had additional rentals on Carondelet Street. Perhaps through their father—a city employee after the Louisiana Purchase and member of the Louisiana Bank's mixed Creole and American board of directors—association with Americans was less of an anomaly

—

for the first-generation Souliés.[57] As for the Dollioles, archival research has yielded a single building commission for a Dolliole in the American Sector—Jean-Louis built a cottage in the 800 block of Magazine Street in 1831.[58]

The Souliés extended their influence and property ownership even farther upriver in Faubourg Annunciation and Faubourg Livaudais as the city's boundaries extended into former plantations that had been created from Sieur de Bienville's large holding above the city that he founded (figure 2.4). Six faubourgs—named primarily after the plantation owners—were platted: Duplantier (1806), Saulet (1810), La Course (1807), Annunciation (1807), Nuns (1809), and Panis (1813/1829).[59] The two latter subdivisions were uptown from Felicity Street and technically in Jefferson Parish.[60] The rapid and successful sale of lots in Faubourgs Nuns and Panis prompted developers to look to the next adjacent plantation upriver. After the Livaudais family encountered financial problems and the plantation owner and his wife divorced in the 1820s, Madame Livaudais turned over the plantation (received in the divorce settlement) to a solicitor who sold the property for development in 1832.[61] Faubourgs Nuns, Panis, and Livaudais were incorporated as the city of Lafayette that same year. In the antebellum era, these upriver neighborhoods were characterized by a range of residences, including Creole plantation houses and cottages as well as rowhouses, single-family homes, and larger villas in a variety of early to mid-nineteenth century architectural styles. The Soulié brothers capitalized on property ownership in these popular neighborhoods during the city's 1840s construction boom. In Faubourg Livaudais, Albin Soulié purchased an entire square in 1847. Norbert followed suit, purchasing several lots in the neighborhood on Chestnut Street, one block riverside of Lafayette Cemetery No. 1 (1833), in 1848. Also that year, he purchased several lots at the corner of Bacchus at Euterpe Streets in Faubourg Annunciation (figure 2.5). These acquisitions place the Souliés' real estate activities in areas of the city not generally considered to have been inhabited by *gens de couleur libres* in the antebellum period.

IN THEIR "PROPER PLACE"

By the height of New Orleans's fame as "America's Western Capital" in the 1850s,[62] the Dolliole and Soulié families had acquired property in several areas of the city. Like many *gens de couleur libres*, their property ownership was predominantly in the Vieux Carré and Faubourg Tremé. To a lesser extent, they were present in Faubourg Marigny and New Marigny (the Dollioles) as well as the Creole suburbs, American Sector, and upriver suburbs (the Souliés). The families' movement, collectively and individually, throughout the city appears to have been fluid, with no overt obstacles or hardships. Still, they were more ensconced in the areas of

Figure 2.4. Faubourg Annunciation (center) and Faubourg Livaudais (left). Detail from *Topographical Map of New Orleans and Its Vicinity*. Charles F. Zimpel surveyor, 1833. The Collins C. Diboll Vieux Carré Digital Survey at The Historic New Orleans Collection.

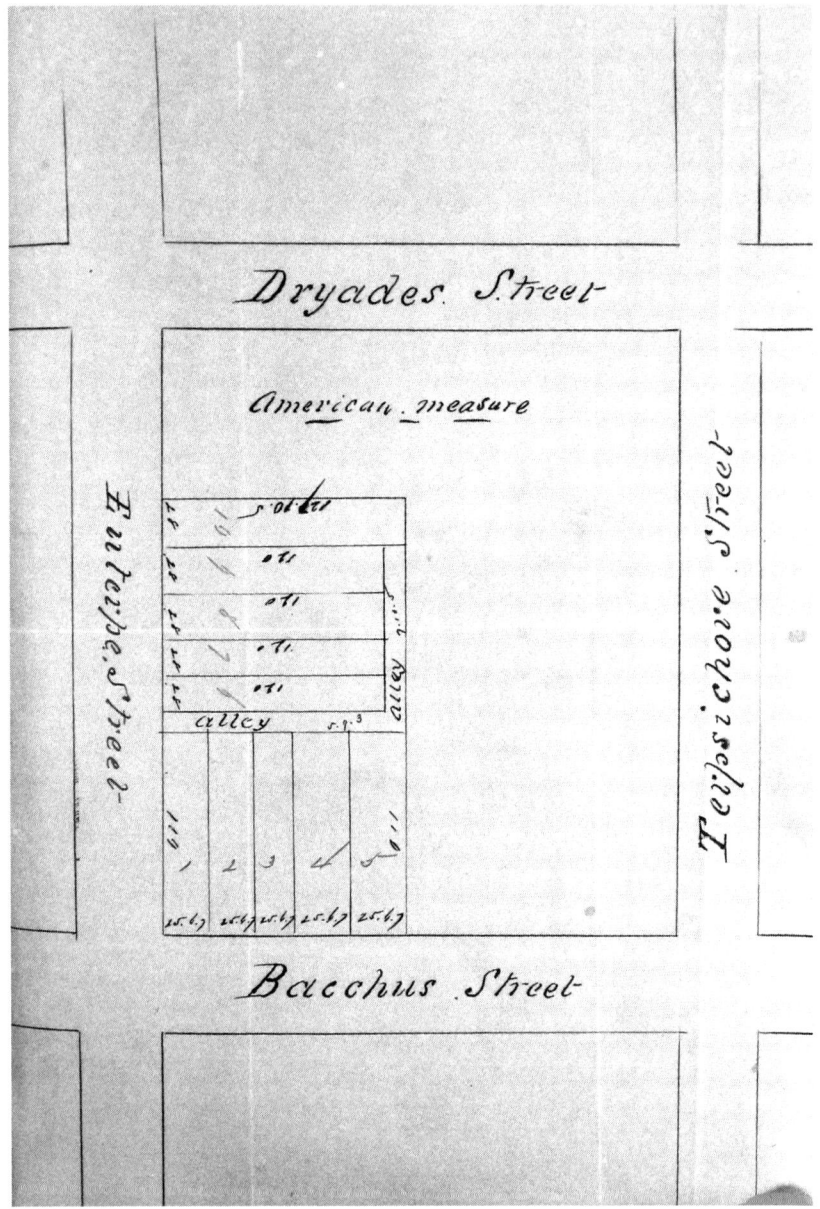

Figure 2.5. Properties purchased by Norbert Soulié at the north corner of Bacchus (now Baronne) and Euterpe Streets. Attached to sale of property from Norbert Soulié to Heinrich Kleinhagan et al., Theodore Guyol notary, volume 11, act 668, May 2, 1846. Courtesy of Hon. Chelsey Richard Napoleon, Clerk of Civil District Court, Parish of Orleans.

the city traditionally associated with free people of color and French-speaking whites. On the one hand, the *gens de couleur libres'* success as property owners and speculators presented a dichotomy in a city becoming more and more American and culturally and racially segregated and attempting to keep free people of color in their "proper place" in daily life.[63] On the other hand, their reality underscored the parity they retained with white Creoles and many Americans. Residential patterns for both families were consistent with the development of the city and patterns of movement of the *gens de couleur libres* to Faubourg Tremé (table 2.2). With few exceptions, both families called the Vieux Carré home until the 1830s, when the Dollioles purchased property on St. Philip Street and Norbert Soulié left New Orleans. For the remainder of the antebellum period, first-generation members of both families lived primarily in one location: Faubourg Tremé.

Likewise, when noted separately from a place of residence, the families' businesses were primarily in one geographic area (table 2.1). Bernard and Albin Soulié's place of business, first as builders, then as commission merchants, remained in the Vieux Carré throughout the antebellum period. Only a second-generation Dolliole, Louis Drausin (son of Jean-Louis), is noted as having a workplace separate from his residence; it was located in Faubourg Tremé on St. Philip Street.

The property ownership of the Dollioles, Souliés, and other *gens de couleur libres* is important, as their antebellum development and settlement patterns were never again as concentrated in some parts of the city but had far-reaching consequences that affected the future of racial geography in New Orleans in other

TABLE 2.1. BUSINESS MOVEMENT OF THE DOLLIOLE AND SOULIÉ FAMILIES FROM CITY OF NEW ORLEANS DIRECTORIES, 1805-1850

Year	Vieux Carré	Faubourg Tremé
1832	Bernard and Albin Soulié (builders) 19 Main	
1838	Bernard and Albin Soulié (merchants) 55 Bienville	
1841	Bernard and Albin Soulié (merchants) 55 Bienville	
1842	Bernard and Albin Soulié (merchants) 55 Bienville (upstairs)	Louis Drausin Dolliole 216 St. Philip
1846	Bernard and Albin Soulié (merchants) 48 Conti	Louis Drausin Dolliole and Emile Errié 216 St. Philip
1850	Bernard and Albin Soulié (merchants) 139 Royal	

TABLE 2.2. RESIDENTIAL MOVEMENT OF THE DOLLIOLE AND SOULIÉ FAMILIES FROM CITY OF NEW ORLEANS DIRECTORIES, 1805-1850

Year	Vieux Carré	Faubourg Tremé	Faubourg Marigny/ Creole faubourgs
1805	Louis Dolliole–67 St. Philip Eulalie Mazange–40 Dumaine		
1811	Pierre Dolliole–63 St. Philip J. L. Dolliole–65 St. Philip Louis Dolliole–67 St. Philip John Souliér [sic]–16 Bourbon		
1822	[Jean] Louis Doriol [sic]–St. Philip below Rampart Jean and Norbert Soulié–114 Bourbon	J. L. Dolliole–80 Bayou Road	Joseph–14 History
1824	Jean and Norbert Soulié–241 Bourbon		
1832	Norbert, Bernard, and Albin Soulié–19 Main		
1834		J. L. Dolliole–92 Bayou Road J. L. Dolliole–216 St. Philip Joseph Dolliole–St. Philip near St. Claude	
1838		Joseph Dolliole–85 Bayou Road Bernard and Albin Soulié–377 Rampart	J. L. Dolliole–103 Love
1841		J. L. Dolliole–corner of Bayou Road and Villeré Louis Drausin–St. Peter near Robertson Joseph Dolliole–corner of Bayou Road and Plauché Street Joseph Dolliole Jr.–Tremé between Ursulines and St. Philip	

1842		J. L. Dolliole–corner of Bayou Road and Villeré Louis Drausin–St. Peter near Robertson Joseph Dolliole–corner of Bayou Road and Plauché Street Joseph Dolliole Jr.–Tremé between Ursulines and St. Philip	Albin Soulié–50 Love
1846		J. L.–Bayou Road near Villeré and Robertson Joseph Dolliole–corner of Bayou Road and Plauché Albin and Bernard Soulié–377 Rampart	J. L. Dolliole–103 Love
		J. L. Dolliole–Bayou Road near Villeré Joseph Dolliole–Bayou Road near Plauché	
1849		J. L. Dolliole–283 Bayou Road Joseph Dolliole–254 Bayou Road	
1850		J. L. Dolliole–283 Bayou Road Joseph Dolliole–254 Bayou Road	

instances. As the city of New Orleans expanded, newly developed suburbs all had duplicate physical features—public squares, cemeteries, canals, and civic and religious institutions.[64] These similarities, however, were not repeated in ownership patterns, especially since the percentage of free persons of color with respect to the city's entire population dropped from 23 percent to 8.5 percent between 1820 and 1850. In the 1850s, *gens de couleur libres* remained concentrated in the First District (Fifth and Seventh Wards) and the Third District (First Ward). The three wards contained more than half of the free Black population and one-seventh of the city's white residents. In contrast, the Second District contained one-ninth of the free Black population and half of the white population.[65] From 1850 to 1870, wealthier free persons of color relocated to the newly fashionable Esplanade Avenue—the dividing line between two traditionally Creole spheres—instead of to the Lower Garden District and Garden District.[66] After the Civil War, a large number of *gens de couleur libres* retained their property holdings in Faubourg Tremé.

Many increasingly sold their homes and land to white Creoles, Americans, and, to a lesser extent, newly manumitted Blacks. Still, it was in this neighborhood where the *gens de couleur libres'* identified new potential for urban development through their construction and development activities (in an in-between area between the original city and swampland) and contributed to the city's growth into the twentieth century.[67]

PART II

ENGAGEMENT

Forming and Transforming the Built Environment

CHAPTER 3

THE ARCHITECTURE OF THE DOLLIOLE AND SOULIÉ FAMILIES

The comfort is a matter of habit.

BENJAMIN HENRY LATROBE, *THE JOURNAL OF LATROBE* (1819)

In his descriptions of early nineteenth-century architecture in New Orleans, Benjamin Henry Latrobe praises the modes of design and layout of Creole domestic architecture, particularly the cottages ubiquitous in the Vieux Carré and Faubourg Marigny.[1] While the older parts of the city gained larger and more sumptuous houses after fires in 1788 and 1794, this simple form persisted. In the residential quarters in new suburbs below and above the Vieux Carré, freestanding houses based on typologies from the American Northeast, but placed at the *banquette* (sidewalk) and with walled side yards as per local convention, became popular after the turn of the nineteenth century. Farther upriver in American-dominated neighborhoods, houses set back in shaded lawns and streets planted with trees were the norm.[2] In addition to the disposition of lots, building forms and architectural styles also changed with the transition of Louisiana from a European colony to an American territory and state. The role of the *gens de couleur libres* builder in the changing architectural character of New Orleans's neighborhoods can be seen in the works built by the Dollioles and Souliés. Aside from acquiring property throughout the city, and staking claim to land and to their birth and legal rights, the *gens de couleur libres* were actively engaged with their property—forming and transforming the built environment to create a place for themselves in the city's architectural heritage. On the one hand, the buildings that Jean-Louis and Joseph Dolliole and Norbert Soulié erected reflect the transitional nature of architectural forms and styles in the territorial and early antebellum periods. On the other hand, their work reveals the builders' backgrounds with regard to learning the building trades, experience with various typological forms, and modes of practice.

LEARNING AND BUILDING

The *gens de couleur libres* formed and transformed themselves and others in the process of acquiring and imparting knowledge of and skills relevant to the building trades. In early nineteenth-century and antebellum New Orleans, educational opportunities were limited for young *gens de couleur libres*, but families found opportunities for their children through apprenticeships or, when possible, through private instruction.[3] Free Black girls might attend day or boarding school or religion classes at the Ursuline convent school until it relocated downriver in 1824.[4] Afterward, Sister Marthe Fortière stayed in New Orleans to operate a school for free girls of color in Faubourg Tremé.[5] Similarly, formal architectural education was unknown in the United States during the antebellum era, and few would have had the opportunity to study the field abroad. No drawing schools or mechanics institutes were located in New Orleans; the latter type of school was not established in the United States until the 1820s.[6] By midcentury, wealthier families could afford to send their children to privately operated schools specifically for free children of color in educators' homes and, after the children made their First Communion in early adolescence, their daughters could be sent to convent schools and their sons to schools of higher learning in the northeastern United States and in Europe, particularly Paris.[7]

Most builders like the Dollioles and Souliés learned through formal or informal apprenticeship. In New Orleans, as throughout the rest of the country, the building trades in the antebellum era were dominated by master craftsmen, not professional architects (table 3.1). In particular, master carpenters often became builders with entrepreneurial skill sets in addition to craft knowledge. They served as general contractors, acquired materials and labor, and directed work. If their work included making drawings and supervising, they were known as architects. Most master craftsmen and builder-architects worked alone and for self-profit or gain.[8] *Gens de couleur libres* in New Orleans followed this same occupational pattern. Most commonly, after completing training with relatives or

TABLE 3.1. ENTRIES FOR BUILDING-RELATED OCCUPATIONS IN CITY OF NEW ORLEANS DIRECTORIES, SELECT YEARS

Occupation	1811	1822	1832
Architect	7	1	3
Builder	1	18	41
Carpenter	51	214	223
Joiner	8	1[1]	8
Cabinetmaker	25	54[2]	74
Carpenter and Joiner	—	6	—
Cabinetmaker and Joiner	—	1	—
Carpenter and Cabinetmaker	—	1	1
Joiner and Architect	—	—	1
Bricklayer	9	41	70
Plasterer	—	—	8
Bricklayer and Plasterer	—	1	—
Slater	1	—	5
Painter	4	—	21
Glazier	—	—	2
Painter and Glazier	5[3]	30[3]	22

Note: This survey of the directories counts single entries, not individuals. For example, partners Mitchell and Le Moyne, builders (1811), or Bernard and Albin Soulié, builders (1832), were counted as one entry.
[1] Listed as a house and ship joiner.
[2] One "late," or retired, cabinetmaker was also noted.
[3] Two were also (wall)paper hangers.

serving as journeymen, craftsmen of color entered the family business or sought self-employment. The first-generation Dolliole and Soulié males certainly could also have been exposed to builders' guides, popular tools for disseminating ideas about form and style in late eighteenth- and early nineteenth-century America, since they were all literate. This type of tool would not have accounted for their initial introductory careers as builders and developers, however.

THE DOLLIOLES

Learning by Doing

Until now, the notation (and repetition) in previous scholarship that Louis Dolliole was an important and prolific builder in the city of New Orleans would indicate that he passed his knowledge of carpentry and the building trades to his sons Jean-Louis, Joseph, and Pierre.[9] No historic documentation indicating that he, or his brother Jean-François, was a builder has been located.[10] Louis is listed as *cabaretier* in the 1811 city directory.[11] In early nineteenth-century New Orleans, a *cabaretier*, or publican, was the owner or manager of an inn or tavern.[12] By 1822, Louis had retired to his Bayou Road home and was listed as a planter. Furthermore, Louis had no formal education and was illiterate; that fact is revealed in that he made his mark on petitions and other documents related to brother Jean-François's estate.[13] Since the Dolliole elders were not builders, Jean-Louis and his brothers (and cousins) would have been self-taught or have learned their trade from another builder, with their inspiration coming from observing the buildings surrounding them in the Vieux Carré.

The Spanish colonial city in which the first-generation Dollioles came of age remained largely French in character. No Spanish architects worked in the city during this time; they were primarily French Creoles and some Anglo-Americans.[14] French military engineers designed most of the buildings in the nascent Louisiana colony.[15] American Robert Jones built the raised Creole cottage (presently known as "Madame John's Legacy") on Dumaine Street in 1789 after a fire devastated the city the previous year (figure 3.1). Truly a Creole building, the raised cottage is an urban version of the French *rez-de-chaussée*—raised timber frame—colonial plantation homes that would have been located outside of the city, built by an American for a Spanish official.[16] After the second fire, in 1794, the colonial government mandated that houses be constructed of brick or of lumber posts infilled with brick (*briquette-entre-poteaux*), be covered with cement (stucco), have roofs covered with tile or brick, and face the street.[17] After these two fires, the Creole (or *banquette*) cottage—a small, single-story house type—came to form the building stock of the Vieux Carré and Creole faubourgs.[18] It is the Creole cottage with which Jean-Louis and Joseph Dolliole would have been most familiar as they came of age and pursued careers as builder-architects in the late eighteenth and early nineteenth centuries.

Figure 3.1. 628–632 Dumaine Street ("Madame John's Legacy"). Photo by John Watson Riley, 2011. The Collins C. Diboll Vieux Carré Digital Survey at The Historic New Orleans Collection.

Proliferation and Perfection of the Creole Cottage

Creole architecture was a direct result of relationships forged between colonizers and colonized and is a result of mixtures of various elements of cultural and building traditions—maritime French, French Canadian, and some Anglo-American.[19] The basis for Creole architecture in the New World actually has origins in the European colonization of Africa. Even before widespread Portuguese exploration, runaway navy and merchant sailors joined West African societies, resulting in the creation of the Luso-African ethnic group. In Africa, native peoples controlled the architectural form of buildings constructed for early European settlers. From the fifteenth through the eighteenth centuries, Europeans adopted local rectangular buildings based on the dwellings of Upper Guinea. The Africans who built these dwellings added their own conventions, which included the porch or gallery. Such changes signified the addition of Africans' own social conveniences and architectural preconceptions to the main rectangular structure. These early forms became the basis for Creole architecture in the New World as European colonization expanded across the Atlantic Ocean. In the late eighteenth century, Europeans in the Caribbean improved on African models by adding casement windows, louvered shutters, and screening. Though the African influence remained strong in colonial architecture throughout various European settlements in the Caribbean, interdependence between forms and conventions from all parties involved was important to the development of Creole architecture that was the source material for builders in New Orleans.[20]

The cohabitation of Hispaniola by the French and Spanish marks an important point of the development of Creole architecture in the New World. The eastern half of the island, Santo Domingo, was established by the Spanish in 1496. With the lack of Spanish settlement and the presence of French buccaneers, the western part of the island became known as Saint-Domingue in 1608. Spain ceded Saint-Domingue to France in 1696.[21] As throughout the rest of the West Indies, the dual occupation of the island, as well as the presence of both natives and enslaved Africans, made for unique cultural adaptations. In fact, according to the anthropologist Jay D. Edwards, the Creole cottage type was influenced more by Caribbean developments than by any direct Spanish or French forms. The most significant contributions of European architecture to the Creole cottage were the Norman plan, with its two-room asymmetrical core, and the Spanish plan, based on a three-room symmetrical nucleus.[22] The Spanish plan influenced the development of the Louisiana raised cottage and, later, larger plantation homes with an encircling gallery and was utilized more by Spanish Caribbean Creoles.[23] The Norman plan was slower to develop, with manifestations based on a two-room (*salle-et-chambre*) asymmetrical core that began to be manipulated in the early days of the Louisiana colony. This two-room core evolved into what has become known as the Creole cottage. European forms were further altered with the addition of living space in the form of galleries present on one or multiple sides of the Caribbean Creole dwelling. Cultural preferences on the dimension, proportion, and arrangement of rooms took precedence as the "idea of the Creole house" spread geographically.[24] The amalgamation of ideas and forms that became the Louisiana Creole cottage was fully developed by the time it became widespread on the North American Gulf Coast. The desire to retain ties to the familiar undoubtedly influenced the use of the Creole cottage by homeowners and builders who immigrated to New Orleans from Saint-Domingue just before and after the turn of the nineteenth century. These refugees added significantly to the already prevalent Creole forms in New Orleans.

Early French and Spanish Colonial cottages had pavilion (hipped) roofs and a layout of four rooms. Each pair of rooms shared a chimney on the center wall. The French Colonial cottage had a steeply pitched roof.[25] Early French Colonial cottages in the city consisted of buildings such as that known today as Lafitte's Blacksmith Shop, circa 1781, located on Bourbon Street (figure 3.2).[26] Following the mandates of Governor Miró after the 1788 and 1794 fires, Spanish Colonial cottages featured shallow or flat roofs covered with barrel tile.[27] Both types

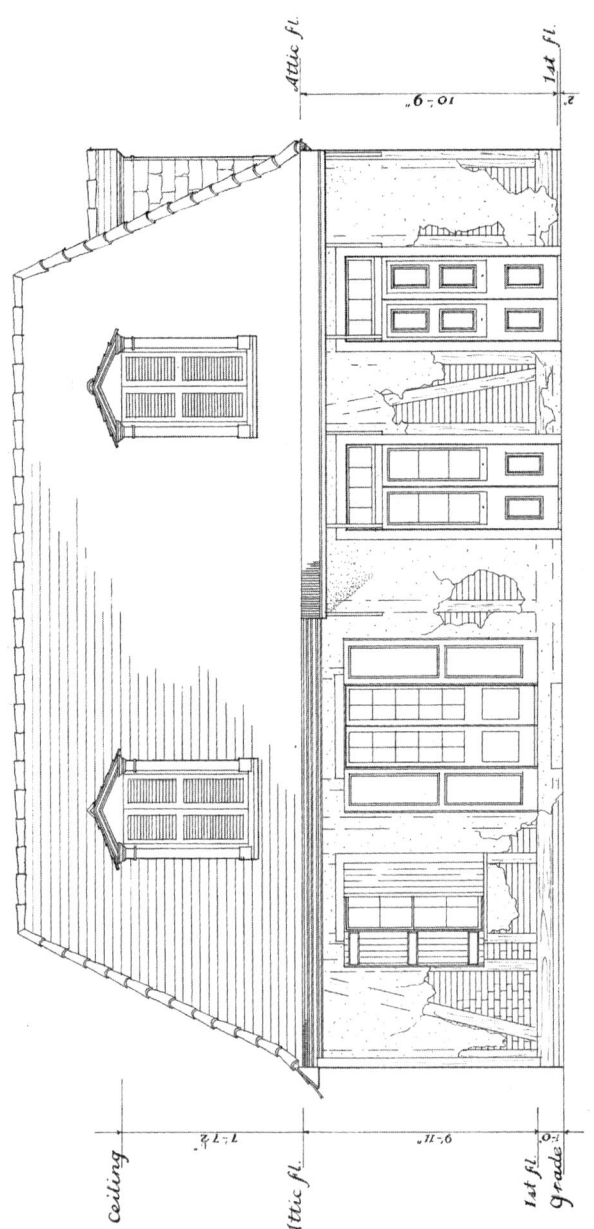

Figure 3.2. 937–941 Bourbon Street ("Lafitte's Blacksmith Shop"), Library of Congress, Historic American Buildings Survey, Index No. HABS, LA,36-NEWOR,13-, Survey No. HABS LA-24.

were placed *en banquette*, flush with the sidewalk, with an *abat-vent*, front roof overhang or extension, over it. In the late 1700s, this house type evolved into the Creole cottage with a steeply gabled roof and a rear loggia flanked by *cabinets*, or storage rooms. Large numbers of these gabled Creole cottages began to be built in New Orleans following the immigration of refugees from Saint-Domingue in 1803, 1804, and 1809.[28] Native sons such as the Dollioles also chose to adopt this form, adding significantly to the already prevalent Creole forms in New Orleans. The creative refashioning of the Creole cottage by the Dollioles and their New Orleans–born peers not only incorporated variations of its architectural form but also considered the living and economic circumstances of the clients.

The Dollioles and their adaptation and interpretation of the Creole cottage form is important because house design and construction in colonial and post-colonial New Orleans, as in the American colonies, was controlled by master carpenters.[29] As no records of earlier property ownership or building contracts have been found, the family's complex of buildings on St. Philip Street in the Vieux Carré was where the Dolliole brothers first constructed buildings. The ca. 1805 Creole cottage at 931–933 St. Philip Street is the oldest of the extant cottages (figure 3.3). The brick-between-post, four-bay house is covered with stucco. The fenestration on the front façade is marked by batten-shuttered openings—two casement doors flanked by casement windows. The Sanborn Fire Insurance Map of 1876 indicates that the cottage had a hipped roof at that time; the present roof with parapet-like, gabled fire walls was in place by 1896. The *abat-vent*, or front façade roof extension, is supported by iron bearers cantilevered from the façade at the roofline.[30] A 1937 sketch plan completed by G. B. Drennan for the Historic American Buildings Survey shows that the cottage has retained its original layout of two-by-two en suite rooms with adjoining fireplaces on the central wall (figure 3.4). Arched openings at the rear loggia originally provided access to a brick courtyard, at the rear of which was a two-story, two-room-wide outbuilding with balcony (now demolished; figure 3.5).[31] The cottage was restored in 1980 by its present owners.[32]

In 1807, Jean-Louis Dolliole built a *maison de maître* on the Bayou Road property he purchased from Claude Tremé.[33] In general terms, the *maison de maître* was the main or master's house of a plantation.[34] This type, however, also refers to a distinct form that was prevalent along the Bayou Road, outside of the city walls, in the first quarter of the nineteenth century. As opposed to the *maison principale*, a "country house" or "manor house" among a complex of buildings on a large *habitation* or plantation, the term *maison de maître* was used in period contracts to describe rectangular-plan houses on smaller properties equal to

Figure 3.3. 931–933 St. Philip Street (Dolliole-Masson Cottage). Jean-Louis Dolliole, ca. 1805. Photo by John Watson Riley, 2010. The Collins C. Diboll Vieux Carré Digital Survey at The Historic New Orleans Collection.

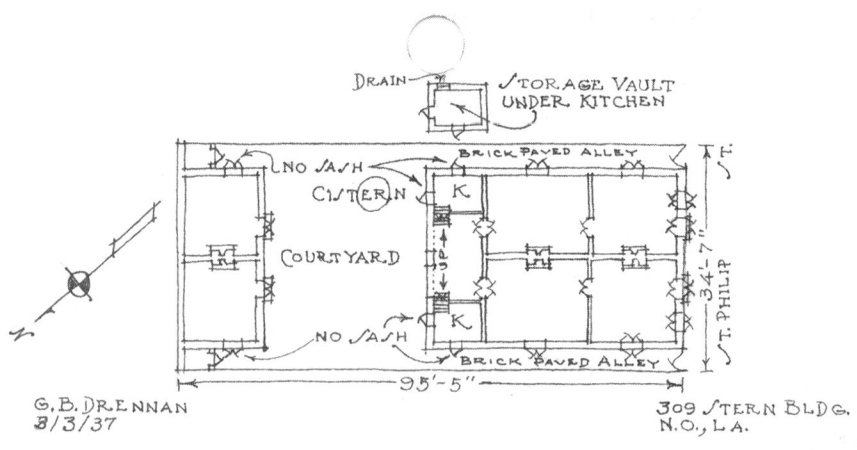

Figure 3.4. Sketch Plan of 931–933 St. Philip Street. Plan drawn by G. B. Drennan, 1937. Library of Congress, Historic American Buildings Survey, Index No. HABS LA,36-NEWOR,72-, Survey No. HABS LA-160.

Figure 3.5. 931–933 St. Philip Street. Photo by Richard Koch, 1938. Library of Congress, Historic American Buildings Survey, Index No. HABS LA,36-NEWOR,72-, Survey No. HABS LA-160.

approximately one-quarter of a New Orleans city square.[35] These raised dwellings, with living quarters on the upper level, had two to four rooms with bonnet roofs (a dual-pitched hipped roof with a double slope on all four sides), a garret, and a full-length porch on one or more sides.[36] The Bayou Road property purchased by Joseph Dolliole from his father's estate in 1806 also featured a *maison de maître*. In Louis Dolliole's estate inventory, the dwelling house was described as a brick-between-post house with a shingle roof containing two apartments as well as front and back galleries. The remainder of the lot was occupied by a garden. The Dolliole's Bayou Road properties and buildings were probably similar in layout (not form) to that depicted on a plan by Eugéne Surgi in 1848 (figure 3.6).[37] Like those of the Dollioles, the lot is elongated, with the shorter frontage facing Bayou Road. The early *maison de maîtres* belonging to the Dollioles—Creole designs that evolved to provide comfort under the local conditions of high temperature and high humidity—would have served as models for their later work. Jean-Louis Dolliole's Bayou Road *maison de maître* supposedly served as his residence while he constructed other houses in the area.[38]

Several of Jean-Louis Dolliole's Creole cottages constructed in the 1820s are still found in Faubourg Marigny. The dwelling at 1436 Pauger is a unique cottage

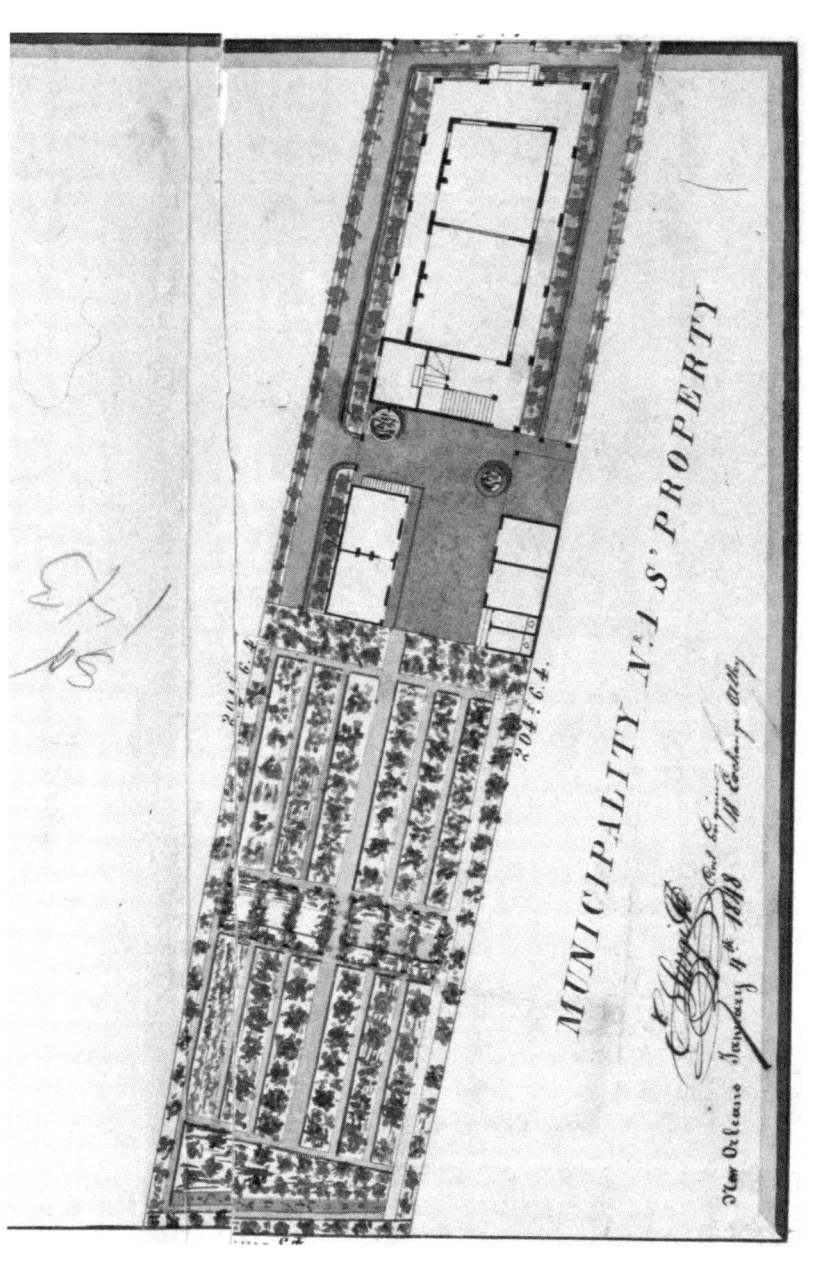

Figure 3.6. Layout of an habitation on Esplanade Avenue similar to that which Louis Dolliole owned on Bayou Road. Source: 1244 Esplanade Avenue. Eugéne Surgi, 1848. Plan Book 65A, folio 63. Courtesy of Hon. Chelsey Richard Napoleon, Clerk of Civil District Court, Parish of Orleans.

Figure 3.7. 1436 Pauger Street. Jean-Louis Dolliole, 1820. Photo by author, 2011.

that shows off his craftsmanship and understanding of Creole building techniques (figure 3.7). Jean-Louis began construction of this building on property owned by his mother-in-law in December 1819 before purchasing the lot from her two months later (his wife, Hortense, had died in August of 1818). This plastered brick cottage is a traditional Creole cottage plan modified to allow for its location on an angled street corner where the extension of Bourbon Street (formerly Bagatelle Street) from the Vieux Carré meets Pauger Street; its roof, fenestration arrangement, and room layout are altered accordingly. The cottage features an irregular five-sided hipped roof with flared edges and wide overhanging eaves over the *banquette* to allow for protection from the elements, as was customary with Creole domestic architecture. The original pan tile covering the roof is still in place; it is not attached with nails but hooked in place on narrow cypress strips. Architectural drawings of the cottage from the Historic American Buildings Survey (HABS) illustrate this technique as well as the mortise-and-tenon timber construction of the roof system (figure 3.8). When built, the cottage featured multilight casement doors and double-hung, twelve-over-twelve, wood-sash windows.[39] The boards of the cypress batten shutters protecting the doors and windows are laid vertically on

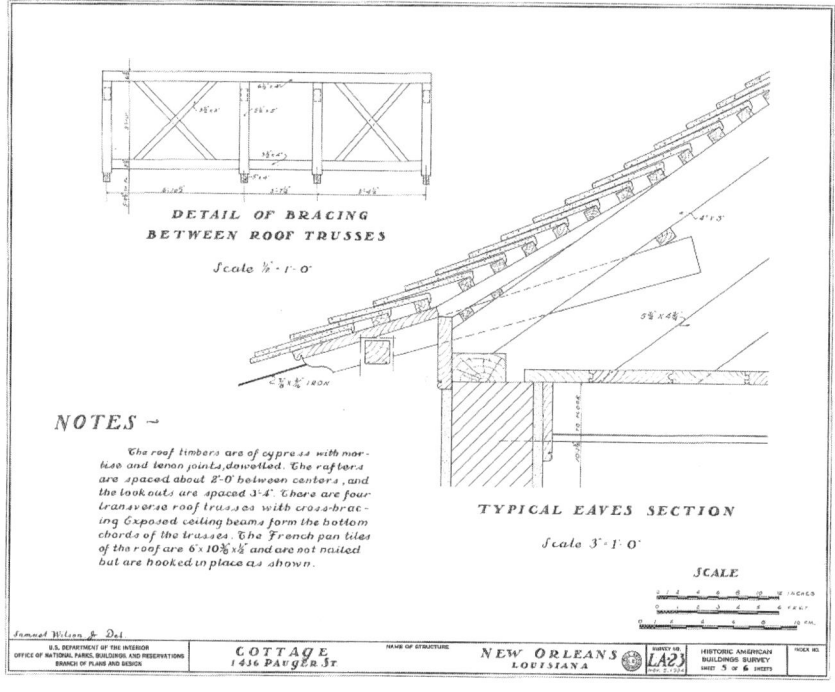

Figure 3.8. Roof system of 1436 Pauger Street. Samuel Wilson Jr., delineator, 1934. Library of Congress, Historic American Buildings Survey. Call No. HABS LA,36-NEWOR,12-. Survey No. HABS LA-23.

the sides that show when closed, and diagonally on the sides visible when open. As opposed to a regular two-by-two layout, the rooms of this cottage originally consisted of a large front chamber with smaller adjacent chambers flanking it (figure 3.9). The space between the small rooms originally served as a loggia; the archways to the rear courtyard had been bricked up and casement doors with transoms and shutters inserted by 1934. Though the cottage has undergone several renovations, it retains the craftsmanship of its builder to a high degree and illustrates the care taken by Dolliole in its design and construction.

Two other Faubourg Marigny cottages that were part of real estate transactions in which Dolliole was involved may have been designed by him as well. Dolliole served as executor for Joseph Prieto, who owned the house and property at 1455–1457 Pauger; he inherited it upon Prieto's death in 1838.[40] The dwelling was constructed between 1810 and 1821.[41] The brick-between-post building is clad

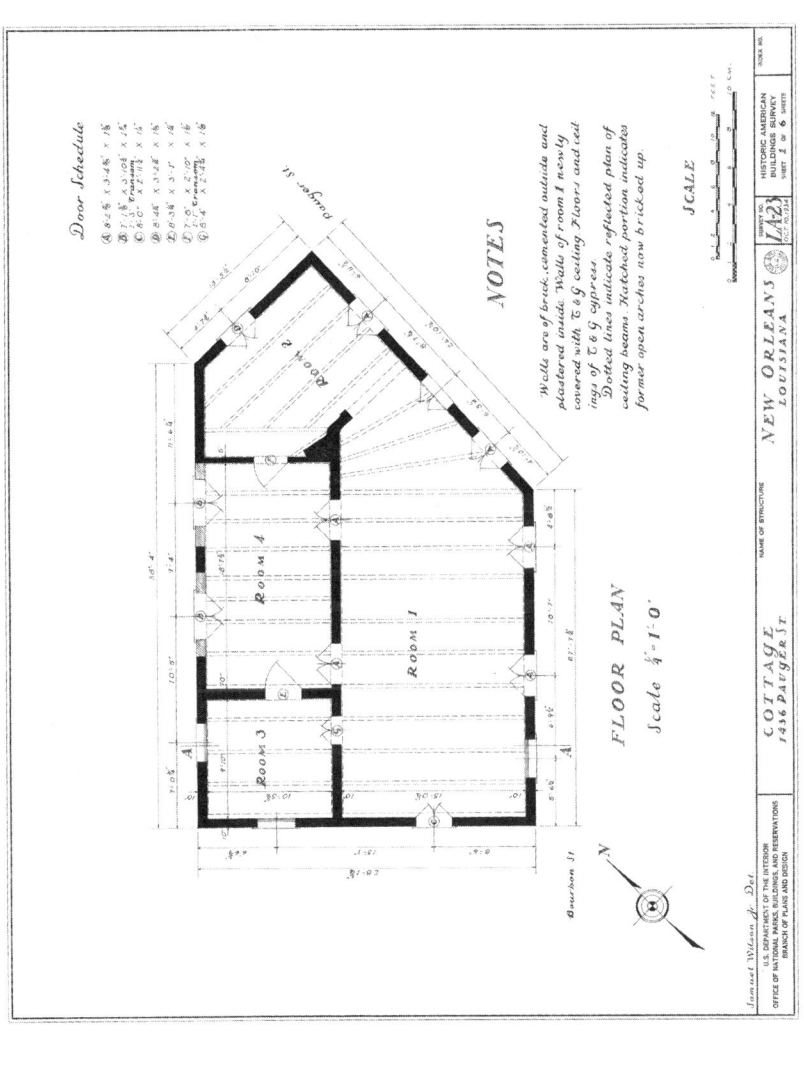

Figure 3.9. Floor plan of 1436 Pauger Street. Samuel Wilson Jr., delineator, 1934. Library of Congress, Historic American Buildings Survey. Call No. HABS LA,36-NEWOR,12-, Survey No. HABS LA-23.

with weatherboard and appears to have the typical four-room cottage layout but a wider than normal street-facing façade. The writers of *New Orleans Architecture*, Volume 4, *The Creole Faubourgs*, attribute it to Dolliole, given the history of its ownership and its similarity in basic style to 1436 Pauger and other Dolliole cottages.[42] Furthermore, the incorporation of a pan-tiled, hipped roof with flared edges appears to have been a rare instance in Faubourg Marigny and was utilized by few builders by 1800.[43] Francisco Tio purchased the house from Jean-Louis Dolliole in 1841.[44] Tio also acquired a cottage at 820 Elysian Fields. Though no specific works of his have been identified, Joseph Dolliole was also active in Faubourg Marigny in the 1820s. For a time, he partnered with another New Orleans–born free builder of color, Henry Fletcher (1791–1853). The men, both listed in the 1822 New Orleans city directory as carpenters, lived at 14 Histoire Street on property that Fletcher owned in Faubourg Marigny.[45]

Despite expanding his work to other areas of the city and being familiar with other building types, Jean-Louis Dolliole continued to build Creole cottages in the Vieux Carré. In April 1822, he was permitted by the city council to turn and move a house on the property he purchased from his father's estate on Burgundy Street between St. Philip and Ursulines the month before.[46] The existing house was to be moved to the rear of the lot so that a new house made of brick and clad with tiles could be constructed at the front of the lot in its place.[47] The form of this new dwelling, formerly at 939–941 St. Philip, is unknown.[48] Since Jean-Louis and other family members resided elsewhere, this new house would have served as an income property until he sold it in 1843. Subsequently, any Dolliole buildings on the property were demolished and replaced by a two-story townhouse and a two-story kitchen-quarters building.[49]

In 1831, Jean-Louis received a commission from John Voisin and Louis Adam to build a cottage on Magazine Street between Julia and Saint Joseph Streets in Faubourg Sainte-Marie. Aside from being the only Dolliole-built building in the Second Municipality, the cottage is also the only edifice for which a building contract involving Jean-Louis Dolliole has been found.[50] The document provides detailed specifications for a four-room cottage with *cabinets* and a rear gallery. Other features of the cottage were to include:

- dimensions: 28½' wide × 46' deep; 2'-high foundation brick-between post construction with cypress timbers; shingle cladding
- *abat-vent* at front façade; 2½' *abat-vent* at rear façade; both capped and covered with shingles
- front doors with glazed transoms accessed by steps

- staircase from each *cabinet* to the attic
- double-hung (sliding sash) windows[51]
- two openings from the rear gallery, each with a solid door and a glazed door surmounted by a glazed transom
- brick interior walls in primary rooms; lath-and-plaster walls in the *cabinets* and gallery
- four fireplaces
- ten interior doors—two paneled double, four paneled single, four simple (at cabinets)

The contract also made provisions for Jean-Louis to construct a two-story, shingle-clad kitchen with two rooms on each level and a double fireplace on the first floor. Jean-Louis possessed the requisite skills to complete this well-thought-out cottage on Magazine Street. Jean-Louis Dolliole's reputation and expertise building Creole cottages made him a suitable choice for this commission in Faubourg Sainte-Marie despite the fact that the neighborhood was already established as an enclave for Anglo-Americans and well on its way to becoming the city's commercial center, with examples of high-style domestic, commercial, and institutional architecture.

The 1830s saw the Dollioles continue to build the traditional four-bay, four-room Creole cottage in Faubourg Tremé, namely on St. Philip Street. Illustrations from properties sold by the succession of Joseph Dolliole clearly depict cottages in the 1100 and 1200 blocks of St. Philip (see figures 1.4 and 1.6). Both lots clearly are occupied by four-bay, four-room cottages with *cabinets*, a kitchen outbuilding, and a two-room latrine. A few subtle differences in the design and layout of the buildings indicate their different uses. The property in the 1100 block, built by 1834, was utilized by several members of the Dolliole family—Joseph lived here in 1834, and Geneviève was in residence at her death in 1838.[52] Therefore, the two-room kitchen outbuilding with front-facing *cabinets* and gallery would have been sufficient to service a single-family home.[53] Joseph's property at 1223–1225 St. Philip, on the other hand, served as a multifamily rental property from the time he acquired the lot and constructed the buildings in 1834 until he sold the improved property in 1854. This is evident in the inclusion of stairways in each *cabinet* so that living space could be added in the attic and tenants could reach their upper chambers privately. Further, the erection of one four-room kitchen building with rear gallery allowed for each tenant to have access to a two-room space.[54] As Joseph owned both properties, he was likely responsible for their construction.

During the 1830s, the Dolliole builders also explored new forms and plans

Figure 3.10. 1227 St. Philip Street. Photo by Liz Jurey, courtesy of the Preservation Resource Center of New Orleans.

for the Creole cottage. In an 1834 act of sale from Joseph Dolliole to Marie Louis Demony, he sold her a half lot in the 1300 block of St. Philip (south side).[55] The transaction stipulated that Joseph was to construct on the lot a brick-between-post house divided into two rooms within three months of the sale (not extant). On narrow properties, the two-bay cottage was a natural progression from the four-room cottage, which was often divided to serve as two residences.[56] The striking proportions resulting from the narrow façade and tall dormered gable of the two-room cottage are visible at the surviving cottage built by Joseph Dolliole at 1227 St. Philip Street (figure 3.10). Restored since 1980 to resemble a more historic appearance, the cottage features a stucco exterior; behind the batten door shutters are modern wood-paneled and glazed casement doors topped with fixed-pane transoms that retain the historic proportions of the front façade fenestration.

When an additional bay was added to the two-bay cottage, reducing the extremes between width and height, the result was the more harmonious three-bay cottage.[57] Jean-Louis Dolliole built a pair of these at 1125 and 1127 St. Philip Street (figure 3.11). The unique nature of the lots prompted construction of these narrower cottages—Jean-Louis erected the two houses on one lot portioned from

Figure 3.11. 1125 and 1127 St. Philip Street. Photo by author, 2011.

Figure 3.12. Side gallery of (and rear addition to) 1125 St. Philip Street. Courtesy of New Orleans Jazz Quarters Hotel.

a larger land purchase.⁵⁸ Each brick house has a single door and two windows at the primary façade and a double-pitched gabled roof where the upturning of the roof extension forms the *abat-vent*.⁵⁹ Each door opens onto a side gallery integrated into the floor plan under the roofline (figure 3.12). This treatment in the Creole cottage resulted in a passage that served "as an additional, 'in-between space,' the kind of refined negotiation between inside and outside that is typical of Creole buildings."⁶⁰ The present disposition in which the galleries are treated as "front porches" and the shuttered casement doors and windows are always closed is contradictory to the cottages' historic use and arrangement.⁶¹ It is no accident that the entry doors were centrally located adjacent to the shared passageway to facilitate communication between the cottages via the facing galleries. This relationship between the buildings would have been ideal if they served as the residences and businesses of Jean-Louis, Joseph, and, in later years, Jean-Louis's son Louis Drausin as city directories indicate.

It is likely that the Dollioles also constructed the three-bay cottage at 1010 Burgundy Street, given their experience with three-bay cottages, their work back and forth between the Vieux Carré and Faubourg Tremé, and their history at the site (figure 3.13). When Jean-Louis sold this lot to his sister Madeleine in 1805, it was unimproved. The buildings on the property would have been constructed under the ownership of Madeleine (1805–1835) or her daughter Victoire Galaud (1835–1842). It follows that whichever woman was responsible would have had her brother or uncle, experienced builders, erect the house and outbuildings. The house at 1010 Burgundy is an elaboration on the three-bay form true to developments of the cottage form in the late to mid-1830s. It is not clear whether the entry door provides access to the front chamber or to an interior hallway. The frame building features Greek Revival detailing unusual for a Creole cottage in the Greek key architrave (trapezoidal) door surround and louvered shutters (the historic pediments over the casement windows have been removed) as well as a Federal style roof dormer at the front of the gabled roof.⁶² This type of gabled dormer—with a double-hung window and segmental arched light usually flanked by pilaster—was introduced from the US East Coast in the early nineteenth century. The arched fanlight and the upper sash of the six-over-six dormer window have been replaced. This stylistic treatment of a Creole cottage would have been unusual for the Dollioles, but they did apply antebellum stylistic conventions from the East Coast in the more traditional four-bay cottage.⁶³

The Dollioles continued building around the corner at the family compound in the 900 block of St. Philip Street in the late 1830s.⁶⁴ While primary source documentation indicates that the family members lived in a house at no. 927–929

Figure 3.13. 1010 Burgundy Street. Photo by author, 2011.

and that a house was built for Pierre Dolliole at no. 935–937 by 1822, the extant houses feature the higher roof profile and stylistic detailing of Creole cottages built in the 1830s. Flanking the cottage that Jean-Louis built in 1805 are two four-bay, brick-between-post cottages featuring fire wall extensions at the end gables, gabled roofs with dormers, and *abat-vents* under an extension of the roof (figures 3.14 and 3.15). Both have Federal and Greek Revival features. The original louvered shutters at no. 927–929, which would have matched those present at no. 935–937, have been replaced with batten shutters. The latter cottage also has wide door lintels characteristic of Greek Revival architecture. Both houses have Federal style gabled roof dormers—the pair at no. 927–929 has period-appropriate replacement windows with curved muntins in the upper sash. The one at no. 935–937 has a six-over-six double-hung unit. The decorative brackets under the *abat-vent* applied in the late nineteenth century are still in place at no. 935–937 but have been removed from no. 927–929. This pair of cottages is among the last buildings known to have been constructed by Jean-Louis or Joseph Dolliole in the antebellum period. Joseph Dolliole did construct a frame cottage with four rooms and an enclosed gallery in Faubourg Tremé in 1839.[65] This house is no longer

Figure 3.14. 927–929 St. Philip Street. Photo by author, 2011.

Figure 3.15. 935–937 St. Philip Street. Photo by author, 2011.

extant, but the two-story, four-room kitchen survives as an excellent example of a period Creole service building.[66]

The first-generation Dollioles specialized in building cottages (table 3.2). Saint-Dominguan émigrés have been given the bulk of the credit for popularizing the cottage form in New Orleans following their arrival in the city at the end of the eighteenth and beginning of the nineteenth centuries.[67] Jean-Louis Dolliole (then in his midtwenties) constructed his first documented cottage in 1805. As such, he was either already familiar with the form before it became widespread in New Orleans or completely mastered it in a short time, adapting it for personal use and professional gain. Jean-Louis's early cottages were the older pavilion or hipped-roof form. Even this type was elaborated through the irregular-plan cottage he built on Pauger Street. By the 1830s, he had followed the evolution of the cottage, building side-gabled houses with steeper roof pitches and utilizing a variety of forms to

TABLE 3.2. CREOLE COTTAGES BUILT BY THE DOLLIOLE FAMILY

Date/ Builder	Location	As-Built Description				
		Form	Plan	Construction	Roof Type	Outbuildings
1805 Jean-L.	931–933 St. Philip	4-bay	4-rooms w/ cabinets	timber; brick-between-post; stucco	pavilion* (now side-gabled)	2-story, 2-room kitchen (d)
1820 Jean-L.	1436 Pauger	irregular	4-rooms w/ cabinets*	timber; brick-between-post; stucco	hipped w/ belcast edges	Not extant
ca. 1820 Jean-L.	1455–1457 Pauger (p)	4-bay	unknown	timber; brick-between-post; weatherboard	dual-pitched hipped	unknown
ca. 1820 Jean-L.	820 Elysian Fields* (p)	4-bay	unknown	timber; brick-between-post	hipped w/ belcast edges	unknown
1822 Jean-L.	939–941 St. Philip (d)	unknown	unknown	brick; tile	unknown	unknown
1831 Jean-L.	800 block Magazine (d)	4-bay	4-rooms w/ cabinets	timber; brick-between-post; shingles	side-gabled	2-story; 4-room kitchen
1831 Jean-L.	1300 block St. Philip (d)	unknown	2-rooms w/ cabinets	timber; brick-between-post; shingles	unknown	kitchen; latrine
by 1832 Jean-L.	1125 St. Philip*	3-bay w/ side gallery	unknown	brick; frame	side-gabled	unknown

TABLE 3.2, CONTINUED

Date/ Builder	Location	As-Built Description				
		Form	Plan	Construction	Roof Type	Outbuildings
by 1832 Jean-L.	1127 St. Philip*	3-bay w/ side gallery	unknown	brick; frame	side-gabled	unknown
by 1832 or 1834	1123 block St. Philip (d)	4-bay	4-rooms w/ cabinets	unknown	side-gabled (p)	1-story kitchen; 2-room latrine
ca. 1834 Joseph	1223–1225 St. Philip (d)	4-bay; 1½ story	4-rooms w/ cabinets	brick	side-gabled (p)	4-room kitchen w/ rear gallery
ca. 1834 Joseph	1227 St. Philip	2-bay	unknown	brick	side-gabled	kitchen
ca. 1835	1010 Burgundy (p)	3-bay	unknown	unknown	gabled; double-pitched	2-story kitchen
by 1838	927–929 St. Philip	4-bay	unknown	timber; brick-between-post; stucco	side-gabled	2-story, 2-room kitchen
by 1838	935–937 St. Philip	4-bay	unknown	timber; brick-between-post; stucco	side-gabled	1-story kitchen
1839 Joseph	923–925 N. Robertson (d)	unknown	4-room w/ closed gallery	frame	unknown	2-story kitchen (extant)

Note: (p) = possible; (d) = demolished; * = altered.

accommodate narrower property dimensions. Joseph also favored the Creole cottage building type and was able to manipulate it as successfully as his older brother.[68] Both native sons were just as capable of and instrumental in spreading the form throughout the city as their counterparts from the French West Indies.

THE SOULIÉS

Architectural Association

Coming of age in the world of the post-fire Vieux Carré, Norbert Soulié and his siblings would also have known the city's French- and Caribbean-influenced Spanish Colonial architecture. The family likely resided in a cottage when they lived on Dumaine Street in 1805. On the property that Jean Soulié owned at the corner of Bourbon and St. Peter Streets from 1808 to 1810, he built two houses: a tile-clad, brick-between-post Creole cottage with four rooms, *cabinets*, and a gallery, and a smaller brick-between-post Creole cottage containing three rooms with a closet and small gallery. The cottages (the former facing Bourbon, the latter facing St. Peter) were separated from one another by a wall with a two-part partition fence.[69]

Unlike the Dollioles, however, the Souliés' kinship ties provided opportunities and exposure to expand their knowledge outside the *gens de couleur libres* community of New Orleans. As a Freemason and city official, Jean Soulié had personal, social, and professional connections to many important individuals. Further, he and Vincent Rillieux, the consort of Soulié's "sister-in-law" Constance Vivant, were veterans of the New Orleans militia; like Jean-Louis Dolliole, they fought in the Battle of New Orleans.[70] Rillieux's father, also Vincent, was a wealthy Creole cotton merchant and plantation owner who had served as a naval captain under Spanish rule.[71] On his mother's side, Norbert was related to Vivants and Chevals, *gens de couleur libres* families long-established in New Orleans. Given the Soulié family's wealth and connections, Norbert may have been sponsored with a trip to France some time before 1811. Younger brother Bernard appears to have gone on one, noting life events of several of his "friends from 1817" in his journal. That year, Bernard would have been sixteen years old, an appropriate age for an educational trip abroad.[72]

If Norbert did not have a "grand tour" and education abroad, he was afforded one of the best opportunities available to a builder-architect of that time. Eighteen-year-old Norbert began working with the architect Henry Sellon Bonneval Latrobe (1792–1817) after the latter arrived in New Orleans in 1811 to oversee the construction of the New Orleans Waterworks Engine House, designed by his father, Benjamin Henry Latrobe (1764–1820). When the younger Latrobe succumbed to yellow fever in 1817, Soulié wrote to the elder Latrobe. In a letter to his New Orleans lawyer, John Rogers, Benjamin Latrobe describes the missive from Norbert:

> I have received [letter] from Mr. Norbert Soulié who appears to have been a principal agent or foreman of my lamented Sons [sic]. He does not say in what capacity, but he says he has been with Henry ever since his arrival in the country, that he was in his office when he last wrote to me, and that he remained until he breathed his last. He also states that my Sons workmen united and in an hour erected a tomb over his grave, which he (Soulié) directed. He also mentions that to Henri he owes chiefly his knowledge of the Arts.[73]

ENGAGEMENT

Figure 3.16. *The Orleans Theatre, 1816.* Details from *Plan of the City and Suburbs of New Orleans from an actual survey made in 1815 by J. Tanesse, city surveyor, 1817.* The Collins C. Diboll Vieux Carré Digital Survey at The Historic New Orleans Collection.

As in the fields of medicine and law, studying with and assisting an established professional was becoming standard in architectural training.[74] It is likely that Soulié obtained the same kind of training that Henry Latrobe received from his father, Benjamin Henry Latrobe, who is considered the first professional architect in the United States responsible for private, civic, and public works in New Orleans; Richmond, Virginia; Philadelphia; Baltimore; and Washington, DC, including the US Capitol (1803–1811, 1815–1817). This training would have included drawing and structural knowledge developed from the study of theory and hands-on practice.[75] He also would have learned the skill of building supervision and how to establish authority with clients and builders.[76] In the senior Latrobe's office, his students were also assistants. They received annual salaries after learning the necessary skills of preparing materials, copying and making drawings, and assisting with land surveying and site supervision.[77] The potential for similar training of Norbert by the younger Latrobe is possible, but no evidence has been found regarding how Henry Latrobe actually ran his practice. One can know, however, the types of buildings that Norbert would have been exposed to. As Henry Latrobe's apparent right-hand man, he would have worked with him on several major projects in New Orleans between 1811 and 1817—New Orleans Waterworks (1811–1812), Charity Hospital (1815), Christ Church (1815), and the Orleans Theatre (1816). These monumental public works were designed in a variety of styles—Federal, Gothic Revival, and Greek Revival (figure 3.16).[78]

Henry Latrobe also designed or built residences for important New Orleanians

THE ARCHITECTURE OF THE DOLLIOLE AND SOULIÉ FAMILIES

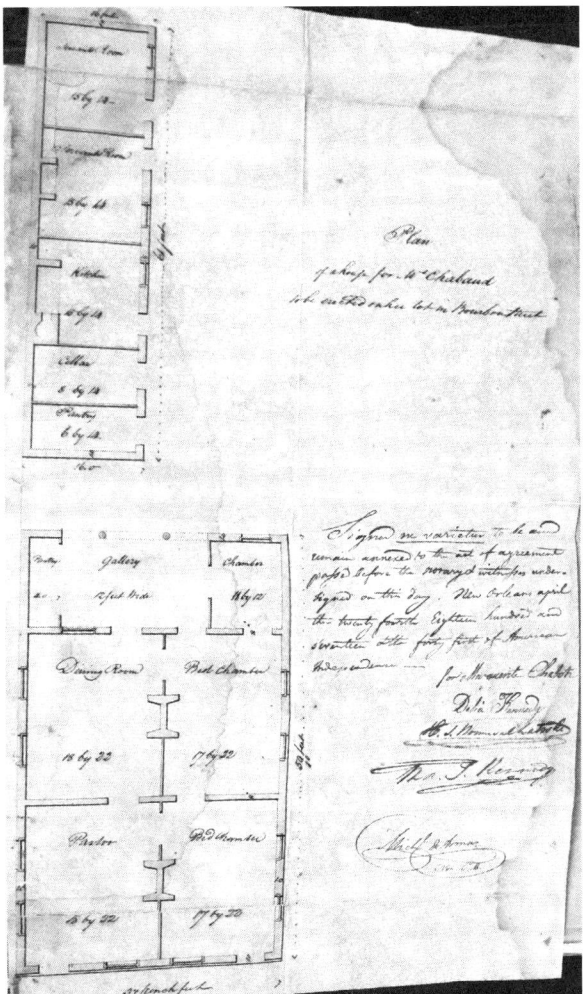

Figure 3.17. Floor plan of Chabot Cottage. Henry Sellon Bonneval Latrobe, 1817. Michel de Armas notary, volume 52, act 212, April 24, 1817. Courtesy of Hon. Chelsey Richard Napoleon, Clerk of Civil District Court, Parish of Orleans.

such as Jean-Baptiste Thierry (1814), Bernard Marigny (1816), William Kenner (1816), Richard Butler (1817), and Margaret Chabot (1817).[79] The contract for the Chabot house was made on April 24, 1817.[80] Latrobe, designated as a "master builder," was commissioned to erect a four-bay, four-room house and an outbuilding in eight months (figure 3.17). In lieu of *cabinets*, the ends of the rear gallery contained a small chamber and a pantry, following Margaret Chabot's specifications.[81] Unlike this typical Creole cottage—which was to have architectural features similar to those of Chabot's existing house and those of her neighbors—Latrobe's house for Jean-Baptiste Thierry is the earliest surviving building with Greek Revival stylistic influences in the city.⁸² Thierry House (721 Governor Nicholls) has the basic form of a four-bay cottage but features a front gallery with an arcade supported by Doric columns and an interior courtyard.⁸³ Latrobe also worked outside of the city, likely designing the detached wings (1811–1819) for Richard Butler's Ormond plantation upriver.⁸⁴ These buildings reflected Henry Latrobe's mastery of the Greek Revival style (courtesy of his father), familiarity with other popular styles (Federal and Gothic Revival), and willingness to work in local vernacular traditions (perhaps with Norbert's knowledge) but also an ability to create individualized buildings as each project demanded. Any of Henry Latrobe's completed works in New Orleans would have served as guides for Norbert Soulié to learn his profession as a builder and architect.

After Henry Latrobe's death, Norbert's "apprenticeship" was complete. His first known individual commission was a private contract with *homme de couleur libre* Jean Longpré to build a *maison à étage* (two-story house) surrounded by galleries on three sides at the corner of St. Peter Street facing the Carondelet Canal.⁸⁵ Although Norbert does not appear to have worked with Benjamin Henry Latrobe after the latter came to New Orleans in 1819 to take over his son's work, Norbert's association with the Latrobes likely opened many other doors for him.⁸⁶ Indeed, when the city of New Orleans solicited bids for the completion of a central clock tower at St. Louis Cathedral in 1819, Soulié was one of the builders or architects that Mayor Augustin Macarty recommended the city council contact.⁸⁷ While the winning bid went to Benjamin Latrobe, the clock tower's designer, Norbert obviously had a positive reputation that enabled him to secure commissions and acquire property.

ARCHITECTURAL ASSIMILATION

Given the sheer number of properties that the Soulié family owned and the inconclusive, inconsistent, or nonexistent nature of building descriptions in land transactions, it is difficult to determine which properties they actually built as opposed to those they only commissioned. In addition, archival research has not brought to light any commissions undertaken by Norbert between 1817 and 1829, though he is listed as a builder in the 1822 and 1824 city directories.⁸⁸

The first of Norbert's works that can be attributed to him with certainty is the extant cottage at 509–511 Burgundy Street. He purchased the property from Marcelin Batigne in 1829. The lot had previously belonged to Norbert's maternal aunt Constance Vivant from 1818 to 1825 (figure 3.18).⁸⁹ When Norbert resold the lot to Vivant in 1831, buildings are mentioned for the first time.⁹⁰ On the site, Norbert built a four-bay, Creole cottage with a partial-hipped roof (it is gabled at the rear)

Figure 3.18. 509–511 Bourbon Street. Norbert Soulié. Photo by author, 2011.

featuring a gabled dormer with arched fanlight window (the dormers on the side faces of the roof were added ca. 1967). As indicated on the 1876 Sanborn map, the house appears to originally have had a rear gallery; the property also contained a series of one- or two-story outbuildings, one of which was likely the standard two-story building housing the kitchen and slave quarters. While maintaining the balance and symmetry of the original fenestration, the existing front and side façades are a skin with Greek Revival entablature and door surrounds added at a later date. At this cottage, Norbert followed traditional design conventions but incorporated some unusual features, including the building's rear roof gable and slightly larger scale.

The architectural historian Edith Long offers no evidence, but states that Norbert Soulié was also responsible for the house at present-day 810 Dumaine Street (figure 3.19).[91] It would have been constructed after Norbert acquired the property in 1830 and demolished the existing buildings. The brick residence is an interesting conundrum, having qualities of two Creole building forms. With its arrangement of four bays across the front and a gabled roof, it is a two-story version of the Creole cottage, although with its massing and verticality it resembles

Figure 3.19. 810 Dumaine Street. Norbert Soulié. Photo by author, 2011.

a townhouse.[92] The Vieux Carré historian Malcolm Heard discusses the development of the Creole townhouse at length, noting that the type developed in the early nineteenth century into a regularized urban type based on the loosely organized Spanish Colonial house.[93] The Creole townhouse typically was two to three and a half stories and three to five bays wide and featured a passageway from one or more of any street-facing façades leading to an interior courtyard around which the interior rooms and staircase loggia were arranged.[94] Unlike the typical Creole townhouse, which shared party walls with adjacent structures, 810 Dumaine Street was originally a completely freestanding building; examination of the roofline indicates that the rear section of the attached outbuilding is an addition; the complex, therefore, did not abut the adjacent property with a party wall when it was built.[95] Comparison of the house's form and roofline with a freestanding "tall cottage" built by Norbert Soulié one block away at 814 Governor Nicholls Street (ca. 1830; figure 3.20) strengthens the evidence that he built the

Figure 3.20. 814 Governor Nicholls Street. Photo by John Watson Riley, 2010. The Collins C. Diboll Vieux Carré Digital Survey at The Historic New Orleans Collection.

house on Dumaine the same way.[96] In these two dwellings, Norbert began moving away from the one-story cottage type and toward increasingly vertical buildings with more complicated massing.[97]

One such dwelling was a house on Bourbon Street. Edith Long notes that "a pleasant pink house, with rather sophisticated detail, on Bourbon in the 300 block . . . was also designed by Soulié."[98] Norbert owned the property at present-day 330–332 Bourbon Street from 1830 to 1858. Earlier transactions note that the lot had buildings, so Norbert would have demolished them to accommodate the two-story brick *porte-cochère* townhouse. It featured a centrally disposed arched carriageway on ground level (a less common example, as the carriageway of a *porte-cochère* townhouse was usually placed to one side) that led to a rear courtyard with a two-story service building at a right angle to the rear of the house. A historic photograph shows that the Federal style house still possessed most of its original window and door openings in 1893 (figure 3.21).[99]

Figure 3.21. 330–332 Bourbon Street (demolished late 1960s). Photographer unknown, ca. 1893. The Collins C. Diboll Vieux Carré Digital Survey at The Historic New Orleans Collection.

The dwelling incorporated several characteristics of Federal style architecture, including exposed brick, header stretcher-end brick lintels, and the carriageway fanlight.[100] This building portrayed Norbert's ability to adapt a style imported from the American East Coast and incorporate it into a more local form—the Creole townhouse—that was suitable for the narrow lot. It became a victim of the cyclical introduction of new forms and types into New Orleans's urban environment—it was demolished when the 300 block of Bourbon Street was razed to make way for the Royal Sonesta hotel in the late 1960s.[101]

The Soulié rowhouses constitute Norbert's interpretation of another vertically oriented urban form (figure 3.22). In the early 1830s, Norbert constructed rowhouses on property that he had purchased in 1819.[102] At 229 and 231 North Rampart Street, two of the rowhouses survive.[103] The three-story, masonry Greek Revival style dwellings originally had cast-iron lintels, dentiled cornices, and wrought-iron balconies.[104] Features and floor plans of the rowhouses when first built can be assessed by comparing them to archival drawings for buildings that once stood a block away at the corner of North Rampart and Conti Streets (figure 3.23).[105] The two groupings of buildings had several features in common, including multiple dwellings behind unified façades in a simplified interpretation of the

THE ARCHITECTURE OF THE DOLLIOLE AND SOULIÉ FAMILIES

Greek Revival style. Both groups of rowhouses also had multistory outbuildings attached to the main dwelling on one side of the courtyard. The rowhouse offered Norbert Soulié the ideal property type to serve as an income property, as he could rent it out as a whole or subdivide it to increase his profit.[106]

In the early 1830s, Norbert received a commission to build a sugar refinery for the partnership owned by Alexander Gordon and Edmund J. Forstall. Norbert and his first cousin Edmond Rillieux were contracted to build the complex's buildings on a portion of Forstall's plantation, located about two miles downriver of the city.[107] The building contract was made in early 1831.[108] This project expanded Norbert's repertoire to industrial works. The "extensive" group of buildings in an "irregular pile," as described by John Gibson in his city directory of 1838, was dominated by a sugarhouse and would have contained the space and apparatus needed for the processing of sugar into raw sugar, molasses, and refined white sugar.[109] The buildings were laid out in a formal arrangement facing the levee (figure 3.24). Entry into the plant complex was via a gabled arcade topped with dormers. Flanking the arcade were two front-gabled wings, each with blind façades at ground level; arched doorways provided access to a balcony at the

Figure 3.22. 229 and 231 North Rampart Street. Norbert Soulié. Photo by author, 2011.

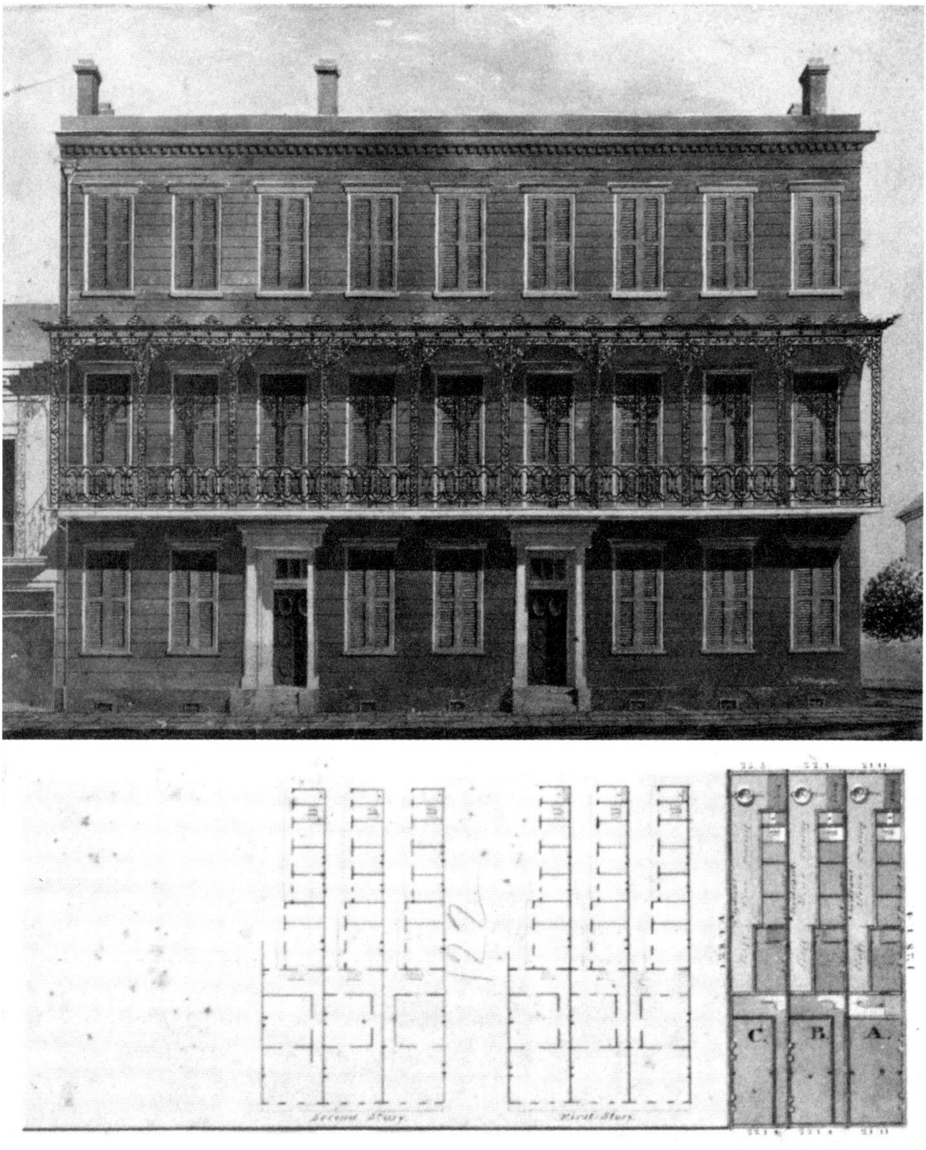

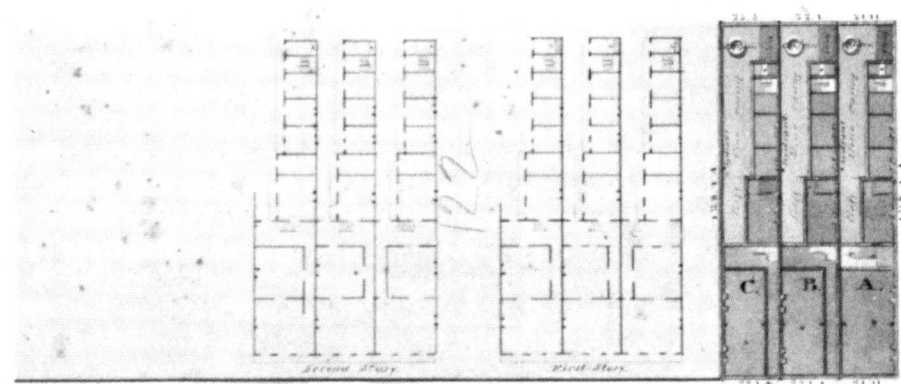

Figure 3.23. Elevations and floor plans of townhouses at Rampart and Conti Streets. Arthur De Armas, February 11, 1870. Plan book 59, folio 11. Courtesy of Hon. Chelsey Richard Napoleon, Clerk of Civil District Court, Parish of Orleans.

Figure 3.24. Louisiana Sugar Refinery. Norbert Soulié and Edmond Rillieux, 1831. Photograph by Theodore Lilienthal, 1867. From Gary A. Van Zante, New Orleans 1867: Photographs by Theodore Lilienthal *(London: Merrell, 2008), page 237.*

second level. Beyond the arcade was a three-story, front-gabled building, probably the main sugarhouse. A four-story, side-gabled building brought up the rear of the building grouping. The disparate buildings were unified by gabled and arched roof dormers and multilight windows. The large smokestack for the boiler was visible between the downriver portion of the front wing and the sugarhouse.[110] According to a description of the plant in the 1838 *Gibson's Guide*, the land, machinery, and buildings cost about $370,000.[111] Greek Revival stylistic characteristics imbued the buildings with an air of formality and dignity not seen in more utilitarian brick mills on sugar plantations. This type of stylistic treatment to an industrial type was repeated in New Orleans at the Levee Steam Cotton Press constructed in 1832.[112] The project had the potential to give Norbert Soulié further prominence in the field of architecture in New Orleans, but it ultimately led to his departure from the city. Some disagreement or altercation, the particulars of which are unknown to posterity, brought the sugar refinery building project to a halt when the buildings were almost complete. Edmond Rillieux disappeared from New Orleans for almost a year and a half.[113] Norbert, meanwhile, began preparing to relocate to Paris, France—permanently.[114]

Having sold the Burgundy Street property back to his aunt in January, Norbert filed a procuration delegating power of attorney over his personal and business affairs to Léon Courcelle, "husband" of his maternal aunt Adelaide Vivant, on April 21, 1831. The following day, he made a joint procuration, again giving Léon Courcelle power of attorney, with older brother Lucien noting

> that they have formed among themselves a society in which they are each half and whose purpose is to use and grow in common the manner most advantageous some capital funds provided each half. And wanting to leave Louisiana . . . they make and form their corporate name of Norbert and Lucien Soulié . . .[115]

Though Norbert's known body of work is incomplete,[116] his building practice and landholdings provided him enough income to live life comfortably as a gentleman in Europe.[117] Upon Norbert's departure for France, his acquisition of property did not cease, but the role of builder was passed on to younger brothers Bernard and Albin. The brothers had privately formed a company, "B. & A. Soulié," to purchase property and enslaved individuals in 1827.[118] Bernard and Albin were listed as "B. & A. Soulié Builders" in the 1832 city directory. Their partnership was legally recognized on April 22, 1833.[119]

Unlike Norbert, who perhaps was the only one of the brothers to receive training from an architect, Bernard and Albin only built Creole cottages. Two cottages built as investment properties can be attributed to Bernard Soulié. He purchased property from the city along an extension of Tremé Street in 1837. Here he built a brick four-bay Creole cottage (figure 3.25). At the rear of the property was a one-story outbuilding.[120] Also in 1837, Bernard acquired a corner lot on Ursulines at Robertson; he sold it to Lucien one year later.[121] Although Lucien owned the property, he lived abroad. So Bernard likely built the one-and-a-half-story brick corner storehouse that subsequently occupied the lot to serve as a rental that generated an income for his absentee older brother. Demolished after 1974, the building form consisted of a typical Creole cottage but with the first floor being reserved for commercial use.[122] As such, the side façade facing the street had an entry (in addition to the doorways at the primary [front] façade) and more windows than usually seen on a Creole cottage. A canopy with signage may have been placed over the corner-facing doorways. The attic space in a storehouse served as a residence, usually for the

Figure 3.25. 1226 Tremé Street. Bernard Soulié, 1837. Photo by Deadria Farmer-Paellmann, 2019.

proprietors of the store; it was accessed via a narrow doorway where a rear *cabinet* was traditionally located. The Tremé Street storehouse marks the only departure from the traditional Creole cottage made by Bernard or Albin in their building activities. Buildings on the brothers' property that they acquired after 1838 are less likely to be attributed to them as builders. For one, they changed their primary means of business and were listed as "B. & A. Soulié" commission merchants from that year onward. Thenceforth, the brothers both frequently traveled to sell and acquire goods.[123] Also, Albin was increasingly in France; he moved to Paris permanently in 1845.[124]

The buildings that are positively credited to the Soulié brothers were constructed mostly in the 1830s (table 3.3). They range from Norbert's more cosmopolitan urban forms to traditional vernacular houses built by Bernard and Albin. While the Souliés' known or extant body of work is much smaller than that of the Dollioles, their contributions to the built environment are not diminished. Jean-Louis Dolliole and, to some extent, Joseph Dolliole explored and perfected the

TABLE 3.3. KNOWN SOULIÉ BUILT WORKS

Current Address or Description	Date	Builder	Form	Style
St. Peter Street (at Carondelet Canal)	1818	Norbert	*Maison à étage*	Vernacular
509–511 Burgundy	1829–1831	Norbert	4-bay cottage	Vernacular
810 Dumaine	ca. 1830	Norbert	Creole townhouse	Vernacular
814 Governor Nicholls	ca. 1830	Norbert	Creole townhouse	Vernacular
330–332 Bourbon (d)	ca. 1830	Norbert	Creole townhouse	Vernacular
229 and 231 N. Rampart	before 1831	Norbert	Rowhouse	Greek Revival
Louisiana Sugar Refinery (d)	1831–1832	Norbert	Sugar mill/refinery	Greek Revival
1226 Tremé	1837	Bernard	4-bay Creole cottage	Vernacular
1529–1533 Ursulines (d)	1838	Bernard	Corner storehouse	Vernacular

Note: (d) = demolished.

range of the Creole cottage. Norbert Soulié was responsible for the architectural assimilation of new concepts such as vertically oriented buildings and the Greek Revival style into familiar forms and existing environments. Albin, too, made his mark, carrying the Creole cottage into newly developed areas of the city and utilizing a traditional form in various ways for financial gain.

Builders in both families constructed houses in the forms and styles with which they were familiar. The antebellum landscape of New Orleans was their pattern book and, in turn, became the site of their contributions to the city's architectural heritage. A survey of properties associated with free people of color (extant in 1974 and 1980) emphasizes the widespread use of the many varieties of the Creole cottage by builders, owners, and developers, as well as its popularity and adaptability by the very nature of its survival (figure 3.26). Of a total of forty-two extant properties in Faubourg Tremé and thirty-eight properties in the Creole faubourgs, the Creole cottage was overwhelmingly the most popular choice. Accordingly, of the known builders of these buildings, most of them constructed Creole cottages (figure 3.27). Jean-Louis and Joseph Dolliole were among those builders who perfected the Creole cottage, increasingly adapting

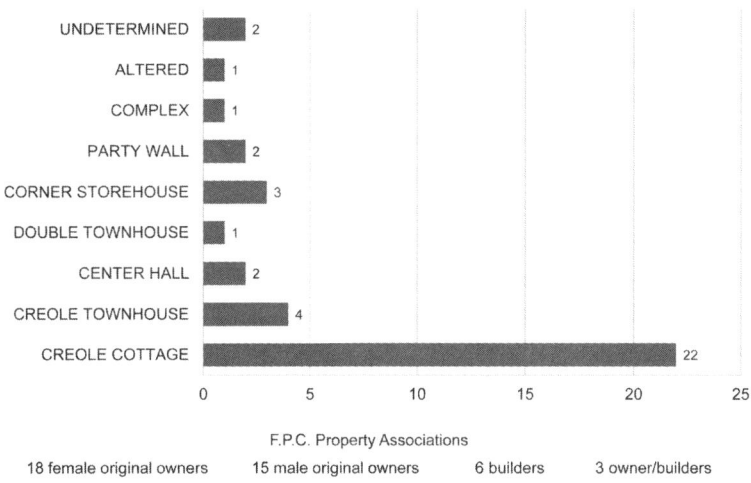
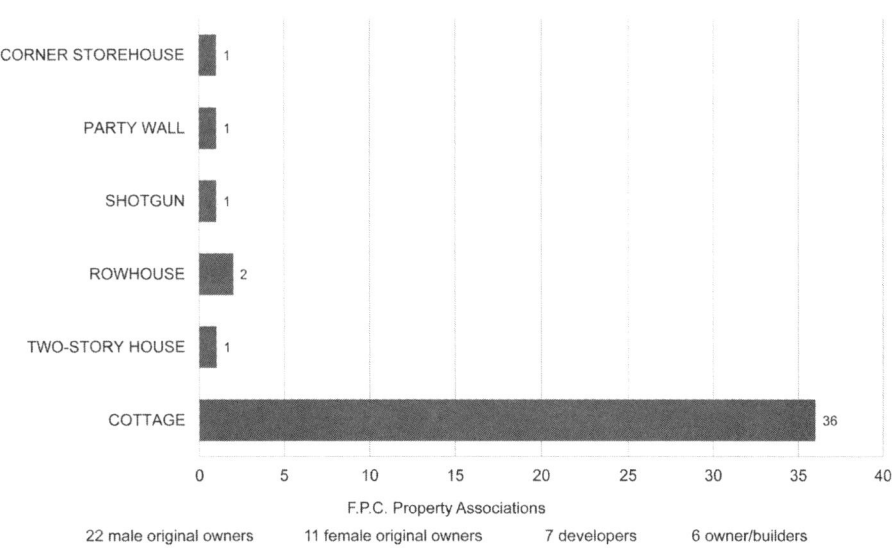

Figure 3.26. Extant gens de couleur libres–associated properties by type. Based on the surveys in New Orleans Architecture, *Volume 4,* The Creole Faubourgs *(top) and* New Orleans Architecture, *Volume 6,* Faubourg Tremé and the Bayou Road *(bottom). Graphs by author.*

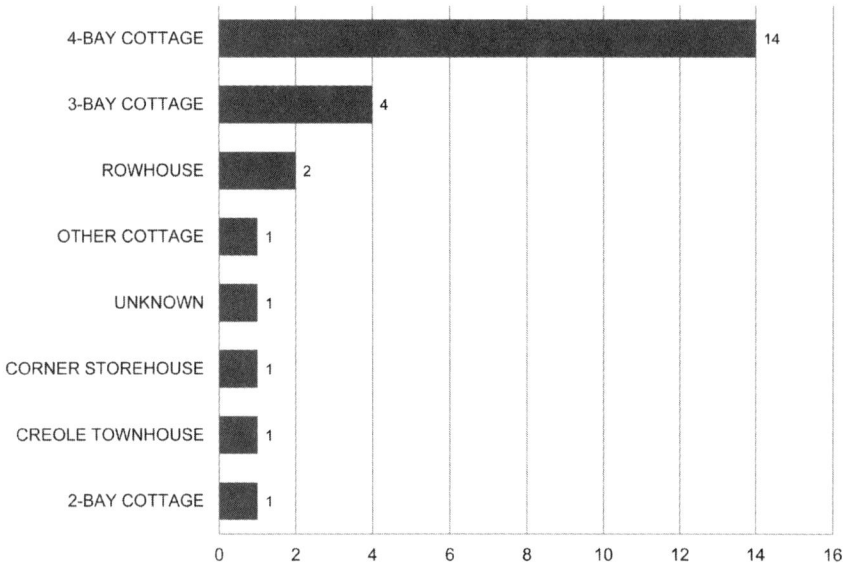

Figure 3.27. Extant building types as constructed by identified gens de couleur libres *builders in Faubourg Tremé and the Creole faubourgs. Graph by author.*

the form to unique property situations and transporting it into newly developed neighborhoods throughout the antebellum period. Bernard Soulié contributed to the continued use of the Creole cottage building type in the 1830s. These three builders' dedication to the Creole cottage form underscores the fact that the *gens de couleur libres* were responsible for the persistence of the Creole cottage in antebellum New Orleans but also brings home the point that not only émigré builders were responsible for its introduction and proliferation.

The *gens de couleur libres* also built in non-Creole forms. Norbert Soulié built only one known Creole cottage and, even then, modified the roof form and scale. Instead, his repertoire consisted primarily of taller building forms—the Creole townhouse and Anglo-influenced rowhouse. Norbert's output is particularly important in that he built the townhouse and rowhouse a few short years before leaving New Orleans. Had he remained in the city, he would likely have been influential in developing these forms even further in the *gens de couleur libres* community. And, with his more formal architectural training, Norbert Soulié was more poised, even more so than his brothers, to utilize American styles such as

Greek Revival, which required greater understanding of the use and application of detailed architectural ornament.

While the Dollioles and Souliés had varying approaches to architectural form, they all worked more or less in vernacular styles and, through varying means, responded to the need for increased housing in a diverse and changing urban environment. The different house types built by the Dollioles, Souliés, and other *gens de couleur libres* are characteristic of the Transitional Period of New Orleans architecture (1820–1835) when colonial and Creole types were increasingly influenced and joined by American traditions (e.g., classical forms and ornamentation and central hall plans).[125] The physical boundaries and urban fabric of New Orleans changed greatly during the first half of the nineteenth century. So, too, did the building forms used in the expanding metropolis. Men like the Dollioles and Souliés ensured the persistence of traditional types. These native sons were prolific builders despite competition from other *gens de couleur libres* builders, many of whom were Saint-Dominguan refugees. With their extensive real estate dealings and connections to white and Black New Orleanians alike, the Dollioles and Souliés appear to have had an advantage over émigrés in their ability to obtain commissions.

CHAPTER 4

"UNCOMMON INDUSTRY"

Gens de Couleur Libres *Builders* in Antebellum New Orleans

His talent in architecture definitely contributed to the beautification of our city.

RODOLPHE DESDUNES, *OUR MEN AND OUR HISTORY* (1911)

The Dollioles were reaching adulthood and the Souliés were coming of age during the territorial period, immediately following the periods of mass migration when thousands of white and Black French Creoles fled to New Orleans from the West Indies during the Haitian Revolution (1791–1804). Many of the "foreign" *gens de couleur libres* were trained as builders who brought their experiences and skills with them to Louisiana. In January 1810, Louisiana's territorial governor William Claiborne lauded the "uncommon industry" of Black carpenters, noting that "many houses have been built in little time and at less cost than before."[1] The need for architecture in the new Louisiana territory provided an opportunity for Black artisans. The architecture built by *gens de couleur libres* was perpetuated by the native builders and the arrival of those from other areas of the Atlantic world seeking refuge in Louisiana in the wake of political turmoil and revolution.

In the colonial United States, most early building artisans were carpenters because of the abundance of wood and its predominant use as a building material. Carpenters in particular were in high demand because they possessed technical and supervisory skills. In New Orleans, their knowledge of producing complicated timber framing as well as local techniques dealing with specific problems such as humidity (i.e., *briquette-entre-poteaux* construction) would have proved useful. Later, others who developed specified skill sets—joiners, bricklayers, masons, glaziers, painters, and plasterers—became prevalent in major colonial cities, including New Orleans.[2] By 1850, almost 64 percent of employed free Black males in the Lower South and in New Orleans were artisans, higher than in all major US cities.[3] Although this number included free men of color who were not mixed-race *gens de couleur libres* or who had skill sets such as tailors and blacksmiths, free builders of color made up a significant portion of this group. Leonard Curry provides three reasons for the large number and the success of free builders of color in the South, specifically in New Orleans as opposed to other regions: (1) Southern whites were fully accustomed to the presence of Black artisans, having been familiar with enslaved labor and the persistence of the *gens de couleur libres* population; (2) the presence of Black artisans ensured secure apprenticeships for young Blacks and allowed those occupations to perpetuate; and (3) New Orleans contained a free community of color largely created by selective manumission not mass emancipation, allowing for artisans to come from the able, energetic, and talented enslaved population or to be individuals educated, trained, and financed due to familial relationships.[4] Thus, the Dollioles and Souliés had many Afro-Creole contemporaries who likewise contributed to New Orleans's antebellum architecture in various ways.

NATIVE SONS

François Boisdoré

François Boisdoré (ca. 1779/1782–1859),[5] natural son of François Dubuisson and Adelaide Boisdoré, was another Louisiana-born *homme de couleur libre* builder and real estate speculator.[6] Boisdoré was Louis Dolliole's and, later, Joseph Dolliole's neighbor on Bayou Road. He appears to have been productive early in the antebellum period and was listed as a builder living on Burgundy Street below Orleans Street in the 1822 city directory. From the late 1820s through the 1840s, he owned numerous properties in the Vieux Carré and Faubourg Tremé—including one small lot on Dumaine Street he sold to Norbert Soulié—and undoubtedly built some of them. Boisdoré contracted to build a *maison de maître* for *femme de couleur libre* Marceline "Marcely" Cornu on Bayou Road in 1828.[7]

His best-known commission, however, was that of a Creole *porte cochère* townhouse for Joseph Soniat Dufossat (1133–1135 Chartres Street) in 1829. Originally,

Figure 4.1. Detail of site plan of 1133–1135 Chartres Street, showing the original façade design and floor plan.

the two-and-a-half-story house displayed an interesting combination of French and Spanish Colonial forms (figure 4.1). The *porte cochère* entrance at the ground floor provided access, through paneled doors, to a courtyard at the rear, at one side of which was a two-story L-shaped outbuilding. The loggia incorporated into the rear of the dwelling provided access to the private floors of the house. Like the carriageway entrance, the ground-floor openings were arched (they were shortened and infilled with rectangular windows after 1965) and had iron or wooden bars in the transoms. Boisdoré also introduced aspects of Anglo-American architecture. By centering the carriageway, the building had ties to French townhouses but also appeared more like a central-plan American house. He also incorporated various aspects of the Federal style—stone door and window

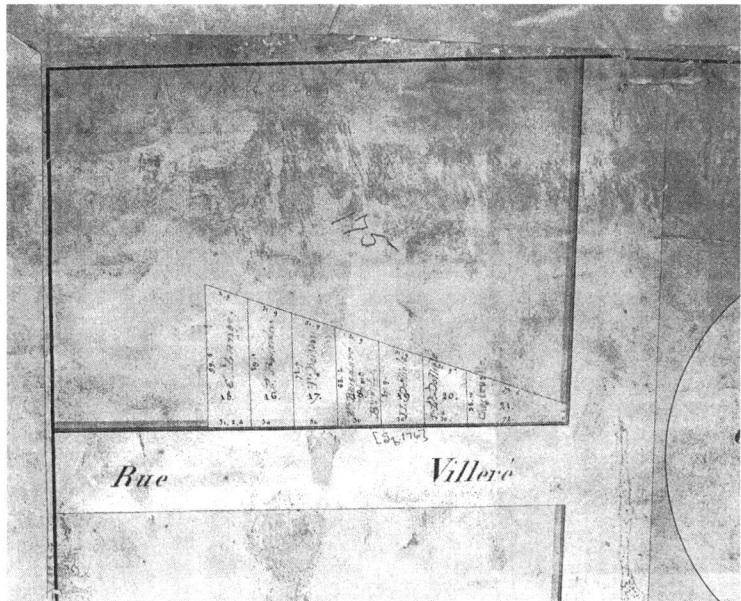

Figure 4.2. Detail of Plan de 14 lots de terre situés au Faubourg Tremé, showing properties owned by François Boisdoré (16–18) and Jean-Louis Dolliole (19–20) on Villeré Street. J. Communy, January 15, 1841. Plan Book 85, folio 14. Courtesy of Hon. Chelsey Richard Napoleon, Clerk of Civil District Court, Parish of Orleans.

lintels, louvered shutters, a main-level entry door with sidelights and a transom fanlight, a projecting dentiled cornice, segmental-arched roof dormers with pilasters and arched windows, and gable-end chimneys—and left the red brick exterior walls exposed. The ground-floor fenestration of the Soniat House has been altered, and the original wrought-iron balcony replaced with a much more ornate one, but the dwelling would still be recognizable to its original owners. Boisdoré continued purchasing land in the 1830s and 1840s, primarily in Faubourg Tremé. In 1841, he acquired three lots near the corner of Villeré Street and Bayou Road, this time abutting property belonging to Jean-Louis Dolliole (figure 4.2).[8] Little real estate activity by François Boisdoré is found after he and Joseph Dolliole sold their Bayou Road properties in the mid-1840s. Boisdoré died in 1859.

Laurent Ursain Guesnon

Laurent Ursain Guesnon (1780–1842) was among the earliest of the builders of color. Guesnon was born in New Orleans on August 10, 1780.[9] He was the natural

ENGAGEMENT

Figure 4.3. 1428 Bourbon Street. Laurent Ursain Guesnon, ca. 1811. Photo by author, 2011.

son of Jacques Guesnon and Marie St. Martin (alias Manon Boisseau).[10] Ursain Guesnon was among the first to purchase property from Bernard Marigny in the latter's newly developed suburb in 1807, making him the neighbor of Catherine Dusuau and, later, Jean-Louis Dolliole on Bagatelle Street.[11] According to Ursain's will, a house was not erected on the lot until after his marriage to Marie Eugenie Reynes (alias Marie/Mathilde Zolla) in 1811.[12] It was there by the time Ursain was listed as a carpenter living on the site—17 Bagatelle near Esplanade—in the 1822 city directory.[13] The four-bay brick cottage on the site at present-day 1428 Bourbon Street is of brick-between-post construction (figure 4.3). The side-gabled roof features a chimney (note the presence of a double fireplace shared by the cottage's two front rooms), segmental-roofed dormers with pilasters and multilight windows topped by fanlights, and a cant in the roofline for the *abat-vent*. The primary façade contains casement doors and windows with fanlight transoms and louvered shutters. While previous scholarship argues that the cottage's fenestration is a retention of the French Colonial tradition of arched openings across the façades of buildings,[14] Guesnon's use of fanlights and the louvered shutters is more indicative of Federal stylistic conventions. In either case, his attention to detail in this cottage was a testament to his skill as a builder and makes this building particularly important, as it is Guesnon's only known extant work. When he died in 1842, Jean-Louis Dolliole served as his testamentary executor. Dolliole was also responsible for building his tomb.[15] The Guesnon family owned their Bourbon Street house until 1854, when his widow sold it.[16] The connection between the two families of builders was strengthened when Dolliole's son Louis Drausin married Guesnon's daughter Marie Eugenie in 1858.[17]

Louis Vivant

Familial connections with free builders of color proved even stronger for the Souliés. Louis Vivant (1796–1870) was a prominent builder in the antebellum period. As the youngest offspring of Louison Cheval and Charles Vivant, Louis was the uncle of the first-generation Souliés, but he was the same age as his nephews. Given his family connections, Louis Vivant could have learned his trade from any number of successful builders—Black or white—in the city. His earliest known work is a two-room, brick-between-post kitchen outbuilding with *cabinets* and a gallery he contracted with N. L. Lauriano to build on Melpomene Street in Faubourg Annunciation in 1832.[18]

In his capacity as a builder, it appears that Louis did a lot of work for his nephews. The Soulié ledger books indicate that in 1843 he earned income providing maintenance and building services for properties owned by Norbert, Bernard, and/or Albin Soulié. On May 8, Vivant enclosed the kitchen of the house on Tremé Street, redoing the gallery and replacing the roof.[19] At the main dwelling, he made repairs to or replaced one stairway, two steps at the façade, two hinges and one hook, and set eight locks and vises. He also made six new keys and covered the northern gable of the house in batten. At the same house, Vivant painted the newly covered gable with two coats, replaced ten panes of glass, and painted the north side of the house. A few months later, in September, he made repairs to the property at 79 Hospital, working on the framework for the well and adjusting two pairs of sashes and two pairs of solid doors.[20] While Vivant likely had learned his trade before working for the Souliés in his late forties, this type of work appears to have gone hand in hand with providing experience and drumming up clientele for his own commissions. Vivant does not appear again in the available Soulié ledgers, and his other known houses were built after 1843.

Vivant constructed a Creole cottage at 1729–1731 Laharpe Street for Joseph Conner, a free Black man, in 1846 (figure 4.4). Conner contracted with Vivant to build the four-bay house for $700.00.[21] Per the specifications, the 26' × 32', four-room cottage was clad in shingles and mounted on a brick foundation. Indicative

ENGAGEMENT

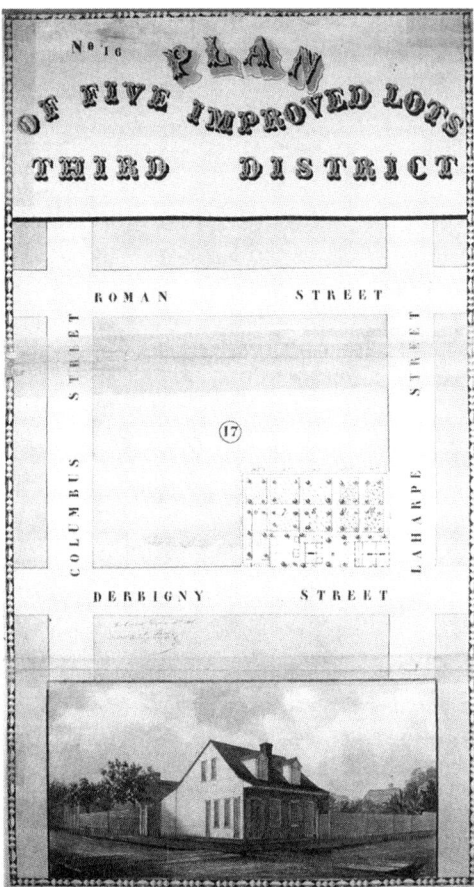

Figure 4.4. 1729–1731 Laharpe Street. Louis Vivant, 1846. Plan of Five Improved Lots, Third District. Adrien Persac, November 15, 1865. Plan book 38, folio 15. Courtesy of Hon. Chelsey Richard Napoleon, Clerk of Civil District Court, Parish of Orleans.

of the period of construction, the Conner cottage featured small dormers and a cant where the *abat-vent* was incorporated into the gabled roof.[22] The dormers may have been added at a later date; they are not noted in the building contract. As depicted in a drawing for the 1865 sale of the property, the cottage was located at the corner of Laharpe and Derbigny Streets and occupied approximately one-quarter of the block. By virtue of its location on a corner, the house also had doors and windows on the façade facing Laharpe (possibly later additions). In addition to the buildings erected by Vivant—the cottage, a two-room kitchen, a well, and a double latrine—the property featured a vegetable garden laid out in squares.

In the fall of 1846, Louis Vivant contracted with *femme de couleur libre* Uranie Roy to build a Creole cottage on Burgundy Street between Ursulines Avenue and St. Philip Street.[23] The contract stipulates that the house was to be a typical brick-between-post, four-room Creole cottage with *cabinets* and a gallery. One of the *cabinets* was to have stairs to a garret lit with four windows. Vivant was also responsible for installing doors "made in the most fashionable way" and hinges and locks "of the best quality." For this "work to be done with the best and soundest material of every kind," Vivant was paid $1,080.00. Aside from the kitchen building and two cottages, little else is known about the building activities of Louis Vivant.[24] The same cannot be said for Soulié kinsman Myrtille Courcelle.

Myrtille Courcelle

Myrtille Courcelle (1805–1872) was a prolific builder of color and property owner. Courcelle lived in Faubourg Tremé, where all of his work was built, at various addresses on St. Philip Street from 1841 to 1858.[25] The oldest son of Adelaide Vivant and Léon Courcelle, he was the first cousin of the first-generation Souliés.[26] The relatives often exchanged property between one another in Faubourg Tremé. One of the many buildings that Courcelle constructed was erected on such a lot. In 1836, Courcelle purchased undeveloped property from cousin Norbert Rillieux. When he sold the lot, and several others, to the Soulié sisters on February 4, 1843, the sale included "the buildings which the owner built since his acquisition."[27] The cottage, still standing at 1509–1511 Dumaine, has the typical four-bay, four-room form. In 1980, it retained many original features, including batten shutters, strap hinges, French doors, and wooden lintel openings. It has been restored since. The two-story outbuilding at the rear of the property line is also extant. The house was probably rented out or occupied by Courcelle relatives. Myrtille Courcelle also built a cottage at present-day 1622 Dumaine that was replaced by a two-story, side hall house in the Italianate style.[28]

Also in 1836, Courcelle purchased an undeveloped lot from the Company of the Architects of the Eighth District (1523–1525 St. Philip).[29] On it, he built an atypical cottage with five bays across the primary façade. It is likely that Courcelle made one of two adaptations to the Creole cottage, the forms of which are obscured by later alterations. The building may have been a dogtrot cottage where a smaller (usually at-grade) central doorway provided access to a passageway between two cottages to a shared rear courtyard. Or, one of the end doors could have opened onto an inset gallery servicing the adjacent dwelling. In any case, this form would have been useful, allowing for Courcelle to maximize the number of units and living spaces to use the cottage as income property.[30] Other details characteristic of an 1830s Creole cottage include the doorways with multilight transom, batten window shutters, and gabled dormers with arched window openings.

In addition to building houses as income property, Courcelle also erected homes for his neighbors. He built a house for Marguerite Boisdoré in the 1600 block of St. Philip Street in 1836 (1609–1611 St. Philip).[31] The roof of the four-bay cottage was canted at the front façade to form the *abat-vent* overhang. The arched dormer fanlight has been infilled. While the other windows and doors on the house have been altered, the transoms over the doorways and the overall proportions of the fenestration have been retained.[32]

On July 9, 1846, Courcelle signed a contract with Charles Henry Daret for the construction of a three-story Creole townhouse (figure 4.5).[33] It was to be built on St. Philip Street between Bourbon and Dauphine Streets on undeveloped property that Daret had purchased the previous year.[34] Though Myrtille served strictly as the builder for the house of someone else's design—French Creole architect Jean-François Correjolles was the supervising architect who furnished plans for the design of the dwelling—the six-page document provides explicit instructions, leaving no doubt as to Courcelle's understanding of building practices and his ability to erect a house of this complexity. The Creole townhouse was a type developed from the traditional Spanish Colonial house that increased the volume of the residence by adding stories and growing upward.[35] Typically, Creole townhouses feature a carriageway, loggia, courtyard, and balcony.[36] This is a later version of the building type with a regularized three-bay façade hiding the Creole features of an open side passage with access to the rear loggia stairway and courtyard behind one of the outer bay doors. Though the house adapted aspects of the increasingly popular American townhouse on its façade, Courcelle was still required by the contract to use French building conventions, such as the cypress framework of the roofing and French glass in the door and window glazing.[37] He also had very careful instructions regarding aspects of the carpentry, including the tongue-and-groove cypress flooring, crown molding, ceiling cornices and rosettes, paneled interior doors, paneled and louvered door and window shutters, and turned mahogany balustrades at the rear loggia.

While he was building what is perhaps his most ambitious work, Courcelle was working in the 1840s for the Souliés in the same capacity as Louis Vivant (also his uncle). Between August 1843 and November 1847, Myrtille did a variety of work on several Soulié properties. He was hired for simple maintenance such as repainting, cleaning, and replacing grills as well as more complicated tasks like repairing roofs and installing new floors at least once a year during this period. Myrtille Courcelle was also a tomb builder. Léon Courcelle's estate files note that Myrtille was paid for building and plastering his father's grave. Myrtille also possessed

Figure 4.5. 830–832 St. Philip Street (Dr. Daret House). Myrtille Courcelle, 1846. Photo by John Watson Riley, 2010. The Collins C. Diboll Vieux Carré Digital Survey at The Historic New Orleans Collection.

some type of drafting ability, for he was also compensated for completing the sepulture drawings.[38]

Aside from his skills as a builder and extant built work, little is known about Myrtille Courcelle's personal life. He appears to have been married twice. On April 29, 1857, a license was granted for Father Rousselon to marry Myrtille Courcelle and Marie Dalcour.[39] He later married Evelina Davis on October 23, 1871.[40] When Myrtille died less than one year later on February 13, 1872, his estate was valued at $36,967.60, leaving no doubt that his career as a builder and property owner had enabled him to be competitive and make substantial earnings.[41]

Joseph Chateau

Though little is known of his background, Joseph Chateau (ca. 1816–unknown) was one of the most prolific free Black builders in antebellum New Orleans. In the 1850 census, Chateau is listed as being a thirty-four-year-old mulatto builder born in the city. His household consisted of his wife and teenage son as well as two men and a teenage boy (all white) with the surname Dupont. Michel and Basset Dupont, both natives of France, were also builders; the two men undoubtedly worked with or for Chateau. Given the fact that at least seventeen contracts documenting his building services were made by New Orleans notaries between 1844 and 1851, Chateau would have needed the extra assistance.[42]

Due to the nature of later work in this block, twin cottages at 416–418 Burgundy can be attributed to Chateau. *Homme de couleur libre* Jean Baptiste Couvertie contracted Chateau to build the houses for him in June 1844.[43] Chateau was tasked to replace an existing *briquette-entre-poteaux* house and wooden kitchen with identical one-and-a-half-story, two-bay, three-room cottages.[44] Each cottage features fire walls at the gable ends and a gabled dormer on the front and rear roof slopes. A passageway between the two houses provides access to the rear courtyards, each with a two-story, shed-roof kitchen outbuilding. The cottages remained in the Couvertie family until 1923.

In April 1845, Chateau contracted with *homme de couleur libre* Ramon Vionnet to build a two-bay *maison de maître* on the latter's property on St. Philip between Burgundy and Rampart (not extant).[45] The contract stipulated that the one-and-a-half-story, side-gabled brick-between-post dwelling was to have three rooms with a brick fireplace painted to imitate marble in each.[46] A plaster rosette and cornice was called for in the front room. The overall proportion of the building was considered, as the height of the roof was to be one-third of the length of the house. The roof featured a dormer window and a four-foot-wide, coffered *abat-vent*. The exterior wall treatment was scored to resemble stone except for the gable ends, which were clad with whitewashed battens. The contract also included the construction of a two-story, brick-between-post kitchen building clad with slate as well as adjacent stables. The outbuilding, at the rear of a brick-paved courtyard, was accessed through a *porte cochère* corridor adjacent to the house. Chateau captured the house's proposed layout and a cross section through the courtyard in a dimensioned plan that was attached to the contract (figure 4.6).

The following month, *femme de couleur libre* Sophia Philips hired Chateau to build another brick-between-post cottage, this one with four bays, on her St. Ann Street property.[47] The framework of the cottage was cypress; the floors, pine.

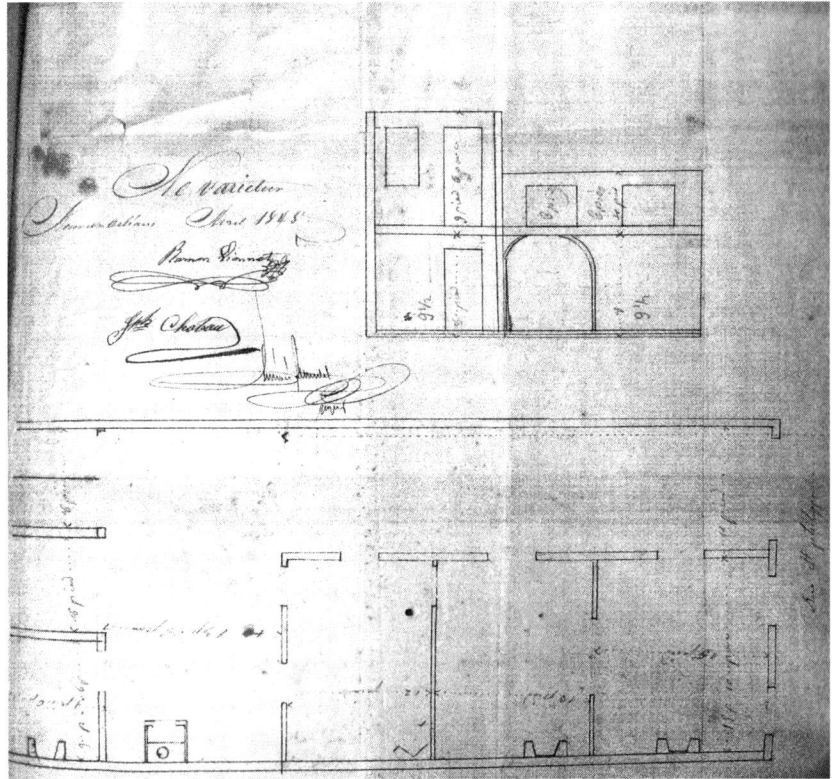

Figure 4.6. Floor plan and section for Roman Vionnet House on St. Philip Street. Joseph Chateau, 1845. Amedee Ducatel notary, volume 27, act 25, September 15, 1845. Courtesy of Hon. Chelsey Richard Napoleon, Clerk of Civil District Court, Parish of Orleans.

Chateau drew a plan depicting the cottage's four first-floor interior rooms, *cabinets*, and gallery as well as a profile of the gabled roof, which had two street-facing dormers (figure 4.7). Again, Chateau was instructed to score the primary façade of the house to imitate stone. This dwelling was intended to serve two families or tenants—a corridor on each side of the dwelling provided separate access for each unit to a shared courtyard. At the rear of the courtyard was one outbuilding; the kitchens were separated by a double latrine at the center.

In July 1845, Chateau returned to Burgundy Street, building a townhouse for Genève Arnault adjacent to Couvertie's twin cottages (412–414 Burgundy).[48] Sharing a party wall with one of the smaller houses, Arnault's three-story home combines elements of the Creole townhouse form with architectural and stylistic

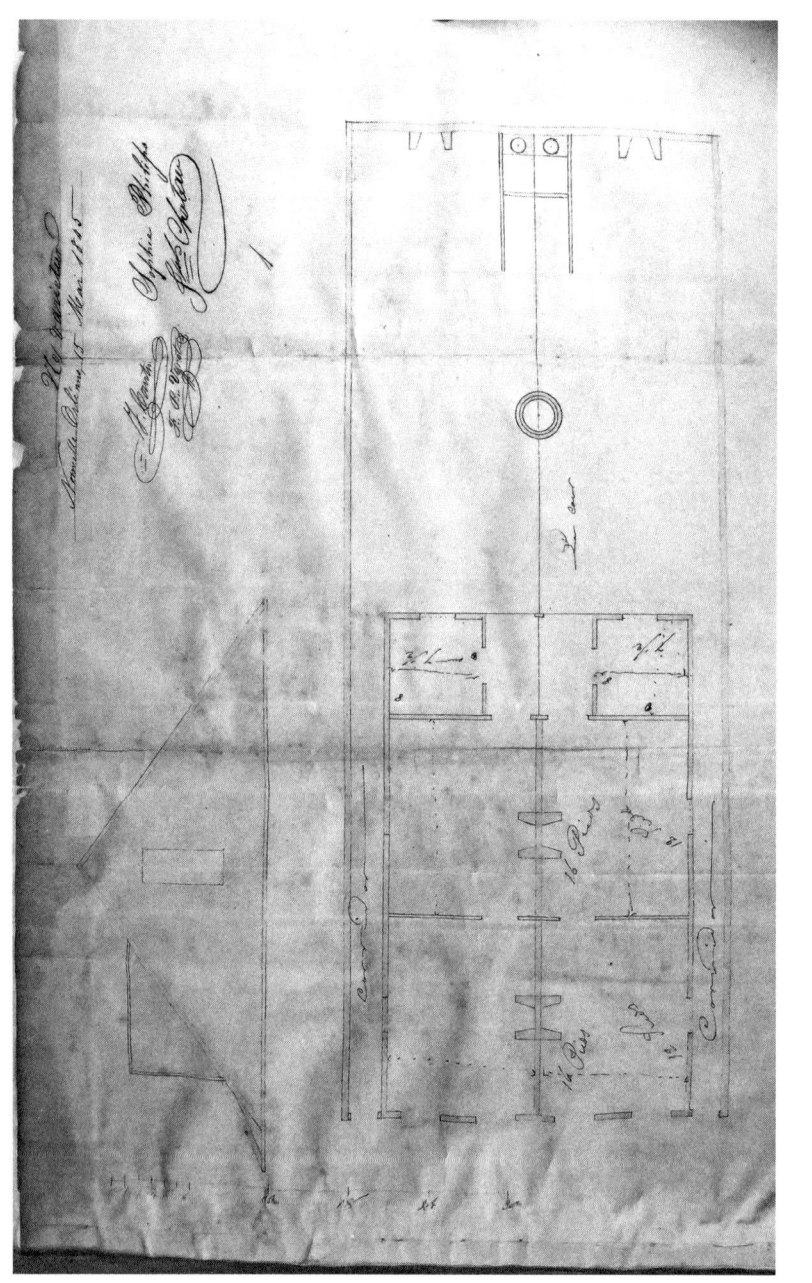

Figure 4.7. Plan of Sophia Philips cottage on St. Ann Street. Joseph Chateau, 1846. Theodore Guyol notary, volume 1, act 256, May 15, 1846. Courtesy of Hon. Chelsey Richard Napoleon, Clerk of Civil District Court, Parish of Orleans.

Figure 4.8. Assembly of houses by Joseph Chateau (from left to right): 422 Burgundy Street, 416–418 Burgundy Street, and 412–414 Burgundy Street. Photo by Liz Jurey, 2020. Courtesy of the Preservation Resource Center of New Orleans.

elements of the American townhouse. The exterior of the building features double-hung windows (perhaps shortened at the ground floor) with stone lintels and sills as well as a dentiled brick cornice and gable-end chimneys. The transomed primary entry door provided access to the ground-floor rooms and exterior staircase in the rear courtyard via a side passage. The ground floor and *banquette* were protected by an *abat-vent* supported by iron rods that also served as a balcony at the first floor.

In January 1846, Chateau was commissioned to build a fourth building on Burgundy Street—another two-bay cottage for Couvertie after the latter added to his property holding on that block in February 1845.[49] In the Vieux Carré Survey, it is assumed that the building's present form was created when half of a four-bay cottage was destroyed by fire. Chateau intentionally built the unique, narrow, four-room linear dwelling with its half-hipped roof.[50] This type of linear dwelling, the *appentis* (shed-roofed) cottage, served as typical postfire emergency housing.[51] This work of Chateau is significant in that it shows a creative response to fitting a house on an extra narrow lot as well as continued Creolization of Caribbean and Gulf Coast forms.[52] The one-story house and kitchen were noted in the act when Couvertie sold the property in 1856. With the completion of this third building for Couvertie, four Chateau buildings were located adjacent to one another. Occupying half of the block, they provide a striking assembly of Chateau's works (figure 4.8).

Chateau's work was in demand even in the newer-settled neighborhoods upriver. In addition to commissions in Faubourg Sainte-Marie, he also built in the city of Lafayette.[53] Andrew Oscar Murphy commissioned Chateau to build a wood-frame American townhouse on Magazine Street between First and Second Streets in 1847.[54] The two-story residence was designed in the Greek Revival style

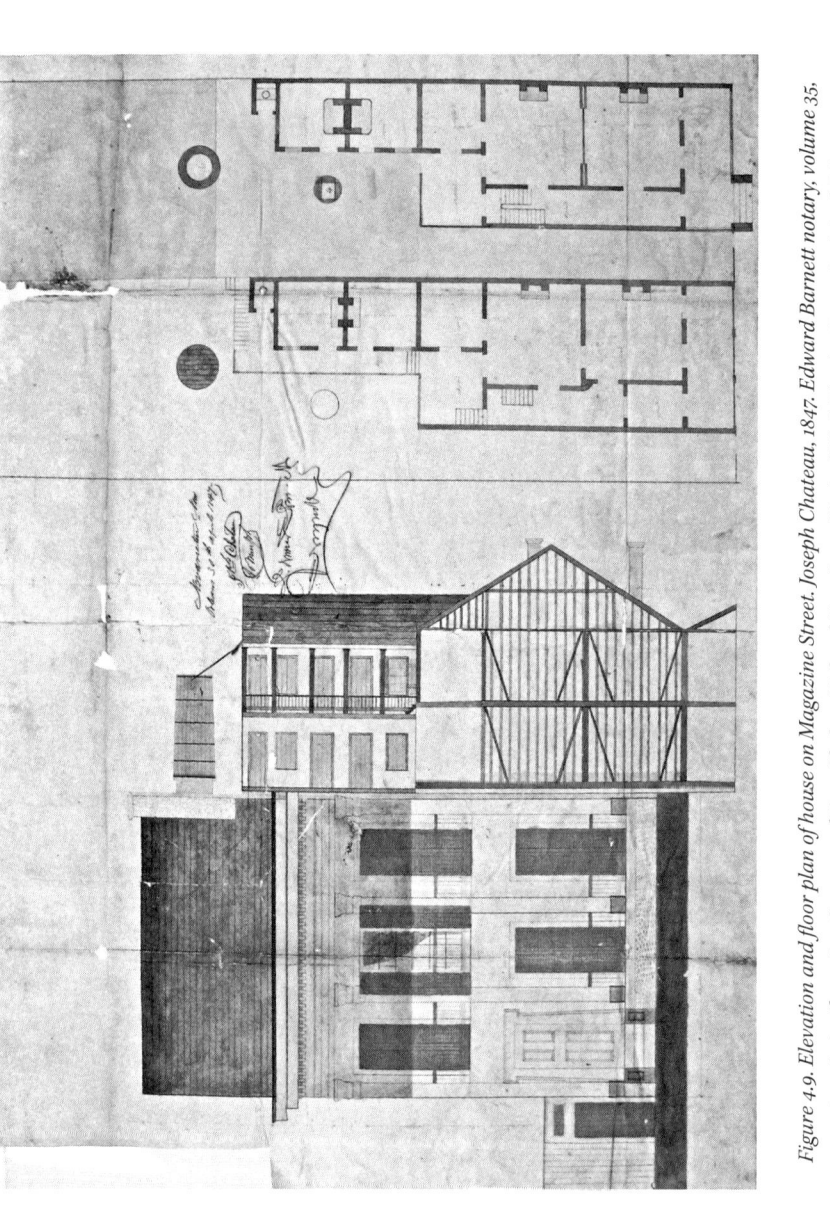

Figure 4.9. Elevation and floor plan of house on Magazine Street. Joseph Chateau, 1847. Edward Barnett notary, volume 35, act 519A, April 30, 1847. Courtesy of Hon. Chelsey Richard Napoleon, Clerk of Civil District Court, Parish of Orleans.

with a five-foot cornice and four full-height pilasters. The front façade was to be scored to resemble stone. Chateau's drawing for the dwelling clearly shows the balloon frame construction, introduced to American architecture in the 1840s, which was to be applied to the building's construction (figure 4.9). This new method of building was responsible for the rapid pace of building in the Garden District in the 1850s.[55]

Joseph Chateau is important as a native-born contemporary of the Dollioles and Souliés for many reasons. He built in several forms and stylistic idioms throughout the city, keeping up with changing local and national trends in architecture. He incorporated new techniques, such as scored or *fleche* façades. He was also a draftsman; over half of the record number of building contracts in his name have drawings with floor plans and, sometimes, elevations and sections.[56] Not least, his work shows a level of sophistication higher than that of both his fellow Louisiana-born and immigrant *gens de couleur libres* builders.

ÉMIGRÉS

Antebellum New Orleans benefited from the design and building skills of those who were bred in the city as well as of individuals (and their descendants) from other parts of the Gulf seeking refuge in Louisiana in the wake of political turmoil and revolution. The skills and abilities of *gens de couleur libres* builders who immigrated to New Orleans from Saint-Domingue, Jamaica, and Cuba in the late eighteenth and early nineteenth centuries have been specifically acknowledged as influencing New Orleans's antebellum architecture in scholarship.[57] The number of specific foreign-born *gens de couleur libres* builders whose names and activities are listed most frequently in secondary source material *and* who were active primarily from 1820 to 1850, however, is relatively small.[58] Among those whose work is touted are Pierre Roup and Nelson Fouché.

Pierre Roup

The Saint-Dominguan native Pierre Roup (ca. 1799–1836) emigrated to New Orleans in 1805.[59] Three years later, he is depicted on Pilié's map as owning property at present-day 1031–1041 Governor Nicholls Street and 1011–1013 Ursulines Avenue.[60] Also in 1808, he purchased property on Hospital Street (present-day 1018–1020 and 1024 Governor Nicholls) and built a *colombage* (half-timbered) *maisonette*. Here, Roup departed from his native- and foreign-born contemporaries in his construction of the type of linear cottage that influenced the development of the shotgun house,[61] which is no longer extant.[62] He resided there until purchasing in 1816 a lot on North Rampart Street (1035 North

Figure 4.10. 1035 North Rampart Street. Pierre Roup, 1816. Auction drawing by Pueyo and Cosnier, April 3, 1845. Plan book 40, folio 11. Courtesy of Hon. Chelsey Richard Napoleon, Clerk of Civil District Court, Parish of Orleans.

Rampart), where he built an urban-style Creole cottage (figure 4.10).[63] The one-and-a-half-story exposed brick house was unusual in that the door surrounds were of articulated stone. The house featured four rooms and a rear gallery as well as double fireplaces with marble mantels in the front rooms. Outbuildings in the brick-paved courtyard included a four-room, shingle-roofed kitchen; washing shed; and double latrine.[64] Roup sold the house to Marc Lafitte in 1823.[65] Between 1823 and 1827, Roup again resided at the Governor Nicholls Street *maisonette*. In December 1827, he purchased property on the newly developing Esplanade Avenue.[66] On the lot, he built a cottage where his family resided until 1835. Roup then moved to North Rampart Street in Faubourg Marigny (at former 374 Love Street), where he died in 1836.[67] He probably built the four-room-deep *maisonette* that was on the property at the time.

Roup's known or extant building stock is not limited to houses he built for himself. In 1823, he built a five-room-deep *maisonette* for *femme de couleur libre* Helen Lepage on a lot that he had subdivided from his Governor Nicholls Street property and sold to her (figure 4.11). The hip-roofed dwelling is possibly the oldest shotgun-type house extant in New Orleans and the nation.

Roup also contributed to his profession as a builder in other ways. With other Saint-Dominguan émigré building artisans, both Black and white, Roup was instrumental in establishing La Loge Persévérance numéro Quatre (Perseverance Lodge No. 4, founded in Saint-Domingue in 1806) in New Orleans in 1808. By 1820, as an officer of the Masonic lodge, he had signed the building contract for the construction of a new meeting hall.[68] In March 1825, Roup's abilities as a builder were recognized when he was selected to serve as the supervisor for the builders Bickel and Hamblet, who had been commissioned to add a story and repair a house owned by Germain Ducatel on Royal Street.[69] Pierre Roup was an immigrant *gens*

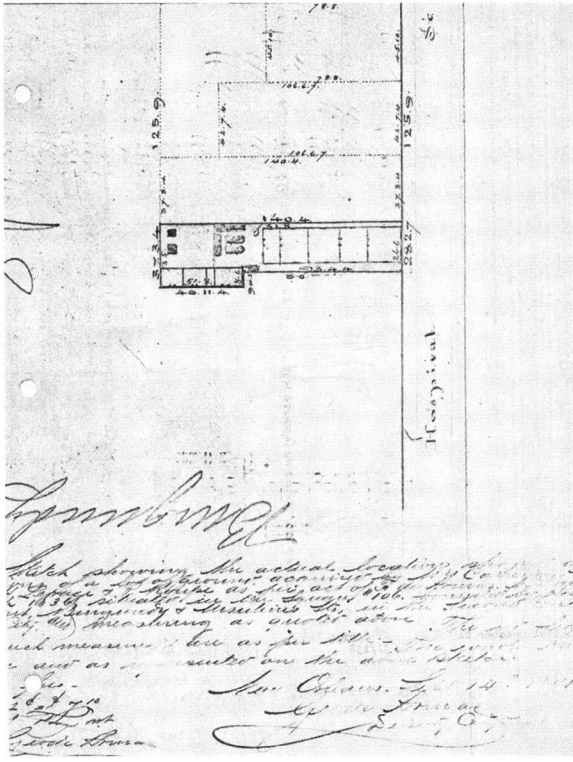

Figure 4.11. 1024 Governor Nicholls Street (Helen Lepage maisonette). Pierre Roup, 1823. The Collins C. Diboll Vieux Carré Digital Survey at The Historic New Orleans Collection.

de couleur libre builder whose skills and ability allowed him to participate in the physical and social aspects of the building profession at high levels.

Nelson Fouché

Nelson Fouché (ca. 1800–1874)[70] was another *homme de couleur libre* who, like the Dollioles and Souliés, was heavily involved in real estate speculation. Born in Jamaica or Cuba, Fouché married a Cuban free woman of color, Françoise Lefebvre, in New Orleans in 1825.[71] Between April 1825 and February 1828, he served as teacher to several young apprentices.[72] He was noted as a bricklayer in the 1832 city directory. Fouché also made many real estate investments, some with his kinsman Louis Dutreuil Fouché.[73] Nelson Fouché owned property in Faubourg Tremé in the 1200 block of North Claiborne Avenue and in the former City Commons.[74] Among Nelson Fouché's dealings was the purchase of several properties from Joseph Dolliole in early 1835.[75] He also jointly acquired lots on Washington Promenade in Faubourg Franklin with Jean-Louis Dolliole in May 1835.

The only example of Fouché's built work known to still be in existence is his own home at the corner of Mandeville and Chartres Streets (2340 Chartres; figure 4.12). Constructed in 1836, the detached two-and-a-half-story townhouse is Creole in form. The primary façade contains four arched openings with doors protected by paneled shutters. Though a cursory survey is not definitive, the fanlight transoms likely concealed an *entresol* storage area that separated the ground floor from the first-floor commercial area. The first floor of the primary façade features shorter double-hung windows with batten shutters; these openings are also present on the first floor of the Chartres Street façade. The façade facing Mandeville Street is actually grander, with four arched and transomed door openings at the ground floor and four rectangular doorways with multilight French doors and vertical board shutters that open onto a balcony (nonoriginal) at the first floor. The different fenestration on the street-facing façades is unified by granite lintels. Rectangular door openings at the rear façade open onto a wood-frame, shed-roof balcony with turned porch supports. On all levels, the attic story is articulated by a projecting string course at the sill level of the rectangular casement windows. Under the hipped roof is a dentiled cornice formed by sawtooth rows of bricks. The roof has gabled dormers with arched windows, two at the front and three at the rear. The townhouse features various influences of Federal style architecture, including the arched openings with fanlights, emphasis on horizontality, and decreasing height of each successive story. Fouché owned the property (which also had a stable and a two-story detached brick kitchen, now demolished) from 1832 to 1838 and again from 1845 to 1858.[76]

Figure 4.12. 2340 Chartres Street. Nelson Fouché. Photo by author, 2011.

Nelson Fouché's personal life becomes less clear, and his building activities diminished over time. Interestingly, he is listed as a beer merchant in the 1850 federal census with real estate holdings valued at $10,000.00.[77] Shortly thereafter, Fouché suffered a change in fortune; he declared bankruptcy in 1853, and ultimately sold the Chartres Street house in 1858.[78] In 1860, he is listed in the census as a kettle setter (with an additional notation that says "mechanic"), and all real estate and personal property values ($10,000.000 and $3,500.00, respectively) are entered under his wife Françoise's name. Historians have confused the names and professions of Nelson and his son, Louis Nelson; it is the latter who was an architect in 1850 at age twenty-six, the first African American, of mixed blood or not, to ever be listed as such in the federal census.[79] Louis Nelson Fouché (1824–1886) is the family member who Rodolphe Desdunes wrote was trained in masonry, architecture, and mathematics.[80] Some historians, however, have imbued the senior Fouché with these skills. Further, it is likely that the draftsman illustrating houses for sale from the 1840s through the 1860s was not the father but the son.[81] Although Nelson Fouché was earmarked by Marie Couvent to serve as one of the founders of the École des Orphelins Indigents (Catholic School for

TABLE 4.1. SELECT BUILT WORKS BY DOLLIOLE AND SOULIÉ CONTEMPORARIES

Builder	Date	Form	Client Time Frame Cost	Current Address or Historic Location	Faubourg
LOUISIANA-BORN BUILDERS					
François Boisdoré	1828	unknown (d)	M. Cornu	Bayou Road at Tremé	Tremé
	1829	Creole townhouse	J. S. Dufossat	1133 Chartres	Vieux Carré
Laurent Guesnon	ca. 1811	4-bay cottage	self no contract	1428 Bourbon	Marigny
Louis Vivant	1832	2-room kitchen building (unknown)	N. L. Lauriano 2 months $500.00	Melpomene	Annunciation
	1846	4-bay cottage (d)	J. Connor, fmc 60 days $700.00	Laharpe at Derbigny	Tremé
	1847	4-bay cottage (d)	U. Roy, fwc 60 days $1,080.00	1031–1033 Burgundy	Vieux Carré
Myrtille Courcelle	ca. 1836	4-bay cottage	self no contract	1509–1511 Dumaine	Tremé
Joseph Chateau	ca. 1836	4-bay cottage	self no contract	1523–1525 St. Philip	Tremé
	1836	4-bay cottage	M. Boisdoré, fwc $900.00	1609–1611 St. Philip	Tremé
	1846	Creole townhouse	C. H. Daret 8 months $10,200.00	832 St. Philip	Vieux Carré
	1844	two 2-bay cottages	J. B. Couvertie, fmc $6,700	416–418 Burgundy	Vieux Carré
	1844	4-bay cottage (unknown)	J. Dowson, fmc	undetermined	undetermined
	1844	4-bay cottage (unknown)	P. Heno, fmc	undetermined	undetermined
	1845	2-bay *maison de maître* (d)	R. Vionnet, fmc 3 months $1,325	St. Philip bet. Burgundy and Rampart	Vieux Carré

Joseph Chateau	1845	Creole townhouse (d)	R. Vionnet, fmc $4,100	St. Philip bet. Rampart and St. Claude	Tremé
	1845	4-bay cottage (double) (d)	S. Philips, fwc	St. Ann bet. Villeré and Robertson	Tremé
	1845	4-bay cottage (d)	Mrs. Johnson $1,700	Jackson bet. Tremé and Marais	Sainte-Marie
	1845	2-bay cottage (d)	V. Perilliat $1,300	Rampart bet. St. Peter and Toulouse	Tremé
	1845	Undetermined (unknown)	V. Perilliat $1,650	Chartres bet. St. Louis and Conti	Vieux Carré
	1845	Creole townhouse	G. Arnault $5,100	412–414 Burgundy	Vieux Carré
	1845	4-bay cottage (d)	J. McLaughlin $2,350	corner of Jackson and Franklin	Tremé
	1846	2-bay appentis cottage	J. B. Couvertie, fmc unknown	422 Burgundy	Vieux Carré
	1847	American townhouse (d)	A. O. Murphy 3 months $2,500	Magazine bet. First and Second	Lafayette
	1847	American cottage (unknown)	C. Morel $3,700	Bayou St. John	Tremé
	1851	2-bay cottage (unknown)	N. Gibbs, fwc $3,500	Bound by St. Claude, Rampart, St. Philip, Dumaine	Tremé
ST. DOMINGUAN ÉMIGRÉS					
Pierre Roup	1808	Shotgun *maisonette* (d)	self no contract	1018–1020 Governor Nicholls	Vieux Carré
	1816	4-bay cottage	self no contract	1035 N. Rampart	Tremé
	1823	Shotgun	Helen LePage, fwc	1024 Governor Nicholls	Vieux Carré

TABLE 4.1, CONTINUED

Pierre Roup	1827	Creole cottage (d)	self no contract	1012–1016 Esplanade	Esplanade Ridge
	Ca. 1829	Shotgun *maisonette*	self no contract	1744 North Rampart	Marigny
Nelson Fouché	1836	Creole townhouse	self no contract	2340 Chartres	Marigny

Note: (d) = demolished; fmc = free man of color; fwc = free woman of color.

Indigent Orphans, founded in 1847) after her death and to serve on the first board of directors, it was his son, Louis, who taught mathematics there.[82] Both of the Fouchés' contributions remain important to the output of émigré builders of color in the antebellum period.

Within this brief examination of specific *gens de couleur libres* builders who practiced contemporaneously with the Dollioles and Souliés, it becomes clear that while the work of émigré builders was important and certainly contributed to the retention of Creole forms and inclusion of Anglo forms as the city expanded in the antebellum years, native builders certainly held their own as far as the use of Creole forms, development of the Creole cottage, adaptation of Anglo architectural elements and style into traditional building, and in sheer numbers. Free builders of color did build large numbers of Creole cottages (table 4.1), but they also increasingly designed or erected buildings of various types, incorporating popular styles and conventions but always working within the conventions of New Orleans's unique cultural and architectural environment.

CHAPTER 5

"RAISED TO THE TRADE"

Building Practices of Gens de Couleur Libres *Builders in Antebellum New Orleans*

Son, once you learn this, ain't nobody can take it away from you.

MR. MARTINEZ, *RAISED TO THE TRADE*

T he building forms or typologies constructed by the *gens de couleur libres* have been widely explored, but the profession of building as it related to the *gens de couleur libres* community is relatively unexamined. Whether born in Louisiana or abroad, *gens de couleur libres* builders had to find ways to obtain work and get the job done to sustain viable careers. What is apparent is that no matter their place of birth, the Dollioles, Souliés, and most of their contemporaries had backgrounds in woodworking. This skill and at least some business aptitude were the only requisites to become successful builders in antebellum New Orleans.

WHAT'S IN A NAME?

Those involved in the construction of buildings were primarily referred to as builders, carpenters, joiners, or cabinetmakers in historic documentation (table 5.1). A carpenter (*charpentier*) employed timber-frame construction using mortise-and-tenon, scarf, and lap joints to construct the frame, walls, and trusses of a building.[1] More specifically, a joiner or carpenter-joiner (*menuisier*) fabricated

TABLE 5.1. TITLES/ROLES OF *GENS DE COULEUR LIBRES* BUILDERS

Builder	Contracts	City Directories	Federal Census
Jean-Louis Dolliole (1779–1861)	building contractor (1831)	joiner (1811) cabinetmaker (1822) carpenter (1832/1838)	builder (1850)
Joseph Dolliole (1790–1868)	—	carpenter (1822/1834/1838)	joiner (1850)
Norbert Soulié (1793–1869)	—	builder (1822/1824)	—
François Boisdoré (1779/82–1859)	—	builder (1822)	carpenter (1850)
Laurent Guesnon (1770–1842)	—	carpenter (1822/1832)	—
Louis Vivant (1796–1870)	building contractor (1832/1846)	—	builder (1850)
Myrtille Courcelle (1805–1872)	building contractor (1844)	builder (1849/1850)	—
Joseph Chateau (1816–unknown)	contractor (1845)	cordwainer (1832) builder (1850)	builder (1850)
Pierre Roup (dates unknown)	builder (1825)	carpenter (1822) builder (1832)	—
Nelson Fouché (ca. 1800–1874)	—	bricklayer (1832)	beer merchant (1850) kettle setter/ mechanic (1860)

decorative portions of a building such as wainscoting, moldings, doors, paneling, sashes, and other trim work.[2] The cabinetmaker (*ébéniste*) was a highly skilled furniture maker with more status than an assistant *menuisier*, who was considered a journeyman.[3] Most of these specialized terms were usually applied to men at higher levels in the building trades as opposed to the simple term *bâtisseur* (builder). The terms "joiner," "cabinetmaker," and "carpenter" were applied to Jean-Louis Dolliole over time, an indication of the increase in his experience and the types of commissions he pursued and obtained by the 1830s. Norbert Soulié and most free builders of color emphasized in this chapter were simply recognized as builders. Joseph Dolliole's identification as a joiner as late as 1850 perhaps signifies that he was no longer actively practicing at this point in his life. Some type of change in status is also reflected for François Boisdoré, who went from being identified as a builder to a carpenter. On the other hand, the term applied to an individual's profession could simply have been at the whim of the individual, directory writer, or census taker—for all intents and purposes, the role of the builder in contractual documents was relatively the same. In the 1830s and 1840s, building contracts referred to a builder as an *entrepreneur* or *entrepreneur en bâtiments/de bâtisses*—contractor or building contractor. This distinction is significant. Mary Woods notes that most master craftsmen were not employers, much less contractors. "They worked alone, but they worked for themselves."[4] However, as builders, some of the men were also general contractors who coordinated all aspects of a building project. In addition to physically taking part in construction, they were in charge of acquiring materials and labor as well as directing work on the site.[5] The professional responsibilities and capabilities of *gens de couleur libres* can be gleaned from examination of building contracts.

CONTRACTING AND CONDUCTING WORK

In his doctoral dissertation, Naohito Okude utilizes building contracts to break down the architectural grammar of buildings built by free people of color in antebellum New Orleans. He analyzes the linguistic components provided in contracts between *gens de couleur libres* builders and their clients—contractual obligations, building types, linguistic preferences, and racial classifications. These data provide information on the social, cultural, and economic aspects of commissioning a building. The surviving building contracts concerning the Dollioles, one private agreement for a commission by Norbert Soulié, and a select group of their contemporaries contain basically the same type of information: identification of the parties involved, specifications outlining the type of building(s) to be erected, and contract terms (schedule and compensation). The contracts assessed for this study underscore the fact that free builders of color built a variety of forms for diverse clients—Black and white, Anglo and Creole, male and female. The documents are generally two to three pages long. Longer and more detailed contracts are usually for a large building or one that has more architectural or stylistic details, like the Creole townhouse that Myrtille Courcelle built for C. H. Daret (eight pages).[6] One exception is the twelve-page contract between Courcelle and Marguerite Boisdoré for her Tremé Creole cottage. As would be expected, more complicated buildings, like Creole townhouses, brought in a larger income, and builders were provided longer periods of time to complete them. Contracts generally stipulated that builders were themselves responsible for acquiring the necessary building materials of good quality. As was typical for master builders of the period, *gens de couleur libres* builders charged a single fee for design (if applicable), contracting, craftsmanship, and supervision.[7] They were paid in increments, sometimes with a deposit to get a job started, and then at various stages of the project's completion. The final payment was typically made when the client approved the work and the builder handed over the keys. More often than not, no plans were included with a building contract. Notable exceptions are the contracts involving Joseph Chateau, who included at least a floor plan if not an elevation or cross section with contracts for buildings he was to construct. This dearth of plans, in addition to their not having theoretical study of architecture, is likely another reason why *gens de couleur libres* builders were not identified as architects. For, in general, master builders/carpenters, even in the colonial and Federal periods, were known as architects if they drafted basic architectural drawings.[8]

Not all building contracts were made at the inception of a new construction project or for actual building for that matter. Both Jean-Louis and Joseph Dolliole were sellers in land transactions in which a building under construction was included in the conveyance. In June 1831, Joseph sold Marie Demony a lot in Faubourg Tremé where he agreed to construct a two-room, brick-between-post cottage, a kitchen outbuilding, latrines, and a well on the property as part of the sale.[9] Similarly, a few months later, in November 1831, Jean-Louis sold Madeleine Rillieux land with a nearly completed house and kitchens that he was obligated to finish within a month after the sale. Instances of these types of building contracts within property sales may exist for other *gens de couleur libres* builders. Agreements for other types of services may not be clearly indicated in the party names of a transaction. Knowledge of Pierre Roup's role as supervisor of other builders' renovations to a property is based on a building contract reference mentioning his name in the chain of title for 600–608 Royal Street in the Vieux Carré Survey. Similar contractual obligations for free builders of color may be found for other buildings in the Vieux Carré that are indexed by the owner or primary builder/architect name or for buildings located in other parts of the city that have not been surveyed in such a manner.

Information regarding Afro-Creole builders' acquisition of work is relatively easy to find in the available building contracts, but facts regarding how the work was actually accomplished are scarce. One property transaction between brothers Jean-Louis and Joseph Dolliole sheds some light on the types of tools and materials they used.[10] In addition to selling two lots of land and two enslaved individuals to his younger brother in September 1814, Jean-Louis also sold him the "funds" from his "shop," consisting of "his carpentry tools, wood and flooring to manufacture, finished and started furniture, and generally all that there is" to add up to the sale price.[11] No historic documentation exists to ascertain why Jean-Louis would have sold his tools, but whether he did so because he was in need of the funds or to aid Joseph in his own career as a builder, his builder's tools and materials were given monetary value. When Joseph Dolliole appraised the estate of his late friend and former business partner Henry Fletcher in 1853, "one trunk of carpenter's tools" was included in the inventory and valued at $15.00.[12] The importance of the tools of a builder's trade was also recognized when Nelson Fouché was allowed to keep his when he filed for bankruptcy in 1853.[13] Fouché noted that the bankruptcy sale liquidated most of his possessions with the exception of personal clothing, "arms and military accoutrements, and the instruments whereby I make a living, which the law authorizes me to keep."[14] This enabled him to continue to pursue work and improve his economic standing. None of the estate inventories available for the Dollioles (or that of Soulié cousin Myrtille Courcelle) in New Orleans succession records contain references to building tools. These three men died at advanced ages, however, so they may no longer have been actively building and may not have retained such items.

There is no doubt that the Dollioles, the Souliés, and their peers were hands-on builders. In his journal, Bernard Soulié notes that in August of 1848 he "made many repairs on the [Rampart Street] house."[15] As such, *gens de couleur libres* builders faced the physical hazards of their work. Bernard Soulié certainly understood and underscored this when he reported that Paul Lacroix, a white builder and acquaintance, died on April 22, 1847, when the framework for a house he was building collapsed on him.[16]

Skilled at what they did, *gens de couleur libres* builders would have needed assistance completing their commissions in a satisfactory manner and on time. Some formed partnerships with other builders, such as Joseph Dolliole with Henry Fletcher or even brothers Bernard and Albin Soulié working together. As seen in chapters 1 and 2, property ownership was a significant indicator of status in the *gens de couleur libres* community; so, too, was slave ownership.[17] Members of the Dolliole and Soulié families owned enslaved men, women, and children and utilized the labor of the men in their professions. The enslaved mulatto youth François was part of the sale between Jean-Louis and Joseph mentioned above. The transaction stipulated that Joseph "should be able to teach a decent trade (such as that of carpenter) to said mulatto François, and that at the age of thirty years, he will be free in all forms of law."[18] Other than this transaction, only one other of the *gens de couleur libres* builders studied is documented as using or hiring out enslaved labor for building construction. In 1816, Pierre Roup received $50.00 from the city of New Orleans for work that two of his enslaved carpenters completed on public works over the course of a month.[19] In 1818, Norbert Soulié purchased a twenty-year-old enslaved mulatto man named Joseph from the estate of his late teacher, Henry Latrobe. Joseph, noted as being a native of St. Domingue and "somewhat a mason," had a value of $1,000.00 on the Latrobe estate inventory; Norbert purchased him for $1,300.00.[20] Undoubtedly, Norbert and Joseph worked together during the former's apprenticeship with Latrobe, so Norbert would have been well aware of Joseph's skill and ability. This transaction is interesting on social and economic levels. For one, no other enslaved individuals are known to have been part of Latrobe's estate. Any other enslaved laborers on his projects were perhaps hired out from their enslavers. Second, although Latrobe had dozens of other creditors, Norbert accomplished and benefited from Joseph's sale. Norbert would have understood and assessed Joseph's value on two levels—as a quasi-professional builder and as a free person of color one generation removed from slavery. Documentation of Joseph's continued work for Norbert has not been located; his fate unknown. No other enslaved men mentioned in the available Dolliole and Soulié estate inventories and files were noted as being skilled in the building trades or, therefore, utilized by the families in their careers as developers and builders.

The small numbers of enslaved adult males (over age ten) listed in census records, slave schedules, or estate inventories do not indicate that the Dollioles or Souliés utilized enslaved labor in any significant way for their building activities (table 5.2). The one exception is Norbert Soulié, who was listed as head of a household with ten enslaved males over the age of ten in 1830. This was at the peak of Norbert's building career before he left for France, so these men could have assisted with his building projects; it is not known if Joseph was among them. For the most part, the Souliés—most of whom were absentee landlords for a majority of the antebellum period—compensated enslaved men owned by others for menial tasks such as cleaning the outhouses on their properties. Such was the case when they compensated "Negro Ned," slave of A. Laucher, as well as other unidentified enslaved men for cleaning the outhouses on some of their properties.[21]

Responsible for all aspects of a building's completion, the Dolliole and Soulié brothers, Courcelle, Vivant, Fouché, and all the others would have hired free Black carpenters, masons, bricklayers, plasterers, woodworkers, and painters. In addition to relatives such as Belsunce Liotau, other builders that the Souliés employed regularly to work on their houses and rental properties included François Loubarde, Charles Etienne, Louis Contat, Louis Petit, Gardes and Lefebvre, S. Maspereau and Co., and T. A. Dupin.[22] It would have been good business on the part of free builders of color to hire dependable subcontractors with whose work they were familiar. The white architect and contemporary James Gallier Sr. (active

TABLE 5.2. NUMBER OF ADULT ENSLAVED MALES OWNED BY *GENS DE COULEUR LIBRES* BUILDERS IN NEW ORLEANS

	1820 Census	1830 Census	1840 Census	1850 Census Slave Schedule	Estate Inventory*
Jean-Louis Dolliole	0 (0)	not found	0 (5)	1 (5)	2 (2)
Joseph Dolliole	not found	0 (5)	2 (9)	not found	0 (0)
Norbert Soulié	not of age	10 (17)	not found	not found	not found
Bernard Soulié	not of age	not found	1 (3)	not found	not found
Albin Soulié	not of age	not found	2 (7)	not found	not found

*New Orleans archival repositories contain portions of the Souliés' French succession records. No estate inventories are included; they are filed in France. Total number of enslaved individuals owned in parentheses.

in New Orleans from 1834 to 1850) mentions the merits of such a practice: "I *let* out the brickwork, stone work, plastering, painting, slating, and ironwork, to persons already established in those several trades, and I made it a practice to employ the same people, when possible, in each department, as long as I remained in business" (emphasis in original).[23] When free builders of color did contract (informally or through other means that did not necessitate notarial documentation), they seem to have employed a range of journeymen, including other *gens de couleur libres*, free Black, French, and American craftsmen.[24]

Like their white counterparts, *gens de couleur libres* builders also established partnerships to successfully obtain and produce work and to acquire property. Any work that the Dolliole brothers or Soulié brothers would have done together for financial gain constituted a business partnership in which the parties were familiar with one another personally and professionally. Though not a legal partnership, Norbert Soulié and Edmond Rillieux formed a joint venture when they worked on the design and construction of the Louisiana Sugar Refinery. In 1831, Lucien and Norbert Soulié created a partnership to enable them to successfully obtain capital as absentee landlords.[25] Similarly, younger brothers Bernard and Albin did the same, creating a formal partnership in 1833, although they had had an informal arrangement since 1827.[26] Initially, Bernard and Albin were primarily builders. Their partnership later expanded to cover their pursuits as landlords and merchants. The practice of forming business partnerships was common in the antebellum *gens de couleur libres* community. Sometimes, collaborations were not restricted to building construction. Julien Colvis and Joseph Dumas were partners from 1830 to 1869. Real estate speculators, the men also were tailors; their shop was located at 124 Chartres Street in 1849.[27] Among work that the firm commissioned were rowhouses on Common Street (1839) and houses on Carondelet Street (1840)—all in the developing business sector of Faubourg Sainte-Marie—in addition to those on their dual-owned properties in Faubourg Tremé.[28] Etienne Cordevielle and François Lacroix also established a partnership as tailors and real estate speculators (ca. 1825–1849).[29] The duo had a successful business on Chartres Street.[30] In addition to their commercial locations, one of their jointly owned properties on which they built was at Architects' Row, where they commissioned a Creole townhouse (2701 Chartres).[31] In her discussion of the emergence of partnerships in nineteenth-century American architectural practice (1820s and 1830s), Mary Woods recognizes that white architects established professional collaborations to "rationalize and specialize" their architectural work.[32] Working less on expansive and complicated projects that required rationalization and specialization of building design and construction, the *gens de couleur libres* formed associations with like-minded family members and peers, strengthening their communal ties to one another and the built environment.

PAYING IT FORWARD: APPRENTICE SUPERVISORS AND FAMILY ROLE MODELS

Teaching the building trades to younger generations was inherent in New Orleans's *gens de couleur libres* community. Although free Black building artisans may not have been involved in the more traditional types of crafts organizations or formal workshops serving white artisans, they did accomplish their work using apprentices and journeymen, a common practice in all areas of the building trades, thereby transferring their skills and knowledge and perpetuating one of few professional careers viable for young free men of color.[33]

Free youth of color were first introduced to the vocation of building in the home. Jean-Louis Dolliole's oldest son, Louis Drausin, born in 1812 from his first marriage, came of age by the 1830s and 1840s. Eventually becoming a builder himself, Drausin (as he is often listed in legal and statistical records) undoubtedly learned his trade from his father (no indentures with Drausin as the student or evidence of other formal education have been found) and was old enough to work with/for his father by the time Jean-Louis was practicing in the 1830s and 1840s. Drausin's assistance would have lessened Jean-Louis's need for enslaved labor and for other free Black builders to complete his commissions and development projects. At the other end of the spectrum is Louis Nelson Fouché, whose father was also a builder but who received formal education in mathematics and architecture. Many young men who became builders had training from the middle of the spectrum—they learned their trades from master builders via apprenticeships.

While family tradition was significant for the continuation of the practice of *gens de couleur libres* in the building trades, in some cases, men learned skills from others outside of their families. Many a document from the indenture books of the Records of the Office of the Mayor of New Orleans arranged for a *jeune de couleur libre* (free youth of color) or *jeune homme creole* (young Creole man) to learn a building skill. The indentures were formal contracts that specified the responsibilities of the teacher, the student, and even the individual sponsoring the youth to pursue a trade. As opposed to the coercive character of apprenticeships for which the South is known, all parties entered into these agreements willingly.[34] Nor were these the "casual arrangements" of the antebellum period illuminated by Mary Woods.[35] Indentures for apprenticeships were spelled out in very specific terms. In an act regulating apprenticeship in 1806, the legislature of the Territory of Orleans created a format that all indentures for "any art, mastery or occupation" were to follow.[36] Each document contains the following information:

- name of apprentice and age;
- consent and name of sponsor (with relationship to apprentice) if apprentice under the age of twenty-one; consent of mayor, judge, or two justices of the peace;
- name and occupation of teacher;
- art or occupation to be learned;
- date of start of term and length of term;
- specifics as to what the apprentice will be taught;
- specifics as to responsibilities of the apprentice and the teacher; and
- other provisions regarding apprentice's care, if applicable (i.e., room, board, clothing, medical care, etc.).

Eight known contracts from the 1810s and 1820s involve Jean-Louis Dolliole, Norbert Soulié, and Myrtille Courcelle (table 5.3). Generally, all of the contracts were similar in that each apprentice was to reside and work with his teacher. Ranging in age from twelve to fourteen, the apprentices served terms of four to six full and consecutive years. Interestingly, the two twelve-year-olds had the shortest apprentice periods (to learn masonry) at four years. The contract between Norbert Soulié and Etienne Gallot was longer at five years despite the fact that the youth was already fifteen years old. The difficulty in learning all of the nuances of the carpentry trade probably prompted the longest term for Augustin Polidor at six years.

TABLE 5.3. APPRENTICESHIP INDENTURES IN THE BUILDING TRADES INVOLVING SELECT *GENS DE COULEUR LIBRES* BUILDERS

Date	Supervisor	Apprentice, Age	Trade	Sponsor (Relationship)	No. Years of Service
1815	Jean-Louis Dolliole	Augustin Polidor, h.c.l. (*homme de couleur libre*), age 14	carpentry	Bastion, *negro libre* (father)	6
1818	Norbert Soulié	Benigno Caldero, h.c.l., age 12	masonry	Heloise Marcos *f.c.l.* (*femme de couleur libre*) (aunt)	4
1819	Myrtille Courcelle	Etienne Gallot, h.c.l., age 15	masonry	Julie Gallot (mother)	5
1821	Myrtille Courcelle	Theogene Fondal, h.c.l., age 12	masonry	Marie Pierre *f.c.l.* (mother)	4

Alfred Hunt notes that "St. Dominguan free Blacks were employed in most of the journeyman trades in New Orleans as a result of apprenticeships that often called for formal education as part of the indenture contract."[37] One documented example is that of Jacques Daniel St. Ermain, who, in July 1811, was apprenticed to the architectural firm of Frenchmen Latour and Laclott for three years as a brick mason and was to be taught construction and drawing in the architects' spare time.[38] None of the contracts with free builders of color, whether for youths who were native born or émigrés, indicated that the youths would be taught drawing or drafting or any building skills related to but not directly applicable to the trade they were to learn. The 1818 indenture between Soulié and Caldero, however, stipulated that Soulié would furnish a schoolteacher to teach the boy to read, write, and cipher; Caldero had at least had some schooling—he was able to sign his name on the contract. Research has indicated that these *gens de couleur libres* builders did not use any significant amount of enslaved labor for their building work. One instance, though, shows Nelson Fouché training an enslaved man, Pros, at the request of his enslaver, F. Dupuis. Myrtille Courcelle was the only one of the builders contracted to train a youth who was not a free person of color. Etienne Gallot and his mother are assumed to have been white—neither has the notation indicating that they were people of color in the indenture.

In addition to mandating the mechanics of trade that a youth was to learn, the indentures included the quality of the student's performance and the teacher's instruction. The contracts stressed that students were to serve faithfully, obey, and not leave service without permission. As a matter of fact, Benigno Caldero's sponsor, his aunt, was required to compensate Norbert Soulié $200.00 for breach of any part of the contract by Caldero. In turn, an apprentice's supervisor promised to teach all aspects of his trade, withholding nothing. In the antebellum period, along with good instruction and constant supervision, "the employer in the building trades could control [an apprentice's] general conduct to the end that a good mechanic should be the result."[39] These contracts between *gens de couleur libres* builders and, particularly, free youths of color, again allowed for the young men to learn viable trades and to become productive and constructive members of the *gens de couleur libres* community. In the case of these indentures between teachers and (mostly) apprentices of color, the value of the apprenticeship for both parties was understood—no financial compensation for gain or profit for either party was specified in any of the documents.

Most frequently, expertise in the building trades passed along male lines via fathers, grandfathers, and uncles (i.e., the Dolliole family) and also by way of male teachers to their students. Women also strengthened ties among builders via marriage. Building skills were inherited through maternal lines as free men of color were invited into the trade by fathers and brothers-in-law.[40] Further, many builders' daughters married other builders or into families of builders. Jean-Louis Dolliole's daughters Marie Eugenie and Marie Rosella married mason Pedro Barthélémy Brue and carpenter Pierre Jean Bonnecaze, respectively.[41] Even Victoire Galaud, daughter of Madeleine Dolliole, was influenced by her uncles' occupations; she married builder Thomas Urquhart.[42] In turn, Jean-Louis's son Louis Drausin married Marie Eugenie Guesnon, the daughter of builder Laurent Ursain Guesnon.[43] In addition, *femmes de couleur libres* saw to the education of their young male relatives as builders. In five of the eight indenture contracts highlighted above, the sponsors were women, four of them free women of color. *Femmes de couleur libres* also apprenticed their sons to free Black and white artisans and firms. Adelaide Duplessis apprenticed her son Pierre Dolliole, age fifteen, to Jean Conrad in 1829 to learn the trade of cabinetry.[44]

One woman's sponsorship of her son with *hommes de couleur libres* builders was particularly beneficial for the Dolliole family. In July 1827, Laurette Baudin sponsored the training of her sixteen-year-old son Emile Errié with the firm of Cherubin and Dessource.[45] He spent three years and four months learning the profession of carpenter-cabinetmaker. On April 9, 1836, Jean-Louis Dolliole and Baudin signed a marriage contract before the notary Carlile Pollock. By 1838, stepbrothers Louis Drausin Dolliole and Emile Errié were working together when they signed a building contract to construct a brick *maison basse avec attique* (one-story house with attic) for Roman Planas at the corner

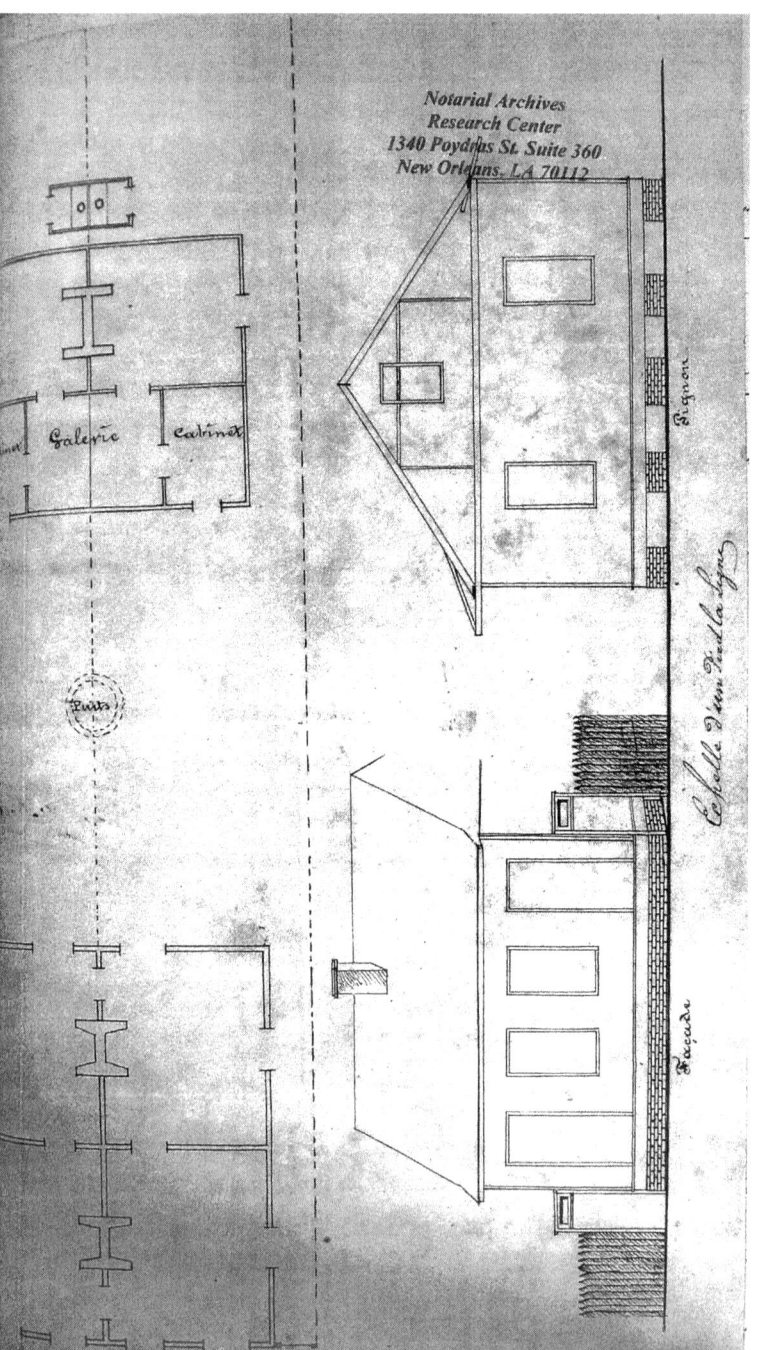

Figure 5.1. Floor plans and elevations for Marguerite Dauphine house. Louis Drausin Dolliole and Emile Errié. Octave De Armas notary, volume 43, act 319, November 23, 1848. Courtesy of Hon. Chelsey Richard Napoleon, Clerk of Civil District Court, Parish of Orleans.

of Frenchmen and Amour (North Rampart) Streets.[46] Jean-Louis Dolliole witnessed and signed the contract to vouch for his sons' work. By 1840, the pair had formed a legally binding partnership. In 1840 and 1841, they contracted to teach young men of color the profession of carpentry building (*"profession de menuisier de bâtiment"*). Another building contract survives for the men's construction of a double Creole cottage and outbuildings—kitchen, double latrine, well, cistern—for Marguerite Dauphine on St. Philip Street between Prieur and Johnson Streets in 1848.[47] Either Drausin or Emile had learned at least the rudiments of architectural drawing, for the contract included specifications with plans (floor plans and elevations) that were prepared by them (figure 5.1). In the 1840s and 1850s, the firm's shop was listed in city directories at Jean-Louis Dolliole's properties on St. Philip Street in Faubourg Tremé. The partnership (alternately referred to as Dolliole and Errié or Errié and Dolliole) last appears in the 1851 city directory; both men continue to be listed individually as carpenters. Through this partnership, the Dolliole family perpetuated familial involvement in the building trades in several ways: via paternal training and support, female (in this case, maternal) sponsorship of education, and intermarriage. This type of passing down of the trades has had far-reaching consequences in the Dolliole family. Young men in every generation have pursued careers in building/construction-related trades (table 5.4). Louis Dolliole's line died out—neither Pierre nor Joseph nor Jean-Louis's sons had male offspring[48]—but continued via Jean François's descendants. Milford Dolliole (1903–1994), a world-famous jazz trumpeter, was a plasterer. As late as 1996, Albert Basam Dolliole Jr. was noted as being a "self-employed construction worker."[49]

The Dollioles and the Souliés were "raised to the trade"—learning the business of building construction, property development, and real estate speculation from their parents, relatives, and other members of the *gens de couleur libres* community. They continued the cycle of tangibly improving the city, enhancing Creole architectural forms and introducing newer popular building types and styles, all while creating enclaves for the *gens de couleur libres* community in the changing physical and social climate of antebellum New Orleans. The distinction between Louisiana-born and foreign *gens de couleur libres* had little effect during the antebellum era. Conflict in the practice and art of building did not exist between native-born and émigré men of color who worked together, hired one another, taught one another. Instead, free men of color builders battled the developing hierarchies in the building profession and the popularization of Anglo forms, two issues that were exacerbated by increasing racial and ethnic tensions in the antebellum South.

TABLE 5.4. OCCUPATIONS OF MALE MEMBERS OF THE DOLLIOLE FAMILY, 1763-1994

Family Member	Occupation
Louis Antoine (1742–1822)	Publican/Planter
Jean-Louis (1779–1861)	**Joiner/Cabinetmaker/Carpenter/Builder**
Louis Drausin (1812–1864)	**Carpenter**
François (1821–unknown)	Unknown
Pierre (unknown–1822)	Shoemaker
Joseph (1790–1868)	**Carpenter/Joiner**
Jean François (1760–1815)	Unknown
Louis Laurent (1806–1828)	Unknown
Etienne Adam (ca. 1799–1871)	**Mason**
Joseph Hypolite (1834–1837)	N/a
Giraud William (1839–unknown)	**Plasterer**/Cigar Maker
Jules R. (1863–unknown)	**Carpenter?**
Mathias (1841–1908)	Cigar Maker
Jean Simon (1870–1919)	Cooper
Joseph Isidore (1873–unknown)	Cooper
Milford (1903–1994)	**Plasterer**
Louis Eugene (1881–unknown)	Cooper
Albert (1876–1881)	N/a
Zepherin Bernard (1843–unknown)	Shoemaker
Bernard (1869–unknown)	Unknown
Joseph Adrien (1846–1879)	Unknown
J. Armand (1873–1878)	N/a
Guy (1871–unknown)	Unknown
Dionis Adrien (1886–unknown)	Unknown
Jules Eveque (1848–1877)	Shoemaker
Jules (1886–unknown)	**Carpenter?**
Joseph Pantheleon (1809–1847)	Clerk
Edmond (1816–1894)	**Carpenter**
Jean Edmond (1842–unknown)	Unknown
Jean François (1844–unknown)	Unknown
Pierre (1848–unknown)	Unknown

Note: Jobs in the building trades are bolded. Milford Dolliole had four brothers whose occupations are unknown to the author. For more biography on Milford Dolliole, see John Ethan Hankins, ed., Raised to the Trade: Creole Building Arts of New Orleans (New Orleans: New Orleans Museum of Art, 2002) and D Obituaries, Orleans Parish, Louisiana, submitted by New Orleans Volunteer Association, accessed January 19, 2011, updated April 2005, http://files.usgwarchives.net/la/orleans/obits/1/d-13.txt.

To keep up with the diversification necessitated by the influx of Americans, northeastern architects, and Federal style architecture, free builders of color expanded their range of work and the economic possibilities of property ownership by buying immense amounts of property. But the restrictions and disadvantages under which urban free Blacks labored in their "occupational opportunity" were of two kinds—legal and societal.[50] In addition, craft training was eventually superseded by educational training.[51] At first, few changes occurred financially as far as the economic standing of well-to-do *gens de couleur libres* entrepreneurs. But in the 1830s, the arrival of Irish and German immigrants in large numbers began to cause the displacement of free persons of color from various vocations, including the building trades; this trend was particularly apparent by the 1840s and 1850s.[52] The status of free builders of color changed in that they were lumped together as craftsmen. The addition of theoretical knowledge to the training of architects and a new degree of corporate (as opposed to communal) organization changed the field from architecture as craft to architecture as profession. For the new American architect, like Benjamin Henry Latrobe ("the first professional" architect), *gens de couleur libres* builders were men "who know nothing but the practice, and whose early life being spent in labor, and in the habits of a laborious life, have had no opportunity to acquire the theory."[53] For one of the few occupational fields in which *gens de couleur libres* did have the "possibilities of enrichment," they came into conflict with builders and architects whose ideas and work quickly became the status quo in the young American city.[54] Latrobe went on to say that the struggle with such mechanics would be "long and harassing."[55] The battle that was more difficult, however, was for *gens de couleur libres* builders to gain and retain the recognition they deserved.

CHAPTER 6

THE STATUS QUO

French, Creole, and Anglo Builders and Architects in Antebellum New Orleans

I have been at war with architecture all my life and will continue so to the end, having all New York in my favor. *(Emphasis in original)*
WILLIAM BRAND, ACCORDING TO BENJAMIN HENRY LATROBE (1819)

... determined to run the hazard of New Orleans.
JAMES GALLIER SR., *AUTOBIOGRAPHY* (1864)

The first architects in New Orleans were French engineers who laid out the city grid and established the vernacular and high-style French architectural vocabularies of the Vieux Carré. Inserting some of their own building sensibility, the Spanish maintained the work and traditions of the French, even after devastating fires destroyed large portions of the city in the late eighteenth century. Spanish rule brought about the birth of the *gens de couleur libres* population and the beginnings of the Creole builder—Black and white. The Treaty of Paris (1763) entitled French immigrants to the status of native-born Louisianans.[1] The Louisiana Purchase in 1803 was followed by an influx of Anglo settlers, as well as new immigrants from Britain and France, seeking economic gains in New Orleans. The newcomers included new builders answering the needs of the growing, nascent American city and looking for their own personal and professional enrichment. From the 1820s through the 1840s, *gens de couleur libres* builder-architects and their white Creole counterparts were simultaneously influenced by American, British, and French architects looking to cater to New Orleans's diverse population and to leave their own stamp on the city.[2] The 1840s brought to the scene additional European immigrants—Irish and German—who transformed the built environment via their settlement patterns and willingness to work in almost any capacity for social and economic advancement. It was in this environment, with the establishment of all these competing groups, that the nineteenth-century prejudice against Black craftsmen—enslaved or free—began.

Little competition existed between free Negroes and whites in the colonial period or in the territorial era (1804–1812).[3] When looking for a builder to construct the new clock tower of the St. Louis Cathedral in the summer of 1819, Norbert Soulié was one of those from whom the city council suggested Mayor Augustin Macarty, member of a prominent Creole family, solicit proposals when no other bids were forthcoming.[4] The other architects recommended were the leading white practitioners of the day—Benjamin Henry Latrobe (English), Claude Gurlie (French), Joseph Guillot (French), and Joachim Courcelle (Creole). While the vague reference to Norbert as "Mr. Soulié, Jr." perhaps denotes some unwillingness on the part of the city's governing body to draw attention to the fact that they were soliciting work from a free man of color whose white father was a staff member of the Macarty administration,[5] the fact remains that they did, and that they considered his work (if not the man) equal to that of the others. The city's request stems from their first-hand knowledge of Norbert's work, familiarity with the services and skills of *gens de couleur libres* builders, and the general labor situation in New Orleans. The fact that most whites harbored little resentment toward labor by men of color "reflected the prevailing shortage of all kinds of labor in America."[6]

Civic improvements, particularly the watering and paving of streets, installation of lamp posts, and improvement of sanitation conditions, were primary goals of Macarty's successor, Louis Philippe Joseph de Roffignac. Early during Roffignac's term (1820–1828), in a change from their hiring practices just a few years earlier, New Orleans's city council, "in an action of little practical economic importance to Blacks—directed the 'municipal labor manager' to employ only white workers" in 1822.[7] While exclusion from working on municipal projects ultimately did not jeopardize the output and economic gain of free builders of color who worked primarily in the residential sphere, this action curtailed any possibility of their involvement in lucrative municipal projects during the city's greatest period of economic growth. Though the city council was still dominated by French Creoles, the decree was likely influenced by the growth of the city outside of the Vieux Carré and the developmental aims of the predominantly Anglo inhabitants of those areas. With the increasing number of white building practitioners in New Orleans, removal of free Blacks from the roster would have eased any competition they had with Anglo builders and architects. The rivalry for physical space and economic prosperity between the French, Creoles, and Americans played a large part in the relegation of *gens de couleur libres* builders to a lesser sphere. Further, most European and Anglo builders and architects (French Creoles being a notable exception) worked in high-style forms and architectural modes that drew on a different building culture than that of the *gens de couleur libres*.

FRENCH ARCHITECTS AND HIGH-STYLE EUROPEAN ARCHITECTURE IN NEW ORLEANS

The city of New Orleans was designed by French engineers and architects, many of whom were in military service. During the Spanish colonial period, Gilberto Guillemard (dates unknown)[8] was responsible for rebuilding the St. Louis Cathedral (1791–1795), the Presbytère (1791–1813), and the Cabildo (1795–1799) after the original buildings were destroyed in the fire of 1788.[9] His designs reflect the Spanish Colonial neoclassicism that was prevalent in the city at the time. In an effort to improve the building's appearance and appeal, a central tower in the same fashion was added by Benjamin Henry Latrobe in 1819 (figure 6.1).[10]

Over the course of the 1810s and 1820s, city surveyors replaced colonial architects and took up the reins of designing for and building in the city. Barthélémy Lafon (1769–1820) immigrated to New Orleans to escape the French Revolution.[11] The engineer and surveyor drew many city plans and maps; he also platted new subdivisions such as Faubourg Sainte-Marie and Faubourgs Duplantier, Saulet, La Course, and Annunciation from former plantations. Lafon's private commissions included designs for homes for prominent New Orleanians such as the notary Pierre Pedesclaux in 1795 and Vincent Rillieux (grandfather of first cousins Norbert Soulié and Edmond Rillieux) in 1800.[12] The Vincent Rillieux residence (ca. 1800; figure 6.2) is Spanish Colonial in form and style. Lafon's work shows that the influence of Spanish architecture, though late to arrive given the persistence of French Colonial architecture, lasted well beyond Spanish rule of the city.

The city surveyor Jacques Tanesse (dates unknown) also created numerous city maps and, in 1813, designed a permanent Halles des Boucheries, or meat market, after the original was destroyed by a hurricane in 1812 (figure 6.3).[13] Tanesse's new building was a simple, classical design and the first building in what has become known as the French Market.[14] Major Arsène Lacarrière Latour, a military engineer, and Jean-Hyacinthe Laclotte were additional Frenchmen who worked both independently and as a team on various New Orleans commissions in the 1810s and 1820s.[15] Lafon, Tanesse, Latour, and Laclotte transferred European architectural sensibilities to the colonial and territorial city, imbuing many civic and religious

Figure 6.1. Cabildo, St. Louis Cathedral, Presbytère. Detail from *Topographical Map of New Orleans and Its Vicinity. Charles F. Zimpel surveyor, 1833*. The Collins C. Diboll Vieux Carré Digital Survey at The Historic New Orleans Collection.

ENGAGEMENT

Figure 6.2. 339–343 Royal Street (Vincent Rillieux House). Barthélémy Lafon, ca. 1800. Photo by John Watson Riley, 2010. The Collins C. Diboll Vieux Carré Digital Survey at The Historic New Orleans Collection.

buildings with grand European styles while at the same time incorporating Creole building forms and design elements, primarily in residential buildings.

French builder-architects productive in the antebellum period maintained the architectural traditions of the city's French founders and Creole progenitors but became increasingly proficient in the Federal and Greek Revival styles introduced by architects from the American eastern seaboard. The builders and partners Jean Felix Pinson and Maurice Pizetta (dates unknown) were among the most popular builders and architects (figure 6.4). In the Vieux Carré, they had a hand in building two *porte cochère* townhouses with a mixture of Creole and Greek Revival style architectural details—one a speculative venture on Royal Street in 1825, the other designed for Paul Lacroix in 1833.[16] The former is clearly a more traditional Creole townhouse (the attic frieze level and molded window lintels were added ca. 1837), while the latter has a Greek Revival style paneled door and surround as well as Creole arched openings. Both houses retain their Creole wrought-iron *garde-de-frise* balconies.[17] On the edge of the Vieux Carré on Canal Street, the team built storehouses—essentially rowhouses adapted for the ground floors to serve as commercial space—in the Federal style in the 1820s.[18] Independently, Pinson and Pizetta were also property developers in Faubourg

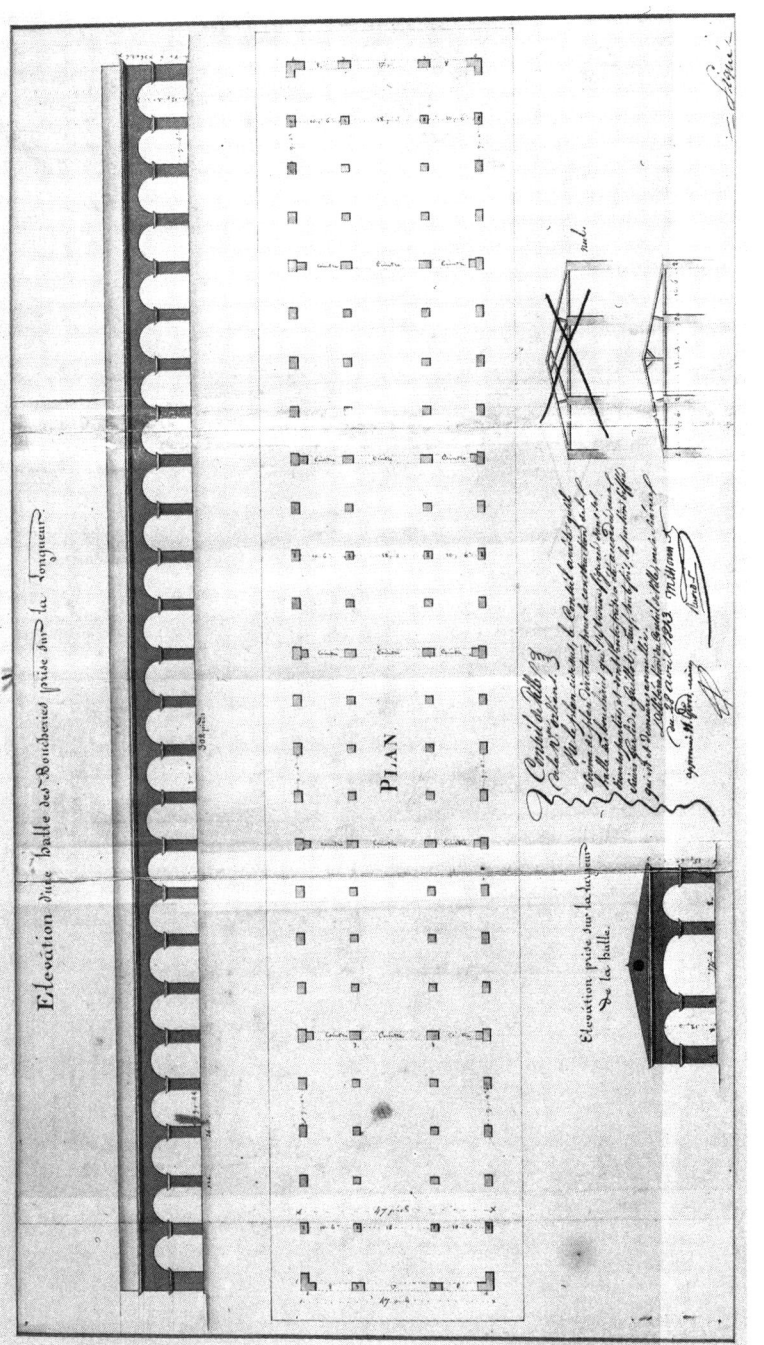

Figure 6.3. Halles des Boucheries (Meat Market)/French Market. Jacques Tanesse, 1813. Possibly delineated by Gurlie and Guillot, contractors. The Collins C. Diboll Vieux Carré Digital Survey at The Historic New Orleans Collection.

 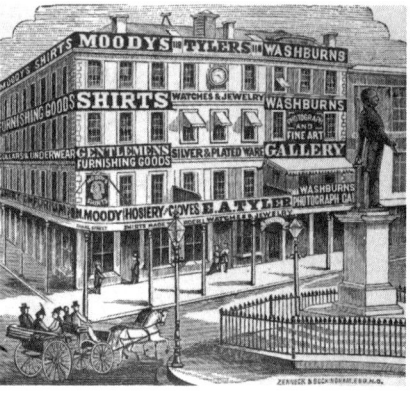

Figure 6.4. Buildings by Jean Felix Pinson and Maurice Pizetta. Left: 501–509 Canal Street (1821). The Collins C. Diboll Vieux Carré Digital Survey at The Historic New Orleans Collection. Right: 633–637 Canal Street (1825). Drawing by Zenneck and Buckingham, from The Stranger's Guide to the City of New Orleans *(J. B. Bradford, 1874). The Collins C. Diboll Vieux Carré Digital Survey at The Historic New Orleans Collection.*

Tremé in the 1820s and 1830s. Like the Dollioles', Pinson's property acquisitions included former Collège d'Orléans property.[19]

Jacques Nicolas Bussière de Pouilly (1804–1875) established a high-profile career designing and building some of the city's greatest landmarks.[20] One of his earliest works was the Greek Revival St. Louis Hotel in the Vieux Carré (1835)—the Creoles' attempt to keep up with building activity in Faubourg Sainte-Marie (figure 6.5).[21] He also designed a Federal style Creole *entresol* townhouse in the middle of the decade.[22] In 1837, he created a master design for a pedestrian approach from Canal Street to the new St. Louis Hotel (figure 6.6). Passage de la Bourse, or Exchange Passage, was an experiment in city planning. For a length of four blocks, the buildings lining Exchange Passage (Place) were to have façades with more or less uniform arcades at ground level and classical architectural features. The design was subsequently realized by de Pouilly and other leading architects, both French and American (618 Conti Street/336 Exchange Place).

De Pouilly's practice expanded when he established a partnership with builder Ernest Goudchaux between 1842 and 1845.[23] The firm of J. N. de Pouilly and Ed. Goudchaux, Architects and Builders, completed contracts for St. Augustine Church (1841–1842), the new American Theatre, and various private residences.[24] The pair continued to work together after the dissolution of the partnership. In 1845, de Pouilly served as superintending architect for the remodel of the Orleans

Figure 6.5. St. Louis Hotel. J. N. B. de Pouilly, 1835. Photographer and date unknown. George François Mugnier Photograph Collection, Louisiana Division/City Archives, New Orleans Public Library.

Figure 6.6. Exchange Place: Entrance to Hotel Royale. *Photographer and date unknown. George François Mugnier Photograph Collection, Louisiana Division/City Archives, New Orleans Public Library.*

Figure 6.7. St. Louis Cathedral. J. N. B. de Pouilly and Samuel Stewart, 1851. Photo by John Watson Riley, 2011. The Collins C. Diboll Vieux Carré Digital Survey at The Historic New Orleans Collection.

Theatre and built a series of five Greek Revival houses on Chartres Street as rental properties.[25] His work is highlighted by two religious buildings. In 1846, he designed Notre Dame des Victoires Church adjacent to the Ursuline Convent. He then redesigned the majority of the front façade of St. Louis Cathedral in an early Classical Revival style in 1850.[26] When the tower and some walls collapsed during construction, de Pouilly was replaced by Samuel Stewart, who completed the work with several modifications (figure 6.7). De Pouilly not only brought French classicism to New Orleans, he gradually incorporated the Greek Revival style into the city's architectural vocabulary, first combining it with familiar Creole forms.[27]

THE STATUS QUO

Frenchmen Claude Gurlie (ca. 1772–unknown) and Joseph Guillot (ca. 1771–1838) began their partnership in 1795.[28] Starting off as builders, they created early works in 1811 that included designs by Latour and Laclotte—the Castillon House and a Creole cottage housing the other designers' atelier.[29] In 1812, Gurlie and Guillot designed the Collège d'Orléans (figure 6.8) with its classically inspired columns, and in 1813, they completed the second floor of Guillemard's Presbytère and supervised construction of Tanesse's meat market.[30] The pair later added a fish market to the complex.[31] Residential commissions in the 1810s included the 1815 *entresol* storehouse for Jean Baptiste Cottin, an 1817 Spanish Colonial townhouse on St. Peter Street, and an 1819 Creole townhouse with Federal style features for Arnaud Magnon.[32] In Faubourg Tremé, they built the Classical Revival style Mortuary Chapel of St. Anthony of Padua (1826–1827), with a first-floor arcade reminiscent of that at the Cabildo (figure 6.9).[33] They designed and built the Gally House in 1830 and implemented the American rowhouse in the Vieux Carré as speculative commercial buildings and housing for the Ursuline nuns (1830–1832). At the Vignié townhouses (1833), Gurlie and Guillot incorporated Federal style ornamentation and architectural details on rowhouses with Creole characteristics (figure 6.10).[34] The pair also designed neighboring townhouses on Royal Street for Jean Baptiste Zenon Cavelier, president of the Bank of Orleans, in 1831.[35] They built a Creole townhouse with Federal style second-story windows for Joseph Adolphe Tricou on Bourbon Street the following year (figure 6.11). Gurlie and Guillot also designed and built commercial buildings in de Pouilly's Exchange Passage. Like de Pouilly, Gurlie and Guillot worked comfortably in traditional Creole forms and colonial styles but increasingly incorporated characteristics of Federal and Greek Revival style architecture—wrought-iron balconies, arcaded ground stories, dormer windows, and wooden cornices with garland ornamental

Figure 6.8. Collège d'Orléans. Gurlie and Guillot, 1812. From Henry Castellanos, New Orleans as It Was: Episodes of Louisiana Life, *2nd edition (New Orleans: L. Graham, 1905).*

Figure 6.9. Mortuary Chapel of St. Anthony of Padua. Gurlie and Guillot. 1819. Confederate Museum, Louisiana Historical Association, New Orleans. From Leonard V. Huber, Louisiana: A Pictorial History (New York: Charles Scribner's Sons, 1975), page 119.

Figure 6.10. 713–719 Royal Street (Vignié townhouses). Gurlie and Guillot, 1833. Photo by John Watson Riley, 2010. The Collins C. Diboll Vieux Carré Digital Survey at The Historic New Orleans Collection.

Figure 6.11. 711 Bourbon Street. Gurlie and Guillot, 1832. Photo by John Watson Riley, 2010. The Collins C. Diboll Vieux Carré Digital Survey at The Historic New Orleans Collection.

detail. While de Pouilly's career extended into the 1840s and 1850s, by the mid- to late 1830s most French architects and builders had quit designing or had died. The field was left open to the city's native-born French Creoles.[36]

CREOLE BUILDERS AND ARCHITECTS

New Orleanians descended from other European nationals (Italian, German, etc.) were also considered Creoles, but, by and large, the French and Spanish dominated that ethnic group. The Spanish presence decreased with the end of Spanish rule when Spanish Creoles, many of the men officials and soldiers, returned to Spain or relocated to other Spanish-ruled dominions.[37] Despite their predominance in the city until the abundant arrivals of Americans and immigrant Europeans, few high-profile white Creole builders or architects can be found in the secondary records of the colonial, territorial, or antebellum periods. The Creoles were known for living leisurely lives as gentlemen. Indeed, many were planters with *habitations* along the Bayou Road and larger plantations on the Mississippi River. But, as the leaders of New Orleans society, many Creole men were political leaders and merchants. Further, in this plantation society, buildings in both rural and urban settings were commonly erected by enslaved labor. Still, French Creoles—émigré and native-born—took part in creating and developing the transitional nature of New Orleans's architecture in the antebellum period.

The Courcelle family, like the Dollioles, consisted of several generations of builders. Achille Courcelle was a master carpenter who immigrated to New Orleans from Véry, France, by 1768, when he married Marie Anne Bernard in St. Louis Cathedral.[38] One of their sons, Joachim Courcelle (ca. 1776–1862),[39] was an important builder throughout his life. In 1818, Courcelle built twelve *entresol* townhouses facing the Marigny Canal (present-day Elysian Fields) for $92,000.00 and is listed on a contract to erect a building in Faubourg Sainte-Marie.[40] He entered into indenture contracts as an apprentice supervisor in 1829, 1830, and 1832. The first-generation Souliés likely acquired some of their building knowledge from Joachim Courcelle, as he was their "uncle by marriage."[41] Etienne François Courcelle and Achille Barthélémy Courcelle, two of Joachim's white nephews (the sons of his older brother Achille Antoine), also followed in his footsteps. Etienne Courcelle (1800–unknown) built two Creole *porte cochère* townhouses for Bernard de Santos on St. Ann Street in 1840, making them the last of that type in the Vieux Carré (figure 6.12).[42] He is listed in the 1842 city directory as a bricklayer and served as the keeper and a tomb builder at St. Louis Cemetery No. 1 in the 1850s.[43] Also present in the directory, residing with his uncle Joachim, is the builder Achille Barthélémy Courcelle (1803–1864). In addition to building, like the Dolliole brothers, A. B. Courcelle speculated heavily in real estate; Bernard Soulié purchased several Tremé properties from him. A. B. Courcelle's influence lasted longer than that of his uncle Joachim or brother Etienne; he built a unique, central-hall house with Classical Revival stylistic detailing at 823 Esplanade in 1853.[44] Edward Schinkel contracted with him for the construction of a Greek Revival townhouse on Esplanade Avenue in 1856.[45]

One of the Courcelles' émigré contemporaries was Jean François Edouard Correjolles; he was born in Baltimore to parents who had fled the turbulence in Saint-Domingue.[46] After relocating to the Caribbean in 1807, the family eventually settled in New Orleans in 1809 when the French refugees were expelled from Cuba. François would have been around fourteen years of age at the time—ripe for training in building or to be sent to France for architectural education. Whichever occurred, he obtained enough skill and reputation to be considered an architect.[47] Correjolles designed many New Orleans buildings. His most well-known design is the residence known today as the Le Carpentier-Beauregard-Keyes House, built in 1826 on Chartres Street (figure 6.13).[48] The transitional house features characteristics of French Colonial and Creole architecture as well as Greek Revival style

Figure 6.12. 1009 and 1013 St. Ann Street. Etienne Courcelle, 1840. Photo by John Watson Riley, 2010. The Collins C. Diboll Vieux Carré Digital Survey at The Historic New Orleans Collection.

architectural details.[49] By 1830, Correjolles had developed a partnership with Jean Chaigneau.[50] The duo built a two-story house with interior kitchen for Perseverance Masonic Lodge No. 4 adjacent to Thibaud's lodge hall. Correjolles built an American townhouse for himself in 1831 but retained the stucco façade of Creole domestic architecture.[51] Two years later, Correjolles built a house for Eulalie Mandeville, half sister of Bernard Marigny and partner of Eugene Macarty, on Barracks Street.[52] The partnership between Correjolles and Jean Chaigneau was dissolved in 1835.[53] Correjolles continued to build vernacular forms—he was the owner-builder of a house in the 600 block of Dumaine Street in Faubourg Tremé in 1836.[54] His abilities extended to serving in a supervisory capacity; Correjolles was the supervising architect for the Uranie Roy House built by *homme de couleur libre* builder Louis Vivant in 1846.[55] Correjolles also served as a teacher to New Orleans youths seeking careers in the building trades. One of them was a *jeune de couleur libre* sponsored by Louise Paul Cheval, a Soulié relation.[56] Samuel Wilson Jr.

Figure 6.13. 1113 Chartres Street (Le Carpentier-Beauregard-Keyes House). François Correjolles, 1826. Photo by John Watson Riley, 2010. The Collins C. Diboll Vieux Carré Digital Survey at The Historic New Orleans Collection.

emphasizes Correjolles's "accidental birth," noting that "he was perhaps the first native born American to achieve success as an architect in New Orleans and his work consistently reflects the American influence in local Creole Architecture."[57] On the one hand, this observation seems to diminish Correjolles's Creole heritage and highlights the problematic distinction that Creole architecture is something separate from American architecture. While Creole architecture was developed during the colonial period, it was still very much in favor and continuing to evolve after Louisiana became a US territory and then state. But, on the other hand, Wilson's statement underscores the fact that Creole architecture and Anglo-American architecture were harmoniously synthesized through the early years of the antebellum period.

ANGLO ARCHITECTS AND THE FEDERAL AND GREEK REVIVAL STYLES

The differences between American Anglos and New Orleans inhabitants of European descent were not so drastic when Americans began to arrive post-Purchase and even more so after the Battle of New Orleans in 1815. The Creoles "realized the advantages of American citizenship. They embraced Americanism with fervent devotion and glorified in the change of status from being a subject to that of being a citizen."[58] While maintaining their building traditions, New Orleans Creoles adapted aspects of popular American styles—Federal then Greek Revival—into and onto their traditional forms. Likewise, they welcomed American architects, many of whom worked in Creole forms in addition to bringing their own methods and practices to the city's antebellum building activity. Among the first group of arrivals who would shape the melding of Creole and Anglo architecture and have influence in the antebellum period were Benjamin Henry Latrobe (1764–1820) and William Brand (1778–1849).

Benjamin Henry Latrobe was complimentary of Creole architecture's adaptation to New Orleans's climate and urban environment. The English-born architect embarked on his US career on the East Coast, designing and building in America's largest cities—Richmond, Virginia; Philadelphia; Washington, DC; and Pittsburgh. He designed the New Orleans Customhouse (1807) and the engine house for the city waterworks (1811–1812). He relocated to the city in 1819 to finish the waterworks project started by his son Henry.[59] Latrobe's admiration of the form and design of Creole domestic architecture is visible in the Creole townhouse he built in 1819 for Vincent Nolte on Toulouse Street (figure 6.14).[60] The architect ushered in the antebellum period with his design for the Louisiana State Bank (1820; figure 6.15).[61] The last work of his career was the central tower for St. Louis Cathedral (1820). Latrobe's residence in New Orleans was brief before he succumbed to yellow fever in 1820. He opened the door for the introduction and acceptance of Federal architecture in New Orleans—used by French, Creole, and Anglo builders alike—early in the post-Purchase period and paved the way for the next wave of American architects in the 1830s.

A Virginia native, William Brand came to New Orleans by 1805, when he is listed in the city directory.[62] His works included the first Orleans Theatre (1809, brickwork); Destrehan House (1811); Orleans Theatre and Ballroom (1817, bricklaying, plastering); and First Presbyterian Church (1819).[63] His domestic and commercial works were also numerous and located in both the Vieux Carré and the American Sector. Three circa 1827 transitional Creole townhouses still stand on St. Louis Street.[64] In 1830, he built a group of warehouses on the corner of Magazine and Poydras Streets for James Maxwell Reynolds.[65] The following year, he designed for commission merchant Samuel Hermann the now-famous Federal style American townhouse, with a central hall, on St. Louis Street (figure 6.16). In 1833, Brand built a row of five Federal style three-story storehouses at the corner of Canal and St. Charles Streets.[66] He also participated in various competitions for municipal buildings. While his early public works were in a variety of

Figure 6.14. 535–541 Royal Street/708–710 Toulouse Street (Vincent Nolte House/"Court of Two Lions"). Benjamin Henry Latrobe, 1819. Photo by Dan Leyrer, 1963. The Collins C. Diboll Vieux Carré Digital Survey at The Historic New Orleans Collection.

Figure 6.15. 403–407 Royal Street (Louisiana State Bank). Benjamin Henry Latrobe, 1820. Photo by John Watson Riley, 2010. The Collins C. Diboll Vieux Carré Digital Survey at The Historic New Orleans Collection.

Figure 6.16. 818–820 St. Louis Street (Hermann-Grima House). William Brand, 1831. Photographer and date unknown. The Collins C. Diboll Vieux Carré Digital Survey at The Historic New Orleans Collection.

styles—Federal and Creole in the Vieux Carré but Gothic Revival in the growing American Sector—his works throughout the city were consistently in the Federal style. Brand's commitment to the latter style was exhibited when he maintained the look of exposed brick by painting the exterior walls "with two good coats of red paint and the joints penciled neatly with white lead."[67] He also disagreed with his good friend Latrobe when the latter criticized Brand over the "London plan" home he was designing for himself on Magazine Street.[68]

Two decades after Latrobe's death, several Anglo architects arrived in New Orleans, including Alexander Thompson Wood, James and Charles Dakin, and James Gallier Sr. This generation ushered the Greek Revival style into the city. Alexander Wood (1804–1854) designed the "Thirteen Sisters," a series of Federal style townhouses on Julia Street in 1833. But by 1847, his design for the US Custom House featured all of the characteristics of Greek Revival architecture (figure 6.17). The building, a significant steel and granite monument occupying a full

Figure 6.17. 423 Canal Street (U.S. Custom House). Alexander T. Wood, 1848. From the Daily Delta, *February 13, 1848. The Collins C. Diboll Vieux Carré Digital Survey at The Historic New Orleans Collection.*

block on the Vieux Carré side of Canal Street, features a temple front façade with a rusticated base and projecting cornice. The lotus capitals on the entry bays' columns are a nod to the simultaneous interest in Egyptian temple architecture during the early nineteenth century. Some of Wood's contemporaries argued that he stole the idea for the Custom House from designs submitted previously by the architectural firm of Dakin and Gallier.

Brothers and New York natives James H. Dakin (1806–1852) and Charles Bingley Dakin (1812–1839) arrived in New Orleans in the mid-1830s via separate routes. Charles arrived in the city in 1834 with James Gallier, an Irish-born architect who had immigrated to the United States via England in 1832. Dakin and Gallier together began an architectural firm that was favored by wealthy members of the Irish-American community. The partners erected a row of three Greek Revival style townhouses on North Rampart in 1834 (figure 6.18).[69] Their works in the mid-1830s included the Verandah Hotel (1835), St. Charles Hotel (1835), and the Merchant's Exchange (1836; figure 6.19). James arrived in New Orleans in 1835, and the Dakin brothers formed their own practice one month later on December 24, 1835. Charles then moved to Mobile, Alabama, in 1836 and subsequently lived in Europe from 1838 to 1839. St. Patrick's Church was completed under Dakin and Dakin in 1838. Charles Dakin died in Iberville Parish in 1839. James Dakin then proceeded to have an illustrious solo career designing Greek Revival buildings in New Orleans, including the Louisiana State Arsenal (1839) as well as Canal Bank and the Medical College of Louisiana in 1843.[70] Shortly thereafter, James Dakin relocated to Baton Rouge to commence work on his design for the Gothic Revival Louisiana State Capitol in 1847. He died in that city in May 1852.[71]

James Gallier Sr. was an Irish-born architect who worked as a carpenter in Dublin, then as an architect in London, in New York (at the firm of Town and Davis), and then in Mobile, Alabama, where he met and worked with Charles Dakin.[72] In his autobiography, Gallier gives the reason for his decision to relocate to New Orleans, "But having heard that any person well acquainted with the practice of building, as well as having a fair knowledge of architecture as an art, could scarcely fail of success in the United States of America, I therefore came to the conclusion that [in New Orleans] lay the proper field for my labours."[73]

After the partnership with Charles Dakin was dissolved, Gallier pursued a successful solo career with architectural offices on Common and Carondelet Streets. He was responsible for a bevy of Vieux Carré residences in diverse forms and styles, including the Angel Xiques House (1830s), Jacques-Philippe Meffre-Rouzan House (1838–1840), James Dick House (1847), Charles Briggs House (1849), and the Michel Musson House (attributed).[74] His civic, commercial, and institutional works were plentiful. When a new waterworks system was designed in the Lower Garden District in the mid-1830s, Gallier did some work on the reservoirs.[75]

Figure 6.18. 228, 232, 236–238 North Rampart (not extant). Photographer unknown, ca. 1920. Courtesy of Louisiana Division/City Archives, New Orleans Public Library, and The Collins C. Diboll Vieux Carré Digital Survey at The Historic New Orleans Collection.

*Figure 6.19. Works of Dakin and Gallier. Top: Verandah Hotel, from
Queen of the South. Bottom: St. Charles Hotel, courtesy of Wikimedia.*

He also assisted with the completion of Dakin and Dakin's Gothic Revival St. Patrick's Church in 1839. He occasionally utilized Creole forms and built two one-and-a-half-story Greek Revival style Creole cottages on Annunciation Street in 1843.[76] In the Lower Garden District, Gallier built Greek Revival style houses in the Coliseum Square area where he lived.[77] He is also responsible for the 1844 design of the Greek Revival townhouse for W. Newton Mercer in the 800 block of Canal Street.[78] Gallier's commercial projects were also numerous. He designed or built

Figure 6.20. 500–546 St. Peter Street (Upper Pontalba Apartment Buildings). James Gallier Sr., 1849–1851. Photo by George François Mugnier, ca. 1890. The Collins C. Diboll Vieux Carré Digital Survey at The Historic New Orleans Collection.

storehouses for R. O. Pritchard (ca. 1835), cotton factor John Hagan (1840), and the City Bank of New Orleans (1844).[79] He also designed a new building for the Canal and Banking Company in 1839 and for the Commercial Bank by 1846.[80] In 1845, the architect made designs for a Commercial Exchange on St. Charles Street. While the building was under construction, Gallier altered the design to accommodate business use on the ground floor and a Masonic lodge on the second.[81]

Gallier's Greek Revival townhouses lent themselves to speculative housing for clients. In this vein, Gallier designed rowhouses for Samuel Moore (1836) and Charles Diamond (1838).[82] On vacant lots adjacent to his offices and building yard, facing Common and Carondelet Streets, he erected buildings to serve as boarding houses, which provided him a "handsome income" at $2,000.00 each per year.[83] The Pontalba Buildings (1849–1851) were Gallier's most influential work in the Vieux Carré (figure 6.20). For the philanthropist Michaela Almonaster, Baroness de Pontalba, Gallier designed sixteen Creole townhouses on each side of the Place d'Armes as speculative properties. With their Greek Revival architectural details, Philadelphia brick exterior walls, and cast-iron balconies supported by granite columns, the rowhouses are a tour de force of urban design.[84] After Gallier's introduction of cast-iron at these buildings, it became ubiquitous in the

Figure 6.21. 545 St. Charles Street (Municipal Hall/City Hall/Gallier Hall). James Gallier, 1850. Photo by Lester Jones, 1940. Library of Congress, Historic American Buildings Survey, Call No. HABS LA,36-NEWOR,21-, Survey No. HABS LA-193.

Vieux Carré, replacing the familiar wrought-iron and *garde-de-frise* work that had been prevalent before. After Gallier quarreled with the difficult baroness, the rowhouses were completed to final designs by Henry Howard (1818–1884). The Irish-born Howard also added his stamp to 1850s New Orleans. Among this work was an addition to the Louisiana Sugar Refinery built by Norbert Soulié and Edmond Rillieux twenty years before.

Completed in 1850, Gallier's Municipal Hall for the Second District (begun in 1845) was New Orleans's last civic stamp of approval of the Greek Revival style and highlighted Gallier's proficiency in the architectural style that he helped establish in the city (figure 6.21). Between 1820 and 1850, New Orleans's most important public buildings were increasingly designed in the Federal and then Greek Revival styles (table 6.1). The Municipal Hall is symbolic of the full transition of New Orleans—economically, socially, culturally, and architecturally—into a

TABLE 6.1. FEATURED PUBLIC BUILDINGS IN NEW ORLEANS, 1820-1850

Date	Building	Architect and/or Builder	Style	Location
1820	Louisiana State Bank	Benjamin Latrobe (architect); Benjamin Fox (builder)	Federal	Vieux Carré
1820	Perseverance Lodge No. 4	Bernard Thibaud (builder)	Federal	Tremé
1821–1824	American Theater	James Caldwell (builder)	Federal	Sainte-Marie
1826	Bank of Louisiana	Benjamin Fox (architect) Bickle and Hamlet (builders)	Federal/ Greek Revival	Vieux Carré
1830	Perseverance Lodge No. 4 *maison à étage*	Correjolles and Chaigneau (builders)	Federal	Tremé
1831–1836	Parish Prison	Pilié/Voilquin/Bourgerol/ Crozet (architects) Slack/Correjolles and Chaigneau/Gobet and Larochette (builders)	Federal	Tremé
1833	Commercial Bank	George Clarkson (architect) Daniel H. Twogood (builder)	Greek Revival	Sainte-Marie
1835	St. Charles Theatre	Antonio Mondelli (architect)	Greek Revival	Sainte-Marie
1835	US Mint	William Strickland (architect) Benjamin Fox/John Mitchell (builders)	Greek Revival	Vieux Carré
1835–1837	Exchange Hotel/ St. Charles Hotel (d)	Gallier and Dakin/James Gallier Sr. (architects)	Greek Revival	Sainte-Marie
1835	Merchant's Exchange (d)	Gallier and Dakin (architects) Daniel H. Twogood (builder)	Greek Revival	Vieux Carré
1836	City Exchange/ St. Louis Hotel	J. N B. and J. I. de Pouilly (architects)	Greek Revival	Vieux Carré
1837	Exchange Passage	J. N. B. de Pouilly (conceived)	Early Classical Revival	Vieux Carré

TABLE 6.1, CONTINUED

Date	Building	Architect and/or Builder	Style	Location
1838–1840	St. Patrick's Church	Dakin and Dakin/James Gallier Sr. (architects)	Gothic Revival	Sainte-Marie
1839	Arsenal	James Dakin (architect)	Greek Revival	Vieux Carré
1839	Tremé Market	A. J. Bourgerol (architect) Gobet and Larochette (builders)	Federal	Tremé
1841	St. Augustine Church	J. N. B. de Pouilly (architect)	Greek Revival	Tremé
1845–1850	Municipal Building/City Hall/ Gallier Hall	James Gallier Sr. (architect)	Greek Revival	Sainte-Marie
1848	US Custom House	Alexander T. Wood (architect)	Greek Revival	Vieux Carré
1849–1851	Pontalba Buildings	James Gallier Sr./Henry Howard (architects)	Greek Revival	Vieux Carré

US city. Two years after the building's completion, the governments of the three city municipalities were merged, and Gallier's building became the reunified metropolis's City Hall.

ANTEBELLUM ARCHITECTURAL PRACTICE OF WHITE ARCHITECTS AND BUILDERS

Learning and Teaching

With the exception of those who trained and worked in formal architectural offices or were educated in institutions of higher learning, French, white Creole, and Anglo architects and builders learned skills as building artisans in similar fashions as the *gens de couleur libres*. Knowledge of the building trades was passed down along male lines. No indenture contracts of apprenticeship have been found for any members of the Courcelle family. One can assume that Joachim Courcelle learned his trade from his father and then passed his knowledge on to his nephews Etienne and Achille Barthélémy. Architects also learned their professions from non-relatives. Claude Gurlie's and Joseph Guillot's service as builders early in their careers for their French predecessors Latour and Laclotte can be viewed as professional apprenticeships and would have afforded them the opportunity to become familiar with the design conventions and technical knowledge needed to design buildings

THE STATUS QUO

in the Early Classical style appropriate for New Orleans and to adapt European architectural conventions to Creole forms.

The formal apprenticeship system was as fruitful for white architects and students as for the *gens de couleur libres*. A survey of the Office of the Mayor's indenture index shows that many white architects and builders served as apprentice supervisors in contracts arranged between 1809 and 1843 (table 6.2). Indentures between white builders/architects and their apprentices followed the same format as those between *gens de couleur libres* builders and their students. One noticeable difference is the matter of compensation. Most indentures for white or Black architects and builders did not involve a stipend for the apprentice. However, in the 1832 contract between Joachim Courcelle and Maurice Populus, a free young man of color, Courcelle had to pay Populus $8.00 at the end of each month for the duration of the apprenticeship.[85] As in an architectural office or other regular course of employment, apprentices were beginning to be compensated monetarily, not just with the knowledge and skills of the trade they endeavored to learn.

TABLE 6.2. APPRENTICESHIP INDENTURES IN THE BUILDING TRADES INVOLVING SELECT BUILDERS, 1809–1843

FRENCH ARCHITECTS				
Latour and Laclotte	Arsène Latour	Gurlie and Guillot	Jean Felix Pinson	Maurice Pizetta
July 1811 (4)	July 1813 (2)	November 1823 March 1830 April 1830	June 1826 September 1827 (s) October 1827 July 1832 (2s) December 1834 (2s)	December 1826 December 1828 May 1829 May 1829 January 1832 February 1833
ANGLO ARCHITECTS		CREOLE ARCHITECTS		
William Brand	Henry B. S. Latrobe	François Correjolles	Joachim Courcelle	Correjolles and Chaigneau
November 1811 March 1812 April 1812 November 1812 August 1817 August 1818 December 1819 May 1820	December 1816	November 1825 September 1826 October 1826 November 1826 November 1827 May 1828 June 1828 September 1828	September 1829 January 1830 November 1832	May 1830 June 1830 (2)

Note: (s) indicates that the apprentice was enslaved.

Of the builders and architects surveyed in this work, those of French origin had the most indenture contracts, and the only contracts in which the apprentice was enslaved.[86] These indentures also spanned the longest time, from 1811 to 1833. Creole architects had the next highest number of indenture contracts, primarily from the mid-1820s to the early 1830s. Interestingly, only two Anglo architects and builders highlighted in *Building Antebellum New Orleans* were engaged as supervisors in apprentice indentures—William Brand in the 1810s and Henry Latrobe with one contract in 1816. The lack of contracts for the latter is understandable in that he died the next year; likewise, his father's tenure in New Orleans was very short and would have lessened his opportunity to serve as an apprentice supervisor. But this dearth of indenture contracts emphasizes the absence of figures like Alexander Wood, the Dakin brothers, and James Gallier Sr., who were actively building before 1843.[87] The reason for this is quite simple. Anglo architects at this time were beginning to develop their practices on a new model. Dakin and Gallier, especially, adopted the more formal office system through which they had been trained on the East Coast and in London. Young men would have gone to work for the architectural firm, gaining their proficiency in particular areas of their employer's expertise, as complex building forms and high-style architecture such as Greek Revival necessitated much more specialized work and training.

The Architectural Office

In his autobiography, James Gallier Sr. discusses his architectural offices. By 1835, he notes that having "bought some lots of ground fronting on Common and Carondelet in New Orleans, I there established my office and workshops, and occupied them as long as I remained in business."[88] In contrast to *gens de couleur libres* builders like the Dollioles or even Creole builders like the Courcelles, whose residences or other small residential buildings served as the hub for their practices, white architects in the antebellum period had practices separate from their homes. Gallier's office complex was quite extensive, containing a commercial building facing Common Street and a building yard with carpenters' shops.[89] Higher-level positions included that of the "foreman carpenter" and, on the business end, the bookkeeper.[90] The firm would also have employed journeymen. One builder with whom Gallier was known to have worked to construct his buildings was Edward Sewell (1805–1864).[91] Gallier did point out the "'difficulties in procuring the services of good workmen to carry out the various contracts I had in hand: I found that mechanics who understood their business, even only tolerably well, preferred taking small contracts on their own account to working for others, so that those who were to be had for hire knew little or nothing of their business.'"[92]

These higher-level builders might have been men such as the Dollioles or Souliés, or even the Courcelles. It is also possible that free craftsmen of color worked under big-name builders like Fox, Brand, and the French builders who hired them as journeymen. In these cases, the names of *gens de couleur libres* builders would not be present on building contracts, providing one explanation for their being less represented in those types of documents.

Gallier's concerns regarding the type of workmen one hired and the idea that certain types of work required certain types of expertise and supervision were certainly not unfounded. The building of the US Mint, designed by William Strickland and started in 1835, was left in the hands of the master carpenter and joiner Benjamin Fox and the master mason and builder John Mitchell.[93] While under construction, the building threatened to collapse because the support system failed. Gallier was called upon to devise a solution to prevent the building's ruin.[94] Other architectural disasters of the time included the collapse of Benjamin Latrobe's central tower for the St. Louis Cathedral in 1850. In turn, de Pouilly's tower for the church collapsed after he took over the project; this accident affected de Pouilly's ability to gain work in the latter part of his career.

Acquiring Large Commissions

The technical knowledge required to successfully construct monumental architecture was one reason *gens de couleur libres* builders (and some of their white contemporaries) had few to no commissions in the way of large public buildings. They simply did not have the knowledge or the means to execute the mastery of wooden piling and wooden cribbing for the foundation support required to make the size and weight of large buildings possible.[95] In addition, the small-scale builder would not have been able to provide all-inclusive services and materials for large buildings with high-style architectural details. Some builders and architects owned interest in related businesses such as lumber yards, sawmills, or brickyards that aided their building, contracting, and developing endeavors.[96] One such individual was James Gallier, who purchased interest in a sawmill; however, the speculative endeavor eventually caused him financial problems.[97] Still, owning or having interest in one's own timber supply would have been particularly helpful, as lumber was short in the years before the Civil War.[98] *Gens de couleur libres* builders, perhaps with the exception of the Souliés, who were mostly absent from the country and developing but not building, did not have at their disposal the materials needed for large, detailed commissions or the funds to acquire them. As evidenced by building contracts, *gens de couleur libres* were perfectly capable of providing labor and materials for modest (domestic) commissions.

Figure 6.22. Advertisement for James Mooney in Paxton's New Orleans City Directory, *1823. From Leonard V. Huber,* Louisiana: A Pictorial History *(New York: Charles Scribner's Sons, 1975), page 141.*

Location also provided an obstacle. The *gens de couleur libres* worked primarily in the Vieux Carré, Faubourg Tremé, and Faubourg Marigny. By the antebellum period, the old quarter of the city was densely built up, leaving little room for the construction of new large buildings without the destruction of others. Tremé, Marigny, and the downriver Creole faubourgs were primarily residential; their distance away from the river and the city's commercial cores would have made them unsuitable for the location of public buildings other than markets and churches. The economic development brought on by the influx of Anglo-Americans spurred development in the areas where they lived and worked *and* that were feasible for development—along Canal Street and in the American Sector. Further, most big commissions were civic projects awarded via competition (table 6.3); the city council's decree of 1822 prevented *gens de couleur libres* from submitting entries.[99] Finally, government agencies, financiers, and other individuals would have sought out the most prominent architects and builders working in the most popular styles. Practitioners were aided in this endeavor by placing advertisements in the city's

TABLE 6.3. SELECT PARTICIPATION IN ANTEBELLUM ARCHITECTURE COMPETITIONS AMONG NEW ORLEANS ARCHITECTS

Date	Building	Known Entrants
1808	Halles des Boucheries (Meat Markets)	**Lafon, Latour**, Brand
1813	Halles des Boucheries	Latrobe, Dujarreau, Gurlie and Guillot (construction), **Tanesse (design)**
1825	Mortuary Chapel of St. Anthony of Padua	**Gurlie and Guillot**, F. Correjolles, Brand, Mooney, and Lissuate
1848	US Custom House	Dakin and Gallier, **Wood**, and others

Note: Winners are highlighted in bold. Source: John Magill, "French Market Celebrates 200th Anniversary," *Preservation in Print* 18, no. 4 (May 1991): 7; Fraiser, *The French Quarter of New Orleans*, 47; Toledano and Christovich, *New Orleans Architecture*, 6:59.

newspapers and directories. James Mooney, a builder-architect, placed a notice in the 1823 city directory announcing his services as an architect, house carpenter, and measurer, highlighting his availability to create architectural drawings (i.e., elevations and sections) and to execute buildings at an affordable price (figure 6.22).[100] Even after returning to New Orleans, Soulié cousins Edmond and Norbert Rillieux placed an ad in the *New Orleans Bee* on May 19, 1834, perhaps to counteract any loss of clientele and damage to their reputations following the Sugar Refinery mishap. Emphasizing skills they learned as a builder and an engineer, the brothers announced that they could "execute 'with neatness, dispatch, and at moderate prices all kinds of maps and plots, of cities, burghs, lots, houses, factories and of machinery of every description.'"[101] Otherwise, advertisements by *gens de couleur libres* builders do not appear to have been standard; most business was gained through word-of-mouth communication as well as familial and community ties.

Gens de Couleur Libres Clientele

By no means did white architects only build large public buildings for the city, the US government, church congregations, or wealthy groups and individuals. They also designed a range of domestic buildings in diverse forms and styles. Further, their clientele was not solely Anglo-Americans. French, French Creole, and Anglo builders and architects had *gens de couleur libres* clientele. The Notarial Archives Research Center and property record searches yield information on building contracts made between several white architects and builders as well as *gens de couleur libres* clients (table 6.4). The contracts examined here were made in the 1830s and 1840s, by which time American architects and builders (and the forms and styles in which they built) would have established strongholds in the building trades and acceptance in non-Anglo communities.

TABLE 6.4. SELECT BUILT WORKS BY WHITE ARCHITECTS FOR NONWHITE CLIENTS

Architect or Builder	Date	Form (status)	Client Time Frame Cost	Current Address/ Historic Location	Faubourg
FRENCH BUILDERS					
Claude Gurlie	1840	5-bay cottage	Milne sisters Unknown $2,000–$3,000	1253–1255 North Villeré	Tremé
Claude Gurlie	1840	undetermined cottage (3)(d)	Milne sisters Unknown $2,000–$3,000	Esplanade	Tremé
J. N. B. de Pouilly	1842	Creole townhouse	Augustine Eugenie Lassize Unknown $ Unknown		Vieux Carré
FRENCH CREOLE BUILDERS					
François Correjolles	1833	unknown	Eulalie Mandeville Unknown $ Unknown	918 Barracks	Vieux Carré
ANGLO BUILDERS					
James Gallier	1836	unknown	Austin Janau Unknown $39,120	Canal at Baronne	Sainte-Marie
W. L. Atkinson (architect) Alexander Baggett (builder)	1839	American townhouses (4)	Norbert Soulié 5 months $29,500	Baronne at Lafayette	Sainte-Marie
Morris Hurley (builder)	1847	townhouse	Magdeleine Oger 2.5 months $1,550	Carondelet at Clio	Saulet

Note: (d) = demolished; (e) = extant.

A builder in his own right, the absentee landlord Norbert Soulié sought the services of a white architect and a white builder when he commissioned speculative properties in 1839. Norbert (with Albin as proxy) contracted with the Virginia native Alexander Baggett (1805–1865) to construct four two-story brick houses with attics and kitchens on the corner of Baronne and Hevia (Lafayette) Streets (figure 6.23).[102]

THE STATUS QUO

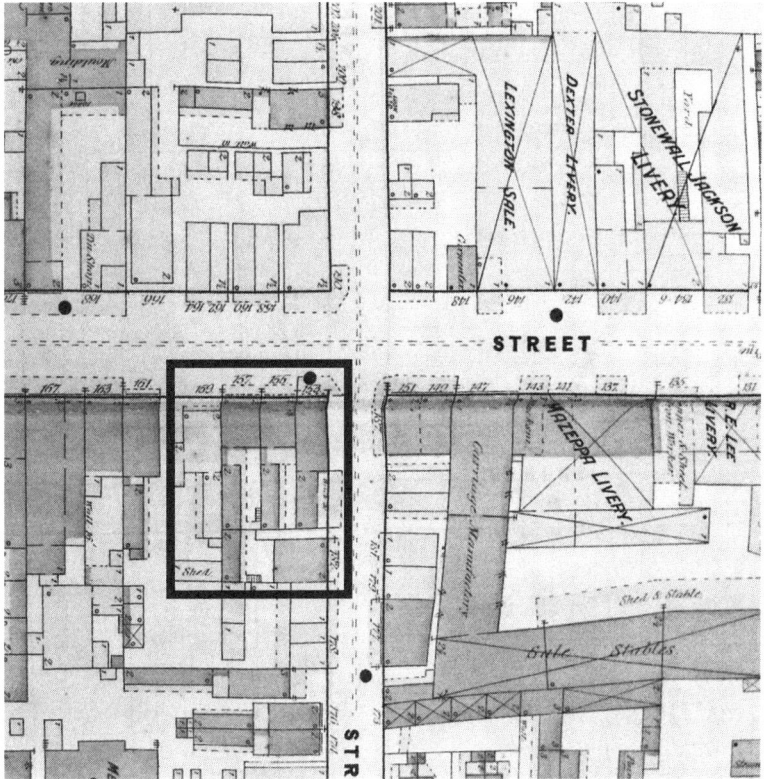

Figure 6.23. Detail of Sanborn Fire Insurance Company Map, Sheet 23, showing location of Norbert Soulié townhouses at corner of Baronne and Lafayette (formerly Hevia) Streets, 1876. Southeast Architectural Archive, Tulane University.

The four-page agreement contained precise specifications, from the dimensions of the foundations, windows, and doors to the type of hardware ("locks shall be the best American manufacture"). Unfortunately, the plans by the architect W. L. Atkinson, an Englishman, cannot be found.[103] One of the buildings was demolished by 1876, and the others have been greatly altered. The contract notes that for these buildings, "All the work [is] to be done after the same Style and the same workmanlike manner of that done to the house of Mr. William Florance in Camp Street." Like Florance's townhouses, Soulié's were to be constructed of country brick, faced with "Lake brick," "jointed & painted & penciled in the best manner," and "trimed [sic] inside with double faced Architraves and plinths."[104] The copycat nature of Greek Revival buildings in New Orleans reflected in the building contracts allows for comparison

Figure 6.24. Above and opposite: Drawings of comparative townhouses in Faubourg Sainte-Marie. Notarial Archive Research Center. Courtesy of Hon. Chelsey Richard Napoleon, Clerk of Civil District Court, Parish of Orleans.

between characteristics of Norbert Soulié's Baronne Street buildings and similar buildings in Faubourg Sainte-Marie.[105] Like Soulié's "tenements," contemporary brick townhouses were also elevated above the *banquette* and featured venetian blinds hung outside the window frames; multilight, double-hung windows (some with the lower sash "down to the floor"); iron galleries; and iron gratings sunk in the flagging (figure 6.24). The repetition of features in these Greek Revival buildings also allowed for a quick turnaround. Baggett was under a tight schedule in that he was required to have Soulié's four townhouses completed in just five months, under penalty of having to pay the rent for the properties if he was late. As recorded in the family ledgers, Norbert Soulié collected rents from these properties in the amount of $40.00 to $50.00 per month.

Renting properties was a consistent means for *gens de couleur libres* to earn income. Like the Soulié sisters, Nancy and Jane Milne were no exception. After the Milne sisters were emancipated, they were entitled to be identified as *gens de couleur libres* regardless of any mixed race.[106] Building contracts from the year 1840 survive for four commissions between the sisters and Claude Gurlie. When Alexander Milne freed the two women "for their services and the great care they had taken of him in his old age and infirmities" in his 1838 will, he stipulated that Gurlie build four houses to serve as income property for them.[107] According to the 1840 building contract between Gurlie and Alexander Milne's executor, the architect was to design and build two brick cottages at a cost of $2,000.00 each and two brick cottages at the cost of $3,000.00 each. One of these houses, a five-bay brick cottage on North Villeré Street, is extant but is altered and in poor condition.[108]

In 1842, J. N. B. de Pouilly designed a two-story Creole storehouse for *femme de couleur libre* Augustine Eugenie de Lassize on St. Peter Street. It was built by his sometime associate Ernest Goudchaux.[109] Built after de Pouilly had designed high-style public buildings like the St. Louis Hotel (1836) and Exchange Passage (1837), this house illustrates the builder-architect's retention of features found in his earlier domestic works.

Toward the end of the antebellum period in 1847, the free woman of color Magdeleine Clemence Oger contracted with Morris Hurley to build a wood house for her in Faubourg Saulet. Hurley's work was to match exactly Oger's current residence on the adjacent lot that *homme de couleur libre* architect William Kincaide had designed for her six years earlier. This commission is significant in that it provides evidence that *gens de couleur libres* lived and worked in a suburb even farther upriver than Faubourg Sainte-Marie during the antebellum period. Furthermore, in an interesting turn, a white architect is building the designs of a very talented *homme de couleur libres* architect.[110]

In the above examples, all of the French architects worked in Faubourg Tremé; the Creole architects, in the Vieux Carré; and the Anglo architects and builders, in the American Sector. So, while their *gens de couleur libres* clients were present in different parts of the city, the architects and builders of all ethnicities appear to have conducted work in the neighborhoods in which they were most familiar, in the forms and styles most prevalent in those neighborhoods.

CHANGE

As far as public architecture is concerned, white architects and East Coast types and styles did not have a problem encroaching on traditionally Creole and, more importantly, Afro-Creole places. For example, numerous buildings were erected in Faubourg Tremé—an area that was historically dominated by free people of color—in non-Creole styles by builders and architects other than *gens de couleur libres*. The Collège d'Orléans, Carondelet Canal, St. Augustine Church, Mortuary Chapel of St. Anthony of Padua, Parish Prison, and Tremé Market were all public works or buildings in which free builders or architects of color were not involved. One reason for this problem was that the building labor force in which *gens de couleur libres* builders and architects participated gained additional competitors. Increasing European immigration in the 1840s and 1850s brought craftsmen and laborers—mostly Irish and German—who sought to capture the labor market of larger towns and cities.[111] With the influx of Irish and other immigrants, racial prejudice developed within the building trades, and the idea that Blacks, including *gens de couleur libres*, were incapable as craftsmen began to take root.

Increasing racial tension played a part in the marginalization of *gens de couleur libres* building artisans and architects, but the city's American economy contributed to it more so. Opportunity and economic development during the antebellum years made growth, prosperity, cooperation, and organization possible for American architects.[112] In this period, economies were extremely localized and undercapitalized; municipal governments often depended on money from private sources for public works. Private projects were funded this way as well, and private investors focused on short-term gains.[113] This affected the more "professional" white architects, like Latrobe, who had to be careful in their expenses when designing and constructing large buildings. Likewise *gens de couleur libres* builders, working on a smaller scale with more limited finances and enterprises, would have been beyond the scope of such financiers. Free men of color like the Dollioles, Souliés, Boisdoré, Guesnon, Vivant, Courcelle, Chateau, Roup, and Fouché did not have the means, nor likely the desire, to try to underwrite ambitious private and public projects that architects like Latrobe, Dakin, and Gallier "considered worthy of their training and talent."[114] In addition to having theoretical knowledge on top of practical skill, this new professional architect became identified with "public buildings of artistic and structural excellence."[115] Like early American cities—Philadelphia, New York, Boston, Washington, DC—New Orleans was developing the East Coast mentality that being an architect carried the expectation of a certain type of elite professionalism that the *gens de couleur libres*, no matter their individual education or skills, did not manifest. Slowly, the city yielded to the mores of East Coast architecture in practice and appearance. This architectural surrender at the end of the antebellum era coincided with another takeover. In the most detailed and lengthy entry in his journal, Bernard Soulié notes that French Creole builder Joachim Courcelle (his uncle by marriage) died at noon on April 29, 1862. After Union troops had occupied the city on the previous day (April 28), "He went to throw himself into the Carondelet Canal, pushed by sadness."[116] New Orleans surrendered to Admiral David G. Farragut on April 30, 1862, officially ending the antebellum era in Louisiana.

Plate 1. Norbert Soulié (1793–1869). Date and photographer unknown. Photograph courtesy of Soulié Family, Paris, France.

Plate 2. Bernard Soulié (1801–1881). Date and photographer unknown. Photograph courtesy of Soulié Family, Paris, France.

*Plate 3. Albin Soulié (1803–1873). Date and artist unknown.
Drawing courtesy of Soulié Family, Paris, France.*

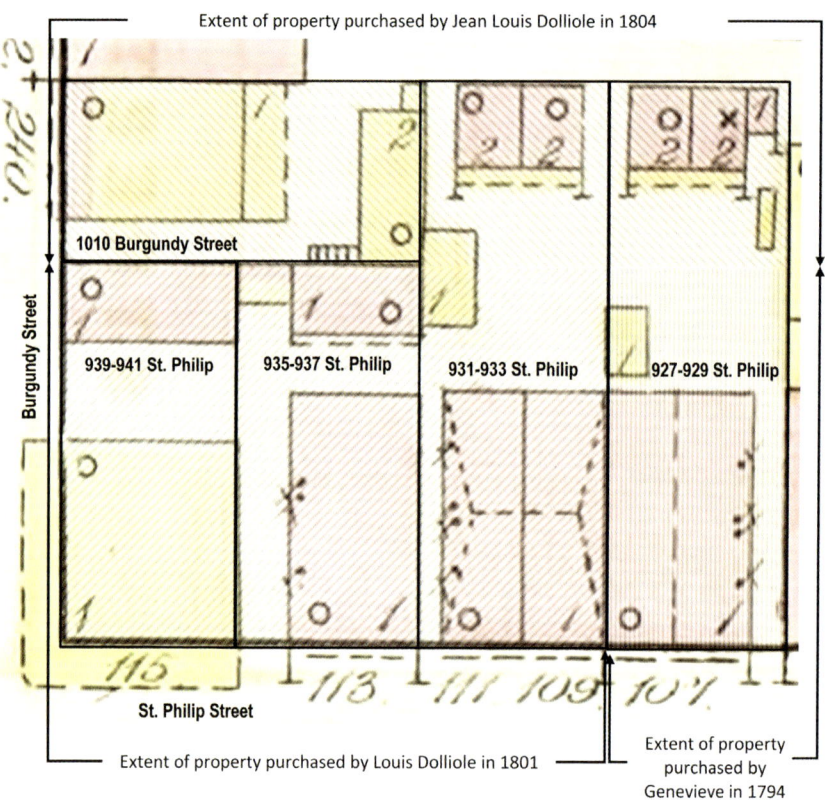

Plate 4. Chronicle of Dolliole-owned property in the 900 block of St. Philip Street, 1794–1854, overlaid on detail of 1876 Sanborn Fire Insurance Company map. Sanborn Fire Insurance Maps, New Orleans, Louisiana, 1876, sheet 34, Collection 125, Southeastern Architectural Archive, Tulane University Special Collections, New Orleans, Louisiana.

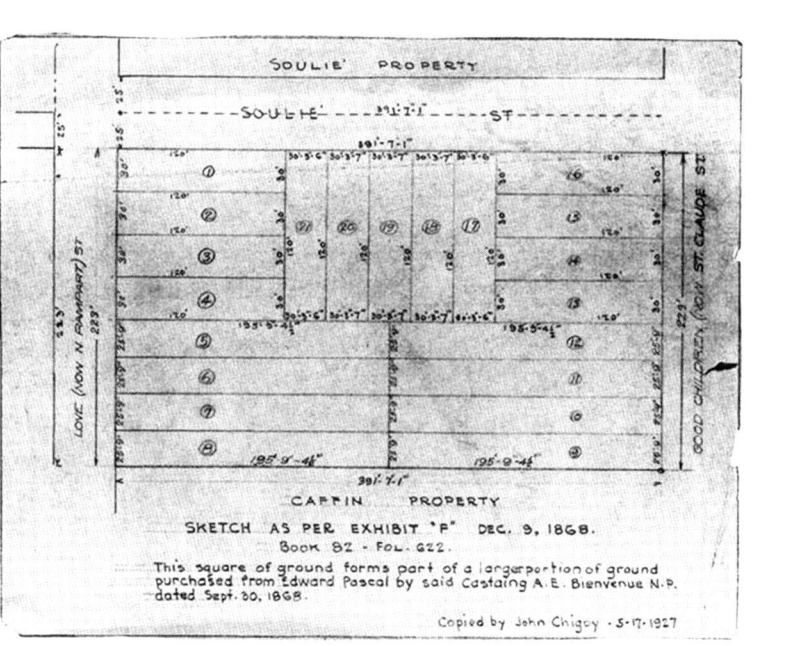

Plate 5. Plan of "Soulié Property" bound by Love (now North Rampart), Soulié, Good Children (now St. Claude), and the Caffin property, 1868. Louisiana Map Collection, Louisiana Division/City Archives, New Orleans Public Library.

Plate 6. 931–933 St. Philip Street (Dolliole-Masson Cottage). Jean-Louis Dolliole, ca. 1805. Photo by author, 2011.

Plate 7. 1436 Pauger Street. Jean-Louis Dolliole, 1820. Photo by author, 2011.

Plate 8. 927–929 St. Philip Street. Photo by author, 2011.

Plate 9. 935–937 St. Philip Street. Photo by author, 2011.

Plate 10. 509–511 Bourbon Street. Norbert Soulié. Photo by author, 2011.

Plate 11. 810 Dumaine Street. Norbert Soulié. Photo by author, 2011.

Plate 12. 1226 Tremé Street. Bernard Soulié, 1837. Photo by Deadria Farmer-Paellmann, 2019.

Plate 13. 1428 Bourbon Street. Laurent Ursain Guesnon, ca. 1811. Photo by author, 2011.

Plate 14. Assembly of houses by Joseph Chateau (from left to right): 422 Burgundy Street, 416–418 Burgundy Street, and 412–414 Burgundy Street. Photo by Liz Jurey, 2020. Courtesy of the Preservation Resource Center of New Orleans.

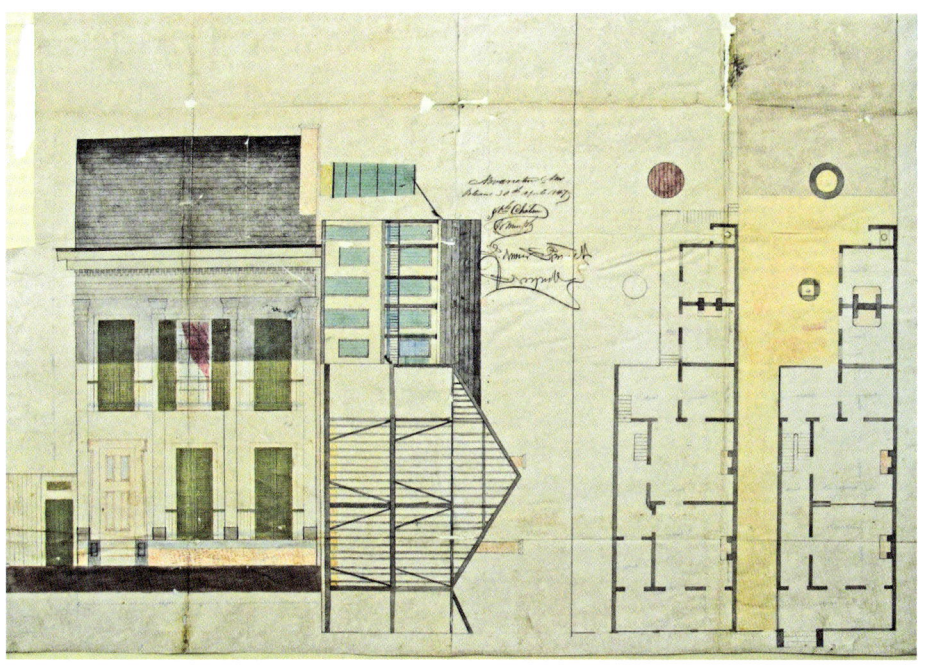

Plate 15. Elevation and floor plan of house on Magazine Street. Joseph Chateau, 1847. Edward Barnett notary, volume 35, act 519A, April 30, 1847. Courtesy of Hon. Chelsey Richard Napoleon, Clerk of Civil District Court, Parish of Orleans.

Plate 16. 2340 Chartres Street. Nelson Fouché. Photo by author, 2011.

*Plate 17. St. Louis Cathedral. J. N. B. de Pouilly and Samuel Stewart, 1851.
Photo by John Watson Riley, 2011. The Collins C. Diboll Vieux Carré
Digital Survey at The Historic New Orleans Collection.*

Plate 18. 713–719 Royal Street (Vignié townhouses). Gurlie and Guillot, 1833. Photo by John Watson Riley, 2010. The Collins C. Diboll Vieux Carré Digital Survey at The Historic New Orleans Collection.

Plate 19. 403–407 Royal Street (Louisiana State Bank). Benjamin Henry Latrobe, 1820. Photo by John Watson Riley, 2010. The Collins C. Diboll Vieux Carré Digital Survey at The Historic New Orleans Collection.

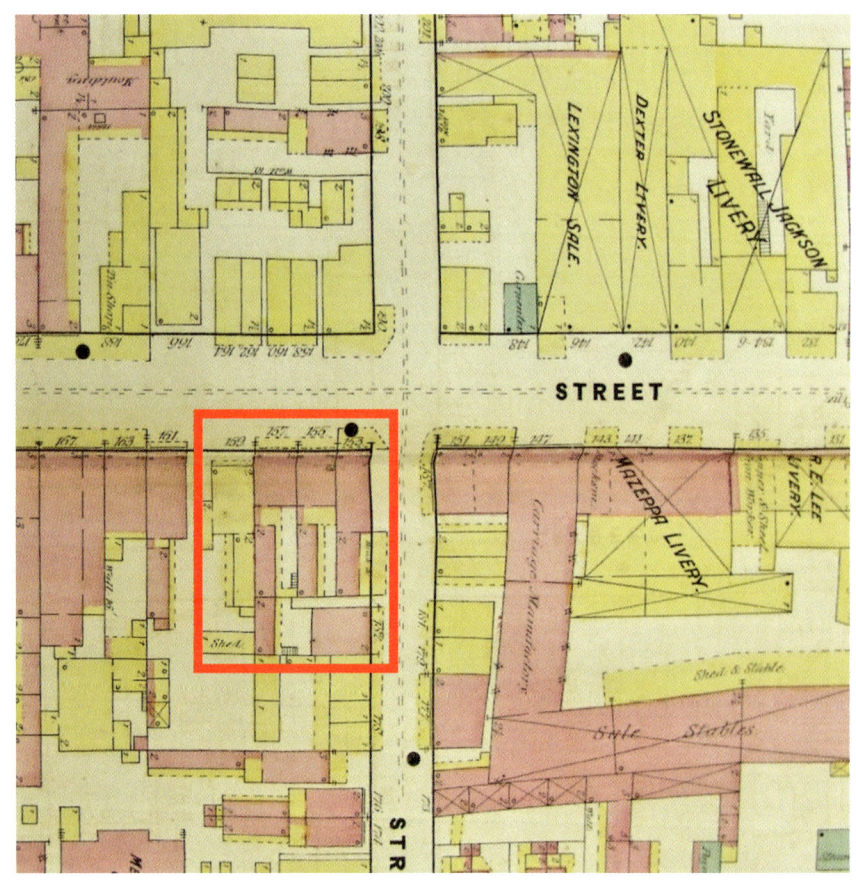

Plate 20. Detail of Sanborn Fire Insurance Company Map, Sheet 23, showing location of Norbert Soulié townhouses at corner of Baronne and Lafayette (formerly Hevia) Streets outlined in red, 1876. Southeast Architectural Archive, Tulane University.

PART III

ENTREPRENEURSHIP

Controlling the Built Environment

CHAPTER 7

MONEY, POWER, AND STATUS IN THE BUILDING TRADES

Property is the basis of power; and this, being established as a cardinal point, directs us to the means of preserving our freedom. (Emphasis in original)

NOAH WEBSTER (1787)

In various historic documents written in French, the term "entrepreneur" is utilized to describe the occupation of known Black and white Creole master builders and property owners.[1] Without knowing the trade of that individual or looking at the original French source material, a literal translation yields the term "undertaker."[2] The word, however, more explicitly describes someone who undertakes a task. More specifically, an entrepreneur is "a person who organizes and manages an enterprise, usually with considerable initiative and risk."[3] In antebellum New Orleans, the skill and prestige of master builders and landowners were recognized by the use of the term *entrepreneur de bâtisses*, regardless of their training or ethnicity. *Gens de couleur libres* acquired wealth and financial security by participating in these enterprises. Risk was involved when bad decisions or an economic downturn affected the practices of building construction; in those circumstances, building and land speculation had the potential to result in financial (or even social) ruin. By and large, however, the *gens de couleur libres* ventures and chances taken in real estate were successful.

Kimberly Hangar notes that three factors, developed in New Orleans's

Spanish colonial period, influenced the ability of free people of color to attain such achievements. The ability of the nascent *gens de couleur libres* community to acquire wealth and financial security relied on: (1) acquisition of a marketable skill before and after being freed, (2) possession of a good reputation in the white community through kinship and patronage, and (3) having access to freedom by being born free or having free kin.[4] The Dollioles and Souliés and their *gens de couleur libres* contemporaries met all of these stipulations—they were born free, attained skills as builders and developers, and gained respectable reputations in the white (Creole and Anglo) communities via their familial associations and clientele. Their privileges as free men affected their professional lives, allowing them to own real estate, enter into business contracts, lease/rent property, and trade on the open market.[5] By these means, the Dollioles and Souliés amassed significant quantities of wealth and became pillars of their communities, exerting a measure of control not seen in other antebellum communities of free persons of color in the United States.

"PERSONS OF POSITION AND QUALITY": WORTH OF *GENS DE COULEUR LIBRES* IN THE BUILDING TRADES

The *gens de couleur libres* builders and property owners of the antebellum period physically transformed the city of New Orleans.[6] Yet the significance of their contributions lies not only in the physical expressions of their work with regard to form, building types, architectural style, and the means of building and construction but also in the personal, communal, social, and cultural motivations behind their choices. The *gens de couleur libres* did not simply act upon their world; they controlled it as much as they were able. Scholarship on New Orleans's free people of color community usually includes discussion of François Lacroix, one of the wealthiest *hommes de couleur libres* in the antebellum city. The business of builders and property owners, and the results of their endeavors, is reflected in his dealings and reputation.

François Lacroix (ca. 1806–1876) and Julien Adolphe Lacroix (ca. 1808–1868) were the natural sons of Elizabeth Norwood and French Creole Paul Lacroix (whose accidental death at a building site in 1847 was recounted in Bernard Soulié's journal). The Lacroix brothers owned and developed many properties throughout New Orleans.[7] François was also a tailor who partnered with sometime builder Etienne Cordeviolle (a mulatto of Afro-Italian ancestry); their firm was located at several locations on Chartres Street. When François Lacroix's wife, Cecile, died in 1856, his estate was valued at over $250,000.[8] At the end of the antebellum period in 1861, though his worth had decreased slightly to

$242,570, Lacroix was still the wealthiest Black man in the city.[9] In addition to his lucrative business as a tailor, through Lacroix's dealings in real estate as a speculator, landlord, and contractor (he individually oversaw many aspects of the construction and maintenance of his properties), he had influence over the city's development and over the ways in which New Orleanians saw and experienced that development. As such, "Lacroix the mere owner of property became Lacroix the proprietor, an exemplar of the social status attributed to ownership and the cultural values conveyed beyond it."[10] Likewise, the Dollioles and Souliés utilized their acts as builders, contractors, and developers to serve not just as actors within and upon their communities but as architects— planners and creators—wielding a significant amount of control and influence. The building-related endeavors of these two families put them among some of the wealthiest citizens of antebellum New Orleans, Black or white.

As *gens de couleur libres* were legally able to enter into contractual agreements, various types of documents shed light on their financial wealth. A starting point for analysis of the Dollioles' and Souliés' value in comparison to other New Orleans residents is examination of marriage contracts. These documents often provide information on the wealth, literacy, and occupations of the contracting parties. Further, they present a particular point in time and are "selective," as wealthier parties were more likely to enter into the competitive marriage market and feel the need to make legal provisions.[11] Of the two families emphasized here, marriage contracts between Bernard Soulié and Eliza Sylvie Courcelle (1832) and between Jean-Louis Dolliole and Marie Eugenie Baudin have been located (1836). The contract between Dolliole and Baudin does not declare the wealth or value of either party; it emphasizes their intent to have communal property and recognizes their three minor children, since they had already been cohabiting for some time.[12] The Soulié-Courcelle contract, on the other hand, is very detailed. On January 19, 1832, Bernard Soulié brought to his marriage $20,000 in property—$19,700 in cash, notes, credits, goods, and merchandise (after deducting debts) and an enslaved individual valued at $300.[13] Already worth $20,000 relatively early in his lifelong occupation as a property developer, real estate speculator, and commission merchant, Bernard ranked among the wealthiest of any New Orleanians. Figure 7.1 shows the average value of property declared in antebellum marriage contracts based on the historian Paul Lachance's database. White grooms declared the most property, an amount three to five times higher than that of free men of color. The value of Soulié's assets was well above the average declared by the wealthiest group. In 1836, 855 *gens de couleur libres* in New Orleans owned a total of $2,462,470 in property and

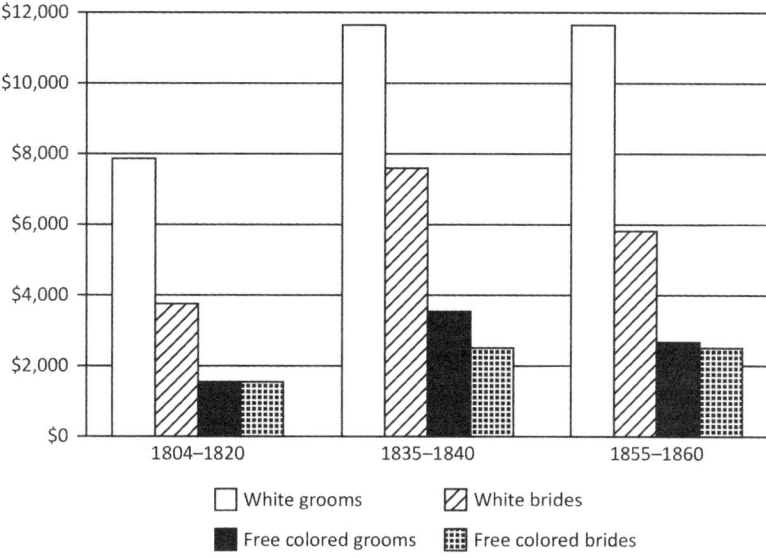

Figure 7.1. Average value of property declared in marriage contracts by period, gender, and race. Courtesy of Paul Lachance, "The Limits of Privilege: Where Free Persons of Color Stood in the Hierarchy of Wealth in Antebellum New Orleans," Slavery and Abolition 17, no. 1 (1996).

620 enslaved individuals.[14] This amounted to an average per person of property valued at $2,880, putting Bernard Soulié above his peers in terms of his value in landed wealth.

In comparison to the marriage contracts from earlier in the antebellum period, the 1850 federal census—the first at which the value of real estate owned by individuals was recorded—illustrates the value of *gens de couleur libres* at the end of the period. New Orleans was the nation's sixth-largest city (the largest in the South) and had the country's largest slave market. At that time, Jean-Louis Dolliole, Joseph Dolliole, and Bernard Soulié owned property worth $10,000, $12,000, and $20,000, respectively. Interestingly, the value of François Lacroix's property was not recorded, though he was at the height of his real estate and commercial activities. No value for real property was recorded for several other free builders of color, including Louis Vivant and Louis Drausin Dolliole, either. In 1850, the *gens de couleur libres* residing in the First Municipality (including the Vieux Carré and Faubourg Tremé) were the wealthiest free people of color in the city (property-wise; table 7.1). Though these individuals accounted for only 28.07 percent of the city's *gens de couleur libres* population, their property

TABLE 7.1. PROPERTY VALUES OF FREE PEOPLE OF COLOR IN NEW ORLEANS, 1850

1860 Wards	1850 Municipalities (M) and Wards	Total FPC Property Value	Total Free Mulatto Property Value	Total Free Black Property Value	Total Free Black Male Property Value	Total Free Black Female Property Value
1	2nd M/Wds 1 & 2	$37,700 (19)	$24,000 (15)	$13,700 (4)	$5,500 (1)	$8,200 (3)
2	2nd M/Wds 3 & 4	19,800 (6)	13,300 (4)	6,500 (2)	1,500 (1)	5,000 (1)
3	2nd M/Wds 5, 6, & 7	980,250 (184)	914,000 (162)	66,250 (22)	28,750 (12)	37,500 (10)
4	1st M/Wds 1 & 2	63,000 (9)	55,000 (8)	7,500 (1)	7,500 (1)	0 (0)
5	1st M/Wds 3, 4, & 5	918,200 (119)	859,750 (103)	44,590 (16)	5,950 (6)	39,000 (10)
6	1st M/Wds 6 & 7	503,600 (73)	471,100 (65)	22,500 (8)	16,000 (4)	8,500 (4)
7	3rd M/Wd 1	407,980 (219)	358,680 (176)	49,300 (43)	23,250 (20)	26,050 (23)
8	3rd M/Wd 2	123,490 (54)	123,490 (44)	19,050 (10)	10,700 (3)	8,350 (7)
9	3rd M/Wds 3 & 4	51,060 (81)	51,060 (50)	21,400 (31)	11,000 (18)	10,400 (13)
Totals		$3,105,080 (762)	2,830,430 (627)	251,150 (97)	110,150 (66)	143,000 (71)

Note: Number of owners in parentheses. Source: Frank Joseph Lovato, "Households and Neighborhoods among Free People of Color in New Orleans: A View from the Census, 1850–1860," Master's thesis, University of New Orleans, 2010.

accounted for 48.82 percent of property values. Residents of the First Municipality's Seventh Ward, the Dolliole brothers and Bernard Soulié contributed to these numbers.

In the intervening decade between 1850 and 1860, at the end of the antebellum period, the wealth of *gens de couleur libres* builders can be ascertained from municipal property tax records and receipts as well as credit reports. Arranged by the names of individual property owners, New Orleans's tax registers of 1852 and 1853 provide specific information as to the location of a property (by ward, block, and, sometimes, street name), the number and worth of any enslaved individuals located on that property (table 7.2), and the property's appraised value, for the purpose of levying taxes. With his ownership of a smaller number of more modest properties, Myrtille Courcelle's landed property is appraised at the lowest amount. The Soulié women (with Eulalie, Celeste, and Coralie having a joint account under Eulalie's name)[15] owned real estate roughly equal to that of their cousin. The values for the real properties of Jean-Louis Dolliole and the partnership of Albin and Bernard Soulié are commensurate with one another's over the year and essentially doubled, since Dolliole and the Soulié partnership owned twice the number of properties. Though the real estate independently owned by Albin Soulié also doubled, the sale of one property worth $6,000 that he owned in 1852 makes the 1853 total seem less proportional. In an interesting twist, Norbert Soulié tops the list with the highest appraised property values. Though he had been an expatriate for twenty years at this point, he continued to buy, develop, and sell a significant number of properties.

R. G. Dun and Company credit reports contain evaluations of the credit worthiness of many of New Orleans's *gens de couleur libres*. The amounts given do not constitute the actual value of personal and real property; they represent the amounts to which it was considered safe to loan money to a person and were *based on* actual values of real and personal property, past creditworthiness,

TABLE 7.2. SELECT ENTRIES FROM 1852 AND 1853 REAL ESTATE TAX REGISTERS FOR NEW ORLEANS

Individual	1852		1853	
	No. of properties	Value	No. of properties	Value
Louise Soulié	1	$3,500	—	—
Eulalie Soulié	2	$2,600	2	$4,300
Myrtille Courcelle	1	$2,500	4	$4,600
Jean-Louis Dolliole	4	$7,700	7	$13,700
Albin Soulié	4	$15,200	7	$12,150
Bernard and Albin Soulié	2	$5,100	6	$13,000
Norbert Soulié	7	$36,900	14	$75,100

Note: The numbers presented in this table do not include the number and value of any enslaved individuals listed with properties. One property, No. 31 Esplanade, was listed on two bills in 1852. The first bill noted that the property was worth $4,500 plus two slaves valued at $800. The second property was worth $2,000 plus two slaves valued at $1,000. The first entry was used in this analysis along with a property valued at $600.

and reputation. The partnership of Bernard and Albin Soulié, who would have needed to acquire credit for their business as commission merchants, is listed; the Dollioles, and most of their other contemporaries, are not. In 1853, Albin and Bernard were "good for" $100,000 in credit. The following year, their worth was estimated between $250,000 and $300,000. Throughout the decade (entries for the firm are present until 1856 and thereafter are absent until 1868, probably due to the Civil War), the brothers were considered "safe" and "first-rate" capitalists with credit in good standing despite their race.[16] An individual entry is also present for Bernard from June 1859. It notes that he owns real estate and enslaved individuals and is considered worth $50,000. Aside from stating his occupation as a broker, the entry includes personal observations indicating that Bernard lives at the corner of Rampart and Barracks, is the agent for parties in France (his siblings), and is "married, steady, sober, honest, and reliable."[17]

The values of individuals' estate inventories at their deaths provide the key to their worth after accumulating (or losing) wealth from a lifetime of business and personal endeavors (table 7.3). As Norbert Soulié remained involved with New Orleans real estate and speculation, enough monies remained from his estate for $63,033.16 in cash legacies to be granted to his heirs in 1869 (only a few thousand dollars shy of François Lacroix's $67,000.00 estate).[18] Based on the appraised value of his property from the tax registers, we know that most of the estate's worth was likely from real property. The personal property of any free person of color was generally less likely to appear in any public record.[19] Free Blacks (of all ethnicities) were among the poorest of the poor, and they rarely appear to have been credited with any personal property except retail merchandise, horses, carts, and, in Southern cities, enslaved individuals.[20] Jean-Louis Dolliole's 1861 estate amounting to $13,959.00 included $2,059.00 in slaves and movable property, mostly furniture and other household goods. Joseph Dolliole's estate (1869) was appraised at $7,726.00 with $226.00 worth of furniture. Based on the comparatively modest value of his property in the 1850s, Myrtille Courcelle died a very wealthy man in 1872 with his estate appraised at $36,957.60! Cash receipts in favor of the succession and unpaid promissory notes accounted for approximately 39 percent and 20 percent of Courcelle's estate, respectively. This indicates that Courcelle was either owed money for building projects or, like his Soulié cousins, was able to use funds generated from his building and real estate activities to serve as a money lender. Instead of branching out in their professional pursuits by building in a variety of types, forms, and styles (i.e., architects such as James Gallier Sr.), *gens de couleur libres* builders and speculators diversified their activities within the building trades via

TABLE 7.3. ESTATE VALUES OF SELECT *GENS DE COULEUR LIBRES* BUILDERS

Individual (year of death)	Assets					Total (less debts)
	Cash	Notes	Moveable	Slaves	Real	
J. L. Dolliole (1861)	n/a	n/a	$59.00	$2,000.00	$11,900.00	$5,426.00 ($13,959.00 −8,533.00)
J. Dolliole (1869)	n/a	n/a	$226.00	n/a	$7,500.00	$7,726.00 ($7,726.00–0)
N. Soulié (1869)	unknown	unknown	unknown	unknown	unknown	$63,033.16 (debts unknown)
M. Courcelle (1872)	$14,595.27	$7,372.33	n/a	n/a	$15,000.00	$33,662.87 ($36,967.60 −3,304.73)

property speculation, lending monies for the purchase of property and serving as mortgage holders.[21] Individuals also took up other professions, depending on their real estate activities, to fund those enterprises. As commission merchants, Bernard and Albin Soulié purchased goods for sale and were compensated for their services by the sale of the goods at a profit or via compensation paid by the owners of the goods. As they became increasingly affluent in this capacity, often traveling abroad, Bernard and Albin spread the demand for building work on their properties to other *gens de couleur libres*, primarily family members. In the antebellum period, "working as a developer involved substantial risks, and architects with little personal capital often found financial disaster, not wealth and leisure, in building."[22] Free persons of color like the Dollioles and Souliés managed to circumvent the risks involved by using modest inheritances of money and property as well as their skills as builders to enhance careers in other professions and to provide employment and income opportunities for other free people of color, for both personal and community gain, thereby becoming some of the wealthiest of the city's *gens de couleur libres*.

EN FAMILLE

An extract from the minutes of death certificates from Paris's Eighth Arrondissement, filed with Bernard Soulié's Orleans Parish Civil District Court succession records, does not include the value of Bernard's estate but does inform that his property was bequeathed to his wife, Eliza Courcelle, as part of their communal property (per their marriage contract and Louisiana's Civil Code laws regarding communal property).[23] The bequeathing of real property and cash legacies (often derived from the acquisition and sale of properties) was one means by which the building and real estate activities of the *gens de couleur libres* provided financial support within families. Within New Orleans's free people of color community, the role of family and its intersection with building and real estate was particularly important. The mixed-race families provided the framework for unique cases of filial and romantic affection to be played out, but those relationships also gained substance and persisted through the inheritance of wealth and property.[24]

Much of the communal nature of the Dollioles' building activities benefited the immediate family. During Louis Dolliole's lifetime, some of his real property was acquired by his sons Jean-Louis, Joseph, and Pierre, providing them with either homes or the means to generate an income. The sons later donated properties to their mother, who, in turn, bequeathed them to her sons. In 1820, Jean-Louis donated his Pauger Street house and land to his minor children from his first marriage.[25] Both Jean-Louis and Joseph made temporary donations of property that they purchased from their father's estate in 1822 to their mother. Various properties (i.e., 1100 block of St. Philip) exchanged hands between the brothers. And when the probate of individual family members' estates ordered the sale of property, other Dollioles purchased it. For example, when Geneviève Azémare died in 1838, her two living sons each purchased one of the two enslaved individuals listed as part of the estate.[26] In addition, Jean-Louis purchased the two properties belonging to Geneviève in the family compound on St. Philip Street that he did not already own. Geneviève's property in the 1100 block of St. Philip Street (which she had purchased from son Pierre) was adjudicated to Joseph Dolliole from her estate. The Dollioles also acted legally on behalf of one another. The year before his death, Pierre gave power of attorney over his affairs to older brother Jean-Louis.[27] Joseph served as Pierre's attorney at their father's estate inventory and was the executor for Charlotte Dolliole (his half sister).[28] Family support also extended to religious obligation—Joseph and his first wife, Madeleine, were the godparents of Jean-Louis's daughter Marie Rosella.[29]

The same kind of support could be found in the Soulié family. While their parents did not bequeath the first-generation Souliés much in the way of real property, the daughters did retain use of their mother's house, and Jean Soulié saw to it that Eulalie Mazange's wishes were carried out on behalf of their children.[30] Having acted on behalf of his sibling living in France since the 1830s, Bernard also functioned as Norbert's testamentary executor when the latter died in Paris in 1869.[31] Brothers Lucien and Norbert formed a partnership to enhance their property and buying power so that they would have adequate income to live abroad.

Younger brothers Bernard and Albin followed suit to fund and supplement their careers as builders and commission merchants in the city of New Orleans.

The Souliés also had a support system formed of extended family members—their maternal aunts, their aunts' partners, their mixed-race cousins, and even, the white relatives of their "uncles." The importance of family ties was established early on when Jean Soulié and Eulalie Mazange served as godparents to Eulalie's younger sister Lucille Vivant and to Eulalie's nephew Norbert Rillieux, son of Constance Vivant.[32] In 1819, Norbert Soulié purchased his aunt Constance Vivant's former cottage on Burgundy from Marcelin Batigne four years after she had mortgaged it to Batigne. Shortly before he relocated to France, Norbert built a house on the lot and resold the property to Vivant, thereby earning money for his departure and restoring her property to her with improvements.

The Souliés also joined forces with their white Creole relatives to secure family property and strengthen ties within the Creole community at large. When Jean Soulié and his two oldest sons moved to France, Léon Courcelle (aunt Adelaide's consort) was given power of attorney over their affairs.[33] Bernard Soulié served as the administrator of Joachim Courcelle's estate when the latter died in 1862.[34] With his father and older brothers gone to France, Bernard's marriage contract with Eliza Sylvie Courcelle (Léon's daughter) on January 19, 1832, was witnessed by Vincent Rillieux (aunt Constance's partner). The first-generation Souliés also entered into many property transactions with their Black and white extended family. Among them were the transfers of properties in Faubourg Tremé and Faubourg Gueno between Bernard and Albin Soulié, Myrtille Courcelle, and the Soulié sisters from 1833 to 1849. On December 27, 1843, Albin was the highest bidder on property sold by the estate of Léon Courcelle that was formerly part of the Cazelar plantation on the right bank of the river.[35]

The familial influences of the Souliés also contributed to their relatives' careers. In his own right, Drausin Barthélémy Macarty (the Souliés' cousin and husband of another of Léon Courcelle's daughters) was a successful developer and land broker. His endeavors were looked upon even more favorably by his kinship and professional ties to the Souliés. Entries from the R. G. Dun and Company credit reports note that Drausin is the brother-in-law of Bernard and Albin Soulié (via Drausin's and Bernard's marriages to sisters) and that he "has a desk at the Office of 'B & A Soulié.'"[36] The Souliés also obviously relied on his trustworthiness and held him in high esteem. Macarty received monies from Bernard to take care of the legacies of Norbert's estate.[37] Drausin Macarty also figures in Bernard Soulié's journal—his many travel activities and death are among the events noted.

BUILDING A COMMUNITY

To legalize and cultivate the benefits of property ownership and building activities, the Dollioles and Souliés also looked to the communal support of their fellow *gens de couleur libres*, other builders and developers in particular. François Boisdoré and the Dollioles figured prominently in one another's lives. In 1800, François Boisdoré purchased property from Claude Tremé on Bayou Road. Louis Dolliole (1806) and Jean-Louis Dolliole (1807) also acquired lots along Bayou Road. In 1822, Joseph became Boisdoré's neighbor when he inherited his father's property. Boisdoré and Jean-Louis Dolliole were also neighbors on the lake side of Villeré Street, near its intersection with Bayou Road, both purchasing lots there in 1841.[38] In other real estate–related activity, Joseph and François together held the mortgage for property being purchased by Charles Harrod and Francis Barber Ogden in Faubourg Lafayette.[39] Boisdoré also held the note for Jean-Louis Dolliole's and Nelson Fouché's purchase of a square in Faubourg Franklin.[40] The Boisdoré-Dolliole relationship also extended to the personal. François Boisdoré witnessed Joseph Dolliole's marriage to Magdeleine Hobe in 1822.[41] In turn, Jean-Louis and Joseph both served as witnesses to the will of Marie Joseph Sophie Olivier, wife of François Boisdoré, on May 25, 1828.[42]

The Dollioles' and Souliés' assistance with probate matters and religious obligations extended into the greater community of free persons of color. Jean-Louis Dolliole was the executor for the estates of Joseph Prieto and the builder Laurent Ursain Guesnon. As native-born Louisianans whose families had been established before 1812, neither the Dollioles nor the Souliés were required to enroll their names in the *Register of Free Persons of Color Entitled to Remain in the State* when the state legislature mandated that measure in 1840. However, as testamentary executor for Jean Baptiste Mallorquin, Jean-Louis Dolliole was ordered to free Mallorquin's enslaved man Daniel Alexis; he then served as witness of Alexis's enrollment in the registry.[43] Influential *gens de couleur libres* supported the Dolliole family as well. When Jean-Louis Dolliole began his second family with Marie Eugenie Baudin, François Lacroix served as the godfather of their son, also François, at the infant's baptism in 1821.[44] In 1832, both Jean-Louis and Joseph appraised the estate of free builder of color Laurent Dessource Quessaire, the same man who had trained Jean-Louis's stepson Emile as a builder.[45]

Among the most significant of these social, institutional, and professional ties that Jean-Louis and Joseph Dolliole maintained with fellow builders of color was the one with Joseph's former partner, the carpenter Henry Fletcher. Both Dolliole brothers attended and witnessed Fletcher's wedding in 1827, and at Henry's death, Jean-Louis served as executor of his estate and Joseph was one of the appraisers.[46] Marie Couvent recognized the status and leadership of these *gens de couleur libres* and additional associates by including them in her legal network to carry out her plans to provide a school for orphans of color on land that she bequeathed in Faubourg Marigny for that purpose. Henry Fletcher served as the executor of Couvent's estate. The builder Nelson Fouché served on the school's founding board of directors. In a related act of networking, Fletcher included his friends Nelson Fouché and Jean-Louis Dolliole—all free builders of color—in a family meeting to support Couvent's property bequest to her former slave Ezaline.[47]

Money Matters

Though less involved in any activities with François Boisdoré (Norbert Soulié purchased property from him on Dumaine Street in 1830) or as witnesses to matters of birth, life, and death in the *gens de couleur libres* community, the Souliés played a large part in the physical growth of the *gens de couleur libres* community and the financial success of its members by financing building and speculation. The Soulié Family Ledgers contain numerous entries regarding the payments made by and on behalf of free persons of color for loans and mortgages. One individual they loaned money to was *femme de couleur libre* Athalie Drouillard. Her name comes up often in the architectural inventory of Faubourg Tremé. Drouillard was the partner of Pierre Passebon and was involved in various real estate ventures with and without him; Mademoiselle Drouillard's holdings were valued at $10,000 in 1850.[48] The Soulié ledgers note that on June 3, 1843, interest was paid on a $2,500 note that the Souliés had previously covered.[49] The note was renewed several times and finally paid off on November 24, 1846.[50] The Souliés' loan to Drouillard helped her cover the mortgage on property she sold to H. Legendre.[51] The Souliés also loaned money to fund specific building projects. Several transactions in the fall of 1845 and most of 1847 appear to relate to one of the contracts Ramon Vionnet made with Joseph Chateau to build a house for him. Apparently, Vionnet owed Chateau monies for one or both contracts, and the Souliés paid that money on his behalf:

> September 20, 1845: (1) notes of Roman Vionnet to the order of Joseph Chateau with *ne varieteur* of Amedee Ducatel from September 15, 1845 at six months; (2) another resembling the preceding at 12 months 180 days of discount at 10% $25.25 and 364 days of discount at 10% $53.25.

November 26, 1845: for 18 months 479 days of discount at 10%.

March 15, 1847: interest on the note of R. Vionnet to his own order from this day for six months in renewal of his note of $525, order of Joseph Chateau, bearing the mortgage due the 18th of this month—185 days at 10%.

September 17, 1847: interest on the note of R. Vionnet, to his own order from the 15th of this month for six months at 12%. In renewal of his two notes each $525 due the 18th of this month and guaranteed by mortgage.[52]

As the Soulié ledgers are not complete, it is not clear if and when Vionnet repaid his loans.

The Souliés' lending extended to the French Creole and American communities. In February 1846, payment was made by Philipe Lacoste, notary public, on a loan that was initiated on November 3, 1845. The note was paid off on September 19, 1846. The Souliés also loaned money to the Anglo builder Edward Sewell.[53] Examination of the account books shows that even James Gallier Sr. sought financial assistance from the Souliés (no mention is made of the family in his autobiography).[54] Sometime prior to June 3, 1843, the Souliés lent Gallier $3,500. On that date, Gallier paid interest on the loan and renewed it for six months at a rate of 10 percent. The loan was renewed on November 30. Gallier then paid $500 toward the principal on June 1, 1844, and renewed the $3,000 balance. The loan was later renewed, this time for a year, on December 4, 1844. The debt appears to have been paid in full on December 8, 1845. One would expect that some of the city's most powerful players in developing the architecture of the city of New Orleans—Black or white, Anglo or Creole—should know (or at least know of) one another well enough to have business dealings together.

Here, then, in their business dealings and in the Soulié ledgers, it should come as no surprise that the lives of the first-generation Dollioles and Souliés intersect. The oldest sons of the two families were born a decade apart, so neither they nor their siblings were immediate contemporaries. But their lives touched in other ways. François Boisdoré and Jean-Louis Dolliole appraised the property of Charles Vivant (the Souliés' maternal "uncle") and Rosette Vivant (the Souliés' maternal aunt) in 1823 and 1828, respectively.[55] Further, Jean-Louis Dolliole sold property on Ursulines Avenue in Faubourg Tremé to the Souliés' "uncle" and fellow Creole builder A. B. Courcelle.[56] However, on October 22, 1835, the first-generation members of the two families came into direct contact when Joseph Dolliole served as surety for a titleless property that the partnership of Bernard and Albin Soulié purchased from Jean Jacques Montfort.[57] Ten years later, on May 17, 1845, the Souliés funded a note for Joseph Dolliole to the order of Jean-Louis Dolliole for 95 days at 18 percent interest.[58] The loan was short-term, as it was paid off on September 20, 1845.[59] It is not certain whether the monies funded a building project or the purchase of property, but the bulk of the Dollioles' antebellum property acquisitions had been made at this point. As involved in the construction and development of the city of New Orleans and the free people of color community as the two families were, one would think that they would have worked together more often. Still, the Dollioles and Souliés found ways for their personal and professional skills and gains to aid the greater *gens de couleur libres* community. The collective nature of the activities of free persons of color is reflected in the types of built works they consistently erected and, by extension, of building in the same areas, that is, the neighborhood enclaves they established. Historical records show that the Dollioles and Souliés understood how to take legal and financial means to protect their personal, familial, and community interests. Using the business of building and speculating as vehicles, they were able to manage the rapid socioeconomic changes taking place around them. Louis and Joseph Dolliole, with François Boisdoré and other neighbors, extended that control into physical space.

As the city started to grow outside of the Vieux Carré in the early nineteenth century, the municipal government and residents sought to settle on the natural ridge that separated the old city and the lakeward back swamp behind it (the upriver side) from Marigny's plantation and new suburbs (the downriver side). Already, Claude Tremé and others owned and were starting to subdivide plantations on the Bayou Road, a natural portage on the upriver side of the ridge. The doors were opened for significant development of the Esplanade Ridge in 1807 when the US government gave the city of New Orleans title to the land from Levee (North Peters) Street to Rampart Street that had formerly been part of the old fortifications and the City Commons.[60] A new street, mapped by Jacques Tanesse in 1810, was cut into these seven blocks. Esplanade Avenue was conceived as a European tree-lined promenade. As the avenue opened, it was improved with residences in the latest styles. Development came to a halt in 1822, however, when the city sought to complete the section of the new promenade from Rampart to Claiborne Streets. Landowners who had acquired property from the former Morand-Tremé plantation along Bayou Road opposed the development, as the rear portions of their land overlapped the projected path of Esplanade Avenue. The road's continuation was made even more difficult when the city was divided into three municipalities: as Esplanade Avenue was the boundary between the First and Third Municipalities, its development required the approval of two autonomous

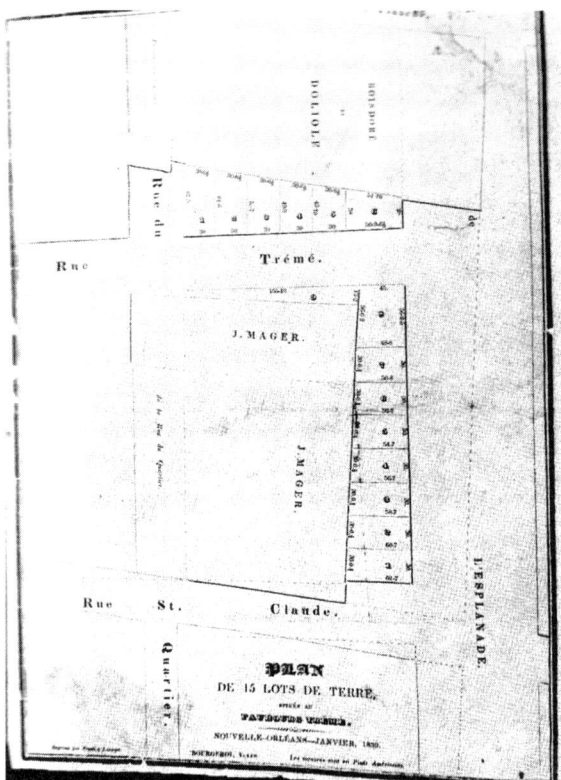

Figure 7.2. Bayou Road properties of Joseph Dolliole and François Boisdoré (top). Plan of fifteen lots in Faubourg Tremé, 1832. Jean Antoine Bourgerol, city surveyor. Courtesy of Hon. Chelsey Richard Napoleon, Clerk of Civil District Court, Parish of Orleans.

governments. Property owners were already up in arms, because the First Municipality proposed the extension of Barracks Street from Rampart to Marais Streets, which would bisect their land. As a result of a suit between the city and Marie Ann Euphrosine Marchand (Madame Plauché), Joseph Dolliole, and François Boisdoré, the land was not acquired and the Barracks Street project was abandoned. This remains evident in the city's landscape today—Barracks Street ends at Marais Street then starts again at North Prieur Street and terminates at Broad Street. On the other hand, Dolliole and Boisdoré were not opposed to the extension of Esplanade Avenue but knew their properties' worth (and, by extension, their own worth) and insisted on being compensated for it; whereas other property owners acquiesced to bartering their land in return for the construction of *banquettes*, the two free men of color demanded full monetary value (figure 7.2). Finally, in a statement from January 1841, the First and Third Municipalities agreed to a sum that amounted to $2,708.25 for the purchase of 10,833 (square) feet of the Dolliole and Boisdoré lands that were required for the project.⁶¹ As financially solvent stakeholders, *gens de couleur libres* like the Dollioles and Souliés manifested their ability to control the physical environment of the city in a spectrum of ways—from their selection and interpretation of forms and styles in the buildings they built for self and others to the broader development of entire neighborhoods and, thus, the city. Legal and financial transactions illustrate that the *gens de couleur libres* were accustomed to coming together for personal and collective gain and to protect their property and interests. They did the same through military and political service and their participation in social organizations and religious life.

EXERTING CONTROL IN THE PUBLIC REALM

"Defenders of the Native Land"

After the outbreak of the War of 1812, Governor Claiborne commissioned four companies of Black militia composed of "certain free people of color."⁶² In defiance of his own militia bill that authorized the Black troops, Governor Claiborne commissioned officers who were not white property owners. Among the three Black second lieutenants was Jean-Louis Dolliole. When the troops were officially mustered by the US Army under the Louisiana Militia, many *gens de couleur libres* became privates in Fortier's First Regiment, including Jean-Louis Dolliole, Joseph Dolliole (orderly sergeant), Pierre Dolliole, Henry Fletcher (corporal), François Boisdoré, Norbert Fortier, Ursain Guesnon, and Charles Vivant.⁶³ These men preserved a tradition of military service; their descendants later formed the Louisiana Native Guards for service during the Civil War, with their ultimate goal being to protect their property and civil rights.⁶⁴

When first developed, Faubourg Tremé had no religious or public educational institutions. Free persons of color and white New Orleanians who resided in the suburb still attended St. Louis Cathedral for their spiritual needs. Further, the city's public school system had not yet been founded. In any case, children of color would not have been allowed to attend, as was the case when the public school system was established in 1841. The block of Bayou Road between St. Claude and Tremé Streets became a nucleus for the educational and religious life of the community and was supported in large part by *gens de couleur libres*. In 1834, Frenchwoman Jeanne Marie Aliquot purchased the former Tremé home and property from the city of New Orleans (which had purchased it directly from Claude Tremé in 1810 and briefly operated the Collège d'Orléans).⁶⁵ She relocated a school for girls and young women of color (established in 1823 by Marthe Fortier, the school also admitted some enslaved individuals) to the site. Aliquot sold the property to the Ursulines (1836), who in turn sold portions to the Sisters of Mount Carmel (1840). In the 1830s, Tremé's *gens de couleur libres*, the area's primary residents, petitioned for a neighborhood church. In the late 1830s, they received permission from Bishop Antoine Blanc to establish a church.[66] The Ursulines donated property that they had retained at the corner of Bayou Road and St. Claude Street (on the former Morand-Tremé plantation) for the edifice designed by Frenchman J. N. B. de Pouilly. Although no persons of color were hired as the architect or contractor, they surely participated in the church's construction. The Dollioles were among the Creole families, Black and white, that contributed to the church's building fund.[67] St. Augustine Catholic Church was dedicated on October 9, 1842; its free patrons of color continued their support and exerted control over the use of the building by purchasing more pews than the white churchgoers and by acquiring all of the pews in both side aisles for enslaved individuals. The Dolliole family was likely involved in other aspects of the church's operation or that of the orders of nuns associated with the church and Faubourg Tremé.[68] A devout parishioner to the end, Jean-Louis Dolliole authorized his estate to pay $50 to the clergy of St. Augustine Church for conducting his funeral services.[69] Jean-Louis Dolliole died on January 9, 1861, the same day that Mississippi became the second state to secede and that artillery fire from Morris Island, South Carolina (the first state to secede) fired on and repulsed a Union supply vessel attempting to approach Fort Sumter.[70] Although the aggressive action did not directly trigger the start of the Civil War, it was a sign of the conflict to come, which ushered in the end of the antebellum era.

CONCLUSION

The Gens de Couleur Libres' *Development of Self and Group Identity through Ownership, Formation, Transformation, and Control of the Built Environment*

> *These men . . . have brought honor and prestige to the Creole of color. Each is justifiably recognized for his merits. Unfortunately, the prejudice of some people and the heedlessness of others seem to have erected a barrier of silence around their illustrious names. But this silence will not always endure. The future will probably inquire into the past. It is to be supposed that the men of tomorrow will ask about the men of yesterday.*
>
> RODOLPHE DESDUNES, *OUR MEN AND OUR HISTORY* (1911)

Historically, the possession of the built world has informed the narratives that are passed on to posterity. With the transfer of buildings from free people of color to white Creoles and Americans, the demolition of portions of the city, and the deliberate erasure of individuals from the historic record, the memory of the builders and original owners has been lost. Social and economic changes in the South and racism before and after the Civil War played significant roles in removing the *gens de couleur libres'* architectural activities from general knowledge. Even when *homme de couleur libre* Rodolph Desdunes wrote his chronicle of the accomplishments of the *gens de couleur libres* in 1911, the antebellum contributions of men like the Dollioles and Souliés were overshadowed by those of Desdunes and his contemporaries, who struggled to retain their identity after the Civil War. It was also heavily weighted toward free persons of color whose ancestors were refugees from Saint-Domingue, Cuba, or other parts of the West Indies. In his account, Desdunes mentions several building artisans but only one architect, Louis Nelson Fouché, who, in the 1850 federal census, became the first Black man in the United States (Creole or not) identified as an architect. By exploring the endeavors of the *gens de couleur libres* via architectural progress and the meaning of architecture on social, cultural, and socioeconomic levels, a new narrative—one that fills in bibliographic and historiographic silences of antebellum free property owners, builders, and developers of color as well as contextual silences regarding their collective influence—is offered.

In *Revolution, Romanticism, and the Afro-Creole Protest Tradition in Louisiana, 1718–1868*, the historian Caryn Cossé Bell chronicles the manner in which free Black intellectual and political protest, spurred by revolutionary ideals, informed and characterized the actions of the community of color in antebellum New Orleans. Coincidentally, I embarked on this journey to learn about the contributions of free people of color to the built environment with my own research in a graduate course titled Architecture in the Age of Revolution. My own ignorance of and assumptions about the *gens de couleur libres* were tied to white supremacist ideals and legislation that began to surface in the 1830s and which Bell ably describes as attempts to obscure the radical manner in which free Black leaders asserted liberty, equality, and brotherhood from New Orleans's founding until the Constitution of 1868.[1] Although the economic and social parity of New Orleans focused more on class and less on race than other Southern metropoles, the dominant social order still attempted to undermine opportunities for free people of color to own property. The manner in which this intermediate class was able to do so suggests a silent form of activism not completely unlike that of more vocal free Black intellects, soldiers, visual artists, and writers. The fact that many of these same individuals were master builders, carpenters, masons, and free men and women of color property owners and developers lends further credence to their contributions to the built environment as a form of protest—concerted objection to the prevailing order—that provided them with economic security and upward mobility. Property ownership and control—considered "inalienable rights" in empire and city building—are suggestive of power and control. History abounds with connections between land and freedom. It follows, then, that along with disenfranchisement, property dispossession of free people of color was a crucial aspect of the destruction of the tripartite racial system and gradual implementation of a biracial, white supremacist order in New Orleans. Through this system, and others institutionalized in urban planning, architecture, historic preservation, and education, the names and contributions of the free men and women who built antebellum New Orleans were hidden or diminished.

The anthropologist Michel-Rolph Trouillot discusses the labor involved in transforming a new narrative out of historiographic silences. He discusses the two sides of history—what happened (historical process) and what is said to have

CONCLUSION

happened (historical narrative/production).² Trouillot explains the means by which those who have the power in history, be they historic figures or historians, have inadvertently or knowingly enabled silence in historical production through fact creation (the making of sources), fact assembly (making of archives), and fact retrieval (making of narratives).³ In the case of the *gens de couleur libres*, who are present in notarial and other historical documentation, silences inherent in sources (artifacts and bodies) and archives (collections of documents and monuments) are circumvented through their reanalysis.⁴ Although few antebellum portraits of New Orleans's free people of color survive, and no known portraits of the first-generation Dollioles and Souliés have been found, physical remembrance abounds in their built works. Extant buildings as well as notarial acts documenting property transactions serve as concrete sources that fill in for those that have disappeared (i.e., demolished buildings and the lack of building contracts). Creative combination of these sources through the city's archives—research repositories and landscape of New Orleans—circumvents the silences created in fact assembly. The *gens de couleur libres* have been silenced in the creation of narrative on several levels. After the Civil War, historians like Creole Charles Gayarré refused to acknowledge the Creole identity of New Orleans *gens de couleur libres* in support of white Creole supremacy.⁵ Still others, such as Henry Clay Warmoth or Donald E. Everett, criticized or misrepresented the aspirations of the free community of color.⁶

I have recast the *gens de couleur libres* as actors and emphasized their actions as an architectural process that erases the dominant narrative and reinforces a new narrative that stresses:

1. Property ownership was a calculated endeavor by the *gens de couleur libres* to establish and maintain birthright.
2. The *gens de couleur libres* primarily owned property in the so-called Creole faubourgs, or suburbs, but their presence in other parts of the city was more pronounced than has been highlighted in previous scholarship.
3. The *gens de couleur libres*' selection of locales for building and developing properties was deliberate and based as much on personal choice and economic opportunity as on racial and geographic divisions.
4. While the *gens de couleur libres* primarily built vernacular forms of architecture derived from colonial "Creolization," or the mixture of various forms, by no means were their works static or purely repetitive. Free builders of color perfected Creole forms based on numerous variables. They also

incorporated and manipulated features of popular architecture such as the Federal and Greek Revival styles.
5. *Gens de couleur libres* builders' work was primarily residential, due in large part to limitations imposed by race and training, but personal preference and financial considerations of the risk and cost involved in building monumental architecture were also factors.
6. Building and real estate activities were means by which the *gens de couleur libres* established and exploited personal and professional relationships to ensure individual economic success and the perseverance and preservation of the community of people of color.

THE PARADOX OF OWNERSHIP

The antebellum period provides a challenging framework in which to view the architecture-related accomplishments of New Orleans's *gens de couleur libres*. They faced a paradoxical situation in which the stability of New Orleans's economy and racial hierarchies affected their success in building, developing, and speculating. Both of these factors were driven by a slave society that devalued Black lives and, thus, the Blackness of the *gens de couleur libres*.[7] Still, free builders and landlords of color "were literally [and physically] invested in New Orleans, and their assets thrived in an Americanizing city where racial codes were becoming stricter."[8] In the antebellum period, the nation's prosperity in trade, manufacturing, and agriculture allowed American artists and architects to explore new markets and become independent entrepreneurs.[9] New Orleans's *gens de couleur libres* were no exception. As they continued to build during the 1830s and 1840s, they exchanged property in significant numbers, creating individual fortunes (large and small) and helping retain Black *and* Creole control in the city. Their success in this was made clear in the *Bee* of March 28, 1836, which observed that

> the property owners in the central municipality [Vieux Carré] will neither sell nor improve, that real estate in the upper municipality [Sainte-Marie] is selling greatly beyond its intrinsic value, and that purchasers would buy lots in the central section if they were put up at auction. Lots in the rear ward [Faubourg Tremé], which a short while ago sold for $300.00, are now selling for $2000.00 and soon resold for $7000.00.[10]

By this time, many of the city's *gens de couleur libres* had moved out of the French Quarter and into Faubourgs Marigny, New Marigny, and (primarily) Tremé. Individuals of greater means, like the Dollioles and Souliés, settled in Tremé. Despite the fact that their status was becoming fragile in an increasingly binary society, property ownership resulted in geographic stability.[11] And though this latter generation was not building on the same scale as their predecessors did from the 1810s through the 1830s, their built work remained relevant as changing styles saw newer buildings in the Vieux Carré and the American Sector come and go. Shirley Thompson notes that "the patterns of ownership and stylish amblings of Creoles of color ... constituted genuine acts of artistic creation not fully captured by characterizations."[12] She observes that literature, particularly poetry and fiction by and about the *gens de couleur libres*, does not adequately reflect their accomplishments, especially those made in possessing, engaging with, and controlling the built environment of antebellum New Orleans. Like François Lacroix, whose real estate activities she highlights, the Dolliole and Soulié families provide exemplary case studies to illustrate secure proprietorship and belonging achieved through legal means as opposed to the lens of anxieties and sentimental expression through which the *gens de couleur libres* are usually examined.[13]

FORMS AND CITYSCAPE: *GENS DE COULEUR LIBRES'* ARCHITECTURAL PRODUCTION

In her master's thesis on building in New Orleans from 1790 to 1830, Corinna Knight says of François Boisdoré's house for Joseph Soniat Dufossat, "This example ... has no distinguishing free-black characteristics or qualities about it."[14] She does not, however, go on to say just what "free-black characteristics" are. The antebellum architecture of the *gens de couleur libres* cannot simply be defined as a form or style or a set few physical features or characteristics. Like all American architecture, it is a response to certain conditions at a certain time, in a particular place, in the development of disparate ideas into an American identity. By the very nature of its synthesis of French and Spanish Colonial, Caribbean, Creole, and Anglo-American architectural attributes, New Orleans's antebellum architecture *is* American architecture. In their contributions to the city's architecture, the *gens de couleur libres* more or less retained the use of Creole forms, albeit with other influences, throughout the antebellum period even with the influx of Classical Revival and other early to mid-nineteenth-century revival styles. Because of their dedication to the use and manipulation of traditional forms, these builders' contributions have been marginalized. Specific study of builders like the Dollioles and Souliés also illuminates the fact that they should be given more credit for unique adaptations of traditionally Creole forms as well as the implementation of Anglo characteristics in combination with and apart from Creole architecture.

Given the many variables that form New Orleans's antebellum architecture, the individual and collective choices of *gens de couleur libres* should not be ignored. The historian Roulhac Toledano argues, "Buildings . . . reveal the economy that provided for the material preferences of the citizens."[15] Builders' and owners' Creole preferences were based on inhabitants' familiarity with French and Spanish Colonial forms and their adaptation—via other exposure to the colonial environment of the Atlantic world—to the geography, climate, and urbanity of New Orleans. The spread of the Greek Revival style and builders' use of the specific elements of classical architecture were aided by the use of pattern books. The practice of "building by analogy" was prevalent and became part of legal and binding agreements in antebellum building contracts as clients requested architectural features or ornamentation that they had seen on another building.[16] *Gens de couleur libres* builders were capable of residential architecture in both veins to satisfy clients from various backgrounds.

The antebellum era saw the rise of New Orleans's ubiquitous townhouse. With the exception of émigré Pierre Roup and his shotgun prototypes, surviving documentation shows that the *gens de couleur libres* did not build *appentis* cottages, *maisonettes*, or shotgun houses. Builders like the Dollioles and Souliés were not tempted by the evolution of linear forms in the first half of the nineteenth century that led to the development of the shotgun house. *Gens de couleur libres* builders were absolutely aware of the shotgun form, especially in Faubourg Tremé, where the Dollioles and Souliés were present throughout the antebellum period and where linear houses coexist with older Creole cottage and townhouse forms. But, where the opportunity presented itself to utilize newer linear forms on narrow lots, the Dollioles choose to build two- and three-bay Creole cottages instead. The *gens de couleur libres* obviously identified with the Creole forms developed before the antebellum period and chose to retain them even as the city grew and other builders turned to the shotgun tradition.

Inasmuch as the specific forms and styles used by a particular individual sheds light on their education and architectural objectives, it is the general effect of the architecture of *gens de couleur libres* as a whole that is unique. What is so significant where the *gens de couleur libres* are concerned is the sheer number of men who participated in the building trades and the individuals of both sexes who were property developers and speculators. Further, they owned and built in all parts of the city, albeit to greater degrees in the older, Creole-dominated parts of the city. That is not to say that separate, biographical study of personalities like Jean-Louis and Joseph Dolliole or of Norbert and Bernard Soulié is not important. On the contrary, it is the individuals' own motivations and experiences that allowed for the Dollioles, the Souliés, Boisdoré, Fouché, and their other contemporaries to contribute to the creation of an entire genre of architecture.

CONCLUSION

COMMITMENT AND CONFLICT

Per the definition of the word, the Dollioles' and Souliés' *engagement* with the built world of antebellum New Orleans signified both commitment and conflict. From their initial acquisition and creation of a family compound as well as an older bachelor's domicile, the Dollioles created their own birthright—transferring real estate among themselves or bequeathing it to one another before selling outside of the family—allowing them to continue to prosper despite increasing hardships facing the *gens de couleur libres* in the decades leading up to the Civil War. Sadly, the lack of male issue, in addition to decreased political and civil rights, played a part in the disappearance of the descendants of Louis Dolliole from New Orleans's building scene. Louis's sons Pierre and Joseph had no known offspring. And although Jean-Louis had two sons, Louis Drausin and François, neither had sons of their own.[17] While the mixed-race children of Jean-François Dolliole, the family's other white progenitor, did not own nearly as much property as their cousins during the antebellum period, it is that branch from whom Dolliole descendants currently living in New Orleans descend and who have perpetuated the family's involvement in the building arts and in community service.

Whatever the reasons behind Norbert Soulié's departure from New Orleans, it served as the impetus for the other family members to follow suit. The marriage contract between Bernard Soulié and Eliza Courcelle in the summer of 1832 notes: "There shall be community of acquests and gains between the parties during this their future marriage, and the said Community shall be governed by the Civil Code now in force in this State and by . . . the Civil Code of France *when they shall have fixed their residence in that Country as their intention is*" (emphasis mine).[18] Just as Bernard embarked on his career as a builder, landowner, and merchant, the other members of the family had already made it their plan to move to France. Even while the city of New Orleans thrived with a bustling boom economy in the 1840s, and the Dollioles and Souliés built and bought on an immense scale, the percentage of *gens de couleur libres* population decreased in comparison to the city's growth. And while individuals and families such as the Dollioles, Courcelles, and Souliés had income greater than most *gens de couleur libres*, the average wealth of persons of color diminished after 1840. The economic decline of the free Black community as a whole continued over the ensuing two decades.[19]

The Civil War brought its own set of problems to the *gens de couleur libres* community, New Orleans, and the South. Identifying with the place of their birth and seeking to support their business interests, *gens de couleur libres* like Bernard and Albin Soulié offered funds for Louisiana's separation from the federal government.[20] Later, others joined the Confederate Army. In an effort to have a stake in the redeveloping personal economies and the state economy after the war ended, many free men of color became involved in Reconstruction politics. Bernard Soulié was among them. Hoping for full enfranchisement, free men of color became involved with the development of the Republican Party. Bernard Soulié, representing the city's Sixth District, was a delegate to the Convention of Universal Suffrage held on September 27, 1865. Bernard was proposed as a vice president for the permanent organization of the convention and was also selected to serve on a committee of five to write an address to the people of Louisiana.[21] His leadership not ending there, Bernard proposed a resolution that would give the convention the name the "Republican Party of Louisiana." He continued to be involved with the organization, along with relatives Edmond Rillieux, Drausin Macarty, Myrtille Courcelle, and Charles Courcelle.[22] Soulié's leadership was not forgotten when he was considered for New Orleans's first post-Reconstruction board of officials in 1869. When selected by Governor Henry C. Warmoth for a position in the mayor's administration (based on a list provided by a committee of fifty citizens), Bernard declined for personal reasons.[23] That Soulié was one of the two men of color selected for seven administrator positions says a lot about his prestige not only in the *gens de couleur libres* population but in the entire city. His stature as a wealthy landowner lent him credibility for the post but also surely played a role in him not accepting the position. For obvious reasons, political office would have taken time from his business pursuits in real estate (according to the R. G. Dun credit reports, he had retired as a merchant and broker by this time).[24] And, surely, with hope diminishing for the kind of city in which he grew up and prospered, Bernard was looking to get his business pursuits in order so he could join his family overseas. Having previously noted to Henry Clay Warmoth in 1866 that "the spirit of Rebellion is alive and dominant," Bernard found his will to fight diminished and his focus now that of his personal survival. Bernard Soulié remained in New Orleans, traveling often, until May 1875, when he permanently relocated to Paris.[25]

For New Orleans's *gens de couleur libres*, they were not working at cross purposes as they continued to seek economic gain and place while continually being disenfranchised and marginalized over the course of the antebellum period. While possessing a great deal of wealth and economic flexibility on the one hand, but faced with diminishing social status on the other, the city's free people of color worked to establish their legacy by transforming contract into birthright.[26] The *gens de couleur libres* undertook the work of acquiring and improving the urban landscape to proclaim birthright and legacy. They became builders and entrepreneurs, bearing personal, financial, and societal risk to establish self and group identity.

IDENTITY: CLAIMING SELF AND PRIVILEGE IN THE BUILT ENVIRONMENT

Two centuries after Louisiana's statehood and Andrew Jackson's ultimate defeat of the British at the battle of New Orleans ushered in the antebellum period in Louisiana, the specific architectural contributions of the *gens de couleur libres* have not been highlighted, and individuals such as the Dollioles and Souliés have rarely been identified and considered as the architects they truly are. In the absence of physical likenesses of the individuals, their buildings and neighborhoods serve as portraits and biographies. By utilizing building as a tool to define individual and communal identity, the *gens de couleur libres* claimed privilege through the built environment and created a lasting impact on the architectural heritage of New Orleans. As such, this work underscores their legacy as architects in two senses. First, in the ancient Greek sense of the word, they were the quintessential master builders who, within the *gens de couleur libres* community, possessed the status and prestige sought by architects at large. And, second, they were indeed architects—planners and creators—of an architectural legacy without which there would be no New Orleans and of an architectural identity that is central to the struggles and tensions inherent in American architecture.

ACKNOWLEDGMENTS

*It's some precious work. It's like a diamond,
like a jewel, and it's for you to preserve it.*

EARL BARTHÉ

When I embarked on this journey to learn more about the contributions of free people of color, little did I know that I would open a treasure trove of history that has enriched my life on professional and personal levels. I have taken to heart the words of master plasterer and self-described "Creole of Color" Earl Barthé (1922–2010). Through this work I seek not only to encourage the preservation of the physical buildings and spaces of New Orleans's antebellum Afro-Creole community but also to illuminate the complex nature of their personal lives. *Building Antebellum New Orleans* is but one perspective of a multifaceted story that offers opportunities for continued study, especially at a time when the significance of African Americans' place in and contributions to this country are yet again being called into question, making sources for knowledge and recognition of Black agency and Black history necessary.

    I owe my gratitude to many for their support of me, my research, and the publication of *Building Antebellum New Orleans*.

    It seems that I have been a lifelong student and even an academic (although I may not have always recognized the latter). I have to thank all of my teachers

ACKNOWLEDGMENTS

through the years who always encouraged me to seek knowledge and to step outside of boxes both literal and figural, whether of my own or society's making. I especially need to acknowledge Rita Canonge, Pam Gremillion, Linda Cormier, Madeline Benjamin, Jean Caruthers, Vicki Jacques, Alice Fischer, Diane Touchet, Bobette Castille, Mathilda Martin, Patricia Colbert-Cormier, Nancy Weiss-Malkiel, and Esther da Costa Meyer, whose involvement along different parts of my journey fostered my growth as a historian, writer, and Black woman. This book is dedicated to my high school English teacher Melinda Mangham. You left us this year, and the emotions that I still have not dealt with prevent me from putting down the words that I have inside knowing that you will take no more "spins around the sun" with us. So, I borrow those of my sister when we wrote what we did not not know would be our last goodbye.

> People will forget what you did, but people will never forget how you made them feel. You made us feel like we could do anything, accomplish any goal, break through any barrier. You will always be more than our teacher, mentor, and friend. You are a family member essential to the process of molding us into the women we are today.

Mrs. M, you always told me that procrastination was a sign of being a perfectionist. Both I and this book are far from perfect, but I will do my best to live up to not only the potential you saw in me but also your amazing legacy. I wish that you were here to see the publication of my first book. I hope that you are proud.

I am grateful to my dissertation committee for acknowledging, through their support of my work, the dearth of scholarship on people of color in our respective fields and how important representing that is to our professions and to me: Christopher Long, Richard Cleary, Michael Holleran, Juliet Walker, and Jay Edwards, thank you. I also wish to thank David Moore Jr. of HHM & Associates, Inc., who encouraged my academic career while I jointly pursued that of a historic preservation professional, and who always emphasized the importance of historic context.

I would like to acknowledge the SRI Foundation and the Graham Foundation for Advanced Studies in the Fine Arts for the financial assistance in support of the dissertation research and writing that was the foundation for *Building Antebellum New Orleans*. I would like to specifically acknowledge Carla Van West (SRI), Terry Klein (SRI), and James Pike (Graham) for personalizing the grants process. I remain humbled by the organizations', and their selection committees', recognition of my scholarship and faith that I would do the topic justice.

ACKNOWLEDGMENTS

The archivists and staff at many repositories aided my research endeavors and responded to scores of long-distance emails and phone calls. I would like to thank Janine Smith, Siva Blake, Juliet Pazera, Sybil Thomas, Erin Heaton, Amanda Picou, and Theresa Butler at the New Orleans Notarial Archives Research Center; Rebecca Smith, Jennifer Navarre, Eric Sieferth, Brian Lavigne, Nina Bozak, and Frances Salvaggio at the Historic New Orleans Collection's Williams Research Center; Christina Bryant, Yvonne Lavoisier, Greg Osborn, Irene Wainwright, Charles Brown, Stephen Kuehling, and Cheryl Picou at the Louisiana Division of the New Orleans Public Library; and Kevin Williams at Tulane's Southeastern Architectural Archive. I am eager for the COVID-19 pandemic to be a thing of the past so that I can return to New Orleans to conduct in-person research.

I am also grateful to several organizations and individuals for their continued recognition of my doctoral research and encouragement of its publication into a book, including the Society of Architectural Historians and the Louisiana Historical Association. I thank Priscilla Lawrence, John Lawrence, and Daniel Hammer at the Historic New Orleans Collection for inviting me to share my work. I also wish to thank Jonn Hankins of the New Orleans Master Crafts Guild as well as Danielle Del Sol and Susan Langenhennig of the New Orleans Preservation Resource Center for creating publication and exhibition platforms to share my research with a wider public audience. Likewise, I am thankful for my homegirl and high school classmate Sharlene Sinegal Decuir, who also provided me a place to lay my head while I was in New Orleans conducting research, all the while on her own journey to becoming a tenured professor in and, now, chair of the History Department at Xavier University.

I am grateful to the University of Texas Press for publishing my first book. I am indebted to director Robert Devens, as well as to editors Sarah McGavick, Lynne Ferguson, and Nancy Warrington for their patience and guidance through the publication process. I wish to thank the series editors as well as all on the press's design and production teams who made this book a reality. I would like to thank my graduate student Ohuntoluwase Oliyide for her assistance with the early preparation of the book manuscript and my best friend Lissa Pearson for her expert mapmaking skills. I would like to thank Furthermore, a program of the J. M. Kaplan Fund, for acknowledging the importance of this book with their grant to fund the color illustration insert.

I am forever indebted to the descendants of the Dolliole and Soulié families whom I have had the opportunity to meet, as well as those I have not. Thank you for entrusting me with the "precious work" of sharing your families' histories.

ACKNOWLEDGMENTS

This book is but a starting point for continued study of their contributions and expansion of their legacies.

And, finally, to my own families, the one that I was born with and the ones that I have made—if anything, my quest for knowledge about our people and desire to tell their stories stem from you; I wrote this history with ours ever on my mind. I thank my sister-friends, Kesha and Rajah Suber, for always having my, and my husband's, back. Thank you to my parents, Paulette and Huey, for fostering the importance of education and being true to one's self. I wish to thank my sisters, Dana and Jana, who have always been supportive of their big sister as we try to live up to our parents' expectations and forge our own paths. I would like to thank my daughters and son, Aria, Zoya, and D'Andre, for inspiring me so that I might inspire them. I will be forever grateful to my husband and best friend, David, who has been with me every step of the way. You continue to give me strength that I do not even know that I have and the drive to constantly strengthen our team, whether at home, work, or school. Thank you for understanding how important this is to me. I hope that you've enjoyed the ride . . . I've got more stories to tell.

NOTES

LIST OF ABBREVIATIONS FOR ARCHIVAL REPOSITORIES

LD/CASP-NOPL (Louisiana Division/City Archives and Special Collections, New Orleans Public Library); http://archives.nolalibrary.org/~nopl/spec/speclist.htm

LDL (Louisiana Digital Library); https://louisianadigitallibrary.org

LHC-LSM (Louisiana Historical Center, Louisiana State Museum); https://www.crt.state.la.us/louisiana-state-museum/collections/historical-center/index

NARC (Office of the Clerk of Civil District Court, Parish of Orleans, Notarial Archives Research Center); http://www.orleanscivilclerk.com/research.htm

WRC-THNOC (Williams Research Center, The Historic New Orleans Collection); https://www.hnoc.org/visit

INTRODUCTION

1. Marriage contract between Bernard Soulié and Eliza Sylvie Courcelle, Theodore Seghers notary, vol. 5, act 12, February 19, 1832, NARC.
2. B. Soulié, "Journal of Bernard Soulié," 323–330, 332, NARC. Soulié's journal was submitted to Susan Laurence Lee Lewis of Biloxi, Mississippi, by his great-great-grandson Edgar Soulié in 1986. It was translated from the French, presumably in its entirety, by Brother Jerome Lepré, S.C. The journal and accompanying letter from Edgar Soulié to Lewis was published in the July 1986 issue of *New Orleans Genesis*. In December 2016, Norbert Soulié, great-great-grandson of Bernard Soulié, provided the author with scans of the handwritten journal.
3. B. Soulié, "Journal of Bernard Soulié," 324.
4. This author assumes that this information is part of the "preamble" to Soulié's journal, as it is the single entry under the heading "1825." It is doubtful that Soulié would have barely begun writing in May 1825 then deliberately eliminated the ensuing six and a half years until January 1832. The year headings that appear in the journal may also

5. The entry reads: "23 January 1832—I was married at 8:00 p.m. to Elisa [sic] Sylvie Courcelles," B. Soulié, "Journal of Bernard Soulié," 324.
6. Toledano and Christovich, *New Orleans Architecture*, 6:93; Kelman, *A River and Its City*, 4; Campanella, *Geographies of New Orleans*, 58–59. Creoles in New Orleans used geographic locators relative to the flow of the Mississippi River as well as other bodies of water such as Lake Pontchartrain. This area was located on the lake side of the Vieux Carré, toward Faubourgs St. John and Pontchartrain, where Gentilly Boulevard, Esplanade Avenue, and Bayou Road come together. Edwards and de Verton, *A Creole Lexicon*, s.v. "geographical locators," 108.
7. New Orleans's population in 1830 was 46,082. Mitchell, *Classic New Orleans*, 31.
8. Roth, *American Architecture*, 151.
9. Christovich, Toledano, and Swanson, *New Orleans Architecture*, 2:70.
10. Fricker and Fricker, Garden District Historic District Additional Documentation, 1974.
11. Campanella, *Time and Place in New Orleans*, 84.
12. For recent scholarship on New Orleans's role in slavery's expansion, see Baptist, *The Half Has Never Been Told*; Johnson, *Slavery's Metropolis*; Marler, *The Merchant's Capital*.
13. Kendall, *History of New Orleans*, 133; Bailey, *Cholera*, 19–20; Rosenberg, *The Cholera Years*, 37; Powell, *The New Orleans of George Washington Cable*, 174.
14. Jean-Pierre Lafitte was born on November 4, 1815. Davis, *The Pirates Laffite*, 479.
15. B. Soulié, "Journal of Bernard Soulié," 324.
16. Historically, the term "Creole" has been fraught with controversy. Some discussions of the term's semantics and use over time include Hall, *Africans in Colonial Louisiana*; Martin, "*Plaçage* and the Louisiana *Gens de Couleur Libre*," 57; and Campanella, *Geographies of New Orleans*, 207–208.
17. For studies specific to the *gens de couleur libres* (particularly in the antebellum period), see Nelson, "People of Color in Louisiana"; Berlin, *Slaves Without Masters*; Schweninger, "Antebellum Free Persons of Color," 345–364; Hirsch and Logsdon, *Creole New Orleans*; Gehman, *Free People of Color*; Kein, *Creole*; Thompson, "The Passing of a People"; Hobratsch, *Creole Angel*; and Thompson, *Exiles at Home*.
18. Edwards et al., "Louisiana's French Creole Architecture"; Edwards and de Verton, *A Creole Lexicon*, s.v. "Creole architecture," 77–78.
19. Aside from New Orleans, Baltimore, Philadelphia, Norfolk, and Charleston were US cities with significant *gens de couleur libres* populations. The communities of *gens de couleur libres* in these cities are highlighted in Curry, *The Free Black in Urban America*; Hunt, *Haiti's Influence on Antebellum America*; Walker, *History of Black Business in America*; Geggus, *Impact of the Haitian Revolution*; and *Common Routes, St. Domingue-Louisiana*.
20. For more on terminology used to describe and distinguish between manumitted Black slaves and free Afro-Creoles during the colonial and Anglo-American periods in New

Orleans, see Spear, *Race, Sex, and Social Order*, 15; Force, "The House on Bayou Road," 31; Ghachem, *The Old Regime and the Haitian Revolution*, 13.

21. Edwards and de Verton, *A Creole Lexicon*, xxi; Hirsch and Logsdon, *Creole New Orleans*, 11.
22. Martin, "*Plaçage* and the Louisiana *Gens de Couleur Libre*," 57.
23. Cohen and Greene, *Neither Slave nor Free*, 5.
24. Thompson, *Exiles at Home*, 190.
25. Gehman, "Visible Means of Support," 213.
26. For scholarship on debunking the myth of *plaçage*, see Clark, *Strange History of the American Quadroon*; Aslakson, "The 'Quadroon-Plaçage' Myth," 709–734; Spear, *Race, Sex, and Social Order*; Johnson, "Death Rites as Birthrights," 233–256; Neidenbach, "'Refugee from St. Domingue,'" 841–862.
27. As a result of the Seven Years' War (1756–1763), or French and Indian War in North America, France lost Canada and all of Louisiana east of the Mississippi except New Orleans to the British. To prevent further English expansion, France secretly ceded the Louisiana colony to Spain by treaty on November 3, 1762. The Spanish did not arrive to take over control of Louisiana until 1765.
28. Huber, *Louisiana: A Pictorial History*, 9.
29. One such law was passed in 1786 that required mulatto women to wear *tignons* (colorful headscarves) and forbade them to wear plumes or jewelry in their hair to distinguish them from their white counterparts. Two years later, a law was enacted that forbade all free persons of color to go out and meet in assemblages at night and that prohibited any free person of color from living in "concubinage." For more details of the *Código Negro*'s regulations governing the rights of slaves, treatment of slaves, rights of the *gens de couleur libres*, and relationships between the city's diverse racial groups, see Spear, *Race, Sex, and Social Order*.
30. Bryan, "Marcus Christian's Treatment," 47–48, 62.
31. Logsdon and Bell, "Americanization of Black New Orleans," 206. Kimberly S. Hanger numbers the *gens de couleur libres* population at 820 of a total population of 5,321 in "Avenues to Freedom," 239, and *Bounded Lives, Bounded Places*, 18, 22.
32. The former province of Provence is now part of Provence-Alpes-Côte d'Azur, one of France's twenty-seven regions. William Dale Reeves gives the year of their immigration as 1760 in *Historic Louisiana*, 17. This date cannot be correct, since the Louisiana colony was not ceded to Spain until 1762. Further, Jean-François Dolliole would have been an infant.
33. Volume 6 of the *New Orleans Architecture* series states that Louis and Jean-François Dolliole were prominent builders in the city. Although that information has been repeated in numerous works, this author has found no primary source evidence (i.e., building contracts, drawings, directory entries, etc.) to give credence to this supposition.
34. Geneviève Azémare is also listed in historic records as Geneviève Laronde, indicating

that she was owned by someone or had a relationship with someone with the Laronde surname.

35. No baptismal entries (with birth dates) were found for the first-generation Dollioles in the sacramental records of the Archdiocese of New Orleans. Jean-Louis's birth year is calculated from his age of seventy-one years at the 1850 census and of eighty-two years at the time of his death in 1861. Joseph Dolliole was fifty-nine years old at the 1850 census and seventy-eight years old at his death in 1868. Madeleine was fifty-two at her death in 1835. No death record for Pierre was located.
36. The Côte des Allemands (German Coast) derived its name from the large number of Germans who settled there in 1721. The area comprises present-day St. Charles, St. John the Baptist, and St. James Parishes.
37. Henriette and Eulalie are identified as her daughters in Louison's will. They are not identified as Charles Vivant's daughters in his will. Various online family genealogical sites have Henriette as the daughter of Juan Prieto and his white wife, Thereze de la Ronde. Together, Louison and Charles had eight children: Rosette, Adelaide, Constance, Lucille, Charles, Louisa, Aimee, and Louis. Charles Vivant last will and testament, 1808, Louisiana Court of Probates (Orleans Parish), General Index of All Successions, 1805–1846, LD/CASP-NOPL. He died in France.
38. Nolan, Dupont, and Bruns, *Sacramental Records*, Vol. 8, *1804–1806*; Benfey, *Degas in New Orleans*, 27.
39. Most of the children's births were recorded in the sacramental records. Two of the children did not live to adulthood: Marie Louise died before 1805, as she does not appear in the family count at the 1805 census. The birth record for the male child Benedic/e was not found, but he died at the age of five in 1807.
40. Lachance, "The Foreign French," 104.
41. Spear, *Race, Sex, and Social Order*, 184.
42. Lachance, "The Foreign French," 104; Spear, *Race, Sex, and Social Order*, 184.
43. Lachance, "The Foreign French," 104; Spear, *Race, Sex, and Social Order*, 184.
44. Spear, *Race, Sex, and Social Order*, 184.
45. Logsdon and Bell, "Americanization of Black New Orleans," 205.
46. Spear, *Race, Sex, and Social Order*, 184.
47. Spear, *Race, Sex, and Social Order*, 184.
48. For more on the legal measures put into place to disenfranchise *gens de couleur libres* in the antebellum period, see Bell, *Revolution, Romanticism, and the Afro-Creole Protest Tradition*, and Stern, *Race and Education in New Orleans*.
49. Thompson, *Exiles at Home*, 14.
50. Thompson, *Exiles at Home*, 138–139.
51. Campanella, *Geographies of New Orleans*, 211.
52. Poesch and Bacot, *Louisiana Buildings, 1720–1940*, 174.
53. Kendall, *History of New Orleans*, 125–126.
54. Campanella, *Geographies of New Orleans*, 212.
55. Published works (aside from the *New Orleans Architecture* series) that focus on the

aesthetics of New Orleans architecture abound, but most feature a very general historical component that, in most cases, does not discuss free people of color at all and focus on specific geographic regions of the city. Such volumes include Ricciuti, *New Orleans and Its Environs*; Bruce, *Great Houses of New Orleans*; Cable, *Lost New Orleans*; Mitchell, *Classic New Orleans*; McCaffety, *The Majesty of the French Quarter*; Vogt, *Historic Buildings of the French Quarter*; Sexton, *New Orleans: Elegance and Decadence*. William Heard, in *French Quarter Manual*, notes contributions of free people of color relevant to specific sites in the Vieux Carré. In "Shotgun: The Most Contested House in America," Jay D. Edwards specifically discusses "The Landlady Effect" or the significance of property ownership and building choices for free women of color in the Early Republican (1803–1819) and antebellum periods.

56. Like many other sources, Sterkx's *Free Negro in Ante-Bellum Louisiana* and Blassingame's *Black New Orleans, 1860–1880* note the prevalence of New Orleans's Black landowners without exploring sense of place. In *Exiles at Home*, the historian Shirley Thompson provides a unique look at *gens de couleur libres*' changing place in society during the antebellum era. Thompson discusses their physical place and space by virtue of their acquisition and ownership of property with a focus on the slipping status of the *gens de couleur libres* in the 1830s and 1840s.

57. After New Orleans was founded in 1718, the initial plan of the city consisted of sixty-six square blocks (or squares). As the city expanded outside of the Vieux Carré, blocks (regular- or irregular-shaped) continued to be referred to as squares. Economic and social differences between the Creoles and the Americans spurred the city's division into three municipalities with different governing bodies. After the city was reunified under one government in 1852, the three municipalities and, later, other newly incorporated areas were known as municipal districts. Here, they are simply referred to as First District, Second District, and so on. The territorial and colonial city and the larger municipalities and districts were further divided into wards for administrative and political purposes. For more on the city's political geographic divisions, see LD/CASP-NOPL, "New Orleans Ward Boundaries, 1805–1880," available at http://nutrias.org/facts/wards.htm.

58. While not limited to the urban environment of New Orleans, Richard Dozier's article "The Black Architectural Experience in America" contains basic biographical information on a handful of former slave artisans and Black planters who influenced architecture in the eighteenth and nineteenth centuries that has since been repeated in studies of free builders of color. In discussions of the professions and building activities of free people of color in Hankins, *Raised to the Trade*, Nick Spitzer and C. Ray Brassieur expand the list through the discussion of a handful of builders and the free Black carpenters, masons, bricklayers, plasterers, woodworkers, and painters that these *gens de couleur libres* practitioners hired. Gehman also mentions these individuals in "Visible Means of Support." The only contemporary account of free artisans of color is found in Rodolphe Lucien Desdunes's *Our People and Our History*.

59. Mark, *"Portuguese" Style and Luso-African Identity*; Edwards, "Creolization Theory,"

50–84; Edwards, "Vernacular Vision," 74, 77, 79–80; and Edwards, "Origins of Creole Architecture," 158.
60. Vlach, "Sources of the Shotgun House"; Okude, "Application of Linguistic Concepts."
61. In addition to Hankins and Dozier, Alfred N. Hunt provides basic historical information and suppositions regarding the training of Black builders and architects in *Haiti's Influence on Antebellum America*.
62. Gehman, "Visible Means of Support," 217; Toledano, Evans, and Christovich, *New Orleans Architecture*, 4:32, 95–97.
63. See Johnson, *Slavery's Metropolis*; Neidenbach, "Life and Legacy of Marie Couvent"; Scott and Hébrard, *Freedom Papers*.
64. Social and economic assessment of the *gens de couleur libres* comes in varied forms. Mary Gehman's chapter "Visible Means of Support" highlights the careers of several antebellum real estate brokers and also discusses the other business endeavors in which they were involved. In *The History of Black Business in America*, Walker places emphasis on the implications of entrepreneurial involvement for Blacks in the United States. She singles out New Orleans's *gens de couleur libres* as being especially business-minded in the decades before the Civil War and provides specific biographical and financial information on men and women who were involved in New Orleans's building trades.
65. Couvent hand-picked these men for the role when she recorded her will in 1832. She died in 1837, and the school opened in 1848. See Neidenbach, "Life and Legacy of Marie Couvent."
66. The many writings of Kimberly Hanger focus on the Spanish period, providing informative background for the antebellum period. In *Neither Slave nor Free*, edited by David Cohen and Jack Greene, Gwendolyn Midlo Hall's chapter on Saint-Domingue explores the circumstances that would have affected free Blacks there before they immigrated to New Orleans. Another important work on Saint Dominguan refugees is Hunt's *Haiti's Influence on Antebellum America*. Alfred Hunt, particularly in the chapter "St. Dominguan Refugees in the Lower South," emphasizes the role that Black and white émigrés played in maintaining the Francophone status quo in New Orleans after the Louisiana Purchase. Hirsch and Logsdon's *Creole New Orleans* focuses on race relations and the interactions between white Creoles, Creoles of color, foreign French, and Americans in the shift from colony to southern state.
67. Adapted from *Random House Webster's College Dictionary* (1996), s.v. "culture."
68. Adapted from *Random House Webster's College Dictionary* (1996), s.v. "social."

CHAPTER 1. THE *GENS DE COULEUR LIBRES'* ACQUISITION OF PROPERTY

1. Spear, *Race, Sex, and Social Order*, 101.
2. Ketcham, *James Madison: A Biography*, 330.
3. Spear, *Race, Sex, and Social Order*, 101.
4. Spear, *Race, Sex, and Social Order*, 102, 109.

5. Toledano and Christovich, *New Orleans Architecture*, 6:87.
6. Spear, *Race, Sex, and Social Order*, 185.
7. Spear, *Race, Sex, and Social Order*, 185–187.
8. *Random House Webster's College Dictionary* (1996), s.v. "ownership" and "possession."
9. *Random House Webster's College Dictionary* (1996), s.v. "birthright."
10. Thompson, *Exiles at Home*, 116–117.
11. The Spanish officially extended the policies of the Code Noir but did not refuse to hear matters related to mixed marriages. Toledano and Christovich, *New Orleans Architecture*, 6:90.
12. Toledano and Christovich, *New Orleans Architecture*, 6:91.
13. *A Digest of the Civil Laws*; *Civil Code of the State of Louisiana*; E. Clark, *Strange History of the American Quadroon*, 110–111; Thompson, *Exiles at Home*, 167.
14. *A Digest of the Civil Laws*; *Civil Code of the State of Louisiana*; E. Clark, *Strange History of the American Quadroon*, 110.
15. Thompson, *Exiles at Home*, 114–115.
16. Thompson, *Exiles at Home*, 115.
17. The death record dated September 28, 1836, and "Petition for the appointment of a tutor & and inventory" filed May 21, 1838, note that she was born in Orleans Parish and around eighty-nine years old at her death on September 1, 1836. Geneviève Dolliole, Estate of 1838, Louisiana, Orleans Parish Estate Files, 1804–1846, LD /CASP-NOPL.
18. Wegmann, "The Vitriolic Blood of a Negro," 205, 214. Louis d'Azémare was the former attorney general for the king of the Isle de la Grenade (present-day country of Grenada) before he came to New Orleans, probably in 1763 when France ceded Grenada to Great Britain after the Seven Years' War. This may account for Dale Reeves's assertion that Geneviève was born in the French West Indies. See Reeves, *Historic Louisiana*, 17. Louis d'Azémare died in November 1868. "Petition," Black Book, vol. 106, September 21, 1768, Colonial Documents Collection, LHC-LSM, https://www.crt.state.la.us/data projects/museum/blackbook/Black_Book_106_1768_Aug-Sep.pdf; various documents in Black Book, vol. 107, Colonial Documents Collection, LHC-LSM, https://www.crt.state.la.us/dataprojects/museum/blackbook/Black_Book_107_1768_Oct-Dec.pdf.
19. No known address for either party has been found prior to that date.
20. The births were not recorded in the registry of St. Louis Cathedral per their absence in the archdiocesan indices and online indices of New Orleans birth records; the reason for the missing entries is not clear. Jean-Louis's birth year of 1779 is derived from his age of seventy-one at the 1850 census and his age of eighty-two per his obituary in the *Bee* on January 10, 1861, one day after his death. This information is further complicated by two separate entries in the death indices that give his age at death as seventy-two and ninety-two. Madeleine's birth year is 1783 based on her age of fifty-two at her death on June 1, 1835, in the death index. Pierre's birth date is unknown (Joseph's 1850 census stats are incorrectly applied to Pierre in volume 6 of the *New Orleans Architecture* series). Based on the listing of the children in Louis Dolliole's probate

records, Pierre was the third born. Joseph was born in 1790 or 1791 based on his age of fifty-nine in the 1950 census and seventy-eight in the 1868 death index.

21. I have used current addresses when referring to properties and locations. Many street names and numbers have changed in New Orleans over time. Dates for changes in street names vary, but the city's street numbers were converted from the "old" numbering system to the present "hundred block system" in 1893–1894. The Louisiana Division of the New Orleans Public Library has an online version of Gray B. Amos's *Alphabetical Index of Changes in Street Names, Old and New, Period 1852 to Current Date, Dec. 1st 1838* located at http://nutrias.org/facts/streetnames/namesa.htm, as well as Gray B. Amos's *Corrected Index, Alphabetical and Numerical, of Changes in Street Names and Numbers Old and New, 1852 to Current Date, April 8, 1938* located at http://neworleanspubliclibrary.org/~nopl/info/louinfo/numberchanges/numberchanges.htm. Additional tools useful for documenting street name and number changes are located in the City Archives at the New Orleans Public Library as well as the Notarial Archives Research Center, New Orleans.

22. Chain of Title, 922–924 Dauphine, from The Collins C. Diboll Vieux Carré Digital Survey, http://www.hnoc.org/vcs/.

23. Hanger, "Patronage, Property, and Persistence," 44.

24. Hanger, "Patronage, Property, and Persistence," 44.

25. Toledano, Evans, and Christovich, *New Orleans Architecture*, 4:95–97.

26. In the Last Will and Testament of Santiago Coursiac, free negro, the property is identified as belonging to Louis Doriole [*sic*], Narcisse Broutin, vol. 15, act 14, January 13, 1801. In the sale of the adjacent land by Coursiac's testamentary executor to Louis Dolliole on July 11, 1801, the initial land is noted as being owned by Genoveva [*sic*] Laronde.

27. Louis Dolliole Estate Inventory, February 22, 1822, filed in the office of Carlile Pollock, February 26, 1822; Chain of Title, 939–941 St. Philip Street, from The Collins C. Diboll Vieux Carré Digital Survey, http://www.hnoc.org/vcs/. This is described as a property in the Vieux Carré on Burgundy Street between St. Philip and Ursulines in Toledano and Christovich, *New Orleans Architecture*, 6:91.

28. "1805 New Orleans City Demographics," submitted by Judith Vinson and Colleen Fitzpatrick, accessed February 22, 2011, http://files.usgwarchives.net/la/orleans/history/directory/1805demo.txt.

29. Either the census taker or the family misreported Jean-Louis's age (he would have been twenty-six years old in 1805) or another teenaged male lived with the family. Geneviève did have another son, François Azémare (alias Dolliole). François is not recognized as a natural child of Louis Dolliole; he and his offspring are mentioned in Geneviève Azémare's succession records.

30. Madeleine Dolliole and Noel Galaud were married on November 3, 1798. Noel, *homme de couleur libre*, was identified as a white male in the 1805 directory and census. The household consists of Noel, a free woman of color over sixteen years of age (Madeleine), two unidentified males of color under the age of sixteen, and one slave girl.

31. Després's ethnicity was gleaned from her estate file, Louison Després, Estate of 1809, Louisiana, Orleans Parish Estate Files, 1804–1846, LD/CASP-NOPL. Her last name is alternately spelled "Dupre" or "Depres" in archival records. This property transaction is noted in the chains of title for the family's other St. Philip Street properties. The original act, completed before notary Narcisse Broutin, could not be located.
32. Noel Gallot [sic], Estate of 1808, Louisiana, Orleans Parish Estate Files, 1804–1846, LD/CASP-NOPL.
33. Noel Gallot [sic], Estate of 1808, Louisiana, Orleans Parish Estate Files, 1804–1846, LD/CASP-NOPL.
34. Jean-Louis Dolliole to Madeleine Dolliole, Narcisse Broutin notary, vol. 10, act 756, November 8, 1805, NARC.
35. Veuve Galaud (née Madeleine Dolliole), Estate of 1835, Louisiana, Orleans Parish Estate Files, 1804–1846, LD/CASP-NOPL.
36. Succession of Victoire Gallaud to Louise Beltremieux, Carlile Pollock notary, vol. 65, act 9, NARC. Jean-Louis Dolliole, her uncle, served as testamentary executor.
37. Geneviève Dolliole to Her Heirs, Order to Sell, Probate Court, November 12, 1838, LD/CASP-NOPL.
38. Succession of Geneviève Dolliole to Jean-Louis Dolliole, Carlile Pollock notary, vol. 61, act 176, NARC; Jean-Louis Dolliole, f.m.c. to Miss Mathilde Duralde, f.w.c., Edward Barnett notary, vol. 26, act 524, December 20, 1844, NARC.
39. Louis Doriol [sic] to Jean-Louis Doriol [sic], Narcisse Broutin notary, vol. 7, act 521, NARC.
40. This date was gleaned by historical and archaeological research by the current owners. Warren and Sexton, "Rooms with a Vieux," 28; Fraiser, *The French Quarter of New Orleans*, 13; Abry, "Cottage Industry," 66–71.
41. Jean-Louis Dolliole to Celestin Saussaye, Amadee Ducatel notary, vol. 64, act 480, December 28, 1854, NARC.
42. Louis Dolliole to Pierre Dolliole, f.m.c. [free man of color], Pierre Pedesclaux notary, vol. 65, act 424, September 20, 1812, NARC.
43. Chain of Title, 935–937 St. Philip Street, from The Collins C. Diboll Vieux Carré Digital Survey, http://www.hnoc.org/vcs/. Pierre Dolliole's succession files could not be located in the probate records at the New Orleans Public Library or in any online indices.
44. Succession of Geneviève Dolliole to Jean-Louis Dolliole, Carlile Pollock notary, vol. 61, act 176, May 11, 1839, NARC.
45. Jean-Louis Dolliole, f.m.c. to Marie Laure Popin, Carlile Pollock notary, vol. 66, act 239, December 21, 1843, NARC.
46. Louis Dolliole inventory; Charles Aicard to Jean-Louis Dolliole, Carlile Pollock notary, vol. 10, act 22, March 9, 1822, NARC.
47. Jean-Louis Dolliole to Louis Sejour, Charles Victor Foulon notary, vol. 12, act 120, April 11, 1843, NARC.
48. No entries for Geneviève Azémare *dit* Laronde (Dolliole) are in the 1811 directory.

49. Only the portion of old Bayou Road lakeside of North Claiborne Avenue retains its original name. Between 1830 and 1850, a new road called Governor Nicholls was carved through the back-of-town plantations. In an attempt to align the new thoroughfare with the older parts of the city, Hospital Street (in the Vieux Carré between the Mississippi River and North Rampart Street) and old Bayou Road (in Faubourg Tremé between North Rampart Street and North Claiborne Street) were renamed Governor Nicholls Street.
50. Christovich, Evans, Toledano, *New Orleans Architecture*, 5:15.
51. Montreuil purchased the property from Tremé on June 11, 1803. Charles Montreuil to Louis Dolliole, Pierre Pedesclaux notary, vol. 53, act 470, June 7, 1806, NARC; this transaction is also mentioned in the Louis Dolliole estate inventory. *New Orleans Architecture*, Vol. 5 notes that Dolliole purchased the Bayou Road property directly from Tremé in 1800 (60, 61) and that this area facing Esplanade "was sold or bequeathed by Tremé to François Boisdoré and Joseph Dolliole" (54). This information is not consistent with the maps and descriptions provided in that volume. Further, archival research has not revealed a direct transaction between Louis or Joseph Dolliole and Tremé. A notarized entry and secondary source maps indicate that Charles Montreuil purchased the property in question from Claude Tremé in June 1803 (Pedro Pedesclaux notary, vol. 44, act 489 or 491, NARC; see also Toledano and Christovich, *New Orleans Architecture*, 6:15, figure 1.
52. Claude Tremé to Jean-Louis Dolliole, Pierre Pedesclaux notary, vol. 54, act 144, March 3, 1807, NARC. See also estate inventory of Jean-Louis Dolliole, Docket No. 17714, Louisiana Second District Court (Orleans Parish), General Index of All Successions, 1846–1880, LD/CASP-NOPL.
53. Toledano and Christovich, *New Orleans Architecture*, 6:xv. The house was still extant on Robinson's 1883 *Atlas of the City of New Orleans, Louisiana* (plate 7).
54. Zaire *dit* Françoise Grammont to Pierre and Joseph Dolliole, Narcisse Broutin notary, vol. 24, act 95, April 15, 1811, NARC.
55. Jean-Louis Dolliole to Joseph Dolliole, John Lynd notary, vol. 11, act 386, September 21, 1814, NARC.
56. Jean-Louis married Hortense Dusuau in February 1818; they already had three children. Hortense died on August 8, 1818, according to petitions filed by Jean-Louis in her succession records. Madame Louis Dolliole (née Hortense Dusuau), Estate of 1819, Louisiana, Orleans Parish Estate Files, 1804–1846.
57. Catherine Dusuau to Jean-Louis Dolliole, Carlile Pollock notary, vol. 2, act 126, February 4, 1820, NARC.
58. Jean-Louis Dolliole to his minor children, Carlile Pollock notary, vol. 2, act 174, April 22, 1820, NARC. Through some arrangement not yet discovered by the author, Jean-Louis regained the property, ultimately selling it in 1858. Toledano, Evans, and Christovich, *New Orleans Architecture*: 4:95; Jean-Louis Dolliole to Patrick Powers, Theodore Guyol notary, May 11, 1858, NARC.
59. Partition between Pierre Dolliole, Jean-Louis Dolliole, and Norbert Fortier, Carlile

Pollock notary, vol. 2, act 524, June 29, 1821, NARC. See drawing by J. A. d'Hemecourt, January 29, 1869, attached to Succession of Joseph Dolliole, Joseph Cuvillier notary, vol. 83, act 7, December 16, 1868, NARC. The partition was made because the property appeared to belong only to Pierre per the language in the original act of sale. In reality, each of the three men had the use of an equal portion. *New Orleans Architecture*, Vol. 6 notes that Jean-Louis Dolliole came into possession of all three lots on July 18, 1821 (page 188). The author found no documentation to support this claim.

60. General Procuration, Pierre Dolliole to Jean-Louis Dolliole, Carlile Pollock notary, vol. 2, act 526, June 29, 1821, NARC.
61. Pierre Dolliole to Joseph Dolliole, Carlile Pollock notary, vol. 2, act 533, June 6, 1821, NARC.
62. Nolan and Dupont, *Sacramental Records of the Roman Catholic Church*, 15:125. A typographical error in *New Orleans Architecture*, Vol. 6 states that Louis Dolliole died in 1832.
63. Louis Dolliole last will and testament, November 4, 1815, Pierre Pedesclaux notary, vols. 70–71, act 964, NARC. For the household inventory and other records related to Louis Dolliole's probate matters, see Louis Dolliole, Louisiana, Court of Probates (Orleans Parish), General Index of All Successions, 1805–1846, and Louis Dolliole, Estate of 1822, Louisiana, Orleans Parish Estate Files, 1804–1846. Original inventory located in the records of Carlile Pollock notary, vol. 8, act 181, NARC. Acceptance by Joseph Aicard, Carlile Pollock notary, vol. 10, act 20, February 23, 1822, NARC.
64. Joseph Aicard to Jean-Louis Dolliole, Carlile Pollock notary, vol. 10, act 22, March 9, 1822, NARC; Joseph Aicard to Joseph Dolliole, Carlile Pollock notary, vol. 10, act 23, March 9, 1822, NARC.
65. Jean-Louis Dolliole to Geneviève Dolliole, Carlile Pollock notary, vol. 10, act 27, March 18, 1822, NARC; Joseph Dolliole to Geneviève Dolliole, Carlile Pollock notary, vol. 10, act 28, March 18, 1822, NARC.
66. Louisiana Corporation to Madeleine Dolliole, Felix De Armas notary, vol. 5, acts 439 and 454, NARC. *New Orleans Architecture*, Vol. 6 claims that Victoire Galaud purchased the lot at number 1205 (page 189).
67. The details of these transactions are found in the Succession of Joseph Dolliole, Joseph Cuvillier notary, vol. 83, act 7, December 16, 1868, NARC. See the accompanying drawing by J. A. d'Hemecourt, January 12, 1869.
68. M. N. N. Destrehan to Joseph Dolliole and Nelson Fouché, Theodore Seghers notary, vol. 12, act 277, May 2, 1835, NARC.
69. Joseph Dolliole and Nelson Fouché to William Lewis, Theodore Seghers notary, vol. 13, act 777, December 29, 1835, NARC; Neidenbach, "Life and Legacy of Marie Couvent," 383.
70. Chain of Title, 822–824 Governor Nicholls, from The Collins C. Diboll Vieux Carré Digital Survey, http://www.hnoc.org/vcs/.
71. A Jean Antoine (Juan Antonio) Soulié died at age forty in New Orleans in September 1787. Woods and Nolan, *Sacramental Records*, Vol. 4. In his will, recorded in the records of notary Fernand Rodriguez (Volume 8, June 3, 1786), Jean Soulié left monetary

NOTES TO PAGES 41–42

bequests to his brothers Antoine and Jean Soulié. See also Maduell, *Marriage Contracts, Wills and Testaments*.

72. The German Coast was a region along the east bank of the Mississippi River settled by German immigrants beginning in 1721; it encompasses present-day St. Charles, St. John the Baptist, and St. James Parishes. Grenoble is located in the French Alps where the Drac and Isère Rivers merge. Ancestry.com., US and Canada, Passenger and Immigration Lists Index, 1500s–1900s [database online], Provo, UT: Ancestry.com Operations, 2010; Ancestry.com., US, Find a Grave Index, 1600s–Current [database online], Provo, UT: Ancestry.com Operations, 2012.

73. Succession of François Liotau, December 20, 1768, Louisiana Colonial Documents Digitization Project, LHC-LSM, accessed July 20, 2020, http://la-state-museum.thecanarycollective.com/document/12911.

74. The Liotau family name appears often in records of the Vivant and Soulié families (also spelled Lioteau, Liatau, Liataud). François Cheval also freed son Paul, Louison's twin, in 1774. In both of those transactions, Jean Baptiste Gauvin served as an intermediary between Cheval and Conant (also spelled Constant and Comptant). He purchased a possible daughter, Prudence, and her two sons in 1790. See Judith Longest Bethea Papers, Manuscript Collections, LD/CASP-NOPL; and Hall, compiler, *Afro-Louisiana History and Genealogy, 1719–1820*, accessed April 1, 2011, database downloaded from http://www.ibiblio.org/laslave/, 2003.

75. Paul Cheval was among early property owners on Bayou Road and in Faubourg Tremé; see Toledano and Christovich, *New Orleans Architecture*, 6:32, 86. Louison's brother Jean Baptiste Meuillon was a prominent landowner in St. Landry Parish. See the Jean Baptiste Meuillon Papers, Louisiana Research Collection, Tulane University, New Orleans, Louisiana, and Christophe Landry, compiler, "Christenings of Known Persons, Cathedral-Basilica of St. Louis King of France, New Orleans, Louisiana, 1750–1790," 2017, http://www.mylhcv.com/wp-content/uploads/2017/07/Christenings-of-Known-Persons.pdf.

76. Emancipation, Maria Luisa Sofia Comptant to Eulalia, Fernando Rodriguez notary, vol. 2A, folio 355, May 7, 1784, NARC. See also Judith Longest Bethea Papers, Manuscript Collections, LD/CASP-NOPL.

77. Per notes in the Judith Longest Bethea Papers.

78. Aside from serving as the notary of record for many of the Liotau family's legal transactions, Leonardo Mazange and his wife, Louise Helene Wiltz, were closely associated with the Chevals, Souliés, and their extended Black and white families. For one, Mazange was one of the sponsors (godfather) for Eulalie's first son, Lucien, at his baptism in 1791. Lucien's godmother was Catalina (Catherine) Milhet, Louison's white first cousin, who was related to the Wiltz family through marriage. Woods and Nolan, *Sacramental Records*, 5:358; "Cheval Family Tree," *Colonial Arkansas Post Ancestry*, Core Family Papers (MC 1380, Box 21, File 6), University Libraries Digital Collection, University of Arkansas Libraries, accessed April 21, 2020, https://digitalcollections.uark.edu/digital/collection/CAPA/id/662/rec/13; Leumas, "Ties That Bind," 183–202.

79. See records of notaries Fernando Rodriguez and Carlos Ximines, NARC; Purchase of slave "Telemaco" by Carlos Vivant & Co. (Charles Vivant, Andre Duclot, and Jean Soulié, referenced in Hall, *Afro-Louisiana History and Genealogy*, http://www.ibiblio.org/laslave/individ.php?sid=23098; various references to slave sales on ancestry.com; Censo-Guía de Archivos de España e Iberoamérica, Duplicados de Gobernadores e Intendentes: Florida, http://censoarchivos.mcu.es/CensoGuia/imprimirFondo.htm?id=985557.
80. Woods and Nolan, *Sacramental Records*, 5:261; 6:258; 7:294, 295; Nolan, Dupont, and Bruns, *Sacramental Records*, 9:373; 10:411, 412; and 11:405. Marie Louise Soulié, whose mother is identified as Eulalie Mazange, was born on August 14, 1791. No death date for this individual has been located, but she is not included with the family at the 1805 census or in either parent's probate records. Five-year-old Benedic Soulié, whose mother is identified in this instance as Eulalie Vivant, was buried on November 11, 1807; his birth date has not been located.
81. Per notes in the Judith Bethea Long Papers, this was at her mother Louison's property at 40 Dumaine Street (present-day 818–822 Dumaine Street).
82. In many cases, the Souliés are not identified as *gens de couleur libres* in archival documents. As such, they are often omitted from free people of color–related finding aids and indices, such as the "Free People of Color Index" at THNOC. More information became available on properties owned by the Soulié family after the Vieux Carré Survey became available electronically. The author searched notary indices where the Notarial Archive Research Center's Bioscope index stated they are included. Otherwise, unless recorded in the Soulié Family Ledgers or secondary materials, specific addresses associated with the Souliés, especially outside of the Vieux Carré, may remain unidentified.
83. Eulalie's mother, Louison, and her sister Adelaide are also *femme de couleur libres* heads of household in 1805, residing at 65 Rue St. Louis and 70 Rue St. Louis, respectively.
84. According to a search of The Collins C. Diboll Vieux Carré Digital Survey, Jean Soulié owned 818–820 Royal Street from 1794 to 1802. He possessed 633 Bourbon Street, 635–637 Bourbon Street, 1221 Dauphine Street, 929–931 St. Louis Street, 933 St. Louis Street, 639–806 St. Peter Street, and 810–814 St. Peter Street in the period between 1808 and 1814.
85. Marie Louise Lioteau will, September 6, 1815, Michel deArmas, notary, Ancestry.com, Louisiana, Wills and Probate Records, 1756–1984 [database online] (Provo, UT, USA: Ancestry.com Operations, 2015). All of these properties were sold in 1828 to settle Eulalie's estate.
86. "Proceedings of the Grand Lodge of Louisiana," 2011, A-1, A-23, accessed October 28, 2020, http://library.la-mason.com/PastProceedings/2010/2011.pdf.
87. "Administrations of the Mayors of New Orleans, James Mather (d. 1821)," LD/CASP-NOPL, accessed July 15, 2012, http://nutrias.org/info/louinfo/admins/mather.htm.

Online version of "Mayors of New Orleans, 1803–1936," compiled and edited by Work Projects Administration.
88. Kendall, *History of New Orleans*, 110, 113, 116.
89. Eulalie Mazange Estate Inventory, Eulalie Mazange, Louisiana, Court of Probates (Orleans Parish), General Index of All Successions, 1805–1846. Original document dated June 8, 1825, filed in office of Carlile Pollock, June 18, 1825.
90. Woods and Nolan, *Sacramental Records*, 16:266. Bernard Soulié notes in his journal that he had his mother's remains moved to a new cemetery on April 10, 1835. Research yields that the only burial ground established in the city that year was Bayou St. John Cemetery. It was active from 1835 to 1844 but vanished by 1880. It was alternately known as Potter's Field, City Cemetery, First Municipality Cemetery, and New Cemetery. La-Cemeteries, "Orleans Parish Cemeteries," accessed July 14, 2012, http://www.la-cemeteries.com/Cemeteries%20Orleans%20Table.shtml.
91. Older brother Norbert Soulié served as their *curator ad litem* (assistant in court).
92. *A Digest of the Civil Laws*; *Civil Code of the State of Louisiana*.
93. Process verbal of sale, May 23, 1828, Eulalie Mazange, Louisiana, Court of Probates (Orleans Parish), General Index of All Successions, 1805–1846; Chain of Title, 819 Bourbon Street, from the Collins C. Diboll Vieux Carré Digital Survey.
94. Chain of Title, 819 Bourbon Street, from the Collins C. Diboll Vieux Carré Digital Survey, https://www.hnoc.org/vcs/. Lafitte appears to have defaulted on the sale. The Collins C. Diboll Vieux Carré Digital Survey chain of title has daughter Eulalie obtaining the property from the estate on June 16, 1828. Eulalie and Norbert later transferred the property between one another in April 1829 and April 1833, with daughter Eulalie finally selling to Azelie Lombard in July 1833.
95. Procuration, Jean Soulié to Norbert Soulié, William Y. Lewis notary, April 16, 1827, referenced in Quittance and Release, Jean Soulié to Miramond O'Duhigg, vol. 4, act 145, April 19, 1831, NARC. NARC notes that "Acts from March 1824 to October 1838 are missing from the bound volumes of this Notary [William Y. Lewis], and were evidently destroyed by fire, which occurred in his office," accessed October 29, 2020, http://www.orleanscivilclerk.com/philpedesclauxindexes/pedesclaux_philippe_book_1.pdf.
96. "An Act to Prevent Free Persons of Colour from Entering into This State and for Other Purposes," March 16, 1830, amended March 25, 1831, in *A Digest of the Ordinances*, 535–544, 559.
97. Ancestry.com, New Orleans, Passenger Lists, 1820–1945 [database online] (Provo, UT: Ancestry.com Operations, 2006); Ancestry.com, New Orleans, Passenger List Quarterly Abstracts, 1820–1875 [database online] (Provo, UT: Ancestry.com Operations, 2011); Ancestry.com, New York Passenger Lists, 1820–1957 [database online] (Provo, UT: Ancestry.com Operations, 2010).
98. Spear, *Race, Sex, and Social Order*, 193.
99. From The Collins C. Diboll Vieux Carré Digital Survey, http://www.hnoc.org/vcs/.
100. From The Collins C. Diboll Vieux Carré Digital Survey, http://www.hnoc.org/vcs/.
101. Soulié ownership is confusing in the block of Dumaine Street between Decatur and

Chartres Streets. According to the Soulié Family Ledgers, nos. 17, 19, and 21 Dumaine Street (present-day nos. 525, 527, and 529–531) were owned by the family and rented out. However, the chains of title from The Collins C. Diboll Vieux Carré Digital Survey note that the properties were owned by Marie Jeanne Coraly Leroy in 1832. *Hommes de couleur libres* and business partners Julien Colvis and Joseph Dumas owned the properties from 1839 to 1846. Norbert Soulié also owned properties across the street, nos. 522, 524, and 526 (old nos. 14 and 16), from 1830 to 1866.

102. Benfey, *Degas in New Orleans*, 27–28. Benfey concludes that Norbert Soulié left New Orleans in 1833, but notarial documents support an earlier departure.
103. Procuration from Lucien Soulié to Léon Courcelle, Theodore Seghers notary, vol. 4, act 151, April 21, 1831, NARC; Procuration from Norbert Soulié to Léon Courcelle, Theodore Seghers notary, vol. 4, act 152, April 21, 1831, NARC; Joint Procuration from Norbert and Lucien Soulié to Léon Courcelle, Theodore Seghers notary, vol. 4, act 153, April 22, 1831, NARC.
104. Bernard and Albin Soulié to Belise Pradel, Ernest Eude notary, vol. 2, act 146, April 11, 1867, NARC; original act, Carlile Pollock notary, March 29, 1838. Duconge, a pharmacist, was a close family acquaintance. When Duconge died in 1874, Bernard Soulié noted in his journal, "F. P. Duconge, another of my friends from 1817, is dead in New Orleans." B. Soulié, "Journal of Bernard Soulié," 330.
105. Toledano and Christovich, *New Orleans Architecture*, 6:148.
106. Nelson Fouché to Bernard and Albin Soulié, Theodore Seghers notary, vol. 11, act 605, October 22, 1835, NARC; Toledano and Christovich, *New Orleans Architecture*, 6:172.
107. First Municipality to Bernard Soulié, Felix De Armas notary, vol. 51, act 88, March 11, 1837, NARC.
108. Andre August Bellonguet to Norbert Soulié, Theodore Seghers notary, vol. 21, act 441, May 1, 1837, NARC.
109. Sale of lots comprising 1529–1533 Ursulines Avenue referenced in Bernard Soulié to Lucien Soulié, Theodore Seghers notary, vol. 25, act 141, March 5, 1838, NARC; Appolinaire Perrault to Lucien Soulié, Charles Victor Foulon notary, vol. 1, act 22, April 21, 1838, NARC; Lucien Soulié to Therese Jourdan, Theodore Guyol notary, vol. 1, act 312, June 9, 1845, NARC; vol. 6, 196. Achille Barthélémy was the son of Achille Antoine Courcelle and the nephew of Léon Courcelle.
110. Bernard and Albin Soulié to Blaise Pradel, Ernest Eude notary, vol. 2, act 146, April 11, 1867, NARC.
111. Building contract between Norbert Soulié and Alexander Baggett, Theodore Seghers notary, vol. 30, act 499, June 4, 1839, NARC. Hevia Street was renamed Lafayette Street by order of City Ordinance O.S. 395, November 1856. Jewell, *Jewell's Digest of the City Ordinances*, 554.
112. Chain of Title, 520 N. Rampart Street, from the Collins C. Diboll Vieux Carré Digital Survey, The Historic New Orleans Collection, http://www.hnoc.org/vcs/. A *fieri facias* ruling is one by which the sheriff is authorized to take property from one against

whom a judgment has been rendered or when a sheriff obtains monies owed by selling sufficient property of the debtor.

113. John Richard Unruh to Norbert Soulié, Lucien Hermann notary, vol. 8, act 20, January 28, 1844, NARC; Norbert Soulié to Benjamin Poydras Delalande, Louis T. Caire, vol. 36, act 312, May 20, 1844, NARC.
114. Etienne Griffin to Albin Soulié, Theodore Seghers notary, vol. 1, act 369, July 7, 1845, NARC.
115. The four sisters are listed as single and living in the household of Albin Soulié in London at the 1871 census of England.
116. Procuration, Celeste, Eulalie, Louise, and Coralie Soulié to Bernard and Albin Soulié, Theodore Seghers notary, vol. 6, act 213, April 29, 1833, NARC (passed in Paris in November 1832). This document notes that the sisters are living in France and gives Bernard permission to act in their name.
117. The exception is Marie Louise, the second sister. For an undetermined reason, Louise does not appear with the other sisters in any transactions researched by the author. She also had a separate account with no real estate activity in the Soulié Family Ledger books.
118. Myrtille Courcelle to Demoiselles Soulié, Charles V. Foulon notary, vol. 12, act 41, February 4, 1843, NARC. Myrtille Courcelle appears to be the first-generation Souliés' first cousin. Courcelle's 1872 will indicates that he left property to his sister Leonide Courcelle, the daughter of Adelaide Vivant (Eulalie Mazange's sister) and Léon Courcelle. No birth records or historical information formally naming Myrtille Courcelle's parents or other siblings have been found, however.
119. Chain of Title, 1131–1133 Dauphine Street, from The Collins C. Diboll Vieux Carré Digital Survey, http://www.hnoc.org/vcs/.
120. Chain of Title, 823–827 Iberville, from The Collins C. Diboll Vieux Carré Digital Survey, http://www.hnoc.org/vcs/.
121. Martineau, *Society in America*, 2:116–117, and *Retrospect of Western Travel*, 1:259; Martin, "*Plaçage* and the Louisiana *Gens de Couleur Libre*," 67; Nelson, "People of Color in Louisiana," 22.
122. Force, "The House on Bayou Road," 35–36.
123. In his journal, Bernard notes that he occupied his house on "Rue des Ramparts" on April 6, 1836; B. Soulié, "Journal of Bernard Soulié," 324. Additional research is needed to determine the exact location of Bernard's residence. In directories from 1834–1859, Bernard's address is 377 North Rampart Street. From 1861 onward, he lived at 301 North Rampart Street. According to the compilers of the *New Orleans Architecture* series, old house number 377 was one of the townhouses in the 200 block of North Rampart Street; Toledano and Christovich, *New Orleans Architecture*, 6:178. Analysis of the 1883 Robinson Atlas, plate 7, suggests that old number 301 would have been on the site of Bernard's property at present-day 1225 North Rampart Street.
124. Love Street, the prolongment of Rampart Street from the Vieux Carré into Faubourg Marigny, and Rampart Street were renamed North Rampart Street as part of an

NOTES TO PAGES 51–60

initiative that streets running parallel to the river have the same names by order of City Ordinance O.S. 395, November 1856. Jewell, *Jewell's Digest of the City Ordinances*, 553.
125. In many cases, the surname of the renter (i.e., Taylor, Daunoy, Labatut), if not the whole name, was noted in the description of the rental property.
126. Soulié Family Ledgers, Book 1, pages 9, 95, WRC-THNOC.
127. The rental income totals for Norbert, Lucien, and the Soulié sisters were calculated by extracting amounts for rents paid from their individual accounts in the ledger books.
128. Lachance, "The Limits of Privilege," 70.
129. Thompson, *Exiles at Home*, 114.

CHAPTER 2. THE RAMIFICATIONS OF USE AND LOCATION

1. Thompson, *Exiles at Home*, 128.
2. Thompson, *Exiles at Home*, 128.
3. Edwards, "Shotgun," 65.
4. Edwards, "Shotgun," 65.
5. Thompson, *Exiles at Home*, 132.
6. Thompson, *Exiles at Home*, 132–133.
7. Christovich, Evans, and Toledano, *New Orleans Architecture*, 5:53.
8. Thompson, *Exiles at Home*, 128.
9. Thompson, *Exiles at Home*, 133.
10. The small antebellum population of this area may account for the small number of antebellum properties associated with free people of color located lakeside of Claiborne Avenue that were analyzed in the Faubourg Tremé/Bayou Road discussions in the *New Orleans Architecture* series.
11. Toledano and Christovich, *New Orleans Architecture*, 6:37, 38.
12. Octave De Armas notary, vol. 25, June 1835, NARC. Bernard Couvent was the husband of Marie Couvent, who is referenced throughout this book.
13. Toledano and Christovich, *New Orleans Architecture*, 6:56.
14. Lewis, *New Orleans*, 41.
15. Toledano and Christovich, *New Orleans Architecture*, 6:56–59.
16. Toledano and Christovich, *New Orleans Architecture*, 6:16. Classes were held in the plantation's *maison principale*.
17. Toledano and Christovich, *New Orleans Architecture*, 6:59.
18. Lewis, *New Orleans*, 45.
19. Lewis, *New Orleans*, 52.
20. Toledano and Christovich, *New Orleans Architecture*, 6:85.
21. The scope of the survey is limited in that it does not include demolished properties or those built by white Creoles or Americans that passed later into the hands of free Black owners.
22. New Orleans city directories indicate that a Joseph Dolliole Jr. (relationship unknown,

since no children are mentioned in the succession records of Joseph Dolliole) did live on Tremé between Ursulines Avenue and St. Peter Street in 1841 and 1842.

23. Toledano and Christovich, *New Orleans Architecture*, 6:142–143. The street named after Faubourg Tremé's founder, St. Claude Street, was renamed between St. Anthony Street and St. Philip Street in 2011 after *femme de couleur libre* and founder of the Catholic Order of the Holy Family Henriette Delille.
24. Smith, *Footprints of Black Louisiana*, 100–101; Crutcher, *Tremé: Race and Place*, 29. Economy Hall was demolished in 1965.
25. Toledano, Evans, and Christovich, *New Orleans Architecture*, 4:9.
26. Thompson, *Exiles at Home*, 142. Marigny's penchant for gambling was recognized in the selection of "Craps" as one of the street names.
27. Latrobe, *Impressions Respecting New Orleans*, 27. By comparison, the Dollioles' undeveloped sixty-foot by three-arpent (576 feet) properties along Bayou Road cost $1,900 and $4,000 in 1806 and 1807, respectively. In 1808, Jean Soulié purchased an undeveloped 75' × 120' lot at the corner of St. Peter and Bourbon Streets for $6,500.
28. Toledano, Evans, and Christovich, *New Orleans Architecture*, 4:9.
29. Eulalie Mazange estate inventory, June 8, 1825, filed in office of Carlile Pollock, June 18, 1825. See also Eulalie Mazange, Louisiana, Court of Probates (Orleans Parish), General Index of All Successions, 1805–1846, LD/CASP-NOPL.
30. Joseph Dolliole and Josefa Rodriguez were married in March 1822.
31. Faubourg Marigny Improvement Association, "Welcome to the Marigny!," accessed March 2, 2012, https://www.faubourgmarigny.org/historyfm.htm.
32. Toledano, Evans, and Christovich, *New Orleans Architecture*, 4:32, 131.
33. Elizabeth Neidenbach provides a thorough analysis of the free Black New Orleanians' property acquisition in Faubourg Marigny in her dissertation, "The Life and Legacy of Bernard Couvent."
34. Lewis, *New Orleans*, 45.
35. Lewis, *New Orleans*, 45.
36. Campanella, *Geographies of New Orleans*, 244.
37. The National Register of Historic Places (NRHP)–listed New Marigny Historic District consists of the historic Nouvelle Marigny, Franklin, and Daunois Faubourgs.
38. Preservation Resource Center of New Orleans, "New Marigny," brochure, accessed July 20, 2020, https://prcno.org/wp-content/uploads/2016/06/NewMarigny.pdf.
39. Building Contract file, NARC.
40. The faubourg's northern, or lakeside, boundary was less clearly defined. Today Florida Avenue is considered the northern boundary. See the City of New Orleans Neighborhood Engagement Office map of "Neighborhood and Community Organizations," accessed October 29, 2020, https://www.nola.gov/neighborhood-engagement/organizations/.
41. Faubourg St. Roch Improvement Association, "A Little History," accessed October 29, 2020, https://sites.google.com/site/fsrianeworleans/about.

42. Faubourg St. Roch Project, "Faubourg St. Roch History." Washington Promenade was later renamed St. Roch Avenue in 1894.
43. Bywater National Register of Historic Places nomination form. While the Bywater neighborhood extends from Franklin Avenue to the Inner Harbor Navigation Canal (also called the Industrial Canal), the NRHP Bywater Historic District is smaller, bound roughly by Montegut Street to the west and Poland Avenue to the east.
44. Toledano, Evans, and Christovich, *New Orleans Architecture*, 4:17. Faubourg Daunois is included in the National Register Faubourg Marigny Historic District. Faubourg Marigny Improvement Association, "Welcome to the Marigny!"
45. Preservation Resource Center of New Orleans, "New Marigny"; Toledano, Evans, and Christovich, *New Orleans Architecture*, 4:20.
46. Toledano, Evans, and Christovich, *New Orleans Architecture*, 4:20.
47. Toledano, Evans, and Christovich, *New Orleans Architecture*, 4:20.
48. Toledano, Evans, and Christovich, *New Orleans Architecture*, 4:20.
49. The neighborhood is named after Holy Cross High School, established on the Reynes plantation in 1859. Holy Cross Historic District National Register of Historic Places nomination form, 1986, National Register of Historic Places Digital Archive on NPGallery, https://npgallery.nps.gov/NRHP/AssetDetail?assetID=80cdeb60-6d48-494b-8fe0-71a81aa2020a.
50. This property was acquired after 1945 when Maurice Harrison's map of New Orleans still shows the undivided plantations. The house and land were sold between 1870 and 1874. Toledano, Evans, and Christovich, 4:147. Pierre Misotiére and Jean Soulié were both recorders under Charles Trudeau's term as Acting Mayor from May 16 to October 8, 1812, "Administrations of the Mayors of New Orleans, Charles Trudeau," LD/CASP-NOPL, accessed March 6, 2012, http://nutrias.org/info/louinfo/admins/trudeau.htm.
51. Christovich et al., *New Orleans Architecture*, 2:7.
52. Toledano, *National Trust Guide to New Orleans*, 89.
53. Christovich et al., *New Orleans Architecture*, 2:10.
54. Christovich et al., *New Orleans Architecture*, 2:10.
55. Nelson, "People of Color in Louisiana," 26.
56. Hémard, "Julie and Julia"; Toledano, *National Trust Guide to New Orleans*, 89.
57. John Soulié, as well as Julien Poydras, James McDonough, and others, was on the board when it was organized in January 1805. Rightor, *Standard History of New Orleans, Louisiana*, 584.
58. Building Contract between John B. D. Voisin and Louis Adam Voisin and Jean-Louis Dolliole, L. T. Caire notary, vol. 17, act 1010, November 9, 1831, NARC.
59. Christovich, Toledano, and Swanson, *New Orleans Architecture*, 1:3–34; Starr, *Southern Comfort*, 18. Faubourg La Course received its name from the plantation owner, Pierre Robin Delogny, who planned to build a racetrack (course) in the suburb.
60. Christovich, Toledano, and Swanson, *New Orleans Architecture*, 1:31.
61. Starr, *Southern Comfort*, 18.
62. Lewis, *New Orleans*, 43.

63. Thompson, *Exiles at Home*, 137.
64. Lewis, *New Orleans*, 46.
65. Curry, *The Free Black in Urban America*, 57.
66. Preservation Resource Center of New Orleans, "New Marigny."
67. Thompson, *Exiles at Home*, 131.

CHAPTER 3. THE ARCHITECTURE OF THE DOLLIOLE AND SOULIÉ FAMILIES

1. Based on the author's analysis of Latrobe's journal and other correspondence, his ramblings through and business in the city do not appear to have taken him to Faubourg Tremé. Latrobe, *The Journal of Latrobe*, 210; Latrobe, *Impressions Respecting New Orleans*; Van Horne, *Correspondence and Miscellaneous Papers*.
2. Fitch, "Creole Architecture 1718–1860," 85.
3. Neidenbach, "Life and Legacy of Marie Couvent," 396.
4. Neidenbach, "Life and Legacy of Marie Couvent," 396.
5. Neidenbach, "Life and Legacy of Marie Couvent," 396–397.
6. Woods, *From Craft to Profession*, 58.
7. The first recorded school for children of color was established in 1813, operated by G. Dorefuille. Marie Justine Sirnir Couvent's School for Indigent Orphans opened in 1848. Michel Séligny operated his Académie Sainte-Barbe from 1834 to 1847. J. L. Marciacq had a school in Faubourg Tremé. In Paris, *hommes de couleur libres* might enroll at the Collège Louis-le-Grand or the University of Paris or often attended specialized schools for the arts (Conservatoire de Paris), engineering (École Centrale), or medicine. New Orleans Public Library, "African Americans in New Orleans: *Les Gens de Couleur Libres*," online exhibit, accessed March 21, 2012, http://nutrias.org/~nopl/exhibits/fmc/fmc.htm; Nelson, "People of Color in Louisiana," 29; Fabre, "New Orleans Creole Expatriates in France"; Hobratsch, "Creole Angel," 17. See also Stern, *Race and Education in New Orleans*, and Neidenbach, "Life and Legacy of Marie Couvent."
8. Woods, *From Craft to Profession*, 12.
9. The extensive article "Free Persons of Color" in Volume 4 of the *New Orleans Architecture* series is the earliest secondary reference to Louis and Jean-François Dolliole being builders. Toledano, Evans, and Christovich, *New Orleans Architecture*, 4:32. Other sources simply cite this work. This information is also presented, uncited, in Toledano, *National Trust Guide to New Orleans*, 16, and also in Patton, *African-American Art*, 58.
10. Neither of the brothers lists his occupation in his last will and testament. Also, no building contracts under their names are found in the building contract index at the Notarial Archives Research Center.
11. Seventy-two other individuals, men and women, are listed with this occupation.
12. *Random House Webster's College Dictionary* (1996), s.v. "publican." The reference staff at the Louisiana Archives, New Orleans Public Library, support this definition, per email correspondence, Irene Wainwright, archivist, to author, October 12, 2012.
13. Louis Dolliole was testamentary executor of Jean-François's estate. Jean-François

Dolliole, Estate of 1816, Louisiana, Orleans Parish Estate Files, 1804–1846, LD/CASP-NOPL.

14. Johnson, "Colonial New Orleans," 50–51.
15. Poesch and Bacot, *Louisiana Buildings*, 18.
16. Poesch and Bacot, *Louisiana Buildings*, 35; Edwards and de Verton, *A Creole Lexicon*, s.v. "rez-de chaussée," 179.
17. Poesch and Bacot, *Louisiana Buildings*, 42.
18. Edwards and de Verton, *A Creole Lexicon*, s.v. "Creole cottage," 78.
19. Johnson, "Colonial New Orleans," 50–51. In his various works, the anthropologist Jay Edwards argues that the adaptation of local building traditions and conventions created the basis for Creole architecture in the New World as European colonization expanded across the Atlantic Ocean. His work also highlights the evolution of Louisiana Creole vernacular houses from their European prototypes via West Indian adaptations.
20. Edwards, "Vernacular Vision," 74, 77, 79–80.
21. Hunt, *Haiti's Influence on Antebellum America*, 9.
22. Edwards, "Origins of Creole Architecture," 158.
23. Edwards, "Origins of Creole Architecture," 155.
24. Edwards, "Origins of Creole Architecture," 188.
25. Heard, *French Quarter Manual*, 25.
26. Heard, *French Quarter Manual*, 25.
27. Heard, *French Quarter Manual*, 4, 25.
28. Hip-roofed Creole cottages continued to be built and were often referred to as *maisonettes*. Edwards, "Origins of Creole Architecture," s.v. "maisonette," 133.
29. Woods, *From Craft to Profession*, 20.
30. Vogt, *Historic Buildings of the French Quarter*, 16.
31. Per the 1876 Sanborn map. Photographs from 1937 depict a one-story, two-room outbuilding. The courtyard presently contains a nonhistoric outbuilding and pool.
32. This cottage is featured in many articles, including W. R. Mitchell Jr., *Classic New Orleans*, 68–71; Warren and Sexton, "Rooms with a Vieux," 28; Abry, "Cottage Industry," 66–71.
33. Toledano and Christovich, *New Orleans Architecture*, 6:xv.
34. Edwards and de Verton, *A Creole Lexicon*, s.v. "maison de maître," 133.
35. Toledano and Christovich, *New Orleans Architecture*, 6:xvi.
36. Toledano and Christovich, *New Orleans Architecture*, 6:xvi; Harris, *McGraw-Hill Dictionary of Architecture and Construction*, s.v. "maison de maître," cross-reference "Creole house," 613.
37. Christovich, Evans, and Toledano, *New Orleans Architecture*, 5:64–65. For an example of the Dolliole *maison de maître*'s floor plan, see the two-room galleried buildings depicted in J. A. Bourgerol's 1844 plan that appears in Toledano and Christovich, *New Orleans Architecture*, 6:46.
38. Toledano and Christovich, *New Orleans Architecture*, 6:xv, xvi.
39. The street façades of the cottage originally had a window-door-door-door-window-door

pattern. When restored in the 1940s or 1950s, the fenestration was altered so that the southwestern window was cut to form a door and the casement doorways were shortened to hold windows. The cottage was renovated again in the 1960s and is prominently featured in Mitchell, *Classic New Orleans*; it is an Orleans Parish Landmark.

40. Toledano, Evans, and Christovich, *New Orleans Architecture*, 4:96.
41. The house was originally located on the property at the corner of Pauger and Dauphine Streets. It was moved to its present location by subsequent owners after 1876. Toledano, Evans, and Christovich, *New Orleans Architecture*, 4:97.
42. Toledano, Evans, and Christovich, *New Orleans Architecture*, 4:96.
43. Toledano, Evans, and Christovich, *New Orleans Architecture*, 4:96–97.
44. Toledano, Evans, and Christovich, *New Orleans Architecture*, 4:96.
45. Neidenbach, "Life and Legacy of Marie Couvent," 349n111, 381.
46. In *New Orleans Architecture*, Volume 4 the petitioner is noted as Louis Dolliole, but he was deceased by the date of the April 16, 1822, city council records.
47. Toledano and Christovich, *New Orleans Architecture*, 6:91n54.
48. The 1876 Sanborn map depicts a one-story house at the site. By the 1896 Sanborn, the property was occupied by a two-story residence. This was probably the two-story townhouse on the property in the 1940s and 1950s. The site is currently occupied by a ca. 1963 building made to look like a Creole cottage.
49. This building was in turn demolished and replaced to look like a period Creole cottage.
50. Building contract between Jean-Louis Dolliole and Jean Baptiste Duforgé Voisin and Louis Adam, L. R. Caire, notary, vol. 17, act 1010, November 9, 1831, NARC.
51. The term used in the contract is *fenêtre à coulisses*.
52. The 1834 directory lists Joseph's address as St. Philip near St. Claude; Geneviève Dolliole estate inventory, Succession of Geneviève Dolliole, 1838, Louisiana, Court of Probates (Orleans Parish), General Index of All Successions, 1805–1846, City Archives and Special Collections, New Orleans Public Library, New Orleans, Louisiana.
53. The house was extant in 1883 but demolished at an unknown date.
54. The main dwelling at 1223–1225 St. Philip was demolished after the 1980 publication of *New Orleans Architecture*, Volume 6.
55. Joseph Dolliole to Marie Louise Demony, Theodore Seghers notary, vol. 4A, act 313, July 29, 1831, NARC. This property was located in Square no. 50 on the uptown side of St. Philip Street. If still extant at the time, it would have been demolished in the late 1960s for the creation of Louis Armstrong Park.
56. Heard, *French Quarter Manual*, 33.
57. Heard, *French Quarter Manual*, 33.
58. Partition between Jean-Louis Dolliole, Joseph Dolliole, and Norbert Fortier, Carlile Pollock notary, vol. 2, act 524, June 29, 1821, NARC. See lot "C" in Figure 46.
59. Vogt, *Historic Buildings of the French Quarter*, 16.
60. Heard, *French Quarter Manual*, 33.
61. The cottage at 1125 also has a nonhistoric rear addition.

62. The phenomenon of the Greek Key architrave door surround is chronicled in Edwards, "Unlocking the History of Greek Key Architecture," 84–91.
63. The south gable of the cottage has been altered since at least the 1940s or 1950s to include doors in place of or cut into existing windows and providing egress from the attic living space to a balcony. A nonhistoric roof dormer was added to the rear of the building at an unknown date. The property historically contained a two-story kitchen building that is extant.
64. The buildings were constructed by the time they were mentioned in Geneviève's estate inventory in 1838.
65. Toledano and Christovich, *New Orleans Architecture*, 6:180.
66. Toledano and Christovich, *New Orleans Architecture*, 6:181.
67. Toledano, *National Trust Guide to New Orleans*, 11, 13; Lachance, "Repercussions of the Haitian Revolution in Louisiana"; Hunt, *Haiti's Influence on Antebellum America*, 45.
68. This dissertation emphasizes the work of Jean-Louis, as more of his work is extant. Additional research may reveal more about the buildings that Joseph constructed, such as those in Faubourg Franklin that are no longer extant.
69. Arthur, *Old New Orleans*, 225; Chains of Title, 633 Bourbon Street, 635–637 Bourbon Street, 639–806 St. Peter Street, from The Collins C. Diboll Vieux Carré Digital Survey, http://www.hnoc.org/vcs/.
70. Benfey, *Degas in New Orleans*, 27.
71. Benfey, *Degas in New Orleans*, 124. The elder Vincent Rillieux was the great-grandfather of the painter Edgar Degas.
72. B. Soulié, "Journal of Bernard Soulié," 330.
73. The letter was dated September 6, 1817. Benjamin Henry Latrobe to John Rogers, October 6, 1817, in Van Horne, *Correspondence and Miscellaneous Papers*, 948. Norbert's letter to Latrobe, dated September 6 and received by Latrobe on October 4, is missing. Latrobe responded to him on October 6, 1817.
74. Woods, *From Craft to Profession*, 60.
75. Woods, *From Craft to Profession*, 18.
76. Woods, *From Craft to Profession*, 19.
77. Woods, *From Craft to Profession*, 60.
78. Mitchell, *Classic New Orleans*, 29; Benfey, *Degas in New Orleans*, 24; Latrobe, *Impressions Respecting New Orleans*, xxii. Latrobe's Orleans Theatre burned in 1816. William Brand's rebuild featured the addition of the Orleans Ballroom. Brand's Theatre was destroyed by fire in 1866; the ballroom is extant. Bruce, *Great Houses of New Orleans*, 33.
79. Index to Richard Butler Papers, 1795–1899, LSU Libraries Special Collections, Louisiana State University, Baton Rouge.
80. Building contract between Margaret Chabot and [Henry Sellon] Bonneval Latrobe, Michel De Armas notary, vol. 2, act 212, April 24, 1817, NARC.
81. The Chabot cottage is not extant. The property (221–225 Bourbon Street) is occupied by a ca. 1834 three-story Creole townhouse.
82. Toledano, *National Trust Guide to New Orleans*, 32.

83. The portico was revealed during the building's renovation in 1940. At that time, the rear outbuilding of the adjacent building had been incorporated into the floor plan of the Thierry House. The house and one-story outbuilding were divided into apartments. The ell connecting the house to the outbuilding is a later addition; from The Collins C. Diboll Vieux Carré Digital Survey, http://www.hnoc.org/vcs/.
84. Latrobe, *Impressions Respecting New Orleans*, xxii.
85. Agreement between Jean-Baptiste Longpré and Norbert Soulié, May 6, 1818, Jean-Baptiste Longpré archive, 1798–1846, WRC-THNOC. Norbert also built a two-story kitchen building and privy on the property.
86. Benjamin Henry Latrobe's last work in New Orleans was the Louisiana State Bank (1819). Jean Soulié was a member of the board of directors. Fossier, *New Orleans: The Glamour Period*, 63–64; Poll, "A Foundational Study."
87. Van Horne, *Correspondence and Miscellaneous Papers*, 1035n1.
88. Norbert's supposed work at Evergreen plantation likely would have been in this period. Samuel Wilson notes: "The names of Norbert Soulié, who worked with Henry S. Latrobe, architect, and Louis Pilié, architect and New Orleans city surveyor, are mentioned in financial statements of the plantation"; Wilson, *Guide to the Architecture of New Orleans*, 54. The nature and duration of his involvement are unknown to this author, as Evergreen plantation is privately owned, and the financial documents are not publicly available. As he left for Paris that year, Norbert Soulié would probably not have been involved in the major remodeling undertaken at the plantation starting in 1832.
89. Constance Vivant acquired a thirty-foot portion from Marie Louis Tavier in 1805 and a fifteen-foot portion from her mother, Louison Cheval, in 1818. Chain of Title, 509 Burgundy Street, The Collins C. Diboll Vieux Carré Digital Survey, https://www.hnoc.org/vcs/; Free People of Color Index, WRC-THNOC.
90. Norbert Soulié to Constant Vivant, Theodore Seghers notary, vol. 4, act 66, February 26, 1831, NARC.
91. Edith Long, "Creole Cottage Blooms under Scott Touch," *Vieux Carré Courier*, March 17, 1967, 2.
92. Heard, *French Quarter Manual*, 35.
93. Heard, *French Quarter Manual*, 37.
94. Heard, *French Quarter Manual*, 38–43; Edwards and de Verton, *A Creole Lexicon*, s.v. "Creole townhouse," 80.
95. This addition was made before 1876, as it appears in the Sanborn Fire Insurance map of that year.
96. Chain of title, 814 Governor Nicholls, from The Collins C. Diboll Vieux Carré Digital Survey, http://www.hnoc.org/vcs/.
97. Heard, *French Quarter Manual*, 35.
98. Long, "Creole Cottage Blooms," 2.
99. The historic photograph shows that the carriageway was marked by double paneled doors topped by an elliptical fanlight. At the flanking doorways, two on each side, were glazed and paneled casement doors fronted by paneled shutters (the leftmost opening

had been replaced by a projecting bay window by 1893). The second-level windows and doors were concealed by louvered shutters, but they were likely casement openings. A wrought-iron balcony extended from the second story at the three central doors. At the roofline was a simple entablature.

100. A 1963 photograph of the house in the Vieux Carré Survey shows that the exterior was later painted. This is noted by Edith Long as well.
101. Long, "Creole Cottage Blooms," 2. The five-story Royal Sonesta (1968–1969) was designed by Curtis and Davis in association with Koch and Wilson Architects to follow the form of traditional row houses built around an interior courtyard, from the Collins C. Diboll Vieux Carré Digital Survey, https://www.hnoc.org/vcs/.
102. In *New Orleans Architecture* (6:178), the authors date the row houses to ca. 1834 based on this information: "The city directories for 1834 and 1837 list Bernard Soulié, Norbert's relative and business associate, at 377 Rampart, *the old address for one of the houses*" (emphasis mine). However, since Norbert had relocated to France in 1831, he was long gone by that time. If built by Norbert before his departure, these row houses constitute very early examples of Greek Revival townhouses (the Greek Revival style did not make an entrance into New Orleans vernacular architecture before ca. 1835). Otherwise, the townhouses would have been built by Bernard and Albin or, in reality, "built" by the Souliés in the sense that they commissioned the buildings.
103. At present, archival research has not revealed if Norbert constructed three or four party-wall townhouses at this site. The 1819 purchase noted the sale of only three lots. However, the Soulié Family Ledgers show that Norbert collected rents as an absentee landlord for four properties here in the 1840s: nos. 41, 43, 45, and 47 Rampart. It appears that Norbert acquired an adjacent lot with an extant building or built a fourth townhouse. Or, he divided his three lots into four.
104. Toledano and Christovich, *New Orleans Architecture*, 6:178.
105. Constructed in 1847, the three-story grouping at North Rampart and Conti contained three individual dwellings, but the street façades were unified by a continuous cornice line and a roofed, wrought-iron balcony at the second level. The multilight windows were uniform in size on each level and protected by louvered shutters. An unpedimented door surround with simple entablature framed each entry doorway, which consisted of a single paneled door topped by a transom. Concealed hallways from the entries provided access to the ground-floor rooms, staircases, and rear courtyards.
106. While the Soulié row houses have retained much of their original form, the ground floors of the extant buildings were severely altered when converted to storefronts by the 1970s. Toledano and Christovich, *New Orleans Architecture*, 6:178. The façades of the row houses have subsequently been restored to their present, more historic, appearance. Alterations to the rear of the buildings have been extensive. At No. 229, the outbuilding was extended into the courtyard (partially by 1876) and the roofline changed. An elevator tower was added between the main dwelling and the outbuilding. At No. 229, a story has possibly been added to the outbuilding (by 1876). The rear

of each courtyard has been infilled with a nonhistoric garage opening onto Basin Street.
107. The site of the refinery was along the levee at St. Peter Street between Reynes and Forstall Streets.
108. Benfey, *Degas in New Orleans*, 27.
109. Gibson, *Gibson's Guide*, 318.
110. The author created this description of the Louisiana Sugar Refinery through comparison with the refinery formerly at Ashland plantation. See http://www.crt.state.la.us/dataprojects/archaeology/virtualbooks/greathou/sugar.htm, accessed October 29, 2020. When Henry Howard made additions to the Louisiana Sugar Refinery in the 1850s, his work included connecting the sugarhouse and rear building and creating an upriver extension in the ell between the front wing and sugarhouse.
111. Gibson, *Gibson's Guide*, 318.
112. Gibson, *Gibson's Guide*, 318. Both buildings were represented on *Topographical Map of New Orleans and Its Vicinity*, Charles F. Zimpel surveyor, 1833, The Historic New Orleans Collection.
113. Benfey, *Degas in New Orleans*, 27, 29.
114. The conflict also created lasting enmity between the Rillieux family and Edmund Forstall. Even after Forstall hired engineer-inventor Norbert Rillieux, Edmond Rillieux's older brother, to serve as head of the refinery in 1833, that business relationship ended unsuccessfully. Forstall later publicly opposed Norbert Rillieux's plans for improving New Orleans's drainage and sewer systems. Benfey, *Degas in New Orleans*, 128; West, "From Sugar Bowl to the International Space Station."
115. Procuration from Lucien Soulié to Léon Courcelle, Theodore Seghers notary, vol. 4, act 151, April 21, 1831, NARC; Procuration from Norbert Soulié to Léon Courcelle, Theodore Seghers notary, vol. 4, act 152, April 21, 1831, NARC; Joint Procuration from Norbert and Lucien Soulié to Léon Courcelle, Theodore Seghers notary, vol. 4, act 153, April 22, 1831, NARC.
116. Among undocumented buildings in New Orleans, research completed by the architect Samuel Wilson Jr. indicates that Norbert also did work at Evergreen plantation in Edgard, Louisiana, based on Soulié's name in the plantation's financial records. The plantation is privately owned, and its records are not available to the public.
117. In French legal documents, Norbert's occupation is noted as "*proprietaire*," or landowner. In the summer of 1834, he was traveling throughout Europe, visiting Italy, Vienna, Dresden, Berlin, Stockholm, and Moscow. Benfey, *Degas in New Orleans*, 23.
118. *Société* (business partnership, enterprise) between Bernard and Albin Soulié, Theodore Seghers notary, vol. 6, act 202, April 22, 1833, NARC.
119. *Société* between Bernard and Albin Soulié, Theodore Seghers notary, vol. 6, act 202, April 22, 1833, NARC.
120. This house was retained by the Soulié family as an income property for many years. It was not sold until 1885, after Bernard had moved to Paris in 1875 and after his death in 1881. After years of alterations and neglect, the cottage was renovated from 2009 to 2011.

121. Toledano and Christovich, *New Orleans Architecture*, 6:196. The author has not found the original acts documenting these transactions.
122. Toledano and Christovich, *New Orleans Architecture*, 6:6, 117.
123. Bernard Soulié's frequent trips, and those of many relatives and close acquaintances, are noted in his journal.
124. Procuration, Albin Soulié to Bernard Soulié, C. V. Foulon notary, vol. 16, act 189, May 20, 1845, NARC. Albin departed on May 26, taking Bernard and Eliza's two young sons with him. B. Soulié, "Journal of Bernard Soulié," 325.
125. Toledano and Christovich, *New Orleans Architecture*, 6:15–16.

CHAPTER 4. "UNCOMMON INDUSTRY"

1. Lachance, "Repercussions of the Haitian Revolution in Louisiana," 214.
2. Woods, *From Craft to Profession*, 11.
3. Curry, *The Free Black in Urban America*, 25, 260, 261.
4. Curry, *The Free Black in Urban America*, 35.
5. Boisdoré's age was given as sixty-eight years at the 1850 federal census, but as eighty years in his death record. USGenWeb, Orleans Parish Death Index, http://www.usgwarchives.org/la/orleans/death-index.htm.
6. The 1850 census notes that he was born in Louisiana. See also Toledano and Christovich, *New Orleans Architecture*, 6:93.
7. Toledano and Christovich, *New Orleans Architecture*, 6:93.
8. Toledano and Christovich, *New Orleans Architecture*, 6:93; Plan Book 84, folio 14, Plan Book Plans Collection, NARC.
9. Ursain Guesnon (1843), "Louisiana, Orleans Parish Estate Files, 1804–1846," index and images, FamilySearch, accessed March 27, 2012, https://familysearch.org/pal:/MM9.1.1/JJZ8-443.
10. Ursain's parents are listed in the death certificate in his estate file. The municipal record notes that on July 9, 1828, Jacques Guesnon was paid $4.00 for the hire of his slave Marie. From the online collection overview of the New Orleans Municipal Records, 1782–1925, Louisiana Research Collection, Tulane University, New Orleans, accessed April 10, 2012, http://specialcollections.tulane.edu/archon/?p=collections/findingaid&id=35&q=&rootcontentid=118621.
11. Toledano, Evans, and Christovich, *New Orleans Architecture*, 4:94. The site plan for the Dussau/Dolliole property identifies the property as belonging to Jacques Guesnon, h.c.l., which means that Jacques Guesnon originally purchased the property and was misidentified as a person of color or that the lot belonged to Ursain, and his father's name was indicated on the plan erroneously.
12. Ursain's death certificate notes that they were married on September 21, 1811.
13. Ursain Guesnon's residence at that address is also accounted for in the 1832 and 1842 city directories.
14. Toledano, Evans, and Christovich, *New Orleans Architecture*, 4:94.

15. "Account and tableau of distribution," Ursain Guesnon (1843), "Louisiana, Orleans Parish Estate Files, 1804–1846," index and images, FamilySearch, accessed March 27, 2012, https://familysearch.org/pal:/MM9.1.1/JJZ8-443.
16. Toledano, Evans, and Christovich, *New Orleans Architecture*, 4:94.
17. New Orleans (La.) Justices of the Peace, Index to Marriage Records, 1846–1880, LD/CASP-NOPL, http://nutrias.org/inv/jpmarrindex/jpmarrindex.htm. They were only married for a year, as Marie Eugenie died on September 24, 1859. USGenWeb, Orleans Parish Death.
18. Building contract between N. L. Lauriano and Louis Vivant, L. T. Caire notary, vol. 21, act 683, June 29, 1832, NARC.
19. Soulié Family Ledgers, Book 1, page 1, WRC-THNOC.
20. Soulié Family Ledgers, Book 1, page 5, WRC-THNOC.
21. Building contract between Louis Vivant and Jesse Connor, Lucien Hermann notary, vol. 12, act 55, February 13, 1846, NARC. The house was completed by the builder André Gregoire for an additional $265. Toledano and Christovich, *New Orleans Architecture*, 6:170.
22. Toledano and Christovich, in *New Orleans Architecture* (6:170), note that the house at 1729–1731 could be the Connor house built by Vivant. Later in the century, Victorian shotguns were added to the neighborhood. It was probably during this period that the cottage was demolished. It does not appear on the 1883 Robinson Atlas.
23. Building contract between Uranie Roy and Louis Vivant, Felix Percy notary, vol. 25, act 344, November 24, 1846, NARC. A search of the Vieux Carré Survey yields that only one property owner with the surname Roy owned property in this block at 1031–1033 Burgundy. The cottage built by Vivant is not extant.
24. Louis Vivant died on June 7, 1870, at the age of seventy-four. USGenWeb, State Archives, Orleans Parish Death Index, accessed March 17, 2011, http://files.usgwarchives.net/la/orleans/vitals/deaths/index/1870disz.txt. Bernard Soulié recorded Louis Vivant's death date in his journal. Louis Vivant was married to Caroline Hastier. They had at least three children: Louise, Madeleine Celeste, and Louis Jr. per this author's survey of the *Sacramental Records* volumes. Louis Jr. is listed with his family at the 1880 census, his occupation that of brick mason.
25. New Orleans city directories, 1841–1858. His address was located between Villeré and Marais Streets from 1841 to 1846. It was 269 St. Philip Street from 1849 to 1858 and then changed to 317 St. Philip Street in 1859.
26. Myrtille Courcelle's succession record and estate file do not identify Léon Courcelle's natural children. The identities of Léon Courcelle's children with Adelaide Vivant are gleaned from analysis of the baptismal records of the archdiocese. Myrtille's name, however, does not appear in these records. The author determined Myrtille Courcelle's parentage from the fact that he bears the last name Courcelle, lists his sister (a confirmed daughter of Adelaide and Léon) as an heir in his will, and is identified as the son of Adelaide and Léon in several genealogical family trees in online searches. Léon Courcelle (1843), Louisiana, Orleans Parish Estate Files, 1804–1846, index and images,

FamilySearch, accessed March 27, 2012, https://familysearch.org/pal:/MM9.1.1/JJZ7-X4C.
27. Toledano and Christovich, *New Orleans Architecture*, 6:161.
28. Toledano and Christovich, *New Orleans Architecture*, 6:161.
29. Toledano and Christovich, *New Orleans Architecture*, 6:189.
30. A nonhistoric rear addition has expanded the house almost to the rear property line, allowing for increased interior space so that it can function as three residences, continuing its use as a multifamily dwelling in the present.
31. Building contract between Marguerite Boisdoré and Myrtille Courcelle, A. Mazareau notary, April 28, 1836, NARC.
32. The cottage is now a wing of the Charbonnet-Labat-Glapion Funeral Home. It has been adjoined to the adjacent building via a connector in the passageway and a rear addition.
33. Building contract between Myrtille Courcelle and Doctor Henry Daret, Lucien Hermann notary, vol. 9, act 266, July 9, 1844, NARC.
34. Chain of Title, 832 St. Philip Street, from the Collins C. Diboll Vieux Carré Digital Survey, http://www.hnoc.org/vcs/.
35. Heard, *French Quarter Manual*, 38.
36. Heard, *French Quarter Manual*, 38.
37. The building contract notes that "La vitrerie sera se premiere qualité en verre francais" and "La charpente pour supporter le toit sera en bois de cypres et fait à la francaise."
38. Léon Courcelle (1843), Louisiana, Orleans Parish Estate Files, 1804–1846, index and images, FamilySearch, accessed March 27, 2012, https://familysearch.org/pal:/MM9.1.1/JJZ7-X4C.
39. University of Notre Dame, Archives Calendar 1857, accessed October 17, 2012, http://archives.nd.edu/calendar.htm. See also Index to marriage records, 1846–1880, LD/CASP-NOPL.
40. Index to marriage records, 1846–1880, LD/CASP-NOPL, accessed December 12, 2011, http://nutrias.org/inv/jpmarrindex/cos_coz.htm.
41. USGenWeb Orleans Parish Death Index, accessed March 18, 2011, http://files.usgwarchives.net/la/orleans/vitals/deaths/index/1872diad.txt; Myrtille Courcelle (No. 35262), Louisiana, Second District Court, Successions, 1846–1880, LD/CASP-NOPL. The date of Myrtille Courcelle's death was also noted in Bernard Soulié's journal.
42. Sally Reeves, "French Speaking '*Hommes de Couleur Libres*' Left Indelible Mark on the Culture and Development of the French Quarter," accessed April 8, 2012, http://frenchquarter.com/history/freepeople.php. Only thirteen contracts with Joseph Chateau as builder are noted in Okude, "Application of Linguistic Concepts."
43. Building contract between Joseph Charles [Chateau] and Jean Baptiste Couvertie, Charles Foulon notary, vol. 14, act 185, June 13, 1844, NARC; Chain of Title, 416–418 Burgundy Street, from The Collins C. Diboll Vieux Carré Digital Survey, http://www.hnoc.org/vcs/. The alias used here may account for the confusion as to the number of Chateau's building contracts, as noted above.

44. The reconstructed floor plans of Joseph Chateau's works are based on Okude's analysis of the building descriptions in the building contracts.
45. Building contract between Ramon Vionnet and Joseph Chateau, Amedee Ducatel notary, vol. 26, act 107, April 11, 1845, NARC.
46. Reeves, "French Speaking '*Hommes de Couleur Libres*.'"
47. Building contract between Sophia Philips and Joseph Chateau, Theodore Guyol notary, vol. 1, act 256, May 15, 1845, NARC.
48. Building contract between Joseph Chateau and Mrs. Geneve Arnault, L. T. Caire notary, vol. 99, act 352, July 12, 1845, NARC.
49. Chain of Title, 422 Burgundy Street, from The Collins C. Diboll Vieux Carré Digital Survey, http://www.hnoc.org/vcs/. Building contract between Joseph Chateau and Jean Baptiste Couvertie, Charles Foulon notary, vol. 18, act 10, January 17, 1846, NARC.
50. Chimneys from the fireplaces in the three front rooms rise from the projecting fire wall on one side of the building. On the other, the roof overhang provides shelter over the corridor to the rear courtyard. Attention to detail is paid at the front façade with projecting sills and lintels at the batten shutter–covered door and window, dentiled cornice, and iron bar–supported *abat-vent*.
51. This temporary linear house form began to be moved from the rear of properties to the street. *Appentis* cottages continued to be built until the 1840s. Edwards, "Shotgun," 70–71; Edwards, "New Orleans Shotgun," 63–64. The *appentis* cottage merged with the Haitian *ti kay* house to form the linear Creole cottage and was a precursor to the shotgun house.
52. Reeves, "French Speaking '*Hommes de Couleur Libres*.'"
53. Building contracts with John Dowson (Octave De Armas notary, vol. 36, act 80, June 20, 1844, NARC), Pierre Heno (Octave De Armas notary, vol. 36, act 83, June 29, 1844, NARC), and Mrs. Nicholas Johnson (L. T. Caire notary, vol. 97, act 337, July 3, 1845, NARC).
54. Building contract between Joseph Chateau and Andrew Oscar Murphy, Edward Barnett notary, vol. 37, act 519A, April 30, 1847, NARC.
55. Starr, *Southern Comfort*, 115.
56. Reeves, "French Speaking '*Hommes de Couleur Libres*.'"
57. Toledano, *National Trust Guide to New Orleans*, 11, 13; Lachance, *The Foreign French*, 104; Hunt, *Haiti's Influence on Antebellum America*, 45.
58. This is based on the author's search of names of specific *gens de couleur libres* builders active primarily from 1820 to 1850 and whose names and activities are listed most frequently in *New Orleans Architecture*, Volumes 4 and 6 on Faubourg Tremé and the Creole faubourgs and in Okude's PhD dissertation.
59. Edwards, "Shotgun," 93n39.
60. Edwards, "Shotgun," 93n39.
61. The single *maisonette* (also called the *maison longue*) is similar to a French Creole cottage in that it has a hipped roof supported by Norman roof trusses and French doors that open onto the banquette. The disposition of the interior rooms, however, is

arranged single-file like the shotgun. Edwards, "Shotgun," 72; Edwards, "New Orleans Shotgun," 69–70.

62. Edwards, "Shotgun," 93n39; Chains of Title, 1018–1020 and 1022–1024 Governor Nicholls, from The Collins C. Diboll Vieux Carré Digital Survey, http://www.hnoc.org/vcs/. Roup is listed as the owner of this property in a private survey conducted by Barthélémy Lafon, *Arpenteur-général dés territoires Sud du Ténnessée*, April 8, 1808, WRC-THNOC.

63. Toledano and Christovich, *New Orleans Architecture*, 6:22. Roup also purchased property in Faubourg Pontchartrain in 1816. Edwards, "Shotgun," 93n39.

64. This description is from the house's subsequent sale in 1845. Toledano and Christovich, *New Orleans Architecture*, 6:179. Today, the cottage's dynamic façade is obscured behind coats of paint, and the entry steps have been removed. The gated wall to the rear courtyard and fire wall have been removed to allow for expansion of the adjacent lot.

65. Toledano and Christovich, *New Orleans Architecture*, 6:179.

66. Christovich et al., *New Orleans Architecture*, 5:48–49. The cottage and outbuilding built by Roup were demolished after 1947.

67. Edwards, "Shotgun," 78. Roup died at age thirty-seven on March 19, 1836. USGenWeb, Orleans Parish Death Index, http://www.usgwarchives.org/la/orleans/death-index.htm. He was married to Catherine Coralie Lafitte, who was the daughter of Pierre Lafitte (brother of pirate Jean Lafitte) and *femme de couleur libre* Marie Louis Villard. Toledano and Christovich, *New Orleans Architecture*, 6:102; see also Davis, *The Pirates Laffite*.

68. Toledano and Christovich, *New Orleans Architecture*, 6:102. Perseverance Lodge is currently part of the Louis Armstrong Park complex in Faubourg Tremé.

69. Building contract between Dr. Germain Ducatel, B. F. Fox, and Bickel and Hamblet, Felix De Armas notary, vol. 3, act 217, March 31, 1825, NARC.

70. Fouché's age and place of birth are not certain, because at the 1850 and 1860 federal censuses, they are noted as age fifty/Jamaica and age fifty-four/Cuba, respectively. Search of the LD/CASP-NOPL Louisiana Biography and Obituary Index and the USGenWeb Orleans Parish Death Records Index did not reveal Fouché's date of death. As he does not appear at the 1870 census, he likely died between 1860 and 1870. Through recent research, the author has located the gravesite of a Thomas Nelson Fouché, but cannot confirm this is the same person. "Thomas Nelson Fouché," *Find a Grave* index, accessed July 20, 2020, https://www.findagrave.com/memorial/165228744.

71. Maduell Jr., *Marriages and Family Relationships of New Orleans, 1820–1830*, 78; Toledano and Christovich, *New Orleans Architecture*, 6:102; marriage contract between Nelson Fouché and Françoise Le Febvre, Marc Lafitte notary, vol. 2, act 145, January 28, 1823, NARC.

72. Lachance, Index to New Orleans Indentures, 1809–1843, LD/CASP-NOPL, http://nutrias.org/~nopl/inv/ indentures/indent-fh.htm#f.

73. Toledano, Evans, and Christovich, *New Orleans Architecture*, 4:32–33.

74. Toledano and Christovich, *New Orleans Architecture*, 6:xv.

75. Theodore Seghers notary, vol. 11, acts 642 and 645, NARC.

76. Toledano, Evans, and Christovich, *New Orleans Architecture*, 4:107.
77. The city directory from the following year indicates that the commercial function of the ground floor of the Chartres Street house was a "beer house."
78. Toledano, Evans, and Christovich, *New Orleans Architecture*, 4:33.
79. The 1850 federal census was the first to list occupations by race. It listed one African American architect in the country who lived in New Orleans. This was Louis Nelson Fouché. Woods, *From Craft to Profession*, 99.
80. Most of the men discussed in any detail in Desdunes's account were still active in their fields after the Civil War and in the late 1800s. Desdunes, *Our People and Our History*, 289.
81. Toledano, Evans, and Christovich, *New Orleans Architecture*, 4:33. A depiction with the elevation, floor plan, and survey of a now demolished cottage in the 700 block of Franklin Street is one example of his output. Louis Nelson Fouché's work in this capacity is documented until 1864.
82. Neidenbach, "Life and Legacy of Marie Couvent," 389–390; Knight, "Builders and Building in New Orleans," 78.

CHAPTER 5. "RAISED TO THE TRADE"

1. Edwards and de Verton, *A Creole Lexicon*, s.v. "charpenterie," 52; s.v. "menuiserie," 137.
2. Edwards and de Verton, *A Creole Lexicon*, s.v. "charpenterie," 52; s.v. "menuiserie," 137; Harris, *McGraw-Hill Dictionary of Architecture and Construction*, s.v. "joinery," 555.
3. Edwards and de Verton, *A Creole Lexicon*, s.v. "ébénisterie," 88. A journeyman was an individual who had completed his apprenticeship and was qualified to work in his trade but under a teacher's employ. Harris, *McGraw-Hill Dictionary of Architecture and Construction*, s.v. "journeyman," 557.
4. Woods, *From Craft to Profession*, 12.
5. Woods, *From Craft to Profession*, 12.
6. Building contract between Myrtille Courcelle and Doctor Henry Daret, Lucien Hermann notary, vol. 9, act 266, July 9, 1844, NARC.
7. Woods, *From Craft to Profession*, 23.
8. Woods, *From Craft to Profession*, 12.
9. Joseph Dolliole to Marie Louis Demony, Theodore Seghers notary, vol. 4A, act 313, July 29, 1831, NARC.
10. Jean-Louis Dolliole to Joseph Dolliole, John Lynd notary, vol. 11, act 386, September 21, 1814, NARC.
11. Translated from Jean-Louis Dolliole to Joseph Dolliole, John Lynd notary, vol. 11, act 386, September 21, 1814, NARC.
12. Jean-Louis Dolliole was Henry Fletcher's executor. Henry Fletcher Estate Inventory, October 17, 1853, Achille Chiapella notary, Ancestry.com, Louisiana, Wills and Probate Records, 1756–1984 [database online] (Provo, UT: Ancestry.com Operations, 2015),

original data: Louisiana County, District and Probate Courts; Neidenbach, "Life and Legacy of Marie Couvent," 381.
13. Toledano, Evans, and Christovich, *New Orleans Architecture*, 4:33.
14. Toledano, Evans, and Christovich, *New Orleans Architecture*, 4:33.
15. B. Soulié, "Journal of Bernard Soulié," 325.
16. B. Soulié, "Journal of Bernard Soulié," 325.
17. Force, "The House on Bayou Road," 36.
18. Jean-Louis Dolliole to Joseph Dolliole, John Lynd notary, vol. 11, act 386, September 21, 1814, NARC.
19. Edwards, "Shotgun" 93n39.
20. Gwendolyn Midlo Hall, compiler, *Afro-Louisiana History and Genealogy, 1719–1820*, database, accessed July 20, 2020, http://www.ibiblio.org/laslave/individ.php?sid=72974 and http://www.ibiblio.org/laslave/individ.php?sid=75507.
21. These additional men were simply identified as "Negro [name]." One example is located in the Soulié Family Ledgers, Book 1, page 7, WRC-THNOC.
22. Soulié Family Ledgers, Book 1, pages 1, 4, 5, 11, 82, 83, 97, WRC-THNOC. Belsunce Liotau was either a relative or close acquaintance. He is the only one of these men mentioned in Bernard Soulié's journal; he recorded Liotau's death on April 10, 1873. B. Soulié, "Journal of Bernard Soulié," 329. No other biographical information could be found on Liotau except that Belsunce Louis Liotau (or Liataud) was married to Charlotte Hudson (1812–1837), the sister of *homme de couleur libre* painter Julien Hudson. Greenwald, *In Search of Julien Hudson*, 12.
23. Gallier, *Autobiography of James Gallier*, 33.
24. Knight, "Builders and Building in New Orleans," 77.
25. *Société* between Lucien and Norbert Soulié, Theodore Seghers notary, vol. 4, act 153, April 22, 1831, NARC.
26. *Société* between Bernard and Albin Soulié, Theodore Seghers notary, vol. 6, act 202, April 22, 1833, NARC.
27. Toledano and Christovich, *New Orleans Architecture*, 6:101.
28. Wilson and Cangelosi, Building Contract Index, NARC; Toledano and Christovich, *New Orleans Architecture*, 6:101.
29. Both men had different careers prior to the partnership. Cordeviolle is listed in the 1822 city directory as the owner of the dry goods store at 127 Bourbon (at the corner of Main), and Lacroix was a cabinetmaker whose address was 23 Bagatelle (at the corner of Peace).
30. The firm can be documented at several addresses over the years: 141 Chartres, 150 Chartres (1832) 123 Chartres (1838). Toledano, Evans, and Christovich, 4:35; "The World of François Lacroix," online exhibit, LD/CASP-NOPL.
31. Toledano, Evans, and Christovich, *New Orleans Architecture*, 4:35, 112.
32. Woods, *From Craft to Profession*, 111.
33. Woods, *From Craft to Profession*, 11.
34. Bardaglio, *Reconstructing the Household*, 104.

35. Woods, *From Craft to Profession*, 55.
36. "The Law on Indentures passed on May 21, 1806," accessed April 16, 2012, http://nutrias.org/~nopl/inv/indentures/ind-law.htm; *Acts Passed at the First Session of the First Legislature of the Territory of Orleans*, 44–56.
37. Hunt, *Haiti's Influence on Antebellum America*, 50.
38. Hunt, *Haiti's Influence on Antebellum America*, 50–51; Lachance, Index to New Orleans Indentures, 1809–1843, LD/CASP-NOPL. The firm of Latour and Laclotte had an atelier in a Creole cottage at 625 Dauphine Street.
39. Woods, *From Craft to Profession*, 55.
40. Brassieur, "Builders' Voices," 113.
41. Brusle's and Bonnecaze's occupations are noted at the 1860 census, when they, their wives, and their children are all living in Jean-Louis Dolliole's household. This might suggest that the men helped their father-in-law with his work if he was still actively building.
42. Urquhart's occupation is listed on the death certificate of Geneviève Dolliole, which he witnessed. Geneviève Dolliole, Estate of 1838, Louisiana, Orleans Parish Estate Files, 1804–1846, LD/CASP-NOPL.
43. Guesnon succession petition found on FamilySearch. The couple was married on February 16, 1858. She died a year and a half later on September 24, 1859. They had no offspring. New Orleans (La.) Justices of the Peace, Index to Marriage Records, 1846–1880, LD/CASP-NOPL, http://nutrias.org/inv/jpmarrindex/jpmarrindex.htm; USGenWeb, Orleans Parish Death Index, http://www.usgwarchives.org/la/orleans/death-index.htm.
44. The author has not found a link to this Pierre Dolliole and the Black descendants of Louis Dolliole and François Dolliole. His name appears in census records and city directories, with his occupation listed as that of carpenter.
45. The firm of Cherubin and Dessource was formed in 1820 between Julien Amothe (alias Chérubin; ca. 1792–1828) and Laurent Dessource Quessaire (ca. 1792–1832). They were listed in the 1822 city directory at 151 Dauphine corner of Ursulines and in 1824 at 325 Dauphine c. Ursulines. The index of indentures shows the men serving as supervisors in six indenture contracts between February 1823 and June 1828. The partnership was short-lived, as both men died young. Julien Amothe died on July 13, 1828, and Laurent Quessaire died on November 3, 1832. Jean-Louis and Joseph Dolliole were the appraisers for Quessaire's estate inventory.
46. Edwards and de Verton, *A Creole Lexicon*, s.v. "maison basse," 133; building contract between Roman Planas and Drausin Dolliole and Emile Errié, Theodore Seghers notary, vol. 29, act 346, September 12, 1838, NARC.
47. Building contract between Dolliole and Errié and Marguerite Dauphine, Octave De Armas notary, vol. 43, act 319, November 23, 1848, NARC.
48. The author did not trace the offspring of Jean-Louis Dolliole's stepson Emile Errié to determine if they were employed in the building trades.
49. D Obituaries, Orleans Parish, Louisiana, submitted by New Orleans Volunteer

Association, updated April 2005, accessed January 19, 2011, http://files.usgwarchives.net/la/orleans/obits/1/d-13.txt.
50. Curry, *The Free Black in Urban America*, 16.
51. Woods, *From Craft to Profession*, 5.
52. Lachance, "The Limits of Privilege," 70.
53. Benjamin Henry Latrobe to Robert Mills, July 12, 1806, in Van Horne, *Correspondence and Miscellaneous Papers*, 239.
54. Lachance, "The Limits of Privilege," 70.
55. Benjamin Henry Latrobe to Henry Ormond, November 20, 1808, cited in Woods, *From Craft to Profession*, 10.

CHAPTER 6. THE STATUS QUO

1. Kendall, *History of Louisiana*, 115.
2. Toledano, *National Trust Guide to New Orleans*, x.
3. Genovese, "Slave States of North America," 263–264; Toledano, *National Trust Guide to New Orleans*, 15.
4. City Council Resolutions, June 16, 1819, cited in Van Horne, *Correspondence and Miscellaneous*, 1035.
5. This was undoubtedly Norbert who was purchasing property and serving as an apprentice supervisor by this time. Soulié "Senior" would have been his father, Jean, who was city recorder during the Macarty administration. The other recommended architects were referred to by their full names. The appellation supplied for Norbert Soulié placed less focus on his individual identity (and race) and more on his white heritage and father's status.
6. Genovese, "Slave States of North America," 264.
7. Roffignac served an uninterrupted eight-year term. "Administrations of the Mayors of New Orleans, Louis Philippe Joseph de Roffignac (1766–1846)," LD/CASP-NOPL, accessed April 23, 2012, http://nutrias.org/info/louinfo/admins/roffignac.htm; Kendall, *History of Louisiana*, 116; Curry, *The Free Black in Urban America*, 17.
8. Guillemard was a French architect in the service of the Spanish government.
9. Patricia Heintzelman and Charles W. Snell, The Presbytère, National Register of Historic Places nomination form, June 30, 1975, National Register of Historic Places Digital Archive on NPGallery, https://npgallery.nps.gov/NRHP/GetAsset/e320109d-87da-4f46-8375-013c18feodfe.
10. These features include two stories, a lower-level arcade with Doric pilasters, a second-story gallery with Ionic pilasters, and a central pediment. The Presbytère was originally called the Casa Curial and was intended to house the priests serving St. Louis Cathedral. This use never transpired; upon completion it was used by the US government. Heintzelman and Snell, The Presbytère.
11. Fraiser, *The French Quarter of New Orleans*, 33.
12. Fraiser, *The French Quarter of New Orleans*, 33, 37.

13. Fraiser, *The French Quarter of New Orleans*, 47.
14. Mitchell, *Classic New Orleans*, 47.
15. Fraiser, *The French Quarter of New Orleans*, 37.
16. Fraiser, *The French Quarter of New Orleans*, 126, 129. Currently known as the Pinson-Pizetta House (at 732 St. Peter), the speculative townhouse was built on the site of the St. Peter Theater (1791–1816). The Lacroix House is located at 837–839 Royal Street. It was built by Joseph Peralta. 837–839 Royal Street, from The Collins C. Diboll Vieux Carré Digital Survey, http://www.hnoc.org/vcs/.
17. The term *garde-de-frise* initially described the wrought-iron spiked lattice placed between the upper floors of adjacent Creole townhouses to prevent thieves from moving between galleries. It eventually came to also describe the wrought-iron railings on the actual balconies placed on Creole townhouses in the first half of the nineteenth century. Edwards and de Verton, A *Creole Lexicon*, s.v. "garde de frise," 107; Fraiser, *The French Quarter of New Orleans*, 40, 92, 109, 126, 130.
18. These commercial buildings are extant at 501–509 Canal Street and 633–637 Canal Street. Christovich et al., *New Orleans Architecture*, 2:134, 137; The Collins C. Diboll Vieux Carré Digital Survey, http://www.hnoc.org/vcs/.
19. Toledano and Christovich, *New Orleans Architecture*, 6:17.
20. De Pouilly was born in France and educated at l'École des Beaux-Arts. He immigrated to New Orleans in 1833 and began making use of his background in architecture and engineering.
21. Fraiser, *The French Quarter of New Orleans*, 141.
22. One of the townhouses was built in 1836 for the Olivier family, the other in 1837 as a business and residence for Louis J. Dulfilho Jr., the first licensed pharmacist in the United States. Fraiser, *The French Quarter of New Orleans*, 146.
23. Goudchaux was born in France in 1813 per his household entry at the 1850 federal census. His death date is unknown.
24. Masson, "J. N. B. de Pouilly."
25. Poesch and Bacot, *Louisiana Buildings*, 181–182.
26. Fraiser, *The French Quarter of New Orleans*, 52.
27. Toledano, Evans, and Christovich, 4:32; Masson, "J. N. B. de Pouilly." Throughout his career, de Pouilly also designed tombs for many notable New Orleans families and taught drawing at Audubon College, which was founded by his son-in-law Simon Rouen in 1853. Huber, McDowell, and Christovich, *New Orleans Architecture*, 3:136–137.
28. Gurlie's dates are taken from a legal document from 1844 that states that he is seventy-two years old and has resided in New Orleans for forty-eight years (which would put his arrival in 1796, after the partnership with Guillot is said to have begun). Benjamin C. Howard, "Benjamin Howard, Antoine Michod et al. vs. Peronne-Bernarding Girod et al.," in *Reports of Cases Argued and Adjudged in the Supreme Court of the United States, January Term, 1846* (Boston: Charles C. Little and James Brown, 1846), 4:533; Toledano, *National Trust Guide*, 15. Guillot's dates were found in his estate file, "Joseph Guillot, 1838," Louisiana, Orleans Parish Estate Files, 1804–1846, FamilySearch,

accessed May 1, 2012, https://familysearch.org/pal:/MM9.1.1/JJZX-XZK. The partners married sisters Marie Louise Paillet (Gurlie) and Catherine Isabel Paillet (Guillot). "Rome, St. Cyr and Early Louisiana Families," accessed April 30, 2012, http://wc.rootsweb.ancestry.com/cgi-bin/igm.cgi?op=SHOW&db= madvintner&recno =39484; Louisiana Genealogical and Historical Society, "St. Louis Cemetery No. 1 Interments January 1–December 31, 1838," accessed April 30, 2012, http://files.usgwarchives.net/la/orleans/cemeteries/louis/00000002.txt, April 1998.

29. Poesch and Bacot, *Louisiana Buildings*, 365, 370.
30. Fraiser, *The French Quarter of New Orleans*, 47; Toledano and Christovich, *New Orleans Architecture*, 6:59.
31. Fraiser, *The French Quarter of New Orleans*, 47.
32. Fraiser, *The French Quarter of New Orleans*, 79–80, 95–101, 190–191.
33. Toledano, *National Trust Guide to New Orleans*, 65.
34. Poesch and Bacot, *Louisiana Buildings*, 368–369, 374; Toledano, *National Trust Guide to New Orleans*, 30; Christovich et al., *New Orleans Architecture*, 2:174; Heard, *French Quarter Manual*, 125; Fraiser, *The French Quarter of New Orleans*, 130–131.
35. Fraiser, *The French Quarter of New Orleans*, 125–126; 633 Royal Street, from The Collins C. Diboll Vieux Carré Digital Survey, http://www.hnoc.org/vcs/.
36. Toledano, *National Trust Guide to New Orleans*, 68.
37. Fossier, *New Orleans: The Glamour Period*, 271.
38. Woods, *Sacramental Records*, 1:62.
39. USGenWeb, Orleans Parish Death Index, http://www.usgwarchives.net/la/orleans/death-index.htm.
40. Toledano, Evans, and Christovich, *New Orleans Architecture*, 4:xiii; Christovich et al., *New Orleans Architecture*, 2:223.
41. Léon Courcelle (Joachim's brother) and Adelaide Vivant (the Souliés' maternal aunt) had a lifetime "left-handed marriage" and several offspring (one of the daughters married Bernard Soulié). *Homme de couleur libre* builder Myrtille Courcelle appears to have been Adelaide and Léon's son.
42. Fraiser, *The French Quarter of New Orleans*, 147–148; Toledano, *National Trust Guide to New Orleans*, 41. The third story was added at a later date. The Courcelles are also associated with the altered cottage at 1126 Marais Street. Toledano and Christovich, *New Orleans Architecture*, 6:172.
43. Fraiser, *The French Quarter of New Orleans*, 145; Christovich et al., *New Orleans Architecture*, 2:223. Fraiser erroneously identifies Etienne Courcelle as an *homme de couleur libre*.
44. Toledano, Evans, and Christovich, *New Orleans Architecture*, 4:142.
45. Christovich et al., *New Orleans Architecture*, 5:45.
46. The Fitzmeyer/Meunier Family Home Page, "Descendants of Gabriel Correjolles, Generation No. 3," accessed April 30, 2012, http://familytreemaker.genealogy.com/users/f/i/t/Linda-M-Fitzmeyer/GENE5-0003.html; Toledano and Christovich, *New Orleans Architecture*, 6:69.
47. François's older brother Gabriel (1780–1842) was also a builder. He contracted with

Jean Chaigneau to build a house on Barracks Street for Louis Moreau in 1831. Gabriel also erected townhouses at the corner of Royal and Governor Nicholls in 1834. Building contract between Jean Chaigneau and Gabriel Correjolles, L. T. Caire notary, March 23, 1831, NARC. Gabriel was born in Fort Dauphine, Saint-Domingue, in 1780. He died in New Orleans in 1842. The Fitzmeyer/Meunier Family Home Page, "Descendants of Gabriel Correjolles, Generation No. 3," accessed April 30, 2012, http://familytreemaker.genealogy.com/users/f/i/t/Linda-M-Fitzmeyer/GENE5–0003.html; 1201 Royal Street, 1205 Royal Street, 713 Governor Nicholls, from The Collins C. Diboll Vieux Carré Digital Survey, http://www.hnoc.org/vcs/.

48. Today the residence, at 1113 Chartres Street, is known as the Le Carpentier-Beauregard-Keyes House and is listed on the National Register of Historic Places.
49. Fraiser, *The French Quarter of New Orleans*, 134.
50. Genealogical and secondary source research did not yield much information on Chaigneau's background.
51. Heard, *French Quarter Manual*, 45; Fraiser, *The French Quarter of New Orleans*, 134.
52. The house was located at 916 Barracks Street. Eugene Macarty acquired the property in 1808 then sold it to Mandeville in 1810. The house and property were transferred to Eulalie's relative Drausin Barthélémy Macarty in 1847. 916 Barracks Street, from The Collins C. Diboll Vieux Carré Digital Survey, http://www.hnoc.org/vcs/; *Encyclopedia Louisiana*, "918 Barracks, Square 912," accessed October 9, 2007, http://www.enlou.com/fq/vc912.htm. This website is no longer active.
53. Christovich et al., *New Orleans Architecture*, 2:223.
54. Toledano and Christovich, *New Orleans Architecture*, 6:161.
55. Correjolles also built nine houses for Louis Gally and Guillaume Marmiche at Decatur and Marigny Streets for $54,000 in 1838. Toledano, Evans, and Christovich, *New Orleans Architecture*, 4:xiii.
56. Contract between François Correjolles and [illegible] Soniat, vol. 3, no. 24, September 17, 1828, Index to New Orleans Indentures, LD/CASP-NOPL.
57. Fitzmeyer/Meunier Family Home Page, "Descendants of Gabriel Correjolles, Generation No. 3," accessed October 19, 2020, https://www.genealogy.com/ftm/f/i/t/Linda-M-Fitzmeyer/GENE5-0005.html.
58. Fossier, *New Orleans: The Glamour Period*, 271.
59. Latrobe's pre-1819 work in the city includes the Customhouse (1809) and Waterworks (1812).
60. Fraiser, *The French Quarter of New Orleans*, 89.
61. Toledano, *National Trust Guide to New Orleans*, 15.
62. "The Dolan Family—From Ireland to Missouri," accessed April 30, 2012, http://familytreemaker.genealogy.com/users/r/a/b/Joni-Rabena-/WEBSITE-0001/UHP-1054.html; Henry L. Abbot, "Biographical Memoir of John Gross Barnard, 1815–1882" (lecture presented before the National Academy of Sciences, April 17, 1902), accessed October 29, 2020, http://www.nasonline.org/publications/biographical-memoirs/memoir-pdfs/barnard-john.pdf; Christovich et al., *New Orleans Architecture*, 2:223.

63. Toledano, *National Trust Guide to New Orleans*, 21; Fossier, *New Orleans: The Glamour Period*, 469; Mitchell, *Classic New Orleans*, 29; Christovich et al., *New Orleans Architecture*, 2:223; Latrobe, *Impressions Respecting New Orleans*, 34n11.
64. Poesch and Bacot, *Louisiana Buildings*, 376. They are now part of Antoine's Restaurant Annex.
65. Christovich et al., *New Orleans Architecture*, 2:185.
66. Christovich et al., *New Orleans Architecture*, 2:12, 139.
67. Christovich et al., *New Orleans Architecture*, 2:13–14.
68. Christovich et al., *New Orleans Architecture*, 2:38.
69. Poesch and Bacot, *Louisiana Buildings*, 179.
70. The latter became part of the University of Louisiana, designed by William Brand in 1847.
71. Toledano, *National Trust Guide to New Orleans*, 16; Ferguson, "Charles and James Dakin."
72. Toledano, *National Trust Guide to New Orleans*, 26.
73. Maynard, *Architecture in the United States*, 25.
74. Toledano, *National Trust Guide to New Orleans*, 19, 27, 28, 104, 134; Fraiser, *The French Quarter of New Orleans*, 155; Christovich et al., *New Orleans Architecture*, 2:40.
75. Christovich, Toledano, and Swanson, *New Orleans Architecture*, 1:92.
76. Christovich, Toledano, and Swanson, *New Orleans Architecture*, 1:144.
77. Christovich, Toledano, and Swanson, *New Orleans Architecture*, 1:45.
78. Christovich, Toledano, and Swanson, *New Orleans Architecture*, 1:16, 142; Toledano, *National Trust Guide to New Orleans*, 36. Today, this building houses the Boston Club; it is the only intact residential building in the business section of Canal Street.
79. Christovich et al., *New Orleans Architecture*, 2:158, 160, 198.
80. Christovich et al., *New Orleans Architecture*, 2:68, 69.
81. Christovich et al., *New Orleans Architecture*, 2:34.
82. Christovich et al., *New Orleans Architecture*, 2:40.
83. Christovich et al., *New Orleans Architecture*, 2:147; Gallier, *Autobiography of James Gallier*, 42.
84. Toledano, *National Trust Guide to New Orleans*, 25.
85. Contract between Joachim Courcelle and Maurice Populus, November 23, 1832, vol. 5, no. 348, Index to New Orleans Indentures, LD/CASP-NOPL.
86. Felix Pinson served as supervisor for all the indenture contracts examined by the author in which the apprentice was a slave.
87. The building contract index ends in 1843.
88. Gallier, *Autobiography of James Gallier*, 27.
89. Gallier, *Autobiography of James Gallier*, 27; Christovich et al., *New Orleans Architecture*, 2:146; Toledano, *National Trust Guide to New Orleans*, 26; Gallier's address in the 1842 city directory is "Common n. Carondelet."
90. Gallier, *Autobiography of James Gallier*, 26.
91. Sewell's built works include the C. H. Taney House (1835), G. R. Stringer House (1836), and 731–733 Street Girod. He had offices in the 600 block of Commercial Place. Poesch

and Bacot, *Louisiana Buildings*, 374; Christovich et al., *New Orleans Architecture*, 2:16, 159, 165.
92. Gallier, *Autobiography of James Gallier*, 26.
93. Christovich et al., *New Orleans Architecture*, 5:13.
94. Christovich et al., *New Orleans Architecture*, 5:14–15.
95. Fitch, "Creole Architecture," 86.
96. Starr, *Southern Comfort*, 127.
97. Gallier, *Autobiography of James Gallier*, 38–32.
98. Starr, *Southern Comfort*, 136–138.
99. The New Orleans chapter of the American Institute of Architects (founded 1857) was responsible for the "removal of responsibility for design of public buildings from the City Engineer's office and establishment of a reasonable method of selecting an architect." AIA New Orleans, "AIA New Orleans History," accessed April 14, 2012, http://www.aianeworleans.org/history.
100. From *Paxton's New Orleans City Directory*, 1823, depicted in Huber, *Louisiana: A Pictorial History*, 141.
101. Benfey, *Degas in New Orleans*, 29–30.
102. Building contract between Norbert Soulié and Alexander Baggett, Theodore Seghers notary, vol. 32, act 499, June 4, 1839, NARC; Christovich et al., *New Orleans Architecture*, 2:222.
103. Atkinson also designed the Atchafalaya Bank and two-story row houses for William Saunders on Camp Street in 1840. Christovich et al., *New Orleans Architecture*, 2:40, 70, 129.
104. Building contract between Norbert Soulié and Alexander Baggett; Christovich et al., *New Orleans Architecture*, 2:193.
105. Florance's house on Camp Street does not appear to be extant; it was not recorded in Volume 2 of the *New Orleans Architecture* series. Other buildings that William Florance commissioned or Alexander Baggett built in Faubourg Sainte-Marie have been demolished or are extant but too greatly altered for historic comparison. Christovich et al., *New Orleans Architecture*, 2:193.
106. Jane Milne is identified in the 1850 census as being a mulatto aged thirty-five.
107. Toledano and Christovich, *New Orleans Architecture*, 6:199.
108. Toledano and Christovich, *New Orleans Architecture*, 6:199.
109. The cast-iron gallery and third story were added later. The latter was Achille Peretti's studio from 1906 to 1923. Tennessee Williams wrote *A Streetcar Named Desire* from his attic rooms. Fraiser, *The French Quarter of New Orleans*, 202; French Creoles of America, "Madame Augustine Eugenie de Lassize," accessed April 12, 2006, http://www.frenchcreoles.com/Early%20Creole%20Homes/632%20st%20peter%20street.htm.
110. William Kincaide is not discussed in depth in this work because the author could find little information about him to serve as a point of comparison. Secondary source and limited archival research indicates that in addition to the house for Oger, he built two townhouses in Faubourg Sainte-Marie (1840) and three cottages on Dauphine Street in Faubourg Tremé (1841). These clients were all white males. Okude, "Application of

Linguistic Concepts," 113; Toledano, Evans, and Christovich, *New Orleans Architecture*, 4:121. Hurley also built townhouses in the 300 block of North Rampart Street that year, near those erected by Norbert Soulié.

111. Genovese, "Slave States of North America," 264. Most of these individuals left Europe as a result of the potato famine in Ireland and the mini revolution brought on by the Professors' War of 1848 in Germany. Toledano, *National Trust Guide to New Orleans*, xiii.
112. Woods, *From Craft to Profession*, 26.
113. Woods, *From Craft to Profession*, 21.
114. Woods, *From Craft to Profession*, 25.
115. Woods, *From Craft to Profession*, 26.
116. B. Soulié, "Journal of Bernard Soulié," 328.

CHAPTER 7. MONEY, POWER, AND STATUS IN THE BUILDING TRADES

1. Building contracts: Jean-Louis Dolliole (1831), Dolliole and Errié (1838, 1848), Louis Vivant (1846).
2. The word "entrepreneur" (undertaker) has been in use since the early eighteenth century when it was first used by a Parisian banker, Richard Cantillon. Stevenson and Amabile, "Entrepreneurial Management," 146.
3. *Random House Webster's College Dictionary* (1996), s.v. "entrepreneur."
4. Hanger, "Patronage, Property, and Persistence," 53.
5. Gehman, "Visible Means of Support," 209.
6. Desdunes, *Our People and Our History*, 80.
7. Among the properties owned by one or both of the brothers, by faubourg were Vieux Carré: 716 St. Philip, 717 St. Louis, 839 Bourbon, 1005 Burgundy, 713 St. Louis, 833 Bienville, 306 Dauphine, 720 Dumaine, 716 Dumaine, 907 Burgundy; Marigny and Creole faubourgs: 2701 Chartres, 1903 Dauphine, 2105 Dauphine, 125–129 Decatur, 2109 Decatur, 503 Esplanade, 501 Frenchmen, 700–706 Frenchmen; Sainte-Marie: 117–119 Decatur.
8. This amounts to approximately six million dollars in early twenty-first-century currency. Thompson, *Exiles at Home*, 114.
9. "The World of the François Lacroix," LD/CASP-NOPL.
10. Thompson, *Exiles at Home*, 113.
11. Lachance, "The Foreign French," 121.
12. Marriage contract between Jean-Louis Dolliole and Marie Eugenie Baudin, Carlile Pollock notary, vol. 53, act 120, April 9, 1836, NARC.
13. Marriage contract between Bernard Soulié and Eliza Sylvie Courcelle, Theodore Seghers notary, vol. 5, act 12, January 19, 1832, NARC.
14. Bryan, *Myth of New Orleans in Literature*, 53.
15. Per the family's ledger books.
16. R. G. Dun and Co. Collection, Louisiana volume 11, 30, Baker Library, Harvard Business School, Boston, Massachusetts.

17. R. G. Dun and Co. Collection, Louisiana volume 11, 19.
18. Docket No. 30844, Louisiana, Civil District Court (Orleans Parish), General Index of All Successions, 1880–1903, LD/CASP-NOPL. Lacroix's estate would be worth $1.2 million in today's currency. Thompson, *Exiles at Home*, 114.
19. Curry, *The Free Black in Urban America*, 38.
20. Curry, *The Free Black in Urban America*, 38.
21. Woods, *From Craft to Profession*, 95.
22. Woods, *From Craft to Profession*, 95.
23. Docket No. 8029, Louisiana, Civil District Court (Orleans Parish), General Index of All Successions, 1880–1903, LD/CASP-NOPL.
24. Thompson, *Exiles at Home*, 11.
25. Jean-Louis Dolliole to his minor children, Carlile Pollock notary, vol. 2, act 174, April 22, 1820, NARC.
26. Succession of Geneviève Dolliole, 1838, Louisiana, Court of Probates (Orleans Parish), General Index of All Successions, 1805–1846, LD/CASP-NOPL.
27. Procuration, Pierre Dolliole to Jean-Louis Dolliole, Carlile Pollock notary, vol. 2, act 526, June 29, 1821, NARC.
28. Succession of Louis Dolliole (1822) and Succession of Charlotte Dolliole (1836), Louisiana, Court of Probates (Orleans Parish), General Index of All Successions, 1805–1846, LD/CASP-NOPL. Joseph Dolliole also witnessed the marriage of Isabelle Macarty and Daniel Nobe. Toledano and Christovich, *New Orleans Architecture*, 6:161. Nobe was undoubtedly related to Joseph's first wife, Magdeleine Hobe (possibly Jove/Nobe).
29. Nolan, Dupont, and Bruns, *Sacramental Records*, 18:124.
30. Albin and Celeste did purchase their mother's four slaves.
31. Docket No. 33792, Louisiana Second District Court (Orleans Parish), General Index of All Successions, 1846–1880, LD/CASP-NOPL.
32. Woods and Nolan, *Sacramental Records*, 4:59; Dupont and Bruns, *Sacramental Records*, 10:376.
33. See Theodore Seghers notary, vol. 4, acts 151, 152, and 153, NARC. Norbert first acted as attorney for his father, Jean Soulié (W. Y. Lewis notary, April 16, 1827). Later, Norbert and Lucien signed procurations (referred to in other legal transactions) giving power of attorney to Bernard and/or Albin (see Theodore Seghers notary, February 28, 1838; April 11, 1840; April 19, 1842). Bernard and/or Albin also acted on behalf of their sisters (see Theodore Seghers notary, November 5, 1832, and Joseph Lisbony notary, August 21, 1846). When he traveled, Bernard signed a procuration in favor of Albin until his return; see Theodore Seghers notary, April 29, 1833. Procurations from Albin to Bernard are filed in the records of C. V. Foulon notary and dated May 18, 1845, and May 20, 1845. Additional procurations between the Soulié siblings are located in the acts of Theodore Seghers notary, vol. 11, NARC.
34. Toledano and Christovich, *New Orleans Architecture*, 6:172.
35. "Sale by Register of Wills," December 27, 1843, Succession of Léon Courcelle (1843),

Louisiana, Court of Probates (Orleans Parish), General Index of All Successions, 1805–1846, LD/CASP-NOPL.

36. The entries are from July 1848 and September 1859, respectively. R. G. Dun and Co. Collection, Louisiana vol. 9, 97.
37. Docket No. 30844, Louisiana, Civil District Court (Orleans Parish), General Index of All Successions, 1880–1903, LD/CASP-NOPL.
38. Plan book 85, folio 14, Plan Book Plans Collection, NARC.
39. Release, Francis Barber Ogden and Charles Harrod to Joseph Dolliole et al., William Boswell notary, vol. 12, act 410, August 24, 1830, NARC.
40. See Sale of Land, M. N. N. Destrehan to Nelson Fouché and Joseph Dolliole, Theodore Seghers notary, vol. 12, act 277, May 2, 1835, NARC.
41. Nolan, Dupont, and Bruns, *Sacramental Records*, 15:125.
42. Marie Josephe Sophie Olivier Boisdoré, "Louisiana, Orleans Parish Estate Files, 1804–1846," accessed April 30, 2012, https://familysearch.org/pal:/MM9.1.1/JJZ6-R66. Sophie's mother was Catherine Cheval, aunt of Eulalie Mazange and great-aunt of the first-generation Souliés, making Sophie the first-generation Souliés' second cousin.
43. New Orleans (La.) Office of the Mayor, Register of Free Colored Persons Entitled to Remain in the State, 1840–1864, 4 vols., vol. 1, 1840–1856.
44. Nolan, Dupont, and Bruns, *Sacramental Records*, 15:125.
45. Laurent Dessource Quessaire, Estate of 1832, Louisiana, Orleans Parish Estate Files, 1804–1846, LD/CASP-NOPL.
46. Neidenbach, "Life and Legacy of Marie Couvent," 349, 381. Neidenbach discusses many other events that brought *gens de couleur libres'* social and economic circles together.
47. See Neidenbach, "Life and Legacy of Marie Couvent."
48. Toledano and Christovich, *New Orleans Architecture*, 6:85.
49. Soulié Family Ledgers, Book 1, page 2, WRC-THNOC.
50. Renewal dates were on December 2, 1843; April 5, 1844; December 7, 1844; April 5, 1845; October 8, 1845; April 11, 1846; July 8, 1846. Soulié Family Ledgers, Book 1, 10, 15, 24, 29, 37, 44, 47, 53.
51. Soulié Family Ledgers, Book 1, page 44, WRC-THNOC.
52. Soulié Family Ledgers, Book 1, pages 37, 39, 59, 68, WRC-THNOC.
53. Soulié Family Ledgers, Book 1, pages 1, 16, 17, 19, WRC-THNOC.
54. Soulié Family Ledgers, Book 1, pages 2, 10, 17, 24, 40, WRC-THNOC.
55. Successions of Charles Vivant (1823) and Rosette Vivant (1828), Louisiana, Court of Probates (Orleans Parish), General Index of All Successions, 1805–1846, LD/CASP-NOPL. Boisdoré also held a mortgage for the heirs of Rosette Vivant. Release of Mortgage, Rosette Vivant heirs to François Boisdoré, Joseph Arnard notary, vol. 1, act 177, April 9, 1828, NARC.
56. Toledano and Christovich, *New Orleans Architecture*, 6:196. The property was located at present-day 1523 Ursulines Avenue.
57. Cautionnement by Jean Jacques Montfort and Joseph Dolliole with Bernard and Albin Soulié, Theodore Seghers notary, vol. 12, act 609, May 2, 1835, NARC.

58. Soulié Family Ledgers, Book 1, page 32, WRC-THNOC.
59. Soulié Family Ledgers, Book 1, page 37, WRC-THNOC.
60. Christovich et al., *New Orleans Architecture*, 5:xiii.
61. The municipal governments paid for 10,633 feet of ground at a rate of 25 cents per foot. Christovich et al., *New Orleans Architecture*, 5:61.
62. Brown, "Youngest of the Great American Family," 226.
63. Louisiana Genealogical and Historical Society, Louisiana Soldiers During the War of 1812, accessed May 1, 2012, http://files.usgwarchives.net/la/state/military/war1812/index.txt. Vincent Rillieux, Joachim Courcelle, and Léon Courcelle also served, Vincent and Joachim in Captain Chauveau's Company (cavalry) and Léon in Morgan's Fourth Regiment. See also French Creoles of America, "The Battle of New Orleans," accessed May 8, 2012, http://www.frenchcreoles.com/CreoleCulture/battalion%20creoles/battalion%20creoles.htm.
64. For more on the *gens de couleur libres'* legacy of military service, see Powell, *The Accidental City*, and Bell, *Revolution, Romanticism, and the Afro-Creole Protest Tradition*.
65. St. Augustine Catholic Church of New Orleans, "The History of St. Augustine Catholic Church," accessed October 28, 2020, https://d2y1pz2y630308.cloudfront.net/20194/documents/2019/11/Insert_History_PRESS%203.pdf.
66. St. Augustine Catholic Church of New Orleans, "The History of St. Augustine Catholic Church."
67. Toledano and Christovich, *New Orleans Architecture*, 6:142.
68. In her 1842 will, Jeanne-Marie Aliquot (founder) noted that Jean-Louis Dolliole owed her 260 piastres (on a note endorsed by Joseph Dolliole) and that his stepson Emile Errié owed her 100 piastres. University of Notre Dame Archives, Archives Calendar 1842, accessed March 20, 2012, http://archives.nd.edu/calendar/cal1842.htm.
69. Jean-Louis Dolliole inventory, Docket No. 17714, Louisiana Second District Court (Orleans Parish), General Index of All Successions, 1846–1880, City Archives and Special Collections, New Orleans Public Library.
70. History.com Editors, "'Star of the West' Is Fired Upon," updated January 7, 2020, accessed July 20, 2020, https://www.history.com/this-day-in-history/star-of-the-west-is-fired-upon.

CONCLUSION

1. Bell, *Revolution, Romanticism, and the Afro-Creole Protest Tradition*, 4–6.
2. Trouillot, *Silencing the Past*, 3–4.
3. Trouillot, *Silencing the Past*, 25.
4. Trouillot, *Silencing the Past*, 48.
5. Gayarré's stance is highlighted in Tregle Jr., "Creoles and Americans," 167–182. His pupil Grace King (1852–1932) likewise promoted pure white Creole supremacy in her writings.
6. Henry Clay Warmoth wrote his memoir *War, Politics, and Reconstruction: Stormy Days in Louisiana* in 1930. Donald E. Everett's article "Demands of the New Orleans

Free Colored Population for Political Equity, 1862–1865" was published in the April 1955 issue of *Louisiana Historical Quarterly*. Both are summarized in Bell, *Revolution, Romanticism, and the Afro-Creole Protest Tradition*, 4–5.

7. Thompson, *Exiles at Home*, 138–139.
8. Thompson, *Exiles at Home*, 138–139.
9. Woods, *From Craft to Profession*, 83.
10. Fossier, *New Orleans: The Glamour Period*, 136–137.
11. Force, "The House on Bayou Road," 36.
12. Thompson, *Exiles at Home*, 129.
13. Thompson, *Exiles at Home*, 129.
14. Knight, "Builders and Building in New Orleans," 79.
15. Toledano, *National Trust Guide to New Orleans*, 89, vii.
16. Toledano, *National Trust Guide to New Orleans*, 69.
17. Louis Drausin had one known daughter, Marie Hortense, with first wife, Françoise Eulalie Asmar alias Dolliole. USGenWeb Archives Project, DH through DQ: Alphabetical Birth Indexes for Orleans Parish 1796–1900, http://files.usgwarchives.net/la/orleans/vitals/births/index/nobidhdq.txt. François died by 1850; he is not listed at that year's census. He would have been around twenty-nine years of age. Furthermore, he is not named as an heir in Jean-Louis's 1861 estate inventory.
18. Marriage contract between Bernard Soulié and Eliza S. Courcelle, Theodore Seghers notary, vol. 5, act 12, July 19, 1832, NARC.
19. Lachance, "The Limits of Privilege," 79.
20. In a letter to Governor Thomas O. Moore dated January 11, 1861, two weeks before the state seceded, the brothers offered a loan of $10,000 to the State of Louisiana in support of the "necessities of our country in the present emergency." The author has not determined if the loan was actually realized. Confederate Papers Relating to Citizens or Business Firms, 1861–65, National Archives and Records Administration, Publication No. M346, Record Group 109, Roll 0964, accessed December 1, 2012, http://www.fold3.com/document/52506234/; Benfey, *Degas in New Orleans*, 10.
21. Republican Party (La.) Convention, *Proceedings of the Convention of the Republican Party of Louisiana held at Economy Hall, New Orleans, September 25, 1865, and of the Central Executive Committee of the Friends of Universal Suffrage of Louisiana, now the Central Executive Committee of the Republican Party of Louisiana* (New Orleans: New Orleans Tribune Office, 1865), 14, accessed April 5, 2012, http://www.archive.org/stream/proceedingsofconoorepurich/proceedingsofconoorepurich_djvu.txt.
22. Republican Party (La.) Convention, *Proceedings of the Convention of the Republican Party*, 37–38. Charles Jules Courcelle (1820–1871) was another son of Léon Courcelle and Adelaide Vivant.
23. His cousin and brother-in-law Drausin B. Macarty did not decline his appointment as Administrator of Assessments, however. Kendall, *History of Louisiana*, 337; "Administrations of the Mayors of New Orleans, Benjamin Franklin Flanders (1816–1896)," LD

/CASP-NOPL, accessed December 1, 2012, http://nutrias.org/info/louinfo/admins/flanders.htm.
24. R. G. Dun and Co. Collection, Louisiana vol. 11, 30.
25. B. Soulié, "Journal of Bernard Soulié," 330.
26. Thompson, *Exiles at Home*, 130.

BIBLIOGRAPHY

PRIMARY SOURCES

Published Sources

Forsyth, Alice Daly, ed. *Louisiana Marriages: A Collection of Marriage Records from the St. Louis Cathedral in New Orleans during the Spanish Regime and the Early American Period, 1784–1806.* 2 vols. New Orleans: Polyanthos, 1977.

Gallier, James. *Autobiography of James Gallier, Architect.* Paris: É. Brière, 1864.

Gibson, John. *Gibson's Guide and Directory of the State of Louisiana, and the Cities of New Orleans and Lafayette.* New Orleans: John Gibson, 1838.

Latrobe, Benjamin Henry. *Impressions Respecting New Orleans: Diary and Sketches, 1818–1820.* New York: Columbia University Press, 1951.

———. *The Journal of Latrobe.* New York: D. Appleton, 1905.

Maduell, Charles R., Jr., comp. *Marriage Contracts, Wills and Testaments of the Spanish Colonial Period in New Orleans, 1770–1804.* New Orleans: Charles R. Maduell Jr., 1969.

———. *Marriages and Family Relationships of New Orleans, 1820–1830.* New Orleans: Charles R. Maduell Jr., 1969.

———. *Marriages and Family Relationships of New Orleans, 1830–1840.* New Orleans: Charles R. Maduell Jr., 1969.

———. *New Orleans Marriage Contracts, 1804–1820.* New Orleans: Polyanthos, 1977.

Nolan, Charles E., Dorenda Dupont, and J. Edgar Bruns, eds. *Sacramental Records of the Roman Catholic Church of the Archdiocese of New Orleans.* Vol. 8, *1804–1806.* New Orleans: Archdiocese of New Orleans, 1993.

———. *Sacramental Records of the Roman Catholic Church of the Archdiocese of New Orleans.* Vol. 9, *1807–1809.* New Orleans: Archdiocese of New Orleans, 1994.

———. *Sacramental Records of the Roman Catholic Church of the Archdiocese of New Orleans.* Vol. 10, *1810–1812.* New Orleans: Archdiocese of New Orleans, 1995.

———. *Sacramental Records of the Roman Catholic Church of the Archdiocese of New Orleans.* Vol. 11, *1812–1814.* New Orleans: Archdiocese of New Orleans, 1996.

BIBLIOGRAPHY

———. *Sacramental Records of the Roman Catholic Church of the Archdiocese of New Orleans.* Vol. 15, *1822–1823*. New Orleans: Archdiocese of New Orleans, 2000.

———. *Sacramental Records of the Roman Catholic Church of the Archdiocese of New Orleans.* Vol. 18, *1828–1829*. New Orleans: Archdiocese of New Orleans, 2000.

Nolan, Charles E., and Dorenda Dupont, *Sacramental Records of the Roman Catholic Church.* Vol. 15, *1822–1823*. New Orleans: Archives of the Archdiocese of New Orleans, 2000.

R. G. Dun and Company Collection. Baker Library, Harvard Business School, Boston, Massachusetts.

Sanborn Fire Insurance Company Map collection. Southeastern Architectural Archive, Special Collections, Howard-Tilton Memorial Library, Tulane University, New Orleans, Louisiana.

Soulié, Bernard. "Journal of Bernard Soulié," *New Orleans Genesis* 25, no. 99 (July 1986): 323–330, 332.

Van Horne, John, ed., *Correspondence and Miscellaneous Papers of Benjamin Henry Latrobe.* Vol. 3, *1811–1820*. New Haven: Yale University Press, 1988.

Woods, Earl C., ed. *Sacramental Records of the Roman Catholic Church of the Archdiocese of New Orleans.* Vol. 1, *1718–1750*. New Orleans: Archdiocesan Historical Archives, 1988.

———. *Sacramental Records of the Roman Catholic Church of the Archdiocese of New Orleans.* Vol. 2, *1751–1771*. New Orleans: Archdiocesan Historical Archives, 1988.

Woods, Earl C., and Charles E. Nolan, eds. *Sacramental Records of the Roman Catholic Church of the Archdiocese of New Orleans.* Vol. 3, *1772–1783*. New Orleans: Archives of the Archdiocese of New Orleans, 1989.

———. *Sacramental Records of the Roman Catholic Church of the Archdiocese of New Orleans.* Vol. 4, *1784–1790*. New Orleans: Archives of the Archdiocese of New Orleans, 1989.

———. *Sacramental Records of the Roman Catholic Church of the Archdiocese of New Orleans.* Vol. 5, *1791–1795*. New Orleans: Archives of the Archdiocese of New Orleans, 1990.

———. *Sacramental Records of the Roman Catholic Church of the Archdiocese of New Orleans.* Vol. 6, *1796–1799*. New Orleans: Archives of the Archdiocese of New Orleans, 1991.

———. *Sacramental Records of the Roman Catholic Church of the Archdiocese of New Orleans.* Vol. 7, *1800–1803*. New Orleans: Archives of the Archdiocese of New Orleans, 1992.

Office of the Clerk of Civil District Court, Parish of Orleans, Notarial Archives Research Center, New Orleans, Louisiana

Attached Plans Database

Bioscope database

Maduell, Charles R., Jr., Indexes of Family Records, 1770–1840

Plan Book Plans Collection

Reeves, Sally Kittredge, research files

Wilson, Samuel, and Robert J. Cangelosi. Building Contract Index, 1767–1970

BIBLIOGRAPHY

Louisiana Digital Library

Free People of Color in Louisiana Project
Maps from the Historic New Orleans Collection

Louisiana Division/City Archives and Special Collections, New Orleans Public Library, New Orleans, Louisiana

Estate Inventories of Orleans Parish Civil Courts, 1803–1877
Louisiana. Court of Probates (Orleans Parish). General Index of All Successions, 1805–1846
Louisiana. Court of Probates (Orleans Parish). Index to Suit Records, Numbered Series, 1823–1845
Louisiana. Second District Court (Orleans Parish). General Index of All Successions, 1846–1880
New Orleans City Directories. 1805, 1811, 1822–1824, 1832, 1834, 1838, 1841–1843, 1846, 1849–1859
New Orleans (La.) Office of the Mayor. Indentures, 1809–1843 (mf AA660)
New Orleans (La.) Office of the Mayor. Register of Free Colored Persons Entitled to Remain in the State, 1840–1864, 4 vols. (mf AA430)
New Orleans (La.) Treasurer's Office. Tax Ledgers, 1852–1861 (CC420)

Louisiana Historical Center, Louisiana State Museum, New Orleans, Louisiana

Colonial Documents Collection

Southeastern Architectural Archive, Southeastern Architectural Archive, Howard-Tilton Memorial Library, Tulane University, New Orleans, Louisiana

Sanborn Fire Insurance Maps (Collection 125)

Williams Research Center, The Historic New Orleans Collection, New Orleans, Louisiana

Antebellum Land Collection, 1836–1862. Nineteen items (MSS 457)
Builder Contract Files
Faubourg Marigny Collection, 1850–1880, 53 items (MSS 484)
Free People of Color Vieux Carré Property Owners
Free Persons of Color in Louisiana Collection, 1793–1867, 12 items (MSS 54)
Soulié Family Ledgers, 1843–1882. 5 vols. (MSS 297)
Surveyors' Sketch Books Collection, 1830–1910, 646 items (MSS 290)

Online Sources

"Administrations of the Mayors of New Orleans." Louisiana Division/City Archives and Special Collections, New Orleans Public Library. http://nutrias.org/info/louinfo/admins/mather.htm. Accessed July 15, 2012. Online version of "Mayors of New Orleans, 1803–1936." Compiled and edited by Work Projects Administration.
Amos, Gray B. *Alphabetical Index of Changes in Street Names, Old and New, Period 1852 to*

Current Date, Dec. 1st 1938. New Orleans: City Archives, 1938. Accessed October 19, 2020. http://nutrias.org/facts/streetnames/namesa.htm.

———. *Corrected Index, Alphabetical and Numerical, of Changes in Street Names and Numbers Old and New, 1852 to Current Date, April 8, 1938*. New Orleans: City Archives, 1938. Accessed October 19, 2020. http://archives.nolalibrary.org/~nopl/info/louinfo/numberchanges/numberchanges.htm.

Ancestry.com. *New Orleans, Passenger Lists, 1820–1945* [database online]. Provo, UT: Ancestry.com Operations, 2006.

———. *New York Passenger Lists, 1820–1957* [database online]. Provo, UT: Ancestry.com Operations, 2010.

City Archives, New Orleans Public Library. Alphabetical and Numerical Index of Changes in Street Names and Numbers, Old and New, 1852 to Current Date [1938]. http://nutrias.org/~nopl/info/louinfo/numberchanges/numberchanges.htm.

———. Louisiana Court of Probates (Orleans Parish). General Index of All Successions, 1805–1846. http://nutrias.org/~nopl/inv/probates.

———. Louisiana. Second District Court (Orleans Parish). General Index of All Successions, 1846–1880. http://nutrias.org/~nopl/inv/2dc/2dcsuccession.htm.

———. New Orleans (La.) Justices of the Peace. Index to Marriage Records, 1846–1880. http://nutrias.org/inv/jpmarrindex/jpmarrindex.htm.

FamilySearch. https://familysearch.org/.

———. Louisiana, Orleans Parish Estate Files, 1804–1846. https://www.familysearch.org/learn/wiki/en/Louisiana,_Orleans_Parish_Estate_Files_%28FamilySearch_Historical_Records%29.

HeritageQuest Online. http://www.heritagequestonline.com/hqoweb/library/do/index.

Historic New Orleans Collection. The Collins C. Diboll Vieux Carré Digital Survey. http://www.hnoc.org/vcs/.

Lachance, Paul, comp. and ed. Index to New Orleans Indentures, 1809–1843. Louisiana Division/City Archives and Special Collections, New Orleans Public Library, http://nutrias.org/~nopl/inv/indentures/ind-intr.htm.

———. "Louisiana Biography and Obituary Index." http://nutrias.org/~nopl/obits/obits.htm.

———. "New Orleans Ward Boundaries, 1805–1800." http://nutrias.org/facts/wards.htm.

———. "The World of François Lacroix," online exhibit. Accessed October 2, 2007. http://nutrias.org/~nopl/exhibits/lacroix/intro.htm.

New Orleans Public Library. "African Americans in New Orleans: *Les Gens de Couleur Libres*," online exhibit. Accessed March 21, 2012. http://nutrias.org/~nopl/exhibits/fmc/fmc.htm.

Notarial Archives Research Center. "Historical Notaries' Indexes, by Notary." http://www.orleanscivilclerk.com/notaryalpha.htm.

Purchase of slave "Telemaco" by Carlos Vivant & Co. (Charles Vivant, Andre Duclot, and Jean Soulié) from Hall, Afro-Louisiana History and Genealogy, http://www.ibiblio.org/laslave/individ.php?sid=23098.

Robinson, Elisha, and Roger H. Pidgeon. *Robinson's Atlas of the City of New Orleans, Louisiana*. New York: E. Robinson, 1883. Office of the Clerk of Civil District Court, Parish of Orleans, Notarial Archives Research Center, http://www.orleanscivilclerk.com/robinson/index.htm.

University Libraries, The University of North Carolina at Greensboro. Digital Library on American Slavery. http://library.uncg.edu/slavery/.

University of Notre Dame Archives: Calendar. http://archives.nd.edu/calendar.htm.

USGenWeb Archives Project; Louisiana, Orleans Parish. "Alphabetical Birth Indexes for Orleans Parish 1796–1900." http://www.usgwarchives.net/la/orleans/birth-alpha.htm.

———. City of New Orleans Census. http://www.usgwarchives.net/la/orleans/census.htm.

———. Soards' New Orleans City Directories. http://www.usgwarchives.net/la/orleans/directry.htm.

———. State Archives, Orleans Parish Death Index. Various years. http://www.usgwarchives.net/la/orleans/death-index.htm.

SECONDARY SOURCES

African American Architectural and Art History

Dozier, Richard K. "The Black Architectural Experience in America." *AIA Journal* 65, no. 7 (July 1976): 162–168.

Greenwald, Erin, ed. *In Search of Julien Hudson: Free Artist of Color in Pre–Civil War New Orleans*. Charlottesville: The University of Virginia Press, 2010.

Patton, Sharon. *African-American Art*. Oxford and New York: Oxford University Press, 1998.

Creole Architecture

Brassieur, C. Ray. "Builders' Voices: Reflections on the Fruits of Labor." In *Raised to the Trade: Creole Building Arts of New Orleans*, ed. John Ethan Hankins, 131–135. New Orleans: New Orleans Museum of Art, 2002.

Edwards, Jay D. "Creolization Theory and the Odyssey of the Atlantic Linear Cottage." *Etnofoor* 23, no. 1 (2011): 50–84.

———. "New Orleans Shotgun: A Historic Cultural Geography." In *Culture after the Hurricanes: Rhetoric and Reinvention on the Gulf Coast*, ed. M. B. Hackler, 44–90. Jackson: University of Mississippi Press, 2010.

———. "The Origins of Creole Architecture." *Winterthur Portfolio* 29, no. 2/3 (Summer/Autumn 1994): 155–189.

———. "Shotgun: The Most Contested House in America." *Buildings and Landscapes* 16, no. 1 (Spring 2009): 62–96.

———. "Unheralded Contributions across the Atlantic World." *Atlantic Studies* 5, no. 2 (August 2008): 161–201.

———. "Unlocking the History of Greek Key Architecture." *Louisiana Cultural Vistas* 19, no. 4 (2008–2009): 84–91.

———. "Vernacular Vision: The Gallery and Our Africanized Architectural Landscape." In *Raised to the Trade: Creole Building Arts of New Orleans*, ed. Jon Ethan Hankins and S. Maklansky, 61–94. New Orleans: New Orleans Museum of Art, 2002.

Edwards, Jay D., and Nicolas Kariouk Pecquet du Bellay de Verton. *A Creole Lexicon: Architecture, Landscape, People.* Baton Rouge: Louisiana State University Press, 2004.

Fitch, James Marston. "Creole Architecture 1718–1860: The Rise and Fall of a Great Tradition." In *The Past as Prelude: New Orleans 1718–1868*, ed. Hodding Carter, 71–87. Gretna, LA: Pelican, 1968.

Hankins, Jon Ethan, ed. *Raised to the Trade: Creole Building Arts of New Orleans.* New Orleans: New Orleans Museum of Art, 2002.

Okude, Naohito. "Application of Linguistic Concepts to the Study of Vernacular Buildings: Architectural Design among New Orleans' Free Persons of Color, 1820–1880." PhD diss., George Washington University, 1986.

Spitzer, Nick. "The Aesthetics of Work and Play in Creole New Orleans." In *Raised to the Trade: Creole Building Arts of New Orleans*, ed. John Ethan Hankins, 96–130. New Orleans: New Orleans Museum of Art, 2002.

Vlach, John Michael. "Sources of the Shotgun House: African and Caribbean Antecedents for Afro-American Architecture." PhD diss., Indiana University, 1975.

New Orleans Architecture

Abry, George. "Cottage Industry." *Old-House Journal* (September–October 2004): 66–71.

AIA New Orleans. "AIA New Orleans History." Accessed April 14, 2012. http://www.aianeworleans.org/history.

Arthur, Stanley Clisby. *Old New Orleans: A History of the Vieux Carré, Its Ancient and Historical Buildings.* Facsimile reprint. Westminster, MD: Heritage Books, 2007.

Bacot, H. Parrott, Barbara SoRelle Bacot, Sally Kittredge Reeves, John Magill, and John H. Lawrence. *Marie Adrien Persac: Louisiana Artist.* Baton Rouge: Louisiana State University Press, 2000.

Bruce, Curt. *The Great Houses of New Orleans.* New York: Alfred A. Knopf, 1977.

Christovich, Mary Louise, Roulhac Toledano, Betsy Swanson, and Pat Holden. *New Orleans Architecture.* Vol. 2, *The American Sector.* Gretna, LA: Pelican, 1972.

Christovich, Mary Louise, Sally Kittredge Evans, and Roulhac Toledano. *New Orleans Architecture.* Vol. 5, *The Esplanade Ridge.* Gretna, LA: Pelican, 1977.

Ferguson, John C. "Charles and James Dakin." *KnowLA: Encyclopedia of Louisiana.* Accessed April 26, 2012. https://64parishes.org/entry/charles-and-james-dakin.

Fraiser, Jim. *The French Quarter of New Orleans.* Jackson: University Press of Mississippi, 2003.

Heard, Malcolm. *French Quarter Manual: An Architectural Guide to New Orleans's Vieux Carré.* New Orleans: Tulane School of Architecture, 1997.

Huber, Leonard V., Peggy McDowell, and Mary Louise Christovich. *New Orleans Architecture.* Vol. 3, *The Cemeteries.* Gretna, LA: Pelican, 1996.

Knight, Corinna. "Builders and Building in New Orleans, Louisiana, 1790–1830." Master's thesis, University of Delaware, 1996.

Lemann, Bernard. *Historic Sites Inventory*. New Orleans: Radar and Associates for Regional Planning Commission, 1969.

Long, Edith K. *Along the Banquette: French Quarter Buildings and Their Stories*. New Orleans: Vieux Carré Property Owners, Residents and Associates, 2004.

———. "Creole Cottage Blooms under Scott Touch." *Vieux Carré Courier*, March 17, 1967, 2–3.

Magill, John. "French Market Celebrates 200th Anniversary." *Preservation in Print* 18, no. 4 (May 1991): 7.

Masson, Anne. "J. N. B. de Pouilly." *KnowLA: Encyclopedia of Louisiana*. Accessed April 26, 2012. https://64parishes.org/entry/j-n-b-de-pouilly.

Mitchell, William R., Jr. *Classic New Orleans*. New Orleans: Martin St. Martin, 1993.

Ricciuti, Italo William. *New Orleans and Its Environs: The Domestic Architecture, 1727–1870*. New York: Bonanza Books, 1967.

Sexton, Richard. *New Orleans: Elegance and Decadence*. Revised edition. San Francisco: Chronicle Books, 2003.

Toledano, Roulhac. *The National Trust Guide to New Orleans*. New York: John Wiley and Sons, 1996.

Toledano, Roulhac, and Mary Louise Christovich, comps. *New Orleans Architecture*. Vol. 6, *Faubourg Tremé and the Bayou Road*. Gretna, LA: Pelican, 1980.

Toledano, Roulhac, Sally Kittredge Evans, and Mary Louise Christovich, comps. *New Orleans Architecture*. Vol. 4, *The Creole Faubourgs*. Gretna, LA: Pelican, 1974.

Vogt, Lloyd. *Historic Buildings of the French Quarter*. Gretna, LA: Pelican, 2002.

———. *New Orleans Houses: A House-Watcher's Guide*. Gretna, LA: Pelican, 1935.

Warren, Bonnie, and Richard Sexton. "Rooms with a Vieux." *Louisiana Life* 17, no. 4 (1997): 28.

Wilson, Samuel, Jr. *A Guide to the Architecture of New Orleans, 1699–1959*. New York: Reinhold, 1959.

Wilson, Samuel, Jr., and Bernard Lemann. *New Orleans Architecture*. Vol. 1, *The Lower Garden District*. Compiled and edited by Mary Louise Christovich, Roulhac Toledano, and Betsy Swanson. Gretna, LA: Friends of the Cabildo and Pelican, 1971.

Louisiana Architecture

Poesch, Jessie, and Barbara SoRelle Bacot, eds. *Louisiana Buildings, 1720–1940*. Baton Rouge: Louisiana State University Press, 1997.

American Architecture

Herman, Bernard L. *Town House: Architecture and Material Life in the Early American City, 1780–1830*. Chapel Hill: University of North Carolina Press, 2005.

Maynard, W. Barksdale. *Architecture in the United States, 1800–1850*. New Haven: Yale University Press, 2002.

Roth, Leland M. *American Architecture: A History*. Boulder: Westview Press, 2001.

Woods, Mary N. *From Craft to Profession: The Practice of Architecture in Nineteenth-Century America*. Berkeley: University of California Press, 1999.

African Architecture

Mark, Peter. *"Portuguese" Style and Luso-African Identity: Precolonial Senegambia, Sixteenth–Nineteenth Centuries*. Bloomington and Indianapolis: Indiana University Press, 2002.

Human Geography

Campanella, Richard. *Geographies of New Orleans: Urban Fabrics before the Storm*. Lafayette: Center for Louisiana Studies, 2006.

———. *Time and Place in New Orleans: Past Geographies in the Present Day*. Gretna, LA: Pelican, 2002.

Colten, Craig E., ed. *Transforming New Orleans and Its Environs: Centuries of Change*. Pittsburgh: University of Pittsburgh Press, 2000.

Crutcher, Michael E., Jr. *Tremé: Race and Place in a New Orleans Neighborhood*. Athens: University of Georgia Press, 2010.

De Bow, J. D. B. *Statistical View of the United States—Compendium of the Seventh Census*. Washington, DC: A. O. P. Nicholson, 1854.

Kennedy, Joseph C. G. *Population of the United States in 1860; Compiled from the Original Returns of the Eighth Census*. Washington, DC: Government Printing Office, 1864.

US Census Bureau. "Aggregate Amount of Persons within the United States in the Year 1810: Aggregate Amount of Each Description of Persons within the Territory of New Orleans, 1810." Government Documents, Howard-Tilton Memorial Library, Tulane University, New Orleans, Louisiana.

———. *Census for 1820*. Washington, DC: Gales and Seaton, 1821.

———. *1880 Census: Volume 1. Statistics of the Population of the United States at the Tenth Census*. Washington, DC: Governmental Printing Office, 1883.

Ethnic Studies

Anthony, Arthé Agnes. "The Negro Creole Community in New Orleans, 1880–1920: An Oral History." PhD diss., University of California-Irvine, 1978.

Bell, Caryn Cossé. *Revolution, Romanticism, and the Afro-Creole Protest Tradition in Louisiana, 1718–1868*. Baton Rouge: Louisiana State University Press, 1997.

Berlin, Ira. *Slaves Without Masters: The Free Negro in the Antebellum South*. New York: Pantheon, 1974.

Brown, Cinnamon. "The Youngest of the Great American Family: The Creation of a Franco-American Culture in Early Louisiana," PhD diss., University of Tennessee, 2009.

Bryan, Violet Harrington. "Marcus Christian's Treatment of *Les Gens de Couleur Libres*." In *Creole: The History and Legacy of Louisiana's Free People of Color*, ed. Sybil Kein, 42–56. Baton Rouge: Louisiana State University Press, 2000.

CETA Artists in the City of New Orleans Project/Owen Murphy and Lyla Hay Own. *Créoles of New Orleans*. New Orleans: First Quarter, 1987.

Christian, Marcus B. "A Black History of Louisiana." Unpublished manuscript. Boxes 35 and 36, Literary and Historical Manuscripts, Earl K. Long Library, University of New Orleans, New Orleans, Louisiana.

Cohen, David W., and Jack P. Greene, eds. *Neither Slave nor Free: The Freedmen of African Descent in the Slave Societies of the New World*. Baltimore, MD: Johns Hopkins University Press, 1972.

Desdunes, Rodolphe Lucien. *Our People and Our History*. Translated from the French by Dorothea Olga McCants. Baton Rouge: Louisiana State University Press, 1973. Translation of *Nos hommes et notre histoire* (Montreal: Arbour and Dupont, 1911).

Dormon, James H., ed. *Creoles of Color in the Gulf South*. Knoxville: University of Tennessee Press, 1996.

Fabre, Michael. "New Orleans Creole Expatriates in France: Romance and Reality." In *Creole: The History and Legacy of Louisiana's Free People of Color*, ed. Sybil Kein, 179–207. Baton Rouge: Louisiana State University Press, 2000.

Foner, Laura. "The Free People of Color in Louisiana and St. Domingue: A Comparative Portrait of Two Three-Caste Societies." *Journal of Social History* 3, no. 4 (Summer 1970): 406–430.

Force, Pierre. "The House on Bayou Road: Atlantic Creole Networks in the Eighteenth and Nineteenth Centuries." *Journal of American History* 100, no. 1 (June 2013): 21–45.

Foreman, Nicholas. "Continuity of Caste: Free People of Color in the *Vieux Carré* of New Orleans, 1804–1820." Master's thesis, University of North Texas, Denton, 2012.

Garrigus, John D. "Colour, Class, and Identity on the Eve of the Haitian Revolution: Saint-Domingue's Free Coloured Elite as *colons américains*." *Slavery and Abolition* 17, no. 1 (April 1996): 20–43.

Gayarré, Charles Etienne. "The Creoles of History and the Creoles of Romance: A Lecture Delivered in the Hall of the Tulane University." New Orleans, 1885.

Gehman, Mary. *The Free People of Color of New Orleans: An Introduction*. New Orleans: Margaret Media, 1994.

Genovese, Eugene D. "The Slave States of North America." In *Neither Slave nor Free: The Freedmen of African Descent in the Slave Societies of the New World*, ed. David W. Cohen and Jack P. Greene, 258–277. Baltimore, MD: John Hopkins University Press, 1972.

Ghachem, Malik W. *The Old Regime and the Haitian Revolution*. Cambridge: Cambridge University Press, 2012.

Hall, Gwendolyn Midlo. *Africans in Colonial Louisiana: The Development of Afro-Creole Culture in the Eighteenth Century*. Baton Rouge: Louisiana State University Press, 1992.

———, comp. *Afro-Louisiana History and Genealogy, 1719–1820*. Accessed April 1, 2011; database downloaded from http://www.ibiblio.org/laslave/, 2003.

———. "Saint Domingue." In *Neither Slave nor Free: The Freedmen of African Descent in the Slave Societies of the New World*, ed. David W. Cohen and Jack P. Greene, 172–192. Baltimore, MD: John Hopkins University Press, 1972.

Hanger, Kimberly S. *Bounded Lives, Bounded Places: Free Black Society in Colonial New Orleans, 1769–1803*. Durham: Duke University Press, 1997.

———. "Household and Community Structure among the Free Population of Spanish New Orleans, 1778." *Louisiana History* 30, no. 1 (Winter 1989): 63–79.

———. "Patronage, Property, and Persistence: The Emergence of a Free Black Elite in Spanish New Orleans." *Slavery and Abolition* 17, no. 1 (1996): 44–64.

———. "*Personas de varias clases y colores*: Free People of Color in Spanish New Orleans, 1769–1803." PhD diss., University of Florida, 1991.

Hirsch, Arnold R., and Joseph Logsdon, eds. *Creole New Orleans: Race and Americanization*. Baton Rouge: Louisiana State University Press, 1992.

Ingersoll, Thomas N. "Free Blacks in a Slave Society: New Orleans, 1718–1812." *William and Mary Quarterly* 48, no. 2 (1991): 173–200.

Johnson, Jerah. "Colonial New Orleans: A Fragment of the Eighteenth-Century French Ethos." In *Creole New Orleans, Race and Americanization*, ed. Arnold R. Hirsch and Joseph Logsdon, 12–57. Baton Rouge: Louisiana State University Press, 1992.

Johnson, Jessica Marie. "Death Rites as Birthrights in Atlantic New Orleans: Kinship and Race in the Case of María Teresa v. Perine Dauphine." *Slavery and Abolition* 36, no. 2 (2015): 233–256.

Kein, Sybil, ed. *Creole: The History and Legacy of Louisiana's Free People of Color*. Baton Rouge: Louisiana State University Press, 2000.

King, Stewart R. *Blue Coat or Powdered Wig: Free People of Color in Pre-Revolutionary Saint Domingue*. Athens: University of Georgia Press, 2001.

Lachance, Paul. "The Foreign French." In *Creole New Orleans, Race and Americanization*, ed. Arnold R. Hirsch and Joseph Logsdon, 101–130. Baton Rouge: Louisiana State University Press, 1992.

———. "The Limits of Privilege: Where Free Persons of Colour Stood in the Hierarchy of Wealth in Antebellum New Orleans." *Slavery and Abolition* 17, no. 1 (1996): 65–84.

———. "Repercussions of the Haitian Revolution in Louisiana." In *The Impact of the Haitian Revolution in the Atlantic World*, ed. David P. Geggus, 209–230. Columbia: University of South Carolina Press, 2001.

Lovato, Frank Joseph. "Households and Neighborhoods among Free People of Color in New Orleans: A View from the Census, 1850–1860." Master's thesis, University of New Orleans, 2010.

Mills, Gary B. *The Forgotten People: Cane River's Creoles of Color*. Baton Rouge: Louisiana State University Press, 1977.

Neidenbach, Elizabeth. "The Life and Legacy of Marie Couvent: Social Networks, Property Ownership, and the Making of a Free People of Color Community in New Orleans." PhD diss., College of William and Mary, 2015.

———. "'Refugee from St. Domingue Living in This City': The Geography of Social Networks in Testaments of Refugee Women of Color in New Orleans." *Journal of Urban History* 42, no. 5 (2016): 841–862.

Nelson, Alice Dunbar. "People of Color in Louisiana." In *Creole: The History and Legacy of Louisiana's Free People of Color*, ed. Sybil Kein, 3–41. Baton Rouge: Louisiana State University Press, 2000.

Pruitt, Dwaine C. "*Nantes noir:* Living History in the City of Slavers." PhD diss., Emory University, 2005.

Rankin, David C. "The Forgotten People: Free People of Color in New Orleans, 1850–1870." PhD diss., Johns Hopkins University, 1976.

Reeves, Sally. "French-Speaking *'Hommes de Couleur Libres'* Left Indelible Mark on the Culture and Development of the French Quarter." Accessed April 8, 2012. http://frenchquarter.com/history/freepeople.php.

Schweninger, Loren. "Antebellum Free Persons of Color in Postbellum Louisiana." *Louisiana History* 30 (Fall 1989): 345–364.

———. "Property Owning Free African-American Women in the South, 1800–1870." *Journal of Women's History* 1, no. 3 (Winter 1990): 13–44.

Scott, Rebecca, and Jean Hébrard. *Freedom Papers: An Atlantic Odyssey in the Age of Emancipation.* Cambridge, MA: Harvard University Press, 2012.

Spear, Jennifer M. *Race, Sex, and Social Order in Early New Orleans.* Baltimore, MD: Johns Hopkins University Press, 2009.

Stern, Walter. *Race and Education in New Orleans: Creating the Segregated City.* Baton Rouge: Louisiana State University Press, 2018.

Tregle, Joseph G., Jr. "Creoles and Americans." In *Creole New Orleans: Race and Americanization*, ed. Arnold R. Hirsch and Joseph Logsdon, 131–185. Baton Rouge: Louisiana State University Press, 1992.

Wegmann, Andrew N. "The Vitriolic Blood of a Negro: The Development of Racial Identity and Creole Elitism in New Spain and Spanish Louisiana, 1763–1803." In *Race and Transatlantic Identities*, ed. Elizabeth T. Kenney, Sirpa Salenius, and Whitney Womack Smith, 8–29. New York: Routledge, 2017.

White, Ashli. "'A Flood of Impure Lava': Saint Dominguan Refugees in the United States, 1791–1820." PhD diss., Columbia University, 2003.

Whitten, David O. *Andrew Durnford: A Black Sugar Planter in Antebellum Louisiana.* Natchitoches, LA: Northwestern State University Press, 1981.

Woods, Frances J. *Marginality and Identity: A Colored Creole Family through Ten Generations.* Baton Rouge: Louisiana State University Press, 1972.

African American History

Blassingame, John W. *Black New Orleans, 1860–1880.* Chicago: University of Chicago Press, 1973.

Curry, Leonard P. *The Free Black in Urban America, 1800–1850: The Shadow of the Dream.* Chicago: University of Chicago Press, 1981.

Dormon, James H., Jr. *The African American Experience in Louisiana: From Africa to the Civil War*, ed. Charles Vincent. Lafayette: Center for Louisiana Studies, 1999–2002.

Schafer, Judith Kelleher. *Becoming Free, Remaining Free: Manumission and Enslavement in New Orleans, 1846–1862.* Baton Rouge: Louisiana State University Press, 2003.

Sterkx, H. E. *The Free Negro in Antebellum Louisiana.* Rutherford, NJ: Fairleigh Dickinson University Press, 1972.

West, Jean M. "From Sugar Bowl to the International Space Station: Norbert Rillieux, African-American Inventor." Accessed April 3, 2012. http://www.slaveryinamerica.org/narratives/bio_norbert_rillieux.htm.

Woodson, Carter G. *The Education of the Negro Prior to 1861: A History of the Education of the Colored People of the United States from the Beginning of Slavery to the Civil War*. Washington, DC: Association for the Study of Negro Life and History, 1919.

Louisiana History

"An Act to Prevent Free Persons of Colour from Entering into This State and for Other Purposes." March 16, 1830, amended March 25, 1831. In *A Digest of the Ordinances, Resolutions, By-laws and Regulations of the Corporation of New-Orleans, and a Collection of the Laws of the Legislature Relative to the Said City*, 535–544, 559. New Orleans: Gaston Brusle, 1836.

Brasseaux, Carl. *The "Foreign French": Nineteenth-Century French Immigration into Louisiana*. Vol. 1, *1820–1839*. Lafayette: Center for Louisiana Studies, 1990.

———. *A Refuge for All Ages: Immigration in Louisiana History*. Lafayette: Center for Louisiana Studies, 1996.

Common Routes, St. Domingue-Louisiana. Exhibition catalog. New Orleans: The Historic New Orleans Collection, 2006.

Crété, Lilian. *Daily Life in Louisiana, 1815–1830*. Translated by Patrick Gregory. Baton Rouge: Louisiana State University Press, 1981.

Davis, William C. *The Pirates Laffite: The Treacherous World of the Corsairs of the Gulf*. Orlando, FL: Harcourt, 2005.

Gayarré, Charles Etienne. *History of Louisiana*. 4 vols. New Orleans: Armand Hawkins, 1885.

Huber, Leonard V. *Louisiana: A Pictorial History*. New York: Charles Scribner's Sons, 1975.

"Proceedings of the Grand Lodge of Louisiana," 2011, A-1, A-23. Accessed October 28, 2020. http://library.la-mason.com/PastProceedings/2010/2011.pdf.

Reeves, William D. *Historic Louisiana: An Illustrated History*. San Antonio: Historical Publishing Network, 2003.

Republican Party (La.) Convention. *Proceedings of the Convention of the Republican Party of Louisiana Held at Economy Hall, New Orleans, September 25, 1865, and of the Central Executive Committee of the Friends of Universal Suffrage of Louisiana, now the Central Executive Committee of the Republican Party of Louisiana*. New Orleans: New Orleans Tribune Office, 1865. Accessed April 5, 2012. http://www.archive.org/stream/proceedingsofconoorepurich/proceedingsofconoorepurich_djvu.txt.

New Orleans History

Acts Passed at the First Session of the First Legislature of the Territory of Orleans. New Orleans: Bradford and Anderson, 1807.

Benfey, Christopher E. G. *Degas in New Orleans: Encounters in the Creole World of Kate Chopin and George Washington Cable*. New York: Knopf, 1997.

Blassingame, John. *Black New Orleans, 1860–1880*. Chicago: University of Chicago Press, 1973.

BIBLIOGRAPHY

Cable, Mary. *Lost New Orleans*. Boston: Houghton Mifflin, 1980.

Castellanos, Henry. *New Orleans as It Was: Episodes of Louisiana Life*. 2nd ed. New Orleans: L. Graham, 1905.

Civil Code of the State of Louisiana: With the statutory amendments from 1825 to 1853. New Orleans: Bloomfield and Steel, 1861.

A Digest of the Civil Laws now in Force in the Territory of New Orleans, with Alterations and Amendments to Its Present System of Government. New Orleans: Bradford and Anderson, 1808. Accessed July 23, 2020. https://digestof1808.law.lsu.edu/?uid=1&tid=1&ver=en#1.

Fossier, Albert Emile. *New Orleans: The Glamour Period, 1800–1840*. New Orleans: Pelican, 1957.

Gibson, John. *Gibson's Guide and Directory of the State of Louisiana, and the Cities of New Orleans and Lafayette*. New Orleans: John Gibson, 1838.

Hollandsworth, James G., Jr. *An Absolute Massacre: The New Orleans Race Riot of July 30, 1866*. Baton Rouge: Louisiana State University Press, 2001.

Johnson, Rashauna. *Slavery's Metropolis: Unfree Labor in New Orleans during the Age of Revolutions*. New York: Cambridge University Press, 2016.

Kelman, Ari. *A River and Its City: The Nature of Landscape in New Orleans*. Berkeley: University of California Press, 2006.

Kendall, John Smith. *History of New Orleans*. Chicago: Lewis, 1922.

King, Grace. *New Orleans: The Place and the People*. New York: Macmillan, 1904.

La-Cemeteries, "Orleans Parish Cemeteries." Accessed July 14, 2012. http://www.la-cemeteries.com/Cemeteries %20Orleans%20Table.shtml.

Leumas, Emilie. "Ties That Bind: The Family, Social, and Business Associations of the Insurrectionists of 1768." *Louisiana History* 47, no. 2 (Spring 2006): 183–202.

Lewis, Peirce F. *New Orleans: The Making of an Urban Landscape*. 2nd ed. Santa Fe: Center for American Places, 2003.

McCaffety, Kerri. *The Majesty of the French Quarter*. Gretna, LA: Pelican, 2000.

Mitchell, Mary Niall. *Raising Freedom's Child: Black Children and Visions of the Future after Slavery*. New York: New York University Press, 2008.

Powell, Lawrence N. *The Accidental City: Improvising New Orleans*. Cambridge, MA: Harvard University Press, 2013.

———, ed. *The New Orleans of George Washington Cable: The 1887 Census Office Report*. Baton Rouge: Louisiana State University Press, 2008.

Reynolds, Donald E. "The New Orleans Riot of 1866, Reconsidered." *Louisiana History* 5, no. 1 (Winter 1964): 5–27.

Rightor, Henry, ed., *Standard History of New Orleans, Louisiana*. Chicago: Lewis, 1900.

Starr, S. Frederick. *Southern Comfort: The Garden District of New Orleans*. Cambridge, MA: MIT Press, 1989.

St. Augustine Catholic Church of New Orleans. "The History of St. Augustine Catholic Church." Accessed October 28, 2020. https://d2y1pz2y630308.cloudfront.net/20194/documents/2019/11/Insert_History_PRESS%203.pdf.

Van Zante, Gary A. *New Orleans 1867: Photographs by Theodore Lilienthal*. London: Merrell, 2008.

American History

Bailey, Diane. *Cholera*. New York: Rosen, 2011.
Baptist, Edward E. *The Half Has Never Been Told: Slavery and the Making of American Capitalism*. Philadelphia: Basic Books, 2014.
Ketcham, Ralph Louis. *James Madison: A Biography*. First paperback ed. Charlottesville: University Press of Virginia, 1990.
Martineau, Harriet. *Retrospect of Western Travel*. Vol. 1. London: Saunders and Otley, 1838.
———. *Society in America*. Vol. 2. London: Saunders and Otley, 1837.
Rosenberg, Charles E. *The Cholera Years: The United States in 1832, 1849, and 1866*. Chicago: University of Chicago Press, 1987.

Race and Identity

Arbery, Glenn Cannon. "Victims of Likeness: Quadroons and Octoroons in Southern Fiction." *Southern Review* 25, no. 1 (January 1989): 52–71.
Berzon, Judith R. *Neither White Nor Black: The Mulatto Character in American Fiction*. New York: New York University Press, 1978.
Bryan, Violet Harrington. *The Myth of New Orleans in Literature: Dialogues of Race and Gender*. Knoxville: University of Tennessee Press, 1993.
Davis, F. James. *Who Is Black: One Nation's Definition*. University Park: Pennsylvania State University Press, 1991.
Domínguez, Virginia R. *White by Definition: Social Classification in Creole Louisiana*. New Brunswick, NJ: Rutgers University Press, 1997.
Fischer, Roger A. "Racial Segregation in Antebellum New Orleans." *American Historical Review* 74, no. 3 (February 1969): 926–937.
Gilman, Susan. "The Mulatto, Tragic or Triumphant? The Nineteenth-Century American Race Melodrama." In *The Culture of Sentiment: Race, Gender and Sentimentality in Nineteenth-Century America*, ed. Shirley Samuels, 221–243. New York: Oxford University Press, 1992.
Guillory, Monique. "Under One Roof: The Sins and Sanctity of the New Orleans Quadroon Balls." In *Race Consciousness: African-American Studies for the New Century*, ed. Judith Jackson Fossett and Jeffrey Tucker, 67–92. New York: New York University Press, 1997.
Hanger, Kimberly S. "Avenues to Freedom Open to New Orleans' Black Population, 1769–1779." *Louisiana History* 31 (Summer 1990): 237–264.
Hobratsch, Ben Melvin. "Creole Angel: The Self-Identity of the Free People of Color of Antebellum New Orleans." Master's thesis, University of North Texas, 2006.
Horsman, Reginald. *Race and Manifest Destiny: The Origins of the American Racial Anglo-Saxonism*. Cambridge, MA: Harvard University Press, 1981.
Logsdon, Joseph, and Caryn Cossé Bell. "The Americanization of Black New Orleans." In *Creole New Orleans, Race and Americanization*, ed. Arnold R. Hirsch and Joseph

Logsdon, 201–261. Baton Rouge: Louisiana State University Press, 1992.
Roach, Joseph. "Slave Spectacles and Tragic Octoroons: A Cultural Genealogy of Antebellum Performance." *Theatre Survey* 33, no. 2 (November 1992): 167–187.
Smith, Norman R. *Footprints of Black Louisiana*. Bloomington, IN: Xlibris, 2010.
Somers, Dale. "Black and White New Orleans: A Study in Urban Race Relations, 1865–1900." *Journal of Southern History* 40, no. 1 (1974): 19–42.
Spain, Daphne. "Race Relations and Residential Segregation in New Orleans: Two Centuries of Paradox." *Annals of the American Academy of Political and Social Science* 441 (January 1979): 82–96.
Thompson, Shirley. *Exiles at Home: The Struggle to Become American in Creole New Orleans*. Cambridge, MA: Harvard University Press, 2009.
———. "The Passing of a People: Creoles of Color in Mid-Nineteenth Century New Orleans." PhD diss., Harvard University, 2001.
Zanger, Jules. "The 'Tragic Octoroon' in Pre–Civil War Fiction." *American Quarterly* 18 (Spring 1966): 63–70.

Gender Studies

Alexander, Adele Logan. *Ambiguous Lives: Free Women of Color in Rural Georgia, 1789–1879*. Fayetteville: University of Arkansas Press, 1993.
Aslakson, Kenneth. "The 'Quadroon-Plaçage' Myth of Antebellum New Orleans: Anglo-American (Mis)interpretations of a French-Caribbean Phenomenon." *Journal of Social History* 45, no. 3 (Spring 2012): 709–734.
Bardaglio, Peter W. *Reconstructing the Household: Families, Sex, and the Law in the Nineteenth-Century South*. Chapel Hill: University of North Carolina Press, 1995.
Bleser, Carol, ed. In *Joy and Sorrow: Women, Family, and Marriage in the Victorian South*. New York: Oxford University Press, 1991.
Cheung, Floyd D. "*Les Cenelles* and Quadroon Balls: 'Hidden Transcripts' of Resistance and Domination in New Orleans, 1803–1845." *Southern Literary Journal* 29, no. 2 (Spring 1997): 5–16.
Clark, Emily. *The Strange History of the American Quadroon: Free Women of Color in the Revolutionary Atlantic World*. Chapel Hill: University of North Carolina Press, 2013.
Cott, Nancy F. *Public Vows: A History of Marriage and the Nation*. Cambridge, MA: Harvard University Press, 2000.
Detiege, Augrey Marie. *Henriette Delille, Free Woman of Color: Foundress of the Sisters of the Holy Family*. New Orleans: Sisters of the Holy Family, 1976.
Garrigus, John D. "Redrawing the Colour Line: Gender and the Social Construction of Race in Pre-Revolutionary Haiti." *Journal of Caribbean History* 30, nos. 1–2 (1996): 28–50.
Gaspar, David Barry, and Darlene Clark Hine, eds. *Beyond Bondage: Free Women of Color in the Americas*. Urbana: University of Illinois Press, 2004.
Gould, Lois Virginia Meachem. "'A Chaos of Iniquity and Discord': Slave and Free Women of Color in the Spanish Ports of New Orleans, Mobile, and Pensacola." In *The Devil's Lane:*

Sex and Race in the Early South, ed. Catherine Clinton and Michele Gillespie, 232–246. New York: Oxford University Press, 1997.

———. "In Full Enjoyment of Their Liberty: The Free Women of Color of the Gulf Ports of New Orleans, Mobile, and Pensacola, 1769–1860." PhD diss., Emory University, 1991.

Hangar, Kimberly S. "Coping in a Complex World: Free Black Women in Colonial New Orleans." In *The Devil's Lane: Sex and Race in the Early South*, ed. Catherine Clinton and Michele Gillespie, 218–246. New York: Oxford University Press, 1997.

———. "Protecting Property, Family, and Self: The 'Mujeres Libres' of Colonial New Orleans." *Revista—Review Interamericana* 22, no. 1 (1992): 126–159.

Hine, Darlene Clark, ed. *Black Women in America: An Historical Encyclopedia*. 3 vols. 2nd ed. New York: Oxford University Press, 2005.

Hodes, Martha, ed. *Sex, Love, Race: Crossing Boundaries in North American History*. New York: New York University Press, 1999.

———. *White Women, Black Men: Illicit Sex in the Nineteenth-Century South*. New Haven: Yale University Press, 1997.

Jones, Jacqueline. *Labor of Love, Labor of Sorrow: Black Women, Work, and the Family from Slavery to the Present*. New York: Vintage Books, 1995.

King, Wilma. *The Essence of Liberty: Free Black Women during the Slave Era*. Columbia: University of Missouri Press, 2006.

Kinney, James. *Amalgamation! Race, Sex, and Rhetoric in the Nineteenth-Century American Novel*. Westport, CT: Greenwood Press, 1985.

Martin, Joan M. "*Plaçage* and the Louisiana *Gens de Couleur Libre*: How Race and Sex Defined the Lifestyles of Free Women of Color." In *Creole: The History and Legacy of Louisiana's Free People of Color*, ed. Sybil Kein, 57–70. Baton Rouge: Louisiana State University Press, 2000.

Mattison, Hiram, and Louisa Picquet. *Louisa Picquet, the Octoroon, or Inside Views of Southern Domestic Life*. New York: H. Mattison, 1861. Reprinted in *Collected Black Women's Narratives*, ed. Henry Louis Gates Jr. New York: Oxford University Press, 1988.

Myers, Amrita. "Negotiating Women: Black Women and the Politics of Freedom in Charleston, South Carolina, 1790–1860." PhD diss., Rutgers University, 2004.

Stoler, Ann Laura. *Carnal Knowledge and Imperial Power: Race and the Intimate in Colonial Rule*. Berkeley: University of California Press, 2002.

Tansey, Richard. "Prostitution and Politics in Antebellum New Orleans." *Southern Studies* 18 (Winter 1979): 449–479.

Economic History

Clark, John G. *New Orleans, 1718–1812: An Economic History*. Baton Rouge: Louisiana State University Press, 1970.

Gehman, Mary. "Visible Means of Support: Businesses, Professions, and Trades of Free People of Color." In *Creole: The History and Legacy of Louisiana's Free People of Color*, ed. Sybil Kein, 208–222. Baton Rouge: Louisiana State University Press, 2000.

Marler, Scott P. *The Merchant's Capital: New Orleans and the Political Economy of the Nineteenth-Century South*. New York: Cambridge University Press, 2013.

Reinders, Robert. "The Free Negro in the New Orleans Economy, 1850–1860." *Louisiana History* 6, no. 3 (1965): 273–285.

Stevenson, Howard H., and Teresa M. Amabile. "Entrepreneurial Management: In Pursuit of Opportunity." In *The Intellectual Venture Capitalist: John H. McArthur and the Work of the Harvard Business School, 1980–1995*, ed. Thomas K. McCraw and Jeffrey L. Cruikshank, 133–162. Cambridge, MA: Harvard Business School Press, 1999.

Walker, Juliet E. K. *The History of Black Business in America: Capitalism, Race, Entrepreneurship*. New York: Macmillan Library Reference, 1998.

———. "Racism, Slavery, and Free Enterprise: Black Entrepreneurship in the United States before the Civil War." *Business History Review* 60, no. 3 (Autumn 1986): 343–382.

Colonial Studies

Brasseaux, Carl, and Glenn R. Conrad, eds. *The Road to Louisiana: The Saint-Domingue Refugees, 1792–1809*. Lafayette: Center for Louisiana Studies, 1992.

Cooper, Frederick, and Ann Laura Stoler, eds. *Tensions of Empire: Colonial Cultures in a Bourgeois World*. Berkeley: University of California Press, 1997.

Geggus, David P., ed. *The Impact of the Haitian Revolution in the Atlantic World*. Columbia: University of South Carolina Press, 2001.

Hunt, Alfred N. *Haiti's Influence on Antebellum America*. Baton Rouge: Louisiana State University Press, 1988.

Pitot, James. *Observations on the Colony of Louisiana, from 1796 to 1804*. Translated by Henry C. Pitot. Baton Rouge: Louisiana State University Press, 1979.

Anthropology

Scott, Rebecca J. "Public Rights and Private Commerce: A Nineteenth-Century Atlantic Creole Itinerary." *Current Anthropology* 48, no. 2 (April 2007): 237–256.

Trouillot, Michel-Rolph. *Silencing the Past: Power and Production of History*. Boston: Beacon Press, 1995.

Preservation Planning Documents

Edwards, Jay D., et al. "Louisiana's French Creole Architecture." National Register of Historic Places Multiple Property Nomination. 1991. National Register of Historic Places Digital Archive on NPGallery. Accessed October 28, 2020. https://npgallery.nps.gov/NRHP/GetAsset/12b0ac97-e048-4c63-9a1d-cc96bf9c9689.

Fricker, Jonathan, and Donna Fricker. Garden District Historic District Additional Documentation (supplement to the 1971 National Register of Historic Places nomination form), 1974. National Register of Historic Places Digital Archive on NPGallery. Accessed October 28, 2020. https://npgallery.nps.gov/GetAsset/1f4df2be-a7ff-44d2-a4a3-c9f90c145b1b.

Heintzelman, Patricia, and Charles W. Snell. The Presbytère, National Register of Historic

Places nomination form, June 30, 1975. National Register of Historic Places Digital Archive on NPGallery. https://npgallery.nps.gov/NRHP/GetAsset/e320109d-87da-4f46-8375-013c18fe0dfe.

Holy Cross Historic District National Register of Historic Places nomination form. 1986. National Register of Historic Places Digital Archive on NPGallery. https://npgallery.nps.gov/NRHP/AssetDetail?assetID=80cdeb60-6d48-494b-8fe0-71a81aa2020a.

Neighborhood Sources

Faubourg Marigny Improvement Association. "Welcome to the Faubourg Marigny." Accessed March 2, 2012. http://www.faubourgmarigny.org/historyfm.htm.

Faubourg St. Roch Project. "Faubourg St. Roch History." Accessed January 30, 2012. http://strochproject.com/neighborhood.html.

Hémard, Ned. "Julie and Julia, or *Amour Sans Dot*." Accessed March 7, 2012. http://www.neworleansbar.org/documents/JulieandJuliaArticle.10–7.pdf.

Preservation Resource Center. *New Marigny*. Online brochure. http://www.prcno.org/neighborhoods/brochures/NewMarigny.pdf.

Rebuilding Together New Orleans. "Faubourg St. Roch." Accessed January 30, 2012. http://www.rtno.org/neighborhoods/faubourg-st.-roch/.

Maps

Diagram Showing Inundated District, Sauvé's Crevasse, May 9, 1849. Ludwig von Reizenstein, delineator. LDL, crediting WRC-THNOC.

Plan de la Nouvelle-Orléans avec les noms des proprietaries. Joseph Pilié, surveyor. 1808. New Orleans: The Historic New Orleans Collection.

Plan du Faubourg Marigny. Copied by Claude Jules Allou d'Hémécourt from an 1807 plan by Barthélémy Lafon. ca. 1870. New Orleans: The Historic New Orleans Collection.

Plan of the city and suburbs of New Orleans, from an actual survey made in 1815 by J. Tanesse. Published by Charles Del Vecchio (New York) and P. Maspero (New Orleans), 1817. New Orleans: The Historic New Orleans Collection.

Plan of the City of New Orleans and the Adjacent Plantations. Drawn by Alexander Debrunner. December 24, 1798. New Orleans: The Historic New Orleans Collection.

Topographical Map of New Orleans and Its Vicinity. Charles F. Zimpel, surveyor, 1833. New Orleans: The Historic New Orleans Collection.

Other

Harris, Cyril M. *McGraw-Hill Dictionary of Architecture and Construction*. 4th ed. New York: McGraw-Hill, 2006.

Jewell, Edwin L., comp. *Jewell's Digest of the City Ordinances*. New Orleans: Edwin L. Jewell, 1881.

Reports of Cases Argued and Adjudged in the Supreme Court of the United States, January Term, 1846. Vol. 4. Boston: Charles C. Little and James Brown, 1846.

INDEX

Adam, Louis, 92
African Americans, free, 4, 5, 6–7, 12–13, 21, 25, 27, 62, 71, 79, 119, 123, 128, 146, 147, 148, 150, 151, 155, 157, 200, 202, 214, 217, 219. See also *gens de couleur libres*
Afro-Creole: definition of, 5; as an ethnic group, 5, 12–13. See also *gens de couleur libres*
Aicard, Joseph, 40
Alexis, Daniel, 206
Aliquot, Marie Jean, 211
Almonaster, Michaela (Baroness de Pontalba), 177
American architecture, professionalization of, 5, 13, 102, 148, 155, 156, 191
American Sector, 53, 66–68, 171, 173, 184, 190, 217. See also Faubourg Sainte-Marie
American Theatre, 15, 162
Andry, Manuel, 65
architects and builders, Anglo, 170–180; architectural practices of, 180–190, 191; competition from, 157, 158; partnerships between, 80, 148, 174, 175; as teachers, 101–102, 146, 169, 181–182; training of, 101–102, 155, 180, 182. See also *individual builders*
architects and builders, enslaved, 119, 145–148, 150, 157, 168; apprenticeship/training of, 150, 181, 182
architects and builders, French, 158–167; partnerships between, 160, 162, 165; as teachers, 181–182; use of enslaved labor by, 181, 182
architects and builders, French Creole, 167–170; partnerships between, 169; as teachers, 169, 180, 181–182. See also *individual builders*
architects and builders, *gens de couleur libres*: and acquisition of work, 123, 143–145, 185; apprenticeship/training of, 18, 20, 79–80, 101, 102, 112, 116, 118, 119, 137, 148–151, 153, 155, 168, 180, 196, 207, 216; architectural forms associated with, 18–19, 21, 79, 83, 85, 93, 97, 99, 107, 108, 113, 114–117, 138–140, 153, 215, 217–218; as draftsmen, 102, 126–127, 133, 137, 144, 150, 153; as entrepreneurs, 19–21, 79, 143, 155, 196, 220–221; financial status of, 20, 35–36, 53, 113, 119, 191, 196, 197–203, 204, 207; hiring practices of, 126, 145, 146, 147, 153; kinship and business ties of, 18, 19, 20, 21, 61, 63, 148, 151, 153, 185, 197, 198, 203, 204, 206–211; limitations posed for, 55, 196, 203, 216;

INDEX

marginalization of, 191; motivations of, 18, 34, 197, 218; occupations of, 79, 80, 119, 149, 154, 155, 196, 198, 202; and ownership of enslaved individuals, 19, 112, 145–147, 148, 150, 201, 203; partnerships between, 40, 80, 92, 112, 145, 147, 153, 197, 201, 202, 205, 207, 209; as teachers, 136, 149–150, 151, 207; in the US South, 119, 149, 153, 213. *See also individual builders*

architects and builders, German, 191

architects and builders, Irish, 174–175, 178, 191

architects and builders, Spanish, 55, 81, 156, 167

Arnault, Genève, 129, 140

Atkinson, W. L., 186, 187

Azémare, Geneviève: association of with Louis Antoine Dolliole, 7, 24, 27, 35, 39, 40; background of, 27; death of, 60, 93, 204; estate of, 204; ownership of enslaved individuals by, 204; ownership of real property by, 16, 27, 28–30, 51, 60, 93, 204

Baggett, Alexander, 45, 186, 188

Batigne, Marcelin, 104, 205

Baudin, Marie Eugenie "Laurette," 151, 198, 206

Bayou Gentilly, 60

Bayou Road: development of, 2, 58–59, 60, 167, 209, 210, 211, 212; Dolliole properties on, 2, 27, 28, 29, 30, 33, 34, 35, 40, 44, 60, 72–74, 81, 85, 87, 88, 115, 206, 210; *gens de couleur libres'* properties on, 60; Soulié properties on, 48–50, 52

Bernard, Marie Anne, 168

Bickel and Hamblet, 134

Bienville, Jean-Baptiste Le Moyne de, 54, 66, 68

Blanc, Bishop Antoine, 212

Boisdoré, Adelaide, 119

Boisdoré, François: association of with the Dolliole family, 20, 206; association of with the Soulié family, 207; background of, 119; as builder, 142–143, 191, 218; as estate appraiser, 208, 209; military service of, 211; ownership of real property by, 2, 121; and property on Bayou Road, 2, 119, 121, 138, 206, 210, 211; works of, 119–121, 138, 217

Boisdoré, Marguerite, 126, 139, 143

Bonnecaze, Pierre Jean, 151

Brand, William, 15, 18, 156, 171, 173, 181, 182, 183, 185

brick-between-post, 33, 85, 90, 92, 93, 96, 100, 122, 123, 125, 128, 144. See also *briquette-entre-poteaux*

Briggs, Charles, House, 175

Briquette-entre-poteaux, 4, 81, 119, 128

Brusle, Pedro Barthélémy, 151

building contracts, 85, 102, 119, 123, 124, 125, 126, 128, 133, 134, 138–140, 142, 162, 168, 182, 183, 185, 188, 190, 207, 215, 218; components of, 143–144; by the Dolliole family, 92–93, 151, 153; by the Soulié family, 104, 109, 187

building traditions: African, 17, 82, 83; Canadian, 82; Caribbean, 82, 83, 100, 131, 217

Butler, Richard, 103, 104

Cabildo, 158, 159, 165

Caldero, Benigno, 150–151

Caldwell, James, 15, 179

Canal and Banking Company, 177

Canal Bank, 174

Canal Street: as a boundary, 15, 66–67; commercial architecture on, 160, 162; development of, 15, 162, 174, 184; residential architecture on, 176

Carondelet Canal, 59, 66, 104, 114, 191, 192

Cathedral-Basilica of St. Louis King of France. *See* St. Louis Cathedral

Catherine (consort of Jean-François

291

Dolliole), 7, 63–64
Cavelier, Jeam Baptiste Zenon, 165
Cazelar plantation, 45, 49, 205
Chabot, Margaret, 103
Chaigneau, Jean, 169, 179, 181
Champs-Élysées, 62
Charity Hospital, 3, 102
Chateau, Joseph: background of, 128; as builder, 142, 191, 207; building contracts of, 144; works of, 128–133, 139, 140
Chemin du Bayou Saint John. *See* Bayou Road
Cherubin and Dessource, 151, 207
Cheval, François, 7, 41
Cheval, Louise Paul, 169
Cheval, Louison: association of with Charles Vivant, 7, 42; background of, 7, 41; family of, 123; manumission of, 41; ownership of real property by, 41
Christ Church, 102
churches, Catholic, 61, 63, 212. *See also specific church names*
City Bank of New Orleans, 2, 177
Civil War, 18, 20, 21, 53, 61, 62, 65, 71, 183, 202, 211, 212, 213, 215, 219
Claiborne, William, 118, 211
coartación, 25
Coliseum Square, 176
Collège d'Orléans, 37, 39, 40, 53, 60, 162, 165, 174, 191, 211
Colvis, Julien, 147
Commercial Bank, 177, 179
Company of the Architects of the Eighth District, 125
Congo Square, 58, 60
Conner, Joseph, 123–124
Conrad, Jean, 151
Contat, Louis, 146
Cordeviolle, Etienne, 148, 197
Cornu, Marceline, 119, 138
Correjolles, Jean-François Edouard, 18, 126, 168–170, 179, 181, 185, 186
Côte des Allemands (German Coast), 7, 41
Cottin, Jean Baptiste, 165
Courcelle, Achille, 168
Courcelle, Achille Antoine, 168
Courcelle, Achille Barthélémy, 45, 168, 180, 208
Courcelle, Charles, 220
Courcelle, Eliza Sylvie, 1, 4, 11, 198, 203, 205, 219
Courcelle, Etienne François, 168, 169, 180
Courcelle, Joachim, 18, 157, 168, 180, 181, 192, 205
Courcelle, Léon, 1, 44, 45, 51, 67, 111, 112, 125, 126, 205
Courcelle, Myrtille: as builder, 142; building contracts of, 149; employment of by Soulié family, 126; estate inventory of, 145; financial status of, 201, 202; ownership of enslaved individuals by, 47; personal life of, 127; political involvement of, 220; property transactions of with Soulié sisters, 47, 58, 205; as teacher, 150; works of, 125–127, 139, 143
Couvent, Bernard, 58
Couvent, Marie, 20, 137, 207
Couvertie, Jean Baptiste, 128, 129, 131, 139, 140
Creole architecture: 21, 168, 170, 171, 217; characteristics of, 4, 5, 85; development of, 82, 83; Norman plan, 83; *salle-et-chambre*, 83; Spanish plan, 83. *See also distinct building forms and types*
Creole cottage, 85, 87, 92, 93, 96, 99, 103, 112, 113, 114, 116, 124, 125, 134, 138, 140, 143, 153, 176, 218; *abat-vent*, 85, 92, 94, 97, 122, 124, 126, 128, 131; adaptations to, 89, 105, 125; *appentis*, 131, 140, 218; Caribbean developments of, 83; characteristics of, 84–85; corner storehouse, 112, 114, 160, 165, 171, 177, 190; *en banquette*, 81, 85; four-bay, 33,

45, 85, 93, 96, 102, 103, 104, 112, 122, 123, 125, 126; four-room, 33, 90, 92, 93, 94, 100, 102, 125, 131; French Colonial, 83; *maisonette*, 133–135, 140, 218; raised, 81, 83; *rez-de-chaussée*, 81; Spanish Colonial, 83; three-bay, 31, 96, 126, 218; two-bay, 40, 94, 128, 131

Creole faubourgs, 21, 54, 61–63, 69, 72–74, 81, 90, 114, 115, 116, 184, 215. *See also individual faubourgs*

Creolization, 5, 19, 131, 215

Cuba, 11, 12, 133, 136, 168, 213

Dakin, Charles Bingley, 173, 174, 175. *See also* Dakin and Dakin

Dakin, James H., 18, 174, 180. *See also* Dakin and Dakin

Dakin and Dakin, 174, 176, 180

Dakin and Gallier, 174, 176, 180, 182, 185, 191

Dalcour, Marie, 127

Daret, Charles Henry, 126, 127, 139, 143

Daunois plantation, 65

Dauphine, Marguerite, 152, 153

Davis, Evelina, 127

Demony, Marie Louise, 94, 144

Desdunes, Rodolph, 118, 137, 213

Deslondes, Maria, 66

Després, Louison, 31

Destrehan, Nicolas, 64

Destrehan House, 171

Diamond, Charles, 177

Dick, James, House, 175

Dolliole (family): architectural training and practice of, 81–100, 116, 153, 191, 218; connections of to Soulié family, 208–209; financial status of, 197, 202, 209, 211; kinship and business ties of, 206, 209; legacy of, 4, 213, 216, 217, 218, 219, 221; legal activities of, 198, 204; occupations of, 154; origins of, 6, 7; and ownership of enslaved individuals, 19, 35, 144, 145, 146, 147, 148, 203, 204; ownership of real property by, 17, 19, 26, 27–41, 53, 55, 58–59, 60–61, 62, 63, 68, 71, 162, 209; and St. Augustine Catholic Church, 212. *See also individual family members*

Dolliole, Albert Basam, Jr., 153

Dolliole, Charlotte, 27, 30, 34, 204

Dolliole, Edmond, 7, 154

Dolliole, Etienne Adam, 7, 154

Dolliole, Geneviève. *See* Azémare, Geneviève

Dolliole, Jean-François, 7, 81, 219

Dolliole, Jean-Louis: architectural training and practice of, 18, 63, 68, 79, 81, 85, 87, 89, 92, 93, 94, 96, 97, 99, 113, 114, 142, 144, 154; association of with François Boisdoré, 121, 206, 208; association of with Marie Couvent, 20; association of with Henry Fletcher, 20, 206–207; association of with Norbert Fortier, 36; association of with Nelson Fouché, 20, 136, 206; association of with Ursain Guesnon, 123; birth of, 7, 27; children of, 3, 20, 63, 148, 151, 153, 204, 219; death of, 212; estate of, 202, 212; as estate appraiser and executor, 19, 20, 123, 206, 207, 208; financial status of, 199, 201, 202; marriages of, 151, 198, 204; military service of, 101, 211; ownership of enslaved individuals by, 35, 144, 145, 147, 204; ownership of real property by, 2, 18, 28–41, 53, 55, 62, 63, 96, 121, 204, 206; as teacher, 148, 149, 150, 153

Dolliole, Joseph: architectural training and practice of, 37, 39, 79, 81, 92, 93, 94, 96, 97, 100, 113, 114, 142, 144, 145, 154; association of with François Boisdoré, 2, 20, 119, 121, 206, 210; association of with Marie Couvent, 20; association of with Henry Fletcher, 20, 92, 145, 206–207; association of with Nelson Fouché, 20, 40, 64, 136; birth of, 7;

293

death of, 27, 60; estate of, 93, 202, 204; as estate appraiser and executor, 19, 206, 207; financial status of, 199; kinship and business and relations of, 209, 210; marriages of, 41, 198, 204, 206; military service of, 211; ownership of enslaved individuals by, 35, 144, 145, 147, 204; ownership of real property by, 2, 3, 20, 28, 29, 35, 37, 39, 40, 41, 55, 60, 63, 68, 87, 93, 121, 144; as teacher, 145
Dolliole, Joseph Pantheleon, 7, 154
Dolliole, Louis Antoine: background of, 7, 27; death and bequests of, 40, 87; descendants of, 153; occupation of, 81, 154; property ownership of, 2, 16–17, 29, 30–34, 87, 88, 119, 204, 206, 219; relationship of with Geneviève Azémare, 7, 24, 27, 35, 40
Dolliole, Louis Drausin: architectural training and practice of, 63, 71, 148, 151, 152, 154; birth of, 148; descendants of, 219; financial status of, 199; marriage of to Marie Eugenie Guesnon, 123, 151; residence of, 37, 71, 96
Dolliole, Louis Laurent, 7, 154
Dolliole, Madeleine: birth of, 7, 27; daughter of, 31, 40, 96, 151; death of, 60; marriage of to Noel Galaud, 31; ownership of real property by, 28, 29, 31, 39, 40, 47, 52, 60, 96, 144
Dolliole, Marie Eugenie: birth of, 3; marriage of to Pedro Barthélémy Brusle, 151
Dolliole, Marie Francoise, 27
Dolliole, Marie Rosella: 204; marriage of to Pierre Jean Bonnecaze, 151
Dolliole, Milford, 153, 154
Dolliole, Pierre: association of with Norbert Fortier, 36, 37; birth of, 7, 27; death and estate of, 39, 40; descendants of, 153, 219; military service of, 211; occupation of, 33, 81, 154; ownership of real property by, 28, 31, 33, 34, 35, 36, 37, 39, 40, 96, 204
Dolliole, Pierre (son of Adelaide Duplessis), 151
Dolliole, Pierre (unidentified), 64
Dolliole, Rosette, 27, 29, 30, 34, 39, 40
Dolliole and Errié, 151–153
Drouillard, Athalie, 207
Dubuisson, François, 119
Ducatel, Germain, 134
Duconge, François Pierre, 1, 45, 47
Dufossat, Joseph Soniat, 119, 138, 217
Dumas, Joseph, 147
Dun, R. G., and Company, 202, 205, 220
Dupin, Félicité, 45
Dupin, T. A., 146
Duplessis, Adelaide, 151
Dupont, Basset and Michel, 128
Dupuis, F., 150
Duralde, Mathilde, 32
Dusuau, Catherine, 35, 38, 122
Dusuau, Hortense, 33, 34

École des Orphelins Indigents, 20, 137
Economy Hall, 61
Errié, Emile: partnership with Louis Drausin Dolliole, 74, 151, 152, 153; training of, 151
Errié and Dolliole. *See* Dolliole and Errié
Esplanade Avenue, 59; development of, 2, 3, 20, 71, 134, 209, 210; properties on, 88
Esplanade Ridge, 60, 140, 209
Etienne, Charles, 146
Everett, Donald E., 215
Exchange Passage/Place (Passage de la Bourse), 162, 163

Farragut, David G., 192
Faubourg Annunciation, 50, 68, 69, 123, 138, 158
Faubourg Carraby, 65
Faubourg Clouet, 64
Faubourg Duplantier, 68, 158

INDEX

Faubourg Franklin, 27, 29, 40, 56, 64, 136, 206
Faubourg Gueno, 50, 58–59, 205
Faubourg La Course, 68, 158
Faubourg Lesseps, 65
Faubourg Marigny, 13, 15, 17, 28, 29, 30, 33, 34, 38, 40, 50, 54, 55, 61–63, 64, 68, 72–74, 78, 87, 90, 92, 134, 138, 140, 184, 207, 216
Faubourg Montegut, 64
Faubourg Montreuil, 64
Faubourg Nouvelle Marigny (New Marigny), 40, 63–64, 216
Faubourg Nuns, 68
Faubourg Panis, 68
Faubourg Sainte-Marie, 1, 2, 15, 54, 66, 92, 93, 131, 139, 148, 158, 162, 168, 179, 180, 186, 188, 190, 216. *See also* American Sector
Faubourg Saulet, 68, 158, 186, 190
Faubourg St. Roch, 64. *See also* Faubourg Franklin
Faubourg Tremé, 7, 13, 15, 17, 21, 28, 29, 30, 33, 34, 48, 49, 50, 53, 54, 59–61, 63, 65, 66, 68, 69, 71, 72–74, 79, 93, 96, 97, 114, 116, 119, 121, 125, 136, 138, 139, 140, 143, 144, 148, 153, 162, 165, 168, 169, 179, 180, 184, 186, 190, 191, 199, 205, 207, 208, 210, 211, 212, 216, 218
Federal style architecture, 15, 96, 97, 107, 120, 136, 155, 160, 162, 165, 171, 173. *See also individual buildings*
femmes de couleur libres: collective influence of, 47, 51; education of, 79, 212; financial status of, 47, 79, 207; property ownership of, 6, 27, 31, 47, 51, 67, 119, 124, 128, 134, 138, 139, 140, 150, 190; and support of male relatives' architectural training, 151. *See also individual women*
Ferrand, Adelaide, 47
Finiels, Nicolas de, 62
First Presbyterian Church, 171
Fletcher, Henry: association of with Marie Couvent, 20, 207; association of with Jean-Louis Dolliole, 20, 206–207; association of with Joseph Dolliole, 20, 92, 145, 206–207; military service of, 211
Fondal, Theogene, 150
Forstall, Edmund J., 44, 65, 108, 109. *See also* Louisiana Sugar Refinery
Fortier, Norbert: and joint property ownership with the Dollioles, 36, 37; military service of, 211
Fortière, Sister Marthe, 79, 211
Fouché, Louis Dutreuil, 136
Fouché, Louis Nelson: architectural training and practice of, 137–138, 140, 148; status of as first Black architect, 213
Fouché, Nelson: architectural training and practice of, 136–138, 142, 145, 146, 148; association of with Marie Couvent, 20, 207; and joint property ownership with Joseph Dolliole, 40, 64, 206; property ownership of, 58; as teacher, 150
Fox, Benjamin, 179, 183
Francophone culture, 12, 13
free people of color. See *gens de couleur libres*
free women of color. See *femmes de couleur libres*
French Colonial style architecture, 41, 83, 122, 158, 168
French Market. *See* Halles des Boucheries
French Quarter. *See* Vieux Carré
French Revolution, 158

Galaud, Noel, 31
Galaud, Victoire: marriage of to Thomas Urquhart, 151; property ownership of, 31, 40, 96
Gallier, James, Sr., 18, 146–147, 156, 173, 174, 175–179, 180, 182, 183, 185, 186, 191, 202, 208
Gallot, Etienne, 149, 150
Gallot, Julie, 150
Garden District. *See* Faubourg Saint-Marie
Garden District, Lower. *See* Faubourg Saint-

INDEX

Marie
Gardes and Lefebvre, 146
Gayarré, Charles, 215
gens de couleur libres: activism and protest tradition of, 214; collective influence of, 16, 20, 21, 71, 209, 211, 214, 217; definition of, 5; disenfranchisement and marginalization of, 191, 214, 217, 220; education of, 79, 101, 211, 212; financial status of, 13, 19, 20, 26, 34, 40, 53, 155, 196–203, 219, 220; immigration of from Saint-Domingue, 11, 15, 85, 99; kinship and business ties of, 203–207; legal restrictions on, 26, 43; legal rights of, 25, 26, 79, 197, 198; marriage contracts of, 1, 151, 198, 199, 204, 205, 219; military service of, 211–212
German Coast. *See* Côte des Allemands
Gordon, Alexander, 108
Gothic Revival–style architecture, 102, 104, 173, 174, 176, 180
Goudchaux, Ernest, 162, 190
Gravier, Beltran, 66, 67
Greek Revival style architecture, 18, 96, 97, 102, 103, 104, 105, 108, 109, 111, 114, 117, 131, 160, 162, 164, 165, 168, 170, 171, 173, 174, 176, 177, 178–180, 182, 188, 216, 218. *See also individual buildings*
Gueno, Pierre, 58
Guesnon, Jacques, 122
Guesnon, Laurent Ursain: architectural training and practice of, 122–123, 138, 142, 191; kinship and business ties of with Dollioles, 123, 151, 206; military service of, 211
Guesnon, Marie Eugenie, 123, 151
Guillemard, Gilberto, 158, 165
Guillot, Joseph, 157, 165, 180. *See also* Gurlie and Guillot
Gurlie, Claude, 18, 157, 165, 180, 186, 190. *See also* Gurlie and Guillot
Gurlie and Guillot, 161, 165, 166, 167, 181, 185

habitation, 58, 85, 88, 167
Hagan, John, 177
Haitian Revolution, 11–13, 61, 118
Halles des Boucheries, 158, 161, 185
Harrod, Charles, 206
Hermann, Samuel, 171, 173
Hispaniola, 83. *See also* Saint-Domingue
Hobe, Magdeleine, 41, 62, 206
Holy Cross (neighborhood), 65
Howard, Henry, 178, 180
Hurley, Morris, 186, 190

immigrants: French, 7, 41, 158, 168; German, 63, 155, 157, 167, 191; Irish, 3, 63, 155, 157, 174, 191; Italian, 167; via Jamaica and Cuba, 11, 12, 133, 168, 213; Saint-Dominguan, 11, 15, 83, 85, 133; Spanish, 58, 167
Independence Place, 64
Inner Harbor Navigation Canal, 65
interracial relationships: cases of, 1, 7, 26, 42, 43, 61, 62, 101, 169, 205, 207; laws regulating, 6–7, 26; origins of in New Orleans, 5–7
Italianate style architecture, 125

Jackson, Andrew, 221
Jamaica, 11, 12, 133, 136
Janau, Austin, 186
Jason, Gabriel, 41
Jason, Helene, 41
Jason, Marguerite, 41
Jefferson Parish, 68
J. N. de Pouilly and Ed. Goudchaux, Architects and Builders, 162, 163
Jones, Robert, 81

Kennedy, Sophia Meisson, 45
Kenner, William, 103
Kincaide, William, 190

Laclotte, Jean-Hyacinthe, 158, 165, 180, 181.

See also Latour and Laclotte
Lacoste, Philipe, 208
Lacroix, François: association of with Dolliole family, 206; community stature of, 217; estate of, 202; financial status of, 197, 198, 199; partnership of with Etienne Cordeviolle, 148
Lacroix, Julien Adolphe, 197
Lacroix, Paul, 145, 160, 197
Lafayette, City of (Orleans Parish), 3, 50, 68, 131. *See also* Garden District
Lafayette Square, 66
Lafitte, Jean, 3
Lafitte, Jean-Pierre, 3
Lafitte, Marc, 43, 134
Lafon, Barthèlèmy, 158, 160, 185
Lake Pontchartrain, 3, 15, 63
Lassize, Augustine Eugenie, 186, 190
Latour, Arsène Lacarrière, 15, 150, 158, 165, 180, 181, 185
Latour and Laclotte, 165, 180, 181
Latrobe, Benjamin Henry: architectural training and practice of, 102, 155; contributions of to New Orleans architecture, 18, 171; death of, 171, 173; reflections on New Orleans architecture by, 54, 78, 171, 173; as teacher, 102; works of in New Orleans, 101, 104, 157, 158, 171, 172, 179, 183, 185, 191
Latrobe, Henry Sellon Bonneval: architectural training and practice of, 101–104; death of of, 104, 146; ownership of enslaved individuals by, 146; as teacher, 102, 181, 182; works of in New Orleans, 101, 102, 103, 104, 171
Lauriano, N. L., 123, 138
Le Carpentier-Beauregard-Keyes House, 168, 170
Lefebvre, Françoise, 136
Legendre, H., 207
Lepage, Helen, 134, 135, 140
Lesseps, A., 65

Levee Steam Cotton Press, 3, 64, 111
Liotau, Belsunce, 146
Liotau, François, 41
Liotau, Marie Louise (née Conant), 41
Livaudais plantation, 3
Locke, John, 24
Longpré, Jean, 104
Loubarde, François, 146
Louisiana: Civil Code of 1808, 26, 204; Civil Code 1825 revision, 26, 204, 219; Code Noir of 1724, 6, 25, 26; Code Noir ou Loi Municipale (1778), 6; Código Negro, 6; Purchase, 2, 5, 13, 15, 25, 67, 156; *Register of Free Persons of Color Entitled to Remain in the State* (1840), 206; statehood, 2, 3, 15, 19, 25, 28, 35, 55, 78, 170, 221; under French dominion, 5, 55; under Spanish dominion, 5, 6, 7, 24, 25, 55, 101, 156, 158, 167
Louisiana Native Guards, 211
Louisiana State Arsenal, 174
Louisiana State Bank, 15, 171, 172, 179
Louisiana State Capitol Building (1847), 174
Louisiana Sugar Refinery, 3, 44, 65, 111, 114, 147, 178
L'Ouverture, Toussaint, 11
Lower Garden District, 71, 175

Macarty, Augustin, 104, 157
Macarty, Delphine, 64
Macarty, Drausin Barthèlèmy, 205, 220
Macarty, Eugene, 52, 169
Macarty, L. B., 64
Madison, James, 24
Magnon, Arnaud, 165
maison à étage, 104, 114, 179
maison basse avec attique, 151
maison de maître, 85, 87, 119, 128, 139
maisonette, 133–135, 140, 218
maison principale, 85
Mallorquin, Jean Baptiste, 206
Mandeville, Eulalie de, 61, 169, 186

INDEX

Mandeville, Pierre Philippe de, 61
Marchand, Marie Ann Euphrosine, 210
Marcos, Heloise, 150
Marigny (de Mandeville), Bernard Xavier Philippe de, 54, 61, 103, 169
Maspereau, S., and Co., 146
Mathew, Julia, 67
Mazange, Eulalie: background of, 7, 41; death of, 43; estate of, 43, 204; family ties of, 7, 41, 42, 205; property ownership of, 16, 42, 43, 47, 51, 62, 67; relationship of with Jean Soulié, 7, 24, 43, 45
Mazange, Leonard, 42
Medical College of Louisiana, 174
Meffre-Rouzan House, Jacques-Philippe, House, 175
Merchant's Exchange, 174, 180
Milne, Alexander, 190
Milne, Jane and Nancy, 186, 190
Minturn, John, 51
Miró, Esteban Rodríguez, 6, 83
Misotiére, Pierre, 66
Mississippi, state of, 5, 212
Mississippi River, 4, 63, 65, 66, 167; as boundary, 55; levees, 15, 60; as trade route, 2, 3, 58; as water source, 62
Mitchell, John, 179, 183
Mitchell and Le Moyne, builders, 80
Mobile, Alabama, 5, 174, 175
Montfort, Charles, 45
Montfort, Jean Jacques, 208
Montreuil, Charles, 35
Mooney, James, 184, 185
Moore, Samuel, 177
Morand-Tremé Plantation, 40, 59, 210, 212
Mortuary Chapel of St. Anthony of Padua, 165, 166, 185, 191
Municipal Hall (Second District), 178
Murphy, Andrew Oscar, 131, 140
Musson, Michel, House, 175

New Orleans: Americanization of, 13, 18, 216; architectural competitions in, 171, 184, 185; Central Business District, 66; cholera epidemics in, 3, 4; City Commons, 59, 66, 136, 209; civic improvements in, 3, 18, 20, 101, 157, 175, 184; cotton trade in, 3; demographics of, 2, 3, 4, 7, 12, 13, 55, 119, 156, 199, 219, 220; division of into municipalities, 15, 54, 55, 58, 60, 179, 210, 216; economy of, 2, 3, 4, 24, 191, 216, 219, 220; Fifth Ward, 71; fire of 1788 in, 27, 66, 78, 81, 83, 156, 158; fire of 1794 in, 55, 78, 81, 83, 156; First Ward, 71; founding of, 54, 66, 160, 214; geography of, 15, 21; incorporation of, 13, 25; Seventh Ward, 59, 64, 71, 200; yellow fever epidemics in, 3, 101, 171
New Orleans Customhouse, 171
New Orleans Navigation Canal (New Basin Canal), 2–3, 65
New Orleans Waterworks, 101, 102, 171
Nolte, Vincent, 171, 172
Norwood, Elizabeth, 197
Notre Dame des Victoires Church, 164

Ogden, Francis Barber, 206
Oger, Magdelcine Clemence, 186, 190
Old Burying Ground, 59. *See also* St. Louis Cemetery No. 1
Olivier, Marie Joseph Sophie, 206
Olmsted, Frederick Law, 54
O'Reilly, Alejandro, 6, 25
Orleans Ballroom, 15, 102, 171
Orleans Parish Prison, 179, 191
Orleans Theatre, 102. *See also* Theatre d'Orleans
Ormond plantation, 104
Our Lady of Guadalupe Church, 60

Paris, France: education of *gens de couleur libres in*, 79; landmarks in, 62; Soulié family immigration to, 112, 113, 220; Soulié family residence in, 1, 47, 204

Passebon, Pierre, 207
Pedesclaux, Pierre, 158
Perrault, Appolinaire, 45
Perseverance Lodge No. 4, 15, 134, 169, 179
Petit, Louis, 146
Philips, Sophia, 128, 130, 139
Pilié, Joseph, 13, 14, 33, 38, 133, 179
Pinson, Jean Felix, 160, 162, 181. *See also* Pinson and Pizetta
Pinson and Pizetta, 160, 162
Pizetta, Maurice, 160, 162, 181. *See also* Pinson and Pizetta
Place Gravier. *See* Lafayette Square
Planas, Roman, 151
Polidor, Augustin, 149, 150
Pontalba Buildings, 177, 180
Pontchartrain Railroad, 3, 63, 64
Popin, Marie Laure, 33
Populus, Maurice, 181
Pouilly, Jacques Nicolas Bussière de, 18, 162–164, 165, 180, 186, 190, 212
Poydras, Julien, 67
Pradel, Belize, 46
Presbytère, 158, 165
Prieto, Henriette, 7, 42
Prieto, Joseph, 63, 90, 206
Pritchard, R. O., 177

Quessaire, Laurent Dessource, 151, 206

Reynes, Marie Eugenie, 122
Reynolds, James Maxwell, 171
Rillieux, Edmond, 3, 44, 65, 109, 112, 147, 158, 178, 185, 220
Rillieux, Norbert, 125, 185, 205
Rillieux, Vincent, 1, 44, 101, 205
Rillieux, Vincent, pére, 158, 160
Rodriguez, Josefa, 40
Roffignac, Louis Philippe Joseph de, 157
Roup, Pierre: architectural training and practice of, 133–136, 140, 142, 191, 218; ownership of enslaved individuals by, 145
rowhouse, 108, 114, 116, 165
Roy, Uranie, 124, 169

Sainet, Emile, 45
Saint-Domingue: cession from Spain to France of, 83; founding of Perseverance Lodge No. 4 in, 134; immigration from, 11, 12, 15, 55, 83, 85, 97, 117, 133, 134, 168, 213; settlement of, 83. *See also* Haitian Revolution
Salkeld, G., 65
Santo Domingo, 83
Santos, Bernard de, 168
Schinkel, Edward, 168
Sewell, Edward, 182, 208
shotgun houses, 133, 134, 140, 218
Sisters of Mount Carmel, 212
slavery and enslaved people: from Africa, 5, 83; Afro-Creole, 13; as artisans, builders, and laborers, 119, 145, 146, 147, 150, 157, 168, 181, 182; demographics of, 12, 199; and Dolliole family, 19, 35, 144, 145, 146, 147, 148, 203, 204; education of, 212; and *gens de couleur libres* enslavers, 19, 202; and German Coast insurrection of 1811, 25; and interracial relationships, 5, 27, 42; laws regulating, 24–25; and manumission, 5, 12–13, 41, 206, 207; and quarters buildings, 104; rights of, 25; and Soulié family, 19, 47, 112, 145, 146, 147, 198, 202; status of in New Orleans, 5, 24, 41, 206, 216; and St. Augustine Church, 212; and trade in New Orleans, 3, 12, 19, 25, 199; value of, 198–199, 201, 202, 203
Société d'Économie et d'Assistance Mutuelle, 61
Soulié (family): architectural training and practice of, 20, 21, 78, 79, 100–114, 116, 117, 141, 145, 153, 168, 183, 191, 198, 218; connections of to Dolliole family,

208–209; and employment of other builders, 123, 126, 146; extended family of, 68, 123, 125, 126, 205, 206; financial status of, 17, 53, 197, 203; immigration to France of, 20, 220; kinship and business ties of, 6, 19, 20, 68, 101, 197, 206–207, 209; legacy of, 4, 20, 213, 216, 217, 218, 219, 221; money-lending activities of, 20, 207–209; origins of, 7, 11; and ownership of enslaved individuals, 19, 47, 112, 145, 146, 147, 198, 202; and ownership of real property, 17, 19, 26, 41–53, 55, 60–61, 62, 63, 65–66, 67–68, 71; rental properties of, 20, 51–52, 146. *See also individual family members*

Soulié, Albin: as absentee landlord, 45; as agent for absentee siblings, 45, 186; architectural training and practice of, 113, 114, 123, 145, 147, 203, 205; birth of, 7, 42; creditworthiness of, 202; financial status of, 201; kinship and business ties of, 205; and ownership of enslaved individuals by, 147; ownership of real property by, 43, 45, 46, 48, 49, 50, 60, 66, 68, 71; rental properties of, 51–52; support for the Confederate States of America by, 219; travel and immigration to France by, 45. *See also* Soulié, B. & A., commission merchants

Soulié, B. & A., commission merchants, 51, 80, 112, 147, 201, 202, 203, 205, 208

Soulié, Benedic, 42

Soulié, Bernard: as agent for absentee siblings, 44, 45, 47, 51, 202; architectural training and practice of, 112, 113, 116, 145, 147, 203, 205; birth of, 7, 42; children of, 3–4; creditworthiness of, 202; education of, 101; as estate executor, 205; financial status of, 51, 53, 198, 199, 200, 201, 220; immigration of to France, 219, 220; kinship and business ties of, 20, 67, 205, 206; marriage of to Eliza Courcelle, 1, 2, 198, 203, 205, 219; ownership of enslaved individuals by, 147, 198, 202; ownership of real property by, 43, 44, 45, 46, 48, 49, 50, 53, 168, 205; political activities of, 220; rental properties of, 51–52; succession records of, 204; support of the Confederate States of America by, 219. *See also* Soulié, B. & A., commission merchants

Soulié, Eulalie: birth of, 7, 42; education of, 45; financial status of, 201; ownership of real property by, 43. *See also* Soulié sisters

Soulié, Gustave Adolph, 3–4

Soulié, Jean: as administrator for his minor children, 43, 204; background of, 1; birth of in France, 1; and Freemasonry, 42, 101; immigration of to New Orleans, 41; kinship and business ties of, 66, 101, 205; military service of, 42, 101; municipal service of, 42–43, 101; and ownership of real property by, 42, 43, 100; partnership of with Jean Charles Vivant, 42; relationship of with Eulalie Mazange, 7, 24, 42, 47; return to France by, 43, 205

Soulié, Lucien: birth of, 7, 42; immigration of to France, 45, 51, 112; occupation of, 43; ownership of real property by, 43, 45, 47, 48, 49, 50, 51, 112; partnership of with Norbert, 112, 147, 204; rental properties of, 51–52, 67

Soulié, Marie Celeste: birth of, 7, 42; education of, 45; financial status of, 201; ownership of real property by, 43. *See also* Soulié sisters

Soulié, Marie Coralie: birth of, 7, 42; education of, 45; financial status of, 201; ownership of real property by, 43. *See also* Soulié sisters

INDEX

Soulié, Marie Louise: birth of, 7, 42; education of, 45; ownership of real property by, 43. *See also* Soulié sisters

Soulié, Norbert: as agent for Jean Soulié, 43; apprenticeship of with Henry Latrobe, 18, 101–102, 104; architectural training and practice of, 7, 79, 100, 101, 102, 104–111, 113, 114, 116, 142, 143, 157, 185, 186; birth of, 7, 42; as client, 186–190; death of, 205; education of, 101; estate inventory of, 202, 205, 206; financial status of, 201, 202; immigration to France of, 45, 51, 71, 111, 219; kinship and business ties of, 3, 100, 123, 205, 207; ownership of enslaved individuals by, 145–146, 147; ownership of real property by, 43, 44, 45, 48, 49, 50, 55, 59, 65, 67, 68, 70, 71, 119, 207; partnership of with Lucien, 112, 147, 204; rental properties of, 51–52, 68, 190; as teacher, 149, 150, 151; work on Louisiana Sugar Refinery by, 1, 44, 65, 108–111, 147, 178, 185

Soulié sisters: and ownership of enslaved individuals, 47; and ownership of real property, 43, 47, 58, 125, 205; rental properties of, 51–52, 68; value of real property of, 201

Spanish Colonial style architecture, 55, 66, 81, 83, 100, 106, 120, 126, 158, 165, 217, 218

St. Augustine Catholic Church, 61, 162, 180, 191, 212

St. Charles Hotel, 174, 176, 179

St. Charles Theatre, 179

St. Ermain, Jacques Daniel, 150

Stewart, Samuel, 164

St. Jean, Mariana, 27

St. Jean's Hospital, 59

St. Louis Cathedral, 55, 104, 157, 158, 159, 164, 168, 171, 183, 211

St. Louis Cemetery No. 1, 59, 168

St. Louis Cemetery No. 2, 60

St. Louis Hotel, 162, 163, 180, 190

St. Martin, Marie (Manon Boisseau), 122

St. Patrick's Church, 174, 176, 180

St. Philip Theatre, 15

Strickland, William, 179, 183

Tanesse, Jacques, 35, 158, 161, 165, 185, 209

Théâtre d'Orléans. *See* Orleans Theatre

Thierry, Jean-Baptiste, 103–104

Tio, Francisco, 63, 92

townhouse, 92, 105, 218

townhouse, American, 116, 126, 131, 140, 168, 169, 171, 176, 186

townhouse, Creole: 107, 114, 116, 126, 130, 136, 138, 139, 140, 143, 148, 160, 162, 165, 171, 186; characteristics of, 105, 106; *entresol*, 136; *porte-cochére*, 107, 119

townhouse, French, 120

townhouse, Spanish Colonial, 165

Treaty of Paris, 156

Tremé, Claude, 2, 35, 54, 85, 206, 209, 211

Tremé Market, 180, 191

Tricou, Joseph Adolphe, 165

Trouillot, Michel-Rolph, 214, 215

Urquhart, Thomas, 151

Ursuline: convent, 65, 79, 165; nuns, 165, 212

US Mint, 179, 183

Verandah Hotel, 174, 176

Vieux Carré, 2, 7, 13, 15, 28–30, 33, 42, 44, 45, 48–50, 54, 55–58, 59, 60, 62, 63, 66, 68, 71, 72–74, 78, 81, 85, 89, 92, 96, 100, 105, 119, 131, 138–140, 144, 156, 157, 160, 162, 165, 168, 171, 173, 174, 175, 177, 178, 179–180, 184, 186, 190, 199, 209, 216, 217

Vionnet, Ramon, 128, 129, 139, 207, 208

Vivant, Adelaide, 67, 111, 125, 205

Vivant, Constance, 101, 104, 205

Vivant, Eulalie. *See* Mazange, Eulalie

Vivant, Jean Charles, 7, 42, 123, 208, 211

Vivant, Louis: architectural training and

practice of, 123–125, 138, 142, 169; employment of by Soulié family, 123, 126; financial status of, 199

Voisin, John, 92

Warmoth, Henry Clay, 215, 220
Washington Square, 62
West Indies, 4, 11, 44, 83, 99, 118, 213
Wood, Alexander Thompson, 173, 183

Xiques, Angel, House, 175